Release gesture implements [tson],
357; i.e. s̲C, sis [vel].

Thova Hulson

Phonological Structure and Phonetic Form: Papers in Laboratory Phonology III brings together work from phonology, phonetics, speech science, electrical engineering, psycho- and sociolinguistics. The chapters in this book are organized in four topical sections. The first is concerned with stress and intonation; the second with syllable structure and phonological theory; the third with phonological features; and the fourth with "phonetic output."

This is the third in the series Papers in Laboratory Phonology. The two previous volumes, like the conferences from which they were derived, have been influential in establishing Laboratory Phonology as a discipline in its own right. *Phonological Structure and Phonetic Form* will be equally important in making readers aware of the range of research relevant to questions of linguistic sound structure.

PAPERS IN LABORATORY PHONOLOGY
SERIES EDITORS: MARY E. BECKMAN AND JOHN KINGSTON

Phonological Structure and Phonetic Form

Phonological Structure and Phonetic Form
Papers in Laboratory Phonology III

EDITED BY PATRICIA A. KEATING

Department of Linguistics, University of California Los Angeles

CAMBRIDGE
UNIVERSITY PRESS

Published by the Press Syndicate of the University of Cambridge
The Pitt Building, Trumpington Street, Cambridge CB2 1RP
40 West 20th Street, New York, NY 10011–4211, USA
10 Stamford Road, Oakleigh, Melbourne 3166, Australia

First published 1994
Reprinted 1995

Printed in Great Britain by Watkiss Studios Ltd., Biggleswade, Beds.

A catalogue record for this book is available from the British Library

Library of Congress cataloguing in publication data

Phonological structure and phonetic form/edited by Patricia A. Keating.
p.   cm. – (Papers in laboratory phonology; 3)
Papers from the Third Conference in Laboratory Phonology held at UCLA.
Includes indexes.
ISBN 0 521 45237 6 (hardback)
1. Grammar, Comparative and general – Phonology – Congresses.
2. Phonetics – Congresses. I. Keating, Patricia A. II. Series.
P217.P484 1994
414–dc20   93-17718 CIP

ISBN 0 521 45237 6

Dedication

The Third Conference in Laboratory Phonology coincided with the retirement from teaching of Peter Ladefoged. Both the conference and this book are dedicated to him in recognition of the role he has played over his career in promoting the linguistic study of sound.

Contents

I. Intonation

Contents

II. Syllables

III. Feature Theory

IV. Phonetic Output

Contents

Contributors

MARY E. BECKMAN   *Department of Linguistics, Ohio State University*

CATHERINE P. BROWMAN   *Haskins Laboratories*

JOHN COLEMAN   *Phonetics Laboratory, Oxford University*

JAN EDWARDS   *Department of Speech and Hearing Sciences, Ohio State University*

LOUIS GOLDSTEIN   *Department of Linguistics, Yale University, and Haskins Laboratories*

BRUCE HAYES   *Department of Linguistics, University of California, Los Angeles*

VINCENT VAN HEUVEN   *Department of Linguistics and Phonetics Lab, Leiden University*

KEITH JOHNSON   *Department of Linguistics, Ohio State University*

ALLARD JONGMAN   *Department of Modern Languages and Linguistics, Cornell University*

PATRICIA A. KEATING   *Department of Linguistics, University of California, Los Angeles*

JOHN KINGSTON   *Department of Linguistics, University of Massachusetts*

D. ROBERT LADD   *Department of Linguistics, University of Edinburgh*

JOHN J. MCCARTHY   *Department of Linguistics, University of Massachusetts*

Contributors

FRANCIS N. NOLAN   *Department of Linguistics, University of Cambridge*

JANET PIERREHUMBERT   *Department of Linguistics, Northwestern University*

ANNIE RIALLAND   *Institute of Phonetics, CNRS, and University of Paris 3*

STEFANIE SHATTUCK-HUFNAGEL   *Research Laboratory of Electronics, MIT*

KENNETH N. STEVENS   *Research Laboratory of Electronics and Department of Electrical Engineering and Computer Science, MIT*

ALICE TURK   *Research Laboratory of Electronics, MIT*

MALCAH YAEGER-DROR   *University of Arizona and Ben Gurion University of the Negev*

Acknowledgments

This collection of papers originated from the Third Conference in Laboratory Phonology at UCLA. A committee consisting of Pat Keating, Bruce Hayes, Peter Ladefoged, Ian Maddieson, and Donca Steriade selected the conference speakers and organized the sessions. Funds for the conference came, via the UCLA Phonetics Laboratory in the Linguistics Department, from the UCLA Division of Humanities and NIDCD grant #DC00029 (Training Program in Phonetics and Speech). The papers in this volume were reviewed anonymously by ad-hoc referees from outside UCLA, too few to name individually, but whose help was essential. Finally, Barbara Blankenship of the UCLA Phonetics Lab provided invaluable editorial assistance in the preparation of the typescript.

In this book we have made a great effort to standardize phonetic transcription using the symbols of the 1989 IPA, even where this goes against standard practice for a particular language. Thanks to all the authors for cooperating in this effort, and apologies to readers for inconsistencies that may inadvertently remain.

I

Introduction

PATRICIA A. KEATING

This volume continues the series *Papers in Laboratory Phonology*, comprising papers and commentaries from the Third Conference in Laboratory Phonology (LabPhon3), which was held at UCLA in June 1991. Most of the papers and some of the commentaries from the conference are included here, in revised versions. Some of the contributors participated in one or both of the previous Laboratory Phonology conferences, while others are new. The conference also included poster presentations, which are not represented in this volume.

The papers have been organized here into four topical sections. The first is concerned in various ways with intonation: a model of stress and accent and its relation to stress shift and to articulatory data (Beckman and Edwards/Shattuck-Hufnagel); pitch accent and its F_0 scaling (Ladd/Hayes); and the acoustics and perception of contrastive focus (van Heuven/Jongman). The second section is concerned with syllable structure and phonological theory: how syllabic affiliations might be determined from phonetic data (Turk/Rialland/Nolan), and the import of statistical regularities in lexical data (Pierrehumbert). The third section is concerned with phonological features: arguments for a natural class of pharyngeal place of articulation, and its phonetic basis (McCarthy/Goldstein), and the relevance of hierarchical representation of features to continuing work on their acoustic correlates (Stevens/Goldstein). The last section is concerned with what can be called "phonetic output": how, as a result of sound change, different speakers realize the same phonological units in different phonetic ways (Yaeger-Dror), how a formant speech-synthesis system can be improved by improving its underlying phonological theory (Coleman/Johnson), how an articulatory speech-synthesis system gets its mouth open (Browman/Kingston).

Some chapters require of the reader knowledge of both phonetics and phonology; others draw on one field in a way accessible to readers from the other field; a few require knowledge of only one of these fields. A phonologist reading this book will be most comfortable knowing how to interpret plots of fundamental frequency (F_0) as the physical correlate of pitch of the voice, and thus of intonational melody; how to interpret graphs of positions of pellets attached to articulators as articulator positions over time; and how formant frequencies relate to articulator positions, and are seen in spectral displays. A phonetician reading this book will be most comfortable knowing about several recent areas of phonological theory, including feature geometry, CV phonology, syllable structure, metrical theory, and prosodic structure. Obviously, no reader will be equally at home with all of these, but a goal of the Laboratory Phonology series is to make readers aware of the range of research relevant to questions of linguistic sound structure. Each reader can then decide which areas of knowledge to develop and apply according to individual interests, following up the references in the individual chapters.

A few of the chapters in this volume are somewhat "self-introducing," containing a fair amount of background information that can be useful in reading other chapters as well. Thus Turk reviews research on syllabification, and her graphs of upper lip movement are a good introduction to articulator movements. McCarthy thoroughly reviews the phonetics of the back of the mouth in introducing his chapter on features of consonants made there, and van Heuven is a good introduction to focus and accent.

Background material in phonetics is provided by some of the standard textbooks in the field. Thus Ladefoged (1993:109ff.) gives explicit help in reading pitch and accent from F_0 traces, while Clark and Yallop (1990:221ff.) effectively introduce resonance frequencies and spectral displays. Aspects of the relation between articulator positions and formant frequencies are covered in Lieberman and Blumstein (1988:172ff.) and Borden and Harris (1984:98) for tube models and perturbation theory respectively.

Background material on several of the phonological topics listed above is provided in tutorial chapters of the previous LabPhon volume: Broe (1992) is an introduction to feature geometry and some aspects of CV phonology, and Ladd (1992) is an introduction to intonational phonology, including pitch range and downtrends. An introductory discussion of syllable structure is given by Goldsmith (1990:104–123), followed by more advanced topics in syllable structure, with other sections of that book treating metrical theory, feature theory, and CV phonology. These sources, like the chapters in the present volume, also give standard references on these topics. For an introduction to prosodic structure, the reader is referred to the opening citations given by Beckman and Edwards (this volume); Hayes (1989:202–220) is a briefer introduction to prosodic hierarchy theory. Most people take "Laboratory Phonology" to refer to the interaction, or "interface," of phonetics and phonology; see, for example, the introduction to the first Laboratory Phonology volume (Beckman and Kingston 1990). The present volume continues this focus, with papers and commentaries by both phoneticians and phonologists and many experimental phonetic studies. However, phonology can be done in a laboratory without phonetics: for example, psycholinguistic phonology and computational phonology. The current volume includes two computational papers (Pierrehumbert, Coleman). Another direction for Laboratory Phonology is the modern study of sound change, a well-established field represented here by Yaeger-Dror. This book thus tries to extend the purview of Laboratory Phonology without diluting its central orientation to phonetics.

An obvious question raised by the appearance of each volume in the series is how the field of Laboratory Phonology has been developing. It seems safe to say that the mutual difficulties between phonetics and phonology discussed by Liberman (1983) and Beckman and Kingston (1990) have waned considerably, even if they have not disappeared. The weakest version of Laboratory Phonology seems securely established: namely, that phonologists might sometimes benefit from collecting their data in a laboratory, and that phoneticians might sometimes enjoy testing the phonetic consequences of phonological hypotheses. There is no longer a general fear requiring written appeals for mutual respect and cooperation. Instead, a bolder version of Laboratory Phonology becomes clearer in the volumes in the series. This is the view that quality work in linguistic phonetics requires nontrivial knowledge of phonology, and vice versa; that results from one field might determine analyses in the other; and that all "ph"-linguists should think of themselves as Laboratory Phonologists at least some of the time. We should not take this too far; phonetics and phonology are not the same thing and there is always the danger of pushing them so much together that we lose depth of expertise from each. Interdisciplinary work always runs the risk of dilettantism. But all in all this is much the risk to be preferred, at least at the moment: how much better off we are to be in fear of dilettantism than of each other!

References

Beckman, Mary E. and John Kingston. 1990. Introduction. In J. Kingston and M.E. Beckman (eds.) *Papers in Laboratory Phonology I: Between the Grammar and Physics of Speech*. Cambridge: University Press.

Borden, Gloria J. and Katherine S. Harris. 1984. *Speech Science Primer*. 2nd edition. Baltimore, MD: Williams & Wilkins.

Broe, Michael. 1992. An introduction to feature geometry. In Docherty and Ladd (eds.).

Clark, J. and C. Yallop. 1990. *An Introduction to Phonetics and Phonology*. Oxford and Cambridge, MA: Basil Blackwell.

Docherty, G.J. and D.R. Ladd (eds.). 1992. *Papers in Laboratory Phonology II: Gesture, Segment, Prosody*. Cambridge: University Press.

Goldsmith, John A. 1990. *Autosegmental and Metrical Phonology*. Oxford: Basil Blackwell.

Hayes, B. 1989. The prosodic hierarchy in meter. In P. Kiparsky and G. Youmans (eds.), *Rhythm and Meter. Phonetics and Phonology*, Vol. 1. San Diego: Academic Press.

Ladd, D.R. 1992. An introduction to intonational phonology. In Docherty and Ladd (eds.).

Ladefoged, P. 1993. *A Course in Phonetics*. Third edition. New York: Harcourt, Brace, Jovanovich.

Liberman, Mark Y. 1983. In favor of some uncommon approaches to the study of speech. In P.F. MacNeilage (ed.) *The Production of Speech*. New York: Springer-Verlag.

Lieberman, Philip and Sheila E. Blumstein. 1988. *Speech Physiology, Speech Perception, and Acoustic Phonetics*. Cambridge: University Press.

Part I
Intonation

2

Articulatory evidence for differentiating stress categories

MARY E. BECKMAN and JAN EDWARDS

2.1 Introduction

Speech is structured both by the grammatical functions of contrast and organization and by the physical medium for those functions, namely sound as produced by the human vocal tract and perceived by the human ear. In investigating sound structure, neither the grammar nor the medium can be ignored. Each is an external source of constraint and explanation for facets of the other. A striking example of the dangers of ignoring either is the difficulty we have had in characterizing stress. It is only within the last ten years or so that phonological accounts of stress patterns have approached the level of descriptive insight afforded to segmental patterns by the phonetic observations of Panini. Conversely, investigations of physical and perceptual correlates of stress have produced many seemingly conflicting results, at least in part because of confusion concerning the phonological categories and structures involved.

In this paper, we will describe our understanding of what a unified theory of (surface) stress patterns must be like in general in order to be able to account for both the phonology and the phonetics of stress. We will then make a few proposals about how to fill in the specifics of the theory for a description of some parts of the English stress system, and show how this description might help account for the phonetics of stress shift. Finally, we will present some articulatory data in partial support for our specific proposals.

2.2 A theory of stress

One of the reasons why stress has been so difficult to characterize phonologically is that its salient function is not the familiar one of

7

contrasting lexical items. That is, stress is not a paradigmatic specification like tone or vowel quality. Rather, it is a syntagmatic structural specification. It is one of the devices that a language can use to set up a hierarchical organization for its utterances.

This view is part of a general understanding of prosody that has emerged clearly only with the development of metrical theory (see *inter alia* Liberman and Prince 1977; Selkirk 1981; Nespor and Vogel 1986; Pierrehumbert and Beckman 1988). In this view, prosody is the organizational framework that measures off chunks of speech into countable constituents of various sizes. So in most languages, native speakers know how many syllables a word has. Or, in English, we can count the intonational phrases. In this, prosodic specifications are fundamentally different from segmental ones: whereas segmental specifications are facts about the phonetic content of an utterance, prosodic specifications are facts about how that content is organized.

In general, we can identify two different devices for creating this structural organization: at any level of the prosodic hierarchy, the number of constituents can be indicated by marking the edges or by marking the heads. In the classical linear phonology of Trubetskoy (1939), these two devices correspond to the demarcative and culminative functions, respectively. In metrical representations, they can be identified roughly with trees versus grids. Edges are more obvious when subconstituents are grouped together under a common node at the next highest level in the tree, and heads are more obvious when the most prominent subconstituent is projected into the next highest level in the grid. The first emphasizes the phrasing and the second emphasizes the stresses. (See Beckman 1986 and Hammond 1986 for two different ideas about how to unify these two different devices in a single metrical representation.)

How do languages actually implement these principles for counting structural constituents? The most salient way of marking edges and heads is by the distribution of content specifications. In all languages, there are phonotactic constraints such that some segments can occur only at certain places in the prosodic structure. For example, in English (and many other languages), an obstruent can occur only near the edge of a syllable; it can never be the syllabic peak. Conversely, a vowel is usually a syllable nucleus, so by counting the vowels, a listener can pretty much know how many syllables there are. Also, in English and many other languages, certain tone segments can occur only at the edges of intonation phrases, and thus indicate how many such phrases there are. Other tone segments can only occur on the most stressed word or syllable, giving it an accentual prominence above the rest of the phrase.

Constituent edges and peaks are also marked in more subtle ways by aspects of the phonetic interpretation of segments that can occur in more than one place in the prosodic organization. For example, in many languages a voiceless stop has more aspiration at the beginning edge of a stress foot. Similarly, a segment is longer near the edge of an intonation phrase, and it has often been noted that when a syllable has the phrase stress it tends to be longer than otherwise.

To summarize what this means as a general characterization of stress, then, we can say, first, that phonologically stress is not an autosegment; it is not a primitive content feature like tone or vowel quality. Rather, stress is a structural feature that is derived from relationships among many different content features. It is a catch-all term for the distributional patterns of phonological specifications that mark head constituents at various levels of the prosodic hierarchy above the syllable and for the rules of phonetic interpretation whose output values are conditioned by position relative to these constituents. A good investigative strategy for discovering the best characterization of the surface stress system of a particular language, therefore, is to look for patterns in the distribution of autosegmental content features that suggest presence versus absence of some absolute structural prominence while designing experiments that test for possible phonetic interpretations in terms of some prominence-lending physical or perceptual attribute.

2.3 Types of stress in English

Applying this strategy to English, we think there is good evidence for distributional patterns that define heads for constituents at three levels of the prosodic hierarchy. The phonological contrast at the lowest level is the one that Liberman and Prince (1977) identified by their feature [±stress], corresponding to [±heavy] in Vanderslice and Ladefoged (1972). A syllable with a full vowel as its nucleus has an absolute prominence over any syllable with a reduced vowel or sonorant consonant. Following Selkirk's (1980) proposal, we represent this level in terms of the constituent *stress foot*, as shown in figure 2.1. This yields a level of stress where the prominence is defined phonologically by the distribution of qualitative features of vowel quality. If a syllable has an associated full specification for vowel height and backness ([æ] is specified as [+ low] and [− back]), it is more prominent than any syllable that does not have such a specification.[1] Phonetically, of course, this specification is realized by the distinctive formant patterns for the full vowel, but there are also accompanying differences in duration and loudness; the low front vowel [æ] in the second syllable in *gymnast* or *mailman* is "inherently" longer and more intense than the [ə] in *tempest* or *German*. Depending on the other segments associated to the syllables, there

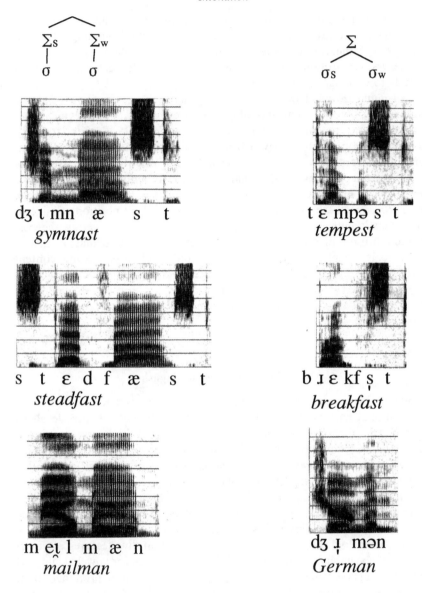

Figure 2.1. Spectrograms and trees for *gymnast* versus *tempest*, *mailman* versus *German*, and *steadfast* versus *breakfast*. (Σ represents a stress foot, σ a syllable.)

can also be marked differences in the phonetic interpretation of other segmental features. If there is no voiced consonant adjacent to the nucleus of a reduced syllable, for example, there may be no period when the vocal folds are audibly vibrating, as shown in the second syllable of *breakfast* in the sample utterance of this word in figure 2.1. Similarly, the second syllable of *German* could have had a syllabic nasal rather than the [ə] that it does in this utterance.

The other two types of strong syllables that we have identified are defined phonologically by the distribution of tones in the intonation contour. The defining features correspond to Vanderslice and Ladefoged's (1972) [±accent] and [±intonation] once we have adjusted for differences in our views of intonation. In the theory of intonation that we adopt (Pierrehumbert 1980; Pierrehumbert and Hirschberg 1990), intonation contours are analyzed as sequences of pitch accents, phrase accents, and boundary tones. A phrase accent or boundary tone is a right-peripheral tone marking the edge of an intermediate-level or a top-level constituent, respectively. (In Pierrehumbert's theory, these two prosodic constituents are called the *intermediate phrase* and the *intonation phrase*.) The tone can be H or L, depending on the pragmatic relationship between its phrase and neighboring material in the discourse. A pitch accent is associated terminally with a syllable in a word or phrase that is under focus locally in the discourse. It is chosen from an inventory of two single-tone (H* and L*) and four bitonal shapes (L* + H, L + H*, H* + L, H + L*) on the basis of the pragmatic relationship between the focused material and the background of mutual beliefs in the discourse.

Although the primary determinants of accentuation thus come from the pragmatics of the discourse context, there are also very strong grammatical constraints on accent placement. One type of constraint comes from the lexicon. A pitch accent cannot dock on a syllable that is not the head of its stress foot. Therefore, if an unusual pragmatic situation requires that accent be placed on a lexically reduced syllable, that syllable will receive a nonce specification for some full vowel quality – i.e. a different stress foot organization is produced. This is the source of the common citation-form pronunciations of the articles *the* and *a* with high and mid tense front vowels, respectively. (Of course, speakers who do not have strong inhibitions against stressed lax vowels in open syllables – i.e. speakers who can contrastively emphasize the first syllable of *Camellia* – could just as easily produce a fully specified low-mid unrounded back vowel [ʌ] in these words.) Also, if a word has more than one full syllable, typically just one of them is marked in the lexicon as a potential association site for a nuclear pitch accent. Words such as *fifteen*, which can readily take nuclear accent on either their first or their second syllables,[2] are the rare exception.

Another type of constraint comes from the phonology of the phrase accent. It is associated not only with the right edge of the intermediate phrase, but also with the right edge of a marked word in the phrase. When these two edges are distant from each other, the H or L phrase tone governs the pitch of the region in between, as if the tone had spread to all intervening syllables, so that no other tones can be associated in that interval, and there can be no further accents until a new phrase starts no matter how many stress feet are included in this interval.

Understanding the English intonation system is essential for understanding surface stress patterns because the association of a pitch accent to a syllable gives it an absolute prominence over any syllable that has no associated tone. In the same way, the syllable associated with the last pitch accent in a phrase (the accent just before the phrase tones) is more prominent than any earlier pitch-accented syllable. It is the tonic syllable or "sentence stress." Phonetically, the prominences at these two levels of the prosodic hierarchy should be realized primarily by the pitch contour. Accented syllables are anchor points for the alignment between the F_0 contour and spectral patterns. If the associated pitch accent is bitonal, there will be a salient rise or fall in pitch around the accented syllable whether the accent is nuclear or prenuclear. A prenuclear single-tone accent makes for a less salient pitch change except when associated to the first accented syllable in the phrase, where there is likely to be a noticeable fall (to a L*) or rise (to a H*), as illustrated in figure 2.2. When interpreted in terms of the intonation contour, these rises and falls are a perceptually salient cue to the accent and thus to the intended discourse focus.

Unlike the theory assumed by Vanderslice and Ladefoged (1972), Pierrehumbert's theory of intonation does not distinguish between pitch-accent shapes that can be associated to nuclear and to prenuclear accented syllables. However, the nuclear-accented syllable is still distinguished phonologically by bearing the last accent before the phrase tone or tones, and thus the last accent in the intermediate phrase.[3] Because of the immediately following phrase tones, moreover, the nuclear-accented syllable is often the locus of the most dramatic changes in pitch within a phrase. Two of the most common intonational contours in English involve a sharp fall in pitch from a nuclear accent H* to a L phrase accent (the canonical "neutral declarative" of the citation form) and a sharp rise in pitch from a L* nuclear accent to a H phrase tone (the "yes–no question" intonation). Phonetically, then, we might think of the pitch excursions resulting from such common sequences of unlike tones as making a perceptual salience or prominence for the nuclear-accented syllable. (Sequences of unlike tones can also create pitch excursions around unaccented syllables – for example, at the

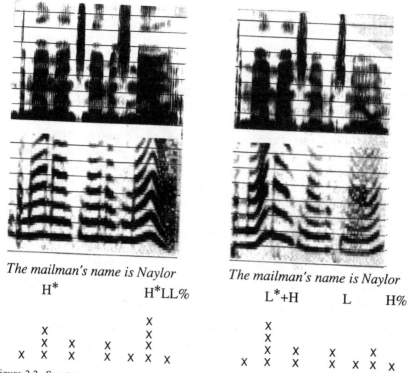

Figure 2.2. Spectrograms and grids for *The mailman's name is Naylor* produced with two different intonation patterns.

confluence of the phrase accent and a high boundary tone when there is a long interval between the nuclear accented syllable and the end of the intonation phrase. In short utterances, however, pitch excursions are more likely to be interpreted in terms of the sequence at a nuclear accent, as in Fry's 1958 experiment showing the salience of the F_0 contour in cueing stress in pairs such as *pérmit* versus *permít*. This is probably a major source of the common misunderstanding in the experimental literature that F_0 excursion is a direct acoustic correlate of the feature "stress", a misunderstanding that has been incorporated into several standard textbooks, such as Pickett 1980).

There can also be many phonetic manifestations of the accent placement in the interpretation of autosegmental features other than the tones. For example, an [h] might be more obstruent-like in an accented syllable, a finding that Pierrehumbert and Talkin (1992) relate to a general strengthening of consonantal features for stressed syllables at all levels. The nuclear-accented syllable can also be markedly longer than it would be if not accented (Klatt 1977). In our own experience, we have found this to be particularly true when the associated pitch-accent tone is L.

2.4 Some consequences

This account of stress (and of these three particular types of stressed syllable in the prosodic hierarchy of English) resolves a fundamental paradox in metrical theory. Earlier structuralist theories, such as that of Trager (1941), recognized only one functional principle, the phonemic principle of paradigmatic contrast among content features. Therefore, these theories viewed stress as a content feature (usually identified as "loudness"), completely on par with contrasts in tone ("pitch") or vowel quality ("timbre"). But as a content feature stress is anomalous. There are no true minimal pairs, in the sense that monosyllabic utterances cannot contrast. Thus, no language uses stresses in the way that Cantonese, for example, uses tones. In this context, the first crucial insight of metrical theory was to recognize that stress is not a paradigmatic distinctive feature. Instead, Liberman and Prince (1977) made it a property of syntagmatic relation, devoid of any necessary phonetic intrepretation in terms of absolute loudness levels. A syllable is weak (or unstressed) only in relationship to its stronger sibling which heads the constituent. It cannot be relatively weaker unless there is some other syllable that is louder and stronger.

When we compare disyllabic utterances, however, this strictly relational view immediately encounters difficulties. Each of the pairs in figure 2.1 above seems to contrast in stress pattern, despite the fact that both words in each have a relationship of stronger first syllable and weaker second syllable. The second syllable in *mailman, steadfast,* or *gymnast* has an absolute degree of strength even though it is weak relative to its leftward sibling. The second innovative insight of metrical theory, then, is the notion of an absolute prominence given by the head-marking features at each level of a strictly ordered prosodic hierarchy, as in Selkirk (1980). In these later metrical accounts, stress is viewed as a specification of a particular prosodic structure, and not just of a particular relationship between stronger and weaker nodes. The phonological content feature that makes the head syllable strong will differ from level to level, but it will share with all other head-marking features the structural property of making the syllable bearing that feature stronger than syllables that do not. The fact that monosyllabic utterances cannot contrast in stress then falls out from the structural requirement that an intonation phrase must have a head syllable. This no longer precludes pairs such as those in figure 2.1, which have the same organization of heads and edges at a higher level but differing organizations at a lower level.

A prediction related to this representation of these words is that categorical contrasts in "primary stress" will be maintained in postnuclear position only if the words differ also in stress-foot structure. For example, *digést* should be categorically perceived as different from *dígest* only if the verb has [ə] rather than the full vowel [aɪ] in its first syllable. The prediction is borne out in the results of Scott (1939) and Huss (1978).

This view of stress also suggests a way to interpret our phonological intuitions about stress shift. Phonologists and phoneticians have long noted apparent stress alternations in phrases such as *Chinése* versus *Chìnese mén*, *Eiléen* versus *Eìleen Náylor*, or *Pennsylvánia* versus *Pènnsylvania législature* (e.g. Kingdon 1958, Bolinger 1965). Experiments by Cooper and Eady (1986), however, suggest that measuring durations or intensities will not yield any strong evidence for a relatively weaker first syllable in *Chinése*, *Eiléen*, or *Pennsylvánia* versus a relatively stronger first syllable in *Chìnese mén*, *Eìleen Náylor*, or *Pènnsylvania législature*.

However, if we think of stress also in terms of possible docking sites for nuclear and prenuclear accents, then we find a plausible account of the perceived shift, as shown in figure 2.3. The word *Eileen* has two full vowels, hence two stress feet. For most speakers, the second foot is the one lexically marked as the potential association site for a nuclear accent. Whether or not the preceding syllable is accented, therefore, it will be the head of the intermediate phrase when uttered in isolation. In a phrase such as *Eileen Naylor*, on the other hand, unless there is a special pragmatic intent to focus narrowly on *Eileen*, the nuclear accent will be later, on the following word. In this case, any accent on *Eileen* will be prenuclear. If there were two prenuclear accents, the first might be perceived as stronger because of the rise in pitch to the first H*, as described above in section 2.3. Or, if there is just one accent, there might be an impetus to associate it to the first readily accentable full syllable. The results of Beckman *et al.* (1990) suggest that this impetus is not strictly a rhythmic one, since the association of a prenuclear accent to the first syllable occurs in *Chinese antique* as easily as in *Chinese dresser*. Rather, the impetus may simply be to give a tonal target as soon as possible in the otherwise unspecified stretch before the nuclear accent. We suspect that such an impetus to have an early tone specification, combined with the greater salience of the first prenuclear H* when there are more than one, is what gives rise to the tendencies that Hayes (1984) observed concerning the spacing of stresses on the "level of scansion." In any case, whether there is an accent on each of the two syllables of *Chinese* or only on the first, the pitch-accent pattern would make the first syllable seem more stressed without any necessary increase in duration or intensity. This account is compatible with results of experiments by Beckman *et al.* (1988, 1990), by Shattuck-Hufnagel (1988, 1989, 1991), and by Horne (1990). It is

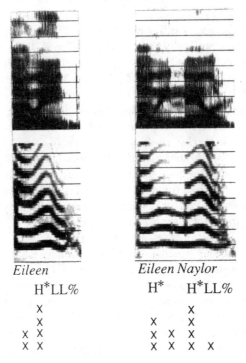

Figure 2.3. Spectrograms and grids for *Eileen* versus *Eileen Naylor* in citation form with hat pattern.

similar in spirit (if not in many details) to the accounts of Vanderslice and Ladefoged (1972) and of Gussenhoven (1991).[4]

This explanation of stress shift in terms of potential for prenuclear accent placement would account for the interaction of stress shift and phonological phrasing that is noted by Selkirk (1984) and many others. If we understand the relevant phrase type to be Pierrehumbert's intermediate phrase, then shifting stress when *Chinese* is separated from the following word by a phrase boundary would mean putting the nuclear accent for the first intermediate phrase somewhere other than on its lexically specified docking site.

The explanation would also account for the asymmetry in possible shift directions (figure 2.4). In theory, prenuclear accents can be placed on any full syllable before the nuclear accent. Therefore, the stress can shift leftward away from the docking site for nuclear accent in the words *Chinese* and *Pennsylvania* when they occur in the rhythmically clashing phrases *Chinese men* and *Pennsylvania legislature*. However, stress does not shift rightward

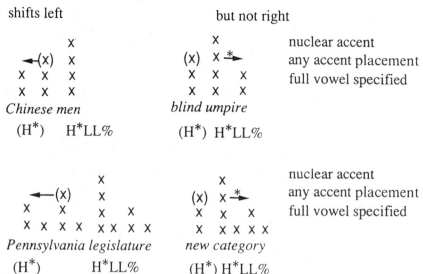

Figure 2.4. The directionality of stress shift.

away from the docking sites in *umpire* and *category* when these words occur in the equally clashing phrases *blind umpire* and *new category*, because that would mean putting a pitch accent in the postnuclear region normally filled by the phrase accent.

A final consequence of this account of the English stress system is that it may help explain the often contradictory results of studies of phonetic correlates of stress. Many previous phonetic studies have compared the intensities, durations, and F_0 excursions in "stressed" versus "unstressed" syllables without controlling systematically for the levels of the stress hierarchy involved. Looking at the lists of phrases or sentences used in these experiments, and trying to guess at the intended readings, we find a rather motley set. In some studies, stress is manipulated by cueing the speaker to shift the nuclear accent from one monosyllabic word to another. Here the comparison between "stressed" and "unstressed" would contrast a nuclear-accented syllable to an unaccented (or perhaps prenuclear-accented) syllable, but both syllables would be full-voweled heads of their stress feet. In other studies, stress is manipulated by using polysyllabic words with the potential nuclear-accent docking site specified lexically for different syllables. Here the "stressed" and "unstressed" syllables often contrast in having full versus reduced vowel specification in addition to (or instead of) the accentual contrast. Therefore, it comes as no surprise when such different corpora yield conflicting results. The first sort of experiment might find that "stressed" syllables have larger F_0 excursions, and that this is a more reliable acoustic correlate than intensity and duration. The second sort of experiment might find the opposite, that greater intensity and longer duration are more reliable measures of stress than F_0 excursion. (See Beckman 1986, pp. 60–62 and 88–89, for a review and discussion of some of this literature.)

The results of articulatory studies of stress have been similarly confusing. Some studies (e.g. Kelso *et al.* 1985) show bigger articulator movements in stressed syllables and a relationship of observed movement speed to size that suggests that the opening gesture into the stressed vowel target is actively targeted as a larger and underlyingly slower movement. Results of other studies (e.g. Summers 1987; Nittrouer *et al.* 1988) suggest that stressed and unstressed vowel gestures might be similar in targeted size and speed, with the main contrast being the duration of the target "hold" before the onset of the gesture into the next segment. We suspect that these apparent contradictions are an artifact of comparing different sets of stress categories. The articulatory patterns involved in making a reduced versus a full vowel specification need not bear any resemblance to those involved in making the minor adjustments in durations of accented versus unaccented full vowels.

In the rest of this paper we will present the results of an experiment in which we compare the articulatory kinematics of stress contrasts at these two different levels in the prosodic hierarchy in English. We will interpret the results in terms of our proposed account of the different head-marking features, and show that the observed patterns are more compatible with it than with an account that posits different values along some scale for a unitary autosegmental feature "stress."

2.5 Examining articulatory kinematics

The data that we will report are part of a larger experiment designed to examine the interaction of various accent-placement patterns with several other prosodic contrasts. Example 1 extracts the relevant sentences from this larger corpus. In these two sentences, there are three target syllables, exemplifying two different stress contrasts. The first syllable of *papa* in sentence (a) is the nuclear-accented head of the intonation phrase and contrasts with the same syllable unaccented in postnuclear position in sentence (b). That syllable, in turn, contrasts with the following reduced second syllable in being the head of the stress foot. (The full syllable contrasts with the reduced syllable also in its position within the word. However, since any effect of position would be to lengthen the word-final reduced vowel, we can be confident that any durational difference between the two must reflect a stress effect that is large enough to counteract the positional one.)

Example 1. Corpus of sentences (and context questions).
    (a) [Was her mama a problem about the wedding?]
        Her PAPA posed a problem.
    (b) [Did his dad pose a problem as far as their getting married?]
        HER papa posed a problem.

We had four subjects repeat these sentences in random order while we tracked the movements of their lips and jaws using the optoelectronic tracking system at Haskins Laboratories. We had the speakers produce the sentences at three different self-selected speaking rates so that we could examine the two stress contrasts across a range of durations and articulator speeds at the different tempi. We listened to the utterances to confirm that the speakers produced the expected intonation pattern of a single intermediate phrase with a $L + H^*$ nuclear pitch accent on the contrastively emphasized word (capitalized in the example) followed by a L phrase accent and L% boundary tone.

We collected various measures of lip and jaw movement in the target syllables and also measured the acoustic duration of each vowel, from the onset of voicing after the release of the syllable-initial [p] to the offset of voicing into the following [p]. One of the articulatory measurements we made was a rough analogue of this acoustic duration measure; we calculated the "lip cycle" duration for each syllable from the time for the peak lower-lip value for the syllable-initial [p] to that for the following syllable's [p]. The other articulatory measurements were the duration, displacement, and peak velocity of the lower-lip movement into the vowel for all four subjects, and the displacement for the jaw-opening movement for three of the four subjects. Note that all but the last of these articulatory measures are defined in terms of the lower lip rather than the jaw. This contrasts with other similar work we have done, where we used jaw position as an estimate of the openness of the vowel. For one subject, however, the jaw trace did not always show a local maximum for the initial [p] or a local minimum for the vowel in the reduced syllable. Since the overall "cycle" duration and the other kinematic measures are defined in terms of excursions from peak to valley and back, therefore, we worked from the lower-lip trace, which always showed clear maxima and minima. Lower-lip position is a more direct index to the consonant target. While it is a less direct index to the vowel target, it does still indicate vocal tract openness through its mechanical coupling to the jaw.

It is a common observation in articulatory studies that movement velocity tends to vary as a function of the movement size; other things being equal, a larger displacement is accomplished with a greater speed. Thus, the raw peak velocity cannot be interpreted directly in terms of the intended movement duration. Also, as Lindblom (1963) and others have suggested, raw displacement cannot be interpreted directly in terms of the intended movement endpoint, because of the potential for "undershoot" when successive gestures involving the same articulators are spaced closely in time. In order to get a quantitative interpretation of the observed kinematic measures in terms of intended durations and target endpoints, therefore, we adopted a model of the underlying dynamics (see Saltzman and Munhall 1989; Browman and Goldstein 1990). This task-dynamic model assumes that speech articulation is best described in terms of an orchestration of gestures for such elementary tasks as labial closure for [p] or pharyngeal constriction for [ɑ], as shown in the top part of figure 2.5. Gestures are specified for three abstract dynamic parameters – stiffness, amplitude, and intergestural phasing – which can be understood roughly as the intended duration of a gesture, its displacement from an intended target position, and the intended temporal spacing between successive gestures.

The lower part of figure 2.5 gives our understanding of how to interpret the kinematic measures of observed movements in terms of the dynamic specifications of underlying gestures. A change in underlying stiffness will affect peak velocity but not displacement; the observed duration will therefore change in direct proportion to the displacement–velocity ratio. A change in underlying amplitude will effect a change in observed displacement, but it will also change the peak velocity, in direct proportion to the displacement, leaving the displacement–velocity ratio and the observed duration both unchanged. A change in phasing will change only the observed duration and not peak velocity or displacement unless the following gesture begins early enough to truncate the preceding gesture before it reaches its targeted displacement.

2.6 Results

Figure 2.6 shows mean lip-cycle durations at each of the three tempi for two of the four subjects. (The mean acoustic vowel durations generally mirrored the patterns of these values very closely, and so will not be shown.) Looking first at the contrast between accented and unaccented vowels, we see a difference between the two subjects. JRE has significantly longer lip-cycle durations at fast and slow tempi, whereas KAJ does not show a consistent durational effect of accent. The other two subjects showed patterns similar to those of JRE. When we look at the contrast between full and reduced vowels, on the other hand, there is a large and consistent durational difference; the vowel in the syllable that heads the stress foot has

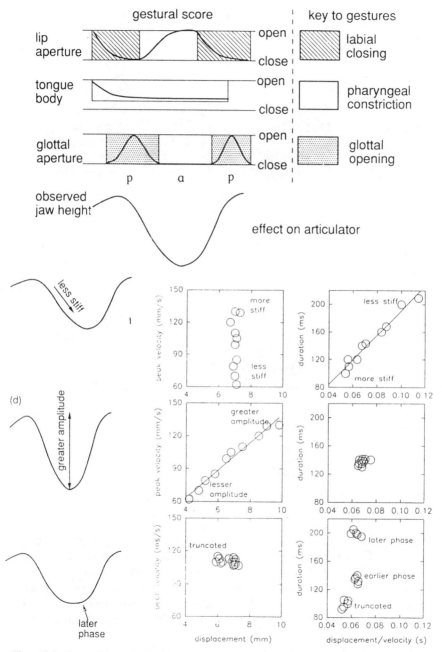

Figure 2.5. Gestural score for [pɑp] and interpretation of observed articulator kinematics in terms of underlying gestures.

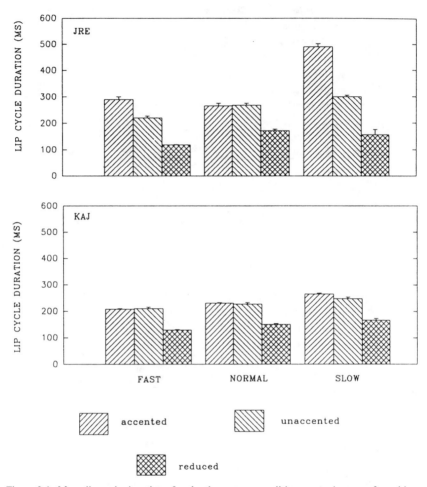

Figure 2.6. Mean lip-cycle durations for the three stress conditions at each tempo for subjects JRE (upper panel) and KAJ (lower panel).

substantially longer lip-cycle durations. This difference is larger than the difference for accented versus unaccented vowels at nearly all tempi and is consistent across all four subjects. The very much shorter duration of the reduced syllable is particularly noteworthy, given the fact that its word-final position should, if anything, make it longer than it would be otherwise. The stress effect at this level is very large, despite the counteracting effect of position within the word.

We now turn to an examination of the kinematics associated with the durational differences at these two levels of stress contrast. Since KAJ showed no durational effect of accent, another subject will be shown instead. Figure 2.7 gives the mean durations, displacements, and peak velocities for the lip-opening movement from the [p] into the vowel for the three syllable types for JRE and this other subject, KDJ. Again, the differences associated with the contrast between accented and unaccented syllables are smaller than those for the other stress contrast, and they are inconsistent across speakers and tempi. KDJ generally has longer movement durations, greater displacements, and larger peak velocities for the accented syllable, but no difference in duration at slow tempo. JRE shows no significant difference in duration at normal tempo, and no difference in the other two measures at normal and slow tempi. The differences associated with full versus reduced syllables, by contrast, are substantial for all three measures, and consistent across speakers and tempi. For both these speakers at all three tempi, the full vowels are associated with longer, more displaced, and faster opening movements. This substantial and consistent difference between full and reduced syllables was true for the other two speakers as well.

The displacement values in figure 2.7 give the correct measure for calculating the underlying stiffness (which we will discuss in conjunction with figure 2.9 below). However, because the lower lip height in the [p] was not constant, the displacements are not the most direct measure of the targeted endpoint of the movement. That is, a larger displacement might reflect a higher position in the consonant and not a lower position due to greater vocal tract openness for the vowel. To understand the differences in movement displacement in terms of differences in the vowel target, therefore, we examined absolute articulator position. For the two subjects shown in figure 2.7 (and one other subject), we could look at absolute jaw position, since the jaw trace showed clear minima even for the reduced vowel. These values are given in figure 2.8.

Again, the differences associated with the contrast between full versus reduced syllables are larger and more consistent than those associated with the contrast between accented and unaccented syllables. For KDJ, there is no consistent stress effect on how high the jaw rises during the consonant, but there is a consistent effect on how low it goes during the vowel. The jaw is somewhat lower for the accented vowel as compared to the unaccented full vowel, and it is very much lower in the unaccented full vowel by comparison to reduced vowel, at all three tempi. For JRE, the jaw tends to be higher during the [p] in the accented syllable by comparison to the unaccented and in the full-voweled syllable by comparison to the reduced (although the effect is more consistent in the latter case). On the other hand, the effect of accent on the vowel position is not consistent, whereas the effect of stress prominence is large and consistent across tempi. (The pattern for

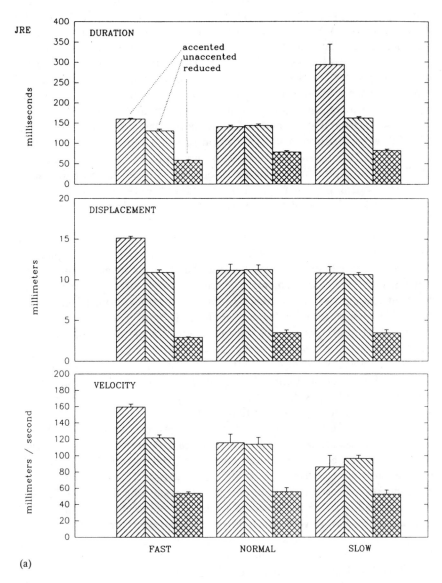

Figure 2.7. Mean durations, displacements, and peak velocities for lip-opening movements in the three stress conditions at each tempo for subjects JRE (a, this page) and KDJ (b, next page).

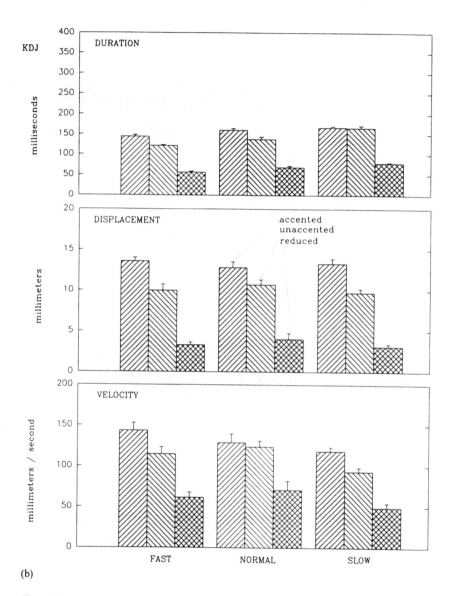

(b)

Figure 2.7. (*continued*)

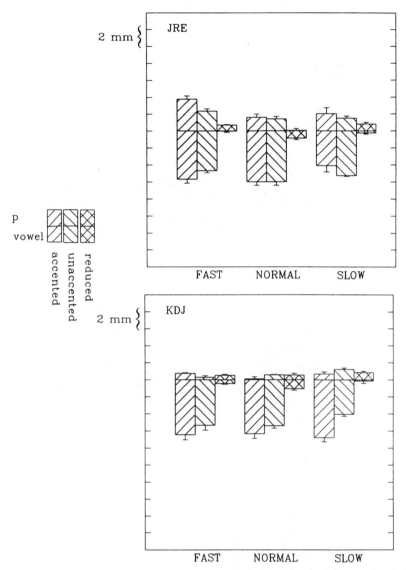

Figure 2.8. Mean jaw positions at maximum value during the [p] and minimum value during the vowel for the three stress conditions at each tempo for subjects JRE (top) and KDJ (bottom).

the other subject who had clear jaw minima is like KDJ's.) Thus in general we can say that the vocal tract tends to be somewhat more open during an accented [ɑ] by comparison to an unaccented [ɑ] (although the effect is not consistent across speakers and tempi), and that it is consistently very much more open during the full vowel than during the corresponding reduced vowel.

We next look at the relationships among the three kinematic measures in order to determine what dynamic specifications might be responsible for the small, inconsistent differences in the durations of the accented versus unaccented (full-voweled) syllables and for the much larger, consistent differences in the durations of the (unaccented) full- versus reduced-vowel syllables. Figure 2.9 plots these relationships for the two subjects whose mean values were shown in figure 2.7.

Looking first at the relationship between peak velocity and displacement, we see that the tokens with reduced vowels form a clearly separate group. They lie below and to the left of the full-voweled tokens, with little overlap in peak velocity values and no overlap in displacement. The values for tokens of the two full-voweled types, by contrast, overlap substantially with each other in both dimensions, although again there is less overlap in displacement than in velocity values. The greater overlap is completely expected given the much closer means for these two types, whereas the common pattern of relatively more overlap in the vertical dimension of the plot is not. That is, for both stress contrasts, the tokens of the less prominent syllable type show larger velocities than would be expected for their displacements given the relationship between velocity and displacement for the more prominent syllable type. This pattern could be interpreted in either of two ways. The movement into the less prominent syllable might have a greater velocity because the underlying gesture is stiffer (i.e. shorter intended duration). Or it could have smaller displacement than expected for its velocity value because it has been cut off by an earlier closing gesture (i.e. closer phasing and truncation).

The other two panels of the figure help to distinguish between these two interpretations. For KDJ, the observed movement durations are a fairly linear function of the durations predicted by their displacement–velocity ratios. A single regression curve would capture fairly well the total trend in the data. Thus, both durational contrasts seem to arise from a difference in underlying stiffness. For JRE, by contrast, two different mechanisms seem to be involved. The reduced and unaccented full-vowel tokens lie on the same line, indicating a difference in stiffness, whereas the accented tokens lie above this trend, suggesting a change in phasing. On the other hand, this difference between the two subjects is not nearly so striking as the aspect of the pattern that both share; for both subjects the full-voweled tokens

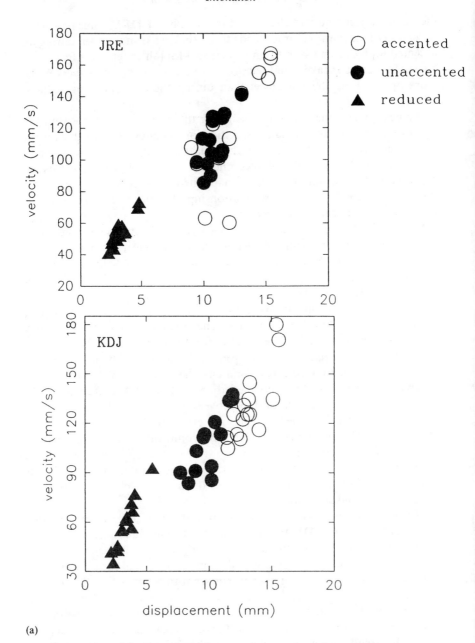

(a)

Figure 2.9. Peak velocity versus displacement (a, this page) and movement duration versus displacement/velocity ratio (b, next page) for opening movements in the three stress conditions for JRE (top) and KDJ (bottom).

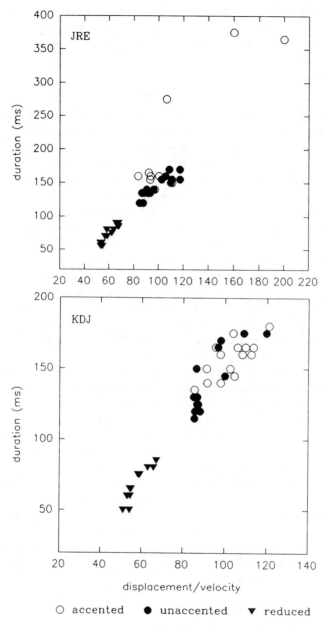

(b)

Figure 2.9. (*continued*)

overlap considerably in both their observed durations and their displace-ment–velocity ratios, and together form a very distinct group from the other stress condition. This is true of the other two subjects as well.

2.7 Conclusion

To summarize these results, we can make the following generalizations. If a syllable with a full vowel is associated to the nuclear accent as the head of its intermediate intonation phrase, other aspects of its production can be affected. For many speakers, the syllable will be longer than a comparable unaccented syllable and have a slightly larger, faster opening movement. However, this effect is not consistent across subjects and tempi, and contrasts sharply with the effect of a prominence contrast at a lower level of the prosodic hierarchy. If a syllable has a full vowel specification as the head of its stress foot, it will necessarily be much longer than a syllable with a reduced vowel, and will have a much larger, faster opening movement.[5]

If interpreted in terms of relative amounts of a content-feature "stress," this difference between the two effects is surprising. Why should the strong syllable at the lower level of the hierarchy be so much longer and larger than unstressed syllables at that level when the strong syllable at the higher level is hardly affected by its structural position? In our account of the stress system of English, however, this pattern is exactly as we would expect. At the lower level, the phonological content of the contrast is one of vowel quality; the full vowel [ɑ] must have a more open vocal tract, and hence a lower jaw and larger lip displacement in going into the vowel. The duration difference, too, is an inherent part of the specification of the prominence contrast at this level. At the higher level, on the other hand, any effect of the prominence on the syllable's duration or on its degree of vocal-tract opening is ancillary to the associated intonation pattern. Speakers can augment the prominence of the accented syllable by making it longer and more open, and thus perhaps louder. And there may be circumstances in which we would expect them to do so to insure that the F_0 contour is correctly interpreted (for example, if there is no sharp F_0 excursion at the nuclear accent, as in a H* H L% contour). On the other hand, the durational prominence is secondary to the phonological marking of the accent, and is clearly optional, since not all speakers make it.

Notes

The work presented in this paper was supported in part by the National Science Foundation under grants IRI-8617852 and IRI-8858109 to Mary Beckman and IRI-

8617873 to Jan Edwards. We thank Haskins Laboratories for generously letting us use the optoelectronic tracking system.

1 Here we assume that [ə] contrasts with vowels such as [æ] in being underspecified (e.g. Borowsky 1986) or targetless (Browman and Goldstein 1992). Note, however, that this definition of the lowest level of stress contrast is somewhat oversimplified, since it ignores cases such as the last syllable of *lackey* (as opposed to *latchkey*) where the high front vowel does not seem to make the syllable the head of its own stress foot. We see these as the analogous problem for the stress foot as that posed for the syllable by [w], [j], and [ɹ], vowel segments which do not constitute heads of their own syllables.

2 We mean here that many American English speakers can put the nuclear accent in words such as *fifteen* on their first syllables even in the absence of special contrastive emphasis, as in counting (*Five, ten, fifteen, twenty...*), although they otherwise produce the forms in isolation with nuclear accent on the second syllable (*The number? Fifteen.*).

3 Meaning that, phonologically, the intermediate phrase is right-dominant (the last accented word is the strongest), just as the stress foot is left-dominant (the first syllable is the strongest). There is a small complication for the theory in general in that prenuclear accented syllables, while clearly being a distinct level of stress from nuclear-accented syllables, do not clearly define any constituent below the intermediate phrase; it is possible to have strings of words with no accented syllables, and it is also possible to have two accented syllables within a word. See Beckman and Pierrehumbert (1986) for a discussion of this problem.

4 One main difference is that ours is a description of pitch-accent placement and other categorical properties of stress as surface phonological phenomena, and we make no claims about how (or whether) accents might be assigned in deep strata of the phonology. Also, the theories of intonation assumed in these two works are both different from Pierrehumbert's, as well as from each other, in the treatment of prenuclear accents and intermediate phrases, among other things. Moreover, Vanderslice and Ladefoged do not make an explicitly hierarchical representation of the relationship between different levels of stress, although their account would be very easily translated into such a representation.

5 The differences perhaps would not be as large in a pair such as *lackey* versus *latchkey* (see note 1 above), but we would be surprised if the other dynamic differences were very much smaller. It is difficult to imagine how else the prosodic contrast could be realized between a "reduced" and "full" [i].

References

Beckman, M.E. 1986. *Stress and Non-Stress Accent*. Netherlands Phonetic Archives 7. Dordrecht: Foris.

Beckman, M.E., K. De Jong and J. Edwards. 1988. Intonational and rhythmic correlates of stress clash. *Journal of the Acoustical Society of America* 83 (Suppl. 1): S113.

Beckman, M.E. and J. Pierrehumbert. 1986. Intonational structure in Japanese and English. *Phonology Yearbook* 3: 255–309.

Beckman, M.E., M.G. Swora, J. Rauschenberg and K. De Jong. 1990. Stress shift, stress clash, and polysyllabic shortening in a prosodically annotated discourse. In *Proceedings of the 1990 International Conference on Spoken Language Processing*, Kobe, 1: 5–8.

Bolinger, D. 1965. Pitch accent and sentence rhythm. In I Abe and T Kanekiya (eds.) *Forms of English: Accent, Morpheme, Order*, 139–180. Cambridge, MA: Harvard University Press.

Borowsky, T.J. 1986. Topics in the lexical phonology of English. Ph.D. dissertation, University of Massachusetts.

Browman, C.P. and L. Goldstein. 1990. Gestural specification using dynamically-defined articulatory gestures. *Journal of Phonetics* 18: 299–320.

1992. "Targetless" schwa: an articulatory analysis. In G. Docherty and D.R. Ladd (eds.) *Papers in Laboratory Phonology II: Gesture, Segment, Prosody*, 26–56. Cambridge: University Press.

Cooper, W.E. and S.J. Eady. 1986. Metrical phonology in speech production. *Journal of Memory and Language* 25: 369–384.

Fry, D.B. 1958. Experiments in the perception of stress. *Language and Speech* 1: 126–152.

Gussenhoven, C. 1991. The English Rhythm Rule as an accent deletion rule. *Phonology* 8: 1–35.

Hammond, M. 1986. The obligatory-branching parameter in metrical theory. *Natural Language and Linguistic Theory* 4: 185–228.

Hayes, B. 1984. The phonology of rhythm in English. *Linguistic Inquiry* 15: 33–74.

Horne, M. 1990. Empirical evidence for a deletion analysis of the rhythm rule in English. *Linguistics* 28: 959–981.

Huss, V. 1978. English word stress in post-nuclear position. *Phonetica* 35: 86–105.

Kelso, J.A.S., E. Vatikiotis-Bateson, E.L. Saltzman and B. Kay 1985. A qualitative dynamic analysis of reiterant speech production: Phase portraits, kinematics, and dynamic modeling. *Journal of the Acoustical Society of America* 77: 266–280.

Kingdon, R. 1958. *The Groundwork of English Intonation*. London: Longmans, Green, & Co.

Klatt, D.H. 1977. Linguistic uses of segmental duration in English: Acoustic and perceptual evidence. *Journal of the Acoustical Society of America* 59: 1208–1221.

Liberman, M. and A. Prince. 1977. On stress and linguistic rhythm. *Linguistic Inquiry* 8: 249–336.

Lindblom, B. 1963. A spectrographic study of vowel reduction. *Journal of the Acoustical Society of America* 35: 1773–1781.

Nespor, M. and I. Vogel. 1986. *Prosodic Phonology*. Dordrecht: Foris.

Nittrouer, S., K. Munhall, J.A.S. Kelso, B. Tuller and K.S. Harris. 1988. Patterns of interarticulator phasing and their relationship to linguistic structure. *Journal of the Acoustical Society of America* 84: 1653–1661.

Pickett, J.M. 1980. *The Sounds of Speech Communication*. Baltimore: University Park Press.

Pierrehumbert, J. 1980. The phonology and phonetics of English intonation. Ph.D. dissertation, MIT. (Distributed 1987 by the Indiana University Linguistics Club.)

Pierrehumbert, J.B. and M.E. Beckman. 1988. *Japanese Tone Structure*. Linguistic Inquiry Monographs 15. Cambridge, MA: MIT Press.

Pierrehumbert, J. and J. Hirschberg 1990. The meaning of intonation contours in the interpretation of discourse. In P. R. Cohen, J. Morgan and M.E. Pollack (eds.) *Intentions in Communication*, 271–311. Cambridge, MA: MIT Press (Bradford Books).

Pierrehumbert, J. and D. Talkin, 1992. Lenition of /h/ and glottal stop. In G. Docherty and D.R. Ladd (eds.) *Papers in Laboratory Phonology II: Gesture, Segment, Prosody*. Cambridge: University Press, 90–116.

Saltzman, E.L. and K.G. Munhall. 1989. A dynamical approach to gestural patterning in speech production. *Ecological Psychology* 1: 333–382.

Scott, N.C. 1939. An experiment on stress perception. *Le Maître Phonétique* 67: 44–45.

Selkirk, E.O. 1980. The role of prosodic categories in English word stress. *Linguistic Inquiry* 11: 563–605.

1981. On the nature of phonological representation. In T. Myers, J. Laver and J. Anderson (eds.) *The Cognitive Representation of Speech*, 379–399. Amsterdam: North-Holland.

1984. *Phonology and Syntax*. Cambridge, MA: MIT Press.

Shattuck-Hufnagel, S. 1988. Acoustic phonetic correlates of stress shift. *Journal of the Acoustical Society of America* 84 (Suppl. 1): S98.

1989. Stress shift as the placement of phrase-level pitch markers. *Journal of the Acoustical Society of America* 86 (Suppl. 1): S49.

1991. Acoustic correlates of stress shift. *Proceedings of the XII International Congress of Phonetic Sciences*, Aix-en-Provence, August 1991, 4: 266–269.

Summers, W.V. 1987. Effects of stress and final-consonant voicing on vowel production: Articulatory and acoustic analyses. *Journal of the Acoustical Society of America* 82: 847–863.

Trager, G.L. 1941. The theory of accentual systems. In L. Spier, A.I. Hallowell and S.S. Newman (eds.), *Essays in Memory of Edward Sapir*, 131–145. New York: Sapir Memorial Publications Fund.

Trubetskoy, N.S. 1939. *Grundzüge der Phonologie*. Travaux du Cercle Linguistique de Prague VII.

Vanderslice, R. and P. Ladefoged. 1972. Binary suprasegmental features and transformational word-accentuation rules. *Language* 48: 819–838.

3

"Stress shift" as early placement of pitch accents: a comment on Beckman and Edwards

STEFANIE SHATTUCK-HUFNAGEL

Beckman and Edwards' paper has two parts: a concise synthesis of an emerging phonological view of prosodic structure, in which the prominent element or head at each level of the prosodic constituent hierarchy is cued by a level-specific set of phonological and phonetic variables, and a description of an experiment aimed at clarifying the articulatory correlates of the level-specific contrasts in stress described in the theory. I will focus here, briefly, on the phonological model and, more extensively, its account of perceived stress shift in terms of the placement of phrase-level pitch accents.

3.1 A model of stress

Beckman and Edwards (henceforth B & E) see prosody as a mechanism for organizing utterances, and "stress" as a term for a number of different types of prominence. They concentrate on two kinds of prominence contrast, presence/absence of a nuclear pitch accent, and presence/absence of a full vowel. Each type of prominence corresponds to the head of a different constituent level in the prosodic hierarchy:

1. the nuclear-pitch-accented syllable (the last and strongest prominence in the constituent "intermediate phrase") versus
2. the non-pitch-accented full-vowel syllable (the first and strongest prominence in the constituent "stress foot") versus
3. the reduced syllable (a nonhead element in the stress foot).

A fourth type of generally recognized prominence, the prenuclear accented syllable, is not included in the discussion of the model but is mentioned by B & E. It is interesting to note in this regard that Vanderslice and Ladefoged

(1972), working in a very different framework, distinguish essentially the same four categories of prominence, using the three separate content features [+intonation] for nuclear pitch accent, [+accent] for nonnuclear accent, and [+heavy] for full-vowel syllables.

B & E note that the prenuclear accented syllable is currently problematic for their theory because they have not identified a constituent (smaller than the intermediate phrase) for which it might be a head. Beckman and Pierrehumbert (1986) discuss the possibility that each accented syllable heads a constituent called the "accentual phrase," but that idea seems to have been abandoned here. A possible avenue of investigation is suggested by the work of Wightman et al. (1992), who found evidence from preboundary lengthening of the syllable rhyme to support several prosodic constituents smaller than the intermediate phrase. Perhaps one of these domains for lengthening is the constituent which would complete B & E's model of stress.

The experimental results by B & E make clear that the effects of prosodic structure on duration are not uniform and incremental. First, the different kinds of "stress" of the model are associated with separate acoustic correlates (duration and F_0). Second, lengthening of segments at the boundaries of prosodic constituents affects the syllable differently from the lengthening related to prominence. In particular, accent-related lengthening affects both the opening and closing gestures of the syllable, while boundary-related lengthening affects just the closing gesture (Edwards et al. 1991; see Wightman et al. 1992 for compatible data from acoustic segment durations in different positions in preboundary syllables). In other words, B & E have shown that two aspects of prosodic structure (prosodic boundaries and nuclear-pitch-accent prominence) have distinguishable effects on what has traditionally been thought of as a single acoustic parameter, duration. B & E's view stands in sharp contrast to a model in which effects on duration simply add together to determine a final segment-duration value, which then has a potentially infinite number of possible interpretations for the listener.

We know from the work of Klatt (1977) and others that many different factors can influence segment duration. The idea that various prosodic effects can be distinguished in the acoustic signal offers a solution to the puzzle of how listeners take apart the resulting duration of a segment in an utterance. B & E's argument that different kinds of stress, traditionally thought of as a unitary phenomenon, are differently signaled by duration versus F_0 is in a similar vein. Their discussion also suggests that fine-grained acoustic analysis of the speech signal may provide even more useful cues to its underlying prosodic structure than we had previously imagined. Thus B & E's experimental results and model are of general importance.

3.2 A model of stress shift as early pitch-accent placement

In what was originally a footnote but has now been expanded into a fuller discussion, B & E discuss the relevance of their theory of stress for the phenomenon called "stress shift." Theoretical treatments of stress shift fall into two general categories. *Rhythm-based theories* relate an apparent leftward shift of stress to the rhythmic context, positing a representation of relative prominence either in terms of binary-branching trees with strong and weak branches, or in terms of a metrical grid, or both (Liberman and Prince 1977; Kiparsky 1979; Prince 1983; Hayes 1984; Selkirk 1984; Nespor and Vogel 1986). When word concatentation and phrasal prominence assignment result in prominent syllables that occur too close together, too far apart, or at intervals that are too irregular, prominence is moved leftward to create a more regular rhythmic pattern (Hayes 1984) or to resolve the "stress clash" or "stress lapse" (Nespor and Vogel 1986). The phonetic correlate of the moved prominence is not generally specified in these phonological theories, which are based on the systematic intuitions that some speakers have about which contexts will induce shifts of prominence within words.

In the second class of theories, apparent stress shift is a matter of phrase-level pitch-accent placement (Bolinger 1965; Vanderslice and Ladefoged 1972; Shattuck-Hufnagel 1989; Horne 1990; Gussenhoven 1991). These *pitch-accent-based theories* account for perceived shift in terms of choices among allowable pitch-accent locations specified for each lexical item. Roughly speaking, these options permit a pitch accent on any syllable that contains an unreduced vowel. The nuclear pitch accent of the phrase, however, must go on the main-stress syllable of its word. When a word like *Massachusetts* is perceived as stress-shifted, it is because the speaker has chosen to place a pitch accent on the earlier syllable, *Mass-*, and not on the main-stress syllable *chu-*.

Pitch-accent-based theories often minimize the role of rhythmic stress clash as an influence on stress shift, suggesting instead that speakers tend to place a pitch accent as early as possible in a phrase. However, even within pitch-accent-based theories, there is room for rhythmic considerations to influence the placement of pitch accents. Gussenhoven (1991) gives an account of this kind, describing apparent shift in terms of deletion of alternate pitch accents leftward from the nuclear accent. For example, in his rule system the middle of three successive accents can be deleted under certain circumstances (see also Vanderslice and Ladefoged 1972). This proposal imposes a rhythmic constraint on pitch-accent placement, with the result that accented and unaccented accent sites tend to alternate.

B & E's view of stress shift belongs to the pitch-accent-placement school. They note that each full-vowel (unreduced) syllable in a word is the head of its own stress foot. One such foot in every word is marked as the "potential association site for a nuclear accent"; its head is the main-stress syllable. When the word is produced in isolation, this syllable is the head of the intermediate phrase and so must receive the nuclear pitch accent, as in the late-stress target word

      Massachusetts
             *

             *

(two asterisks indicate the location of a nuclear pitch accent). B & E note that the earlier stress foot may also receive a prenuclear accent.

When the target word is combined with additional words to form a longer phrase, so that the nuclear accent falls on a later word, B & E note that neither, either, or both syllables of the earlier word may receive a prenuclear accent. If only the first syllable does, due to a preference for an early accent, then the main-stress syllable of the target word may be left without one:

      the Massachusetts miracle.
          *   *

                *

Note that there has been no shift of prominence from -*chu-* to -*Mass-* in the longer phrase. If anything has "shifted," it is the nuclear pitch accent, now located on the *mir-* of *miracle*, rather than on the -*chu-* of *Massachusetts*.

An analogy could be drawn with apparent cross-word-boundary shift in the phrase

      a new Massachusetts miracle,
       *   *

                  *

with an even earlier placement of the initial or "onset" pitch accent in the phrase, and complete deaccentuation of the word *Massachusetts*. For all three of these phrases, the pattern of pitch-accent placement is the same: an initial pitch accent on an early full-vowel syllable, and the nuclear pitch accent on a later main stress syllable.

Bolinger (1965) originally suggested that speakers choose to locate the onset accent on the earliest possible syllable of a new phrase in order to create the preferred intonation contour, one with pitch markers both early and late in the contour. Selkirk (1984) argued that such a model cannot account for the occurrence of shift in a phrase-medial word, as in "THIRteen TENNessee MINers," because the medial word must be deaccented. However, pitch-accent-based models do not necessarily predict deaccenting of the medial word. As B & E note, the speaker has a number of options, including (1) deaccenting, (2) placing a single accent on the early syllable, (3) placing a single accent on the main-stress syllable, or even (4) double-accenting a target word. These accentual alternatives can provide an account for the phrase-medial stress shifts Selkirk discusses. In the example above, the speaker has chosen option (2) for both *thirteen* and *Tennessee*.

Since many options for accent placement are available to the speaker, empirical predictions regarding F_0 comparisons between shifted and nonshifted versions of a target word are difficult. If the early syllable is accented in the same way in both cases, the F_0 pattern for that syllable in the two renditions may differ very little. In addition, the *type* of pitch accent matters: if the speaker accents the early syllable with a high pitch accent in the nonshifted case, but a low pitch accent in the shifted case, there is no sense in looking for a higher F_0 level in the shifted case. These problems can be addressed by phonologically labelling the prosodic structure and tonal options actually implemented for the utterances and comparing only appropriate instances.

2.3 Experimental test of apparent "stress shift" as early pitch-accent placement in the phrase

Empirical exploration of the hypothesis that apparent stress shift arises from the "unmasking" of an early-in-the-word pitch accent by (a) disappearance of the nuclear pitch accent from the main-stress syllable, combined with (b) a tendency to locate a pitch accent as early in the phrase as available options permit, must focus on three questions:

1. Is apparent stress shift in fact perceived by naive listeners?
2. Does it occur in contexts predicted by early accent placement?
3. Does it exhibit the acoustic correlates that an accent-placement view predicts?

2.3.1 Is apparent shift perceived?

Although many speakers report systematic intuitions about apparent stress shift, others do not, so it is important to demonstrate that apparent shift is perceived even by listeners who are naive about the theory. In work that I have been doing with Mari Ostendorf and Ken Ross of Boston University, and Patti Price of Stanford Research Institute, analysing a corpus of FM-radio-news-style speech produced by two different speakers, we found that in 47 utterances of *Massachusetts* judged by naive listeners, 29% were shifted (the rest were deaccented or judged to have their major prominence on the main-stress syllable). While it is interesting that many speakers do not have intuitions about this phenomenon, clearly it occurs for some speakers and listeners.

2.3.2 Does apparent shift occur in non-clash contexts?

The early pitch-accent placement view predicts that apparent shift may occur in onset positions, whether or not there is a rhythmic clash. Beckman *et al.* (1990) report apparent shift without clash (in *Chinese antique*), and I have found a similar result for *Mississippi legislation* (Shattuck-Hufnagel 1991). But the fact remains that many speakers consistently report intuitions that shift is associated with clash environments. In support of these claims, Ross *et al.* (1992) report a greater tendency for early accent placement in clash contexts than in other contexts, although their results also show early accent placement without clash. Taken together, the available empirical results support the view that more than one factor determines the location of pitch accents in an utterance.

If accent placement is influenced by a number of factors, certain speaking situations may bring one factor to the fore. For example, in the special experimental situation where linguistic intuitions are elicited for short phrases in isolation, with no focus determined by the discourse and with minimal prosodic structure to require an onset signal, rhythmic factors may prevail, dictating that target words will shift only in clash contexts.

Additional factors are suggested by speakers who report that shift can occur in non-pitch-accented stretches of speech. These intuitions need to be tested empirically. For example, if the middle word in the phrase *good-looking Massachusetts governor* is deaccented, can it also undergo a stress shift? Rhythmic considerations predict it can (because there is a clash); pitch-accent-based theories rule it out (because there can be no early pitch-accent placement); perceptual tests combined with acoustic measures will determine the answer.

2.3.3 Are the acoustic correlates of perceived stress shift compatible with early pitch accent placement?

As B & E point out, the view of apparent stress shift as the unmasking of early pitch accent by the relocation of nuclear pitch accent rightward is compatible with several sets of published experimental results. Cooper and Eady (1986) report no increase in prominence-related parameters in contexts that should elicit shift, and in utterances where shift is actually perceived, Shattuck-Hufnagel (1991) reports similar results. Horne (1990) also examined the F_0 contour of the words perceived to have undergone stress shift. She found that the F_0 rise on the main-stress syllable was greatly reduced for the shifted case in comparison with the nonshifted case. This finding supports the claim that when early prominence is heard, there is no nuclear pitch accent on the main-stress syllable.

The phonological theory of stress presented by B & E suggests that at least some instances of perceived stress shift can be seen as the result of placing a pitch accent early in the word, perhaps to signal the onset of a new prosodic constituent. Experimental results from both these authors and others support this view of prosodic-constituent structure as a factor in pitch accent placement decisions. Ross *et al.* (1992) report a second factor: pitch-accent rhythm. In their sample of FM-radio-news-style speech, speakers tend to place a pitch accent early in the word to avoid a pitch-accent clash, i.e. in contexts where the initial syllable of the immediately following word is pitch accented. How the two factors of prosodic constituent structure and pitch-accent rhythm interact with semantic-pragmatic focus to determine patterns of accent placement across the phrase remains to be determined.

What does seem clear is that speakers have a number of options for pitch-accent placement in phrases. Thus, it is not possible to say with certainty what "the" pitch-accent pattern for a given phrase will be. Similarly, the same phrase may undergo apparent stress shift when spoken by some speakers and not when spoken by others, or by the same speaker on some occasions and not on others. In order to carry out meaningful investigations of the acoustic correlates of perceived prominence, it is important to study specific utterances, i.e. particular renditions of the phrases of interest, and to determine which of the possible prosodic constituent structures, pitch-accent types and boundary tone types were actually implemented by the speaker. This will ensure a precise specification of which prosodic phenomenon's acoustic correlates are being measured.

Not only do investigators need to know what prosodic options have been chosen by the speaker in the utterances they study; readers of papers also need to know what the cited examples sounded like. This, of course, requires a generally agreed-on scheme for prosodic transcription, since readers cannot rely on their intutions about how they would produce orthographi-cally transcribed examples. A system for transcribing the basic prosodic facts about an utterance has recently been proposed (Silverman *et al.* 1992). Perhaps this system, along with F_0 contours marked with word boundaries, would characterize an example utterance well enough to reproduce its prosody in the mind's ear.

References

Beckman, M. and J. Pierrehumbert. 1986. Intonational structure in Japanese and English. *Phonology Yearbook* 3: 255–309.

Beckman, M., M.G. Swora, J. Rauschenberg and K. De Jong. 1990. Stress shift, stress clash and polysyllabic shortening in a prosodically annotated discourse. In *Proceedings of the 1990 International Conference on Spoken Language Processing*, Kobe, 1: 5–8.

Bolinger, D. 1965. Pitch accent and sentence rhythm. In D. Bolinger, *Forms of English: Accent, Morpheme, Order*. Ed. Isamu Abe and Tetsuya Kanekiyo. Tokyo: Hokuou.

Cooper, W. and S.J. Eady. 1986. Metrical phonology in speech production. *Journal of Memory and Language* 25: 369–384.

Edwards, J., M. Beckman and J. Fletcher. 1991. The articulatory kinematics of final lengthening. *Journal of the Acoustical Society of America* 89(1): 369–382.

Gussenhoven, C. 1991. The English Rhythm Rule as an accent deletion rule. *Phonology* 8: 1–35.

Hayes, B. 1984. The phonology of rhythm in English. *Linguistic Inquiry* 15: 33–74.

Horne, M. 1990. Empirical evidence for a deletion formulation of the rhythm rule in English. *Linguistics* 28: 959–981.

Kiparsky, P. 1979. Metrical structure assignment is cyclic. *Linguistic Inquiry* 10: 421–442.

Klatt, D. 1977. Linguistic uses of segmental duration in English: Acoustic and perceptual evidence. *Journal of the Acoustical Society of America* 59: 1208–1221.

Liberman, M. and A. Prince. 1977. On stress and linguistic rhythm. *Linguistic Inquiry* 8: 249–336.

Nespor, M. and I. Vogel. 1986. *Prosodic Phonology*. Dordrecht: Foris.

1989. On clashes and lapses. *Phonology* 6: 69–116.

Prince, A. 1983. Relating to the grid. *Linguistic Inquiry* 14: 19–100.

Quene, H. and R. Kager. 1990. Automatic prosodic sentence analysis, accentuation and phrasing for Dutch text-to-speech conversion. *Final report 17, Research Institute for Language and Speech, Rijksuniversiteit Utrecht*, The Netherlands.

Ross, K., S. Shattuck-Hufnagel and M. Ostendorf. 1992. Factors affecting pitch accent placement. *Proceedings of the International Congress on Spoken Language Processing*, Banff, 1, 365–368.

Selkirk, E. 1984. *Phonology and Syntax: The Relation Between Sound and Structure*. Cambridge, MA: MIT Press.

Shattuck-Hufnagel, S. 1988. Acoustic-phonetic correlates of stress shift. *Journal of the Acoustical Society of America* 84 (Suppl. 1): S98.

1989. Stress shift as the placement of phrase-level pitch markers. *Journal of the Acoustical Society of America* 86 (Suppl. 1): S49.

1991. Acoustic correlates of stress shift. *Proceedings of the XII Congress of Phonetic Sciences*. Aix-en-Provence, August 1991, 4: 266–269.

Silverman, K. *et al.* 1992. A standard scheme for labelling prosody. *Proceedings of the International Conference on Spoken Language Processing*, Banff, 2, 867–870.

Vanderslice, R. and P. Ladefoged. 1972. Binary suprasegmental features and transformational word-accentuation rules. *Language* 48: 819–838.

Wightman, C., S. Shattuck-Hufnagel, M. Ostendorf and P. Price. 1992. Segmental durations in the vicinity of prosodic phrase boundaries. *Journal of the Acoustical Society of America* 91(3): 1707–1717.

4

Constraints on the gradient variability of pitch range, or, Pitch level 4 lives!

D. ROBERT LADD

4.1 The Free Gradient Variability hypothesis

One of the central assumptions of most work on intonation is that pitch range can vary gradiently to convey differences in emphasis or prominence. Indeed for most investigators this is not a "central assumption" but simply an indisputable fact: it is trivial to observe that when you raise your voice your utterance sounds more emphatic, and also – this is the gradient part – that the more you raise your voice the more emphatic it sounds. I don't propose to dispute either this fact, or the often tacit assumption that such variation in pitch range is "paralinguistic" and largely beyond the scope of phonological analysis.

However, the general observation that pitch range can vary gradiently and paralinguistically – which I don't dispute – has found its way into many theories of intonational phonology in the form of a much more specific assumption about the nature and extent of gradient variability – which I have been disputing for some years now. The assumption is this: the pitch range *on any pitch accent* can be gradiently varied to convey differences in "emphasis" or "prominence," and this variation is largely independent of, or unconstrained by, the pitch-range variation on any other part of the utterance. I will refer to this assumption as the Free Gradient Variability (FGV) hypothesis.

The FGV hypothesis is illustrated in the following two quotes, which display strikingly similar assumptions despite the differences due to the three decades of theoretical change that separate them.

[W]hen emphasis is desired *on any part* of any utterance, several procedures can be used. . . . One can say the whole utterance, *or certain parts of it*, with greatly increased loudness and accompanying extra high, or, in some cases, extra low, pitch; this is often represented by special typography: I said JOE, not Bill. When this happens, the whole utterance *or portion of it* is stretched out horizontally and vertically, as it were; this is then the point at which we draw the line between microlinguistics and metalinguistics: the phenomena that are segmentable were analyzed as phonemes of one kind or another; the phenomena that transcend segments are now stated to be metalinguistic, matters of style, and not part of the microlinguistic analysis. *Here, then, phonology ends.* (Trager and Smith 1951: 52; all emphasis supplied.)

The amount of difference in phonetic value between one accent and another accent which is metrically subordinated to it is continuously variable.... What controls this variation is something like 'amount of emphasis'....[I]ntonation patterns with only one pitch accent can be produced with different amounts of emphasis, with consequent variation in the height of the accent. It is not surprising that *this kind of variation also plays a role where there are several accents.*

[T]he term 'prominence' will be used to refer to the aggregate of metrical strength and emphasis, as it pertains to the control of tonal values. We will assume that *each pitch accent* has an associated prominence value, that prominence is continuously variable, and that the prominence of a metrically stronger accent is at least as great as that of a weaker accent, though not necessarily greater. We will not attempt to explain where prominence values come from, but *will leave this task to pragmaticists and semanticists.* (Pierrehumbert 1980: 39–40; all emphasis supplied.)

The most obvious problem with the FGV hypothesis, as I observed in Ladd 1990, is its falsifiability. *Unrestricted recourse to gradient pitch-range variability makes it nearly impossible to falsify quantitative models* of the phonetic realization of intonation: any observed F_0 target value that deviates from the predictions of a model can be said to have had its pitch range modified.[1] Furthermore, there is a pernicious corollary to the FGV hypothesis, which is that almost any "vertical scale" effect in the phonetic realization of intonation is automatically assumed to be a case of FGV. This actively discourages potentially fruitful investigation: because variation in the vertical scaling of pitch accents *may be* a matter of unpredictable, paralinguistic, gradient variation, phonologists generally assume that any variation in vertical scale *is* a matter of unpredictable, paralinguistic, gradient variation, and consequently do not look more closely at cases where the vertical scaling may actually be subject to more systematic constraints.

Finally, there is something paradoxical about the place of the FGV hypothesis in most work, which in a sense makes the case against it even more damning. The paradox is that, in practice, variation in prominence plays very little role in the detailed workings of quantitative models. On the one hand, such models all assume that any individual pitch accent *can* vary gradiently if the speaker chooses to vary it. On the other hand, they all adequately describe a wide range of speech data and hardly ever have to say that it *does* vary in this way. This surely makes the whole idea suspect. That is, if most of the data on which the quantitative models are based shows little or no evidence of Free Gradient Variability, then FGV is much too powerful a wild card to be included in the model as a little-used option.

The rest of the paper is devoted to presenting evidence against the hypothesis of FGV. In section 4.2 I discuss some general theoretical problems with the version of FGV embodied in Pierrehumbert's approach to the description of intonation. In section 4.3 I present some new and puzzling experimental findings that are seriously inconsistent with the assumption that pitch-range variation is interpreted accent by accent, and propose an explanation in terms of a categorical distinction between normal High tone and "Overhigh." In section 4.4 I relate this explanation to earlier proposals for the description of emphatic pitch range in English intonation.

4.2 The FGV hypothesis in Pierrehumbert's model

In order to focus the argument more specifically on current work, it will be useful to frame the discussion in terms of the model of intonational phonology developed by Pierrehumbert and her colleagues (e.g. Pierrehumbert 1980, 1981; Liberman and Pierrehumbert 1984; Beckman and Pierrehumbert 1986, 1992). I assume familiarity with the basic ideas of this model: the idea that a pitch contour is phonologically a string of tones, aligned in certain well-defined ways with the segmental string (Bruce 1977); that the only tones are H (high) and L (low), organized into "pitch accents" and arranged in various specified sequences; and that the F_0 targets corresponding to the tones are determined by phonetic realization rules, such that one H tone need not have the same F_0 as another. What I wish to focus on is Pierrehumbert's treatment of the relative height of tonal targets in pitch accents.

In Pierrehumbert's model, such differences of relative height effectively arise in only two different ways. First, one accent can be *downstepped* relative to an immediately preceding one. Recognition of the existence of downstep in English intonation, and the proposal of a quantitative model for it, was one of the important contributions of Pierrehumbert's thesis. In Pierrehumbert's conception, downstep is a phonetic realization rule applying to certain sequences of tones within a single phrase. Since downstep is phonologically conditioned (triggered by the occurrence of certain tonal sequences), it is categorically either present or absent. It is the only such categorical effect on vertical scale that Pierrehumbert's model recognizes.

The other way in which vertical scaling can be modified is by gradient modification of the overall pitch range. The quantitative details have evolved since Pierrehumbert's (1980) dissertation but the underlying theory has not. If two pitch accents within a phrase are not in a downstep relationship but have different peak levels, they are assumed to have different degrees of "prominence." If two phrases have similar accent patterns but the overall level of one is different from that of the other, they are assumed to have different "initial pitch-range settings." If two utterance contours are identical but for overall range, they too are assumed to have different pitch-range settings, reflecting the speaker's choice of different degress of "overall emphasis," different discourse organization or paragraph structure, etc. With one exception, the different degrees of prominence, emphasis, initial range, and so on are (a) assumed to be paralinguistic, and hence outside the realm of phonology, and (b) modeled as effects on a single parameter in the quantitative phonetic realization model. (The one exception is that metrical strength – which of course is phonological, not paralinguistic – is assumed to contribute, along with paralinguistic emphasis, to the prominence of individual accents. I will return to this point at the very end of the paper.)

In short, vertical scale effects in Pierrehumbert's model, unless they involve phrase-internal downstep, are assumed to be a matter of FGV. This assumption has a number of unfortunate consequences, of which I will briefly discuss two. For more detail on these two issues see Ladd (1993).

4.2.1 *Nested downstep*

First, consider Beckman and Pierrehumbert's decision to ignore what might be called "nested downstep" in their intonational phonology. It is well established that F_0 downtrends can be nested, so that for example a sentence consisting of three distinct intonational phrases can show downtrends within each phrase and an overarching downtrend across the three phrases. Since the work of Pierrehumbert (1980), as just noted, it has been widely accepted that downtrending pitch contours within short phrases are the result of downstep – accent-by-accent lowering of the pitch register. However, there is good evidence that the downtrends from phrase to phrase also involve stepwise register lowering (e.g. Van den Berg *et al.* 1992; Monaghan 1988, 1991).

In order to express this similarity between accent-by-accent and phrase-by-phrase register shifts, I have elsewhere (Ladd 1988, 1990, 1993) proposed that downstep is a high–low phonological relation between two constituents in a prosodic tree, comparable to the weak–strong and strong–weak relations familiar from metrical phonology. For example:

(1)

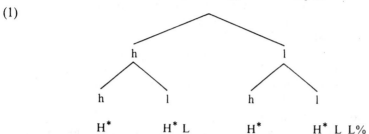

We WOULD have CALLED but there WASn't a PHONE.

As can be seen from this example, the constituents in such a downstep relation can be either terminal elements (individual pitch accents within a phrase) or nonterminal elements (phrases within a larger domain). That is, I see the existence of nested downstep as evidence about the phonological nature of downstep, and my analysis treats downstep – at any level in the prosodic hierarchy – in a uniform way.

In Pierrehumbert's phonological analysis, as just noted above, downstep is a phonetic-realization rule that only applies to certain tonal sequences *phrase-internally*. Obviously, by this definition, downstep is not something that can occur from one phrase to the next. Yet since phrase-to-phrase downstep, or something looking very much like it, manifestly does occur, it must be handled in a different way – and the only other way is as a reflection of FGV. Specifically, according to Beckman and Pierrehumbert (1986) the pitch range for each "intermediate phrase" is selected *independently* according to general discourse principles, and these "phrasal manipulations of overall pitch range *mimic catathesis* [= accent-to-accent downstep]" (299–300, emphasis supplied). The similarity of the accent-to-accent and phrase-to-phrase downtrends is thus ascribed to "mimicry," but why the one should mimic the other is left unexplained.

4.2.2 Pitch-range expansion experiments

Another problem for Pierrehumbert's model is the well-established finding that the relative height of pitch targets is preserved when overall utterance pitch range is experimentally modified. Pierrehumbert (1980), Bruce (1982), Liberman and Pierrehumbert (1984), and Pierrehumbert and Beckman (1988) all include reports of experiments in which specific intonation contours were uttered in varying overall ranges. In all of these experiments, two types of intonation-related variables were manipulated. First, the test utterances involved differences of emphasis, discourse structure, phrasing, length, etc. – differences that affect the height of accent peaks *relative to each other*. Second, each of the test utterances was pronounced in two or more overall pitch ranges – which affects the height of all the accent peaks in an utterance *relative to the speaker's voice range*. In every case, the two manipulations of the contour can be distinguished quite clearly in the experimental results. The patterns of relative F_0 within contours – the patterns that signal relative prominence, discourse, status, etc. – remain extraordinarily constant, while the overall range varies from just a few semitones to (in some cases) a few octaves.

The discovery of this constancy was another of the important contributions of Pierrehumbert's (1980) dissertation, and its role in establishing the significance of target levels in intonational phonology should not be underestimated. The fact that Pierrehumbert's original findings (which were based on English) have been replicated not only in English but also in Swedish and Japanese should guarantee them a central role in our theorizing about the control of pitch range. Yet for the standard Pierrehumbert analysis, incorporating the assumption of FGV, these results now pose a problem.

The problem is that the constancy of F_0 relationships when pitch range is modified is found not only in cases of phrase-internal downstep, but also in other cases involving accentual prominence, phrase-to-phrase relationships, and so on. As we saw, according to Pierrehumbert only the downstepping relationship within a phrase reflects a linguistic effect on vertical scale; everything else – including both relationships between phrases and nondownstepping relationships within phrases – reflects paralinguistic modifications. The constant patterns that emerge in the experimental data are therefore merely the consequence of consecutive paralinguistic choices within an utterance. It is, in theory, only a remarkable coincidence that all these choices bear the same relation to one another whether the voice is lowered or raised; Beckman and Pierrehumbert (1992) are able to suggest only that speakers somehow adopt a "uniform strategy" for dealing with such tasks.

4.2.3 An alternative to FGV

As manifested in Pierrehumbert's analysis of intonational phonology, then, the FGV hypothesis leads us to the conclusion that various quantitative regularities observed in production data from several languages are the result of unexplained mimicry of one contour by another, or of unexpected similarities in the way experimental subjects approach certain kinds of utterances. For a theory as ambitious and as productive of new insights as Pierrehumbert's, this is surely unsatisfactory.

But there is an obvious alternative. This is to assume that only the *overall* modifications of pitch range are gradient and paralinguistic, and that the relative height of accents within phrases and of phrases within sentences is part of the *linguistic* specification of the contour – i.e. part of intonational phonology. This requires us to give up the idea that almost anything to do with vertical scaling is gradient, paralinguistic, and therefore safe to ignore, but it permits us to treat nested downstep as nested downstep, and to make straightforward sense of constant relative F_0 under range expansion rather than be forced to describe it as a curious coincidence. Experimental evidence for this alternative view is presented in the next section of the paper.

4.3 The limits of Free Gradient Variability

4.3.1 The Gussenhoven–Rietveld effect

The story begins with a perceptual effect discovered more or less accidentally by Gussenhoven and Rietveld (1988). In a set of experiments designed to test various hypotheses about the implementation of declination, they asked listeners to judge the *prominence* of pitch accents in stimulus sentences. The sentences were "reiterant" nonsense utterances of the form da-DAH-da-da-da-DAH-da, i.e. seven-syllable utterances with two accent peaks; the two peaks are henceforth referred to as P1 and P2. Various acoustic parameters were manipulated, in particular the F_0 on P2; the listeners' task was to judge the prominence of P2. One of the central findings is that in any given stimulus continuum the average listener ratings of P2's prominence correlate very well with P2's F_0. A typical graph is shown in figure 4.1. This result is scarcely surprising, and is entirely consistent with the FGV hypothesis. However, Gussenhoven and Rietveld's experiments also shed light on what happens to the perceived prominence of P2 when we manipulate the acoustic properties of *P1*, and this is what is of interest here.

Suppose that P2 is held constant but the F_0 on P1 is raised or lowered, as in figure 4.2. What will subjects say about the prominence of P2 as a function of the modification of P1? Pretheoretically, one could imagine three possible types of effects. First, there could be no effect whatsoever: a given pitch level on P2 signals prominence level *p*, and the fact that the prominence on some neighbouring accent changes is irrelevant. This would be the strongest possible confirmation of the hypothesis of FGV, since according to that hypothesis the prominence on each accent can be modified independently. Second, there might be some sort of syntagmatic comparison, similar to so-called "contrast effects" in psychophysics: if P1

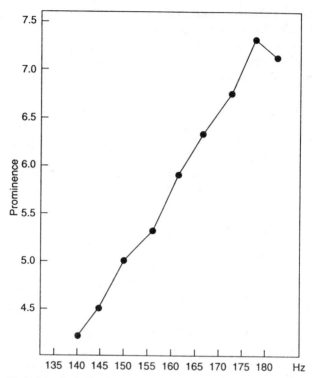

Figure 4.1. Typical results in Gussenhoven and Rietveld's experiment, showing the close correlation between P2's perceived prominence (y-axis) and F_0 on P2 (x-axis).

is made more prominent by increasing its F_0, then the prominence of a given P2 will be correspondingly reduced. I imagine that this is the effect most phonologists and phoneticians would predict if they were forced to think about it; note that the existence of some such comparison of accent peaks in context, though it might make for problems of quantitative detail, would not seriously undermine the FGV hypothesis.

Finally, there is the remaining logically possible effect, which is that increasing the F_0 on P1 would *increase* the perceived prominence of *P2*, while lowering P1 would *decrease* it. That is, instead of some sort of psychophysical contrast effect, there would be a sort of global effect of raising the F_0 on any accent that would affect the prominence on all accents. This seems fairly unlikely; it is certainly difficult to imagine how one might reconcile such a finding with the FGV hypothesis, because it would appear to make it impossible to increase the prominence of an individual accent relative to the prominence of its neighbors. However, the accidental

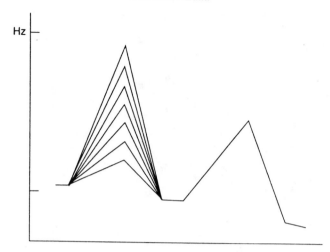

Figure 4.2. Schematic representation of a set of experimental two-peak contours in which P2 is held constant and P1 is systematically varied.

discovery made by Gussenhoven and Rietveld was precisely that changes in the F_0 of P1 have this global effect on the prominence of P2.

For reasons not relevant to the discussion here, Gussenhoven and Rietveld's experiments involved five different stimulus continua, in each of which P1 had different acoustic properties, and P2 had the same range of peak F_0 values. One of the continua – the one for which results are shown in figure 4.1 – may be regarded as having a "normal" P1; in it, P1 had a pitch accent with an F_0 excursion that at each step in the continuum was slightly smaller than the F_0 excursion on P2. In two other continua, the F_0 of P1 was reduced relative to this "normal" version, to "Low" and "Very Low" respectively. Taking these two reduced-P1 continua together with the normal version therefore provides us with a continuum of experimental comparisons of the sort sketched in figure 4.2. (The last two continua involved variations in intensity and will not be discussed here.)

Gussenhoven and Rietveld's results seem quite unambiguous. Informally speaking, what they found is that in stimulus pairs like

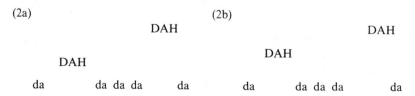

(2a)   (2b)

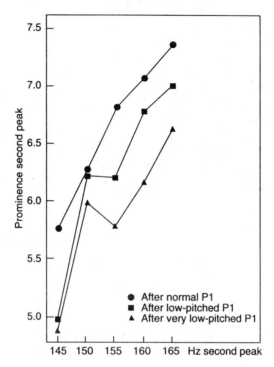

Figure 4.3. The Gussenhoven–Rietveld effect. For a given F_0 value of P2, the perceived prominence of P2 is lower when P1 is lower.

listeners judge the prominence of P2 in (2a), where P1 is relatively low, to be *lower* than the prominence of P2 in (2b), where P1 is somewhat higher. As we move from the continuum with "Very Low P1" through that with "Low P1" to that with "Normal P1," the perceived prominence for any given P2 *steadily increases.* That is, the peaks of F_0 on P1 and P2 do not function independently, nor do they set up a psychophysical contrast effect: rather, the perceived prominence of *P2* appears to correlate with the F_0 on *P1.* This finding, which I refer to as the Gussenhoven–Rietveld effect, is shown in figure 4.3. Gussenhoven and Rietveld acknowledge that this effect is somewhat puzzling but do not really pursue the matter further.

4.3.2 A possible account of the Gussenhoven–Rietveld effect

A possible explanation for the Gussenhoven–Rietveld effect, consistent with the idea that gradient variability of pitch range is actually severely constrained, would be as follows. First suppose that all the contours investigated by Gussenhoven and Rietveld are instances of "nondownstepped" P2, i.e. all instances of a single phonological relationship between P1 and P2. (This is not an unreasonable supposition, as Gussenhoven and Rietveld themselves are at pains to point out that they are not dealing with downstep.) Suppose further that, at least in such cases, the perceived prominence of P2 is not purely a function of the peak F_0 *on P2*, but is rather a function of some sort of *overall* (utterance-level) pitch range. That is, in order to increase the prominence on the nuclear accent, it is sufficient to increase the pitch range on the phrase as a whole. (To put it somewhat differently, overall increases in pitch range are felt by listeners to apply primarily to the nuclear accent.) If this is the case, then the perceived prominence of P2 can be increased or decreased by increasing or decreasing the peak F_0 on *either* pitch accent: the F_0 on both peaks contributes to a unitary impression of phrasal pitch range, which in turn affects the perceived prominence of P2.[2]

This explanation is obviously deeply incompatible with the view that the prominence of each pitch accent is gradiently variable independently of other pitch accents. It would be unwise, though, to go too far in theorizing on the basis of Gussenhoven and Rietveld's results alone. Since the effect was an inadvertent by-product of their study, it needs to be replicated and investigated more closely before we consider it to be one of the phenomena that a theory of pitch range and prominence should be able to account for.

4.3.3 Replicating and extending the Gussenhoven–Rietveld effect

In an experiment done under my direction for an Undergraduate Honours dissertation in the Linguistics Department at Edinburgh, Karen Jacobs (1990) carried out a systematic attempt to replicate the Gussenhoven–Rietveld effect. The basic idea of the experiment was to create a continuum in which *P2* was held constant and *P1* was varied, but in which listeners were still asked, as in Gussenhoven and Rietveld's experiment, to rate the prominence on *P2*.[3] In fact, however, we used two such continua with different values of P2, mixing the stimuli randomly on the test tape, because we thought it likely that otherwise listeners would rapidly become aware that P2 was always the same.

Though we intended the two continua simply as distractors for each other, it turned out that they produced puzzlingly divergent results. In the continuum with the lower (140 Hz) value of P2, there is a trend consistent with the Gussenhoven–Rietveld effect: as the F_0 on P1 increases, the perceived prominence of P2 increases as well. While the data are rather noisy, one might be prepared to accept this as a replication of the Gussenhoven–Rietveld effect. However, in the continuum with the higher (160 Hz) value of P2, no such effect can be observed. If anything, increases in the F_0 on P1 produce a slight *decline* in the perceived prominence of P2, so that the result curves for the two levels of P2 converge as P1 increases. This is shown in figure 4.4.

It is by no means clear what to make of these findings. One defensible conclusion would be that the original Gussenhoven–Rietveld effect was simply an experimental artifact of some sort, and that the attempted replication has failed. In support of this conclusion one might cite the lack of agreement between the two continua, the generally noisy data, and in particular (because it is entirely consistent with the notion of FGV), the fact that the largest effect on the perceived prominence of P2 is the F_0 level of P2 itself.

However, one might at least consider taking seriously the apparent convergence of the two curves in figure 4.4, and conclude that something interesting is going on. Specifically, suppose that in using two different values of P2 we inadvertently introduced two distinct experimental conditions, one in which P2 represents normal High tone, and one in which it represents some sort of "Overhigh" or emphatic tone. When P2 is normal High, we get the Gussenhoven–Rietveld effect: increases in the F_0 of P1 produce increases in the perceived prominence of P2. But when P2 is Overhigh, the Gussenhoven–Rietveld effect does not appear; instead, we get something like a psychophysical contrast effect whereby increases in the F_0 of P1 bring about slight decreases in the perceived prominence of P2. In

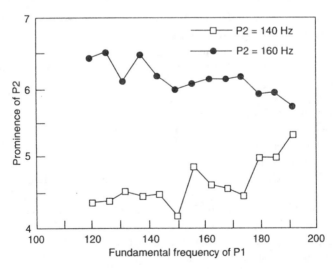

Figure 4.4. Results of the experiment by Jacobs. The lower curve seems to display the Gussenhoven–Rietveld effect (see Figure 4.3), but the upper one seems to show the reverse.

statistical terms, we have an interaction: the effect of P1 on the perceived prominence of P2 is different for different F_0 values of P2.

Extending the explanation offered in the previous section for the Gussenhoven–Rietveld effect, we might suggest that when P2 is normal High, P1 and P2 are in a fixed phonological relationship that does not permit of gradient modification except as applied to the contour as a whole. When P2 is Overhigh, on the other hand, gradient pitch-range effects can apply to it independently, and the listener evaluates the prominence of an Overhigh P2 at least partly on the basis of a direct comparison with P1. In any case it is clear that the attempt to replicate the Gussenhoven–Rietveld effect has – like Gussenhoven and Rietveld's study itself – led unexpectedly to a puzzling result, which itself needs replicating.

In order to determine the robustness of the apparent interaction, therefore, Jo Verhoeven, Karen Jacobs and I did a much larger study, involving nine levels of P1 and four levels of P2. The results, in figure 4.5, show very clearly that the interaction discovered by Jacobs is replicable. The data are far less noisy because more subjects were used, and the picture seems unmistakable. For the lowest of the four values of P2, the perceived prominence of P2 *increases* as P1 increases: this is the Gussenhoven–Rietveld effect. For all three higher values of P2, as P1 increases the perceived prominence of P2 *decreases* slightly; this is the psychophysical contrast effect. An analysis of variance on the results suggests that this difference is real: despite the massive main effect of P2 on perceived prominence, the interaction with P1 is also statistically significant.

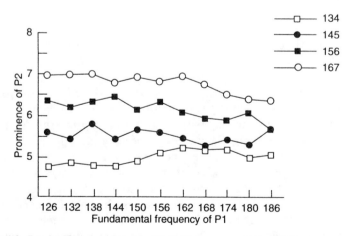

Figure 4.5. Results of the experiment by Ladd, Verhoeven, and Jacobs. The lowest curve shows the Gussenhoven–Rietveld effect (see Figure 4.3), but the three upper curves show the reverse.

4.3.4 Summary

These experimental results can be summarized as follows: if one presents listeners with an utterance containing two accent peaks, in which *both peaks* are of *moderate height*, one can produce an increase or decrease in the perceived prominence of the second or nuclear peak by increasing or decreasing the F_0 on *either* peak. If, however, the second or nuclear peak is very high, then increases in the perceived prominence of the second or nuclear peak must be produced in two different ways: either by increasing the F_0 on the already very high second peak, or by *decreasing* the F_0 on the first peak.

The proposed explanation for these findings takes the form of three theoretical conjectures:

1. Gradient modification of pitch range can be a property either of phrases or of individual accents.
2. When it is a property of the phrase, it affects the perceived prominence of the phrase's nuclear accent, *irrespective of where the gradient variability is phonetically manifested*. This implies that within the phrase there is only a limited range of possible *phonological* vertical-scale relationships (e.g. downstepped, nondownstepped) between the nuclear accent and any prenuclear ones.
3. Gradient pitch-range variability can be a property of an individual accent only when the accent is both (a) nuclear, and (b) Overhigh.

4.4 Overhigh tone?

The weak spot in the account just sketched is obviously the notion of Overhigh tone. How can a "very high" peak be distinguished from a peak that is "moderately high"? The very use of such terms seems to cry out for an analysis in terms of gradient variability of a single underlying category High tone – as in the standard FGV view. In this final section of the paper I wish to explore the possibility of Overhigh tone in greater depth.

First of all, it is worth stressing that the idea is not *a priori* ridiculous. We know that there are many languages, especially in Africa, in which categorically distinct levels of lexical tone are extracted from the continuum of the speaking range. We even know that some such languages (e.g. Chaga, McHugh 1990) have a distinction between a lexical High tone and a contextually raised "Overhigh" tone. That is, human listeners are in principle capable of putting a distinction between "moderately high" and "very high" to phonological use. The suggestion being made here is that that is exactly what they are doing in European intonation systems.

The idea of Overhigh tone in English intonational phonology is not new, of course, having originated in the work of Kenneth Pike in the early 1940s (published as Pike 1945). Pike's original analysis of English intonation involved four phonologically distinct levels, which we may call Low, Mid, High, and Overhigh. This idea was promptly taken over by Wells (1945), Trager and Smith (1951), and others, and – with the pitch levels treated as "phonemes" – it became the standard post-Bloomfieldian analysis of intonation in a variety of languages. Pike originally numbered the four levels from 4 at the bottom to 1 at the top, but in the standard version the numbering was reversed, so that pitch level 4 was Overhigh. This is the usage implied in my alternative title, and the one I will continue with here.

The four-level analysis was the subject of a fundamental critique by Bolinger (especially 1951), which led to the so-called levels-versus-configurations debate that simmered unresolved for roughly thirty years. Bolinger argued that, since sequences of pitch levels like 21, 31, and 41 are in theory phonemically distinct, they should be categorically distinct semantically as well – or even semantically unrelated. In fact, of course, all three seem to be instances of a falling contour, a single broad category with an identifiable (if hard-to-state) common element of meaning. Consequently, Bolinger argued, any representation in which the three are phonemically distinct is misleading.

In place of phonemic levels, Bolinger proposed that the units of intonation are pitch "configurations" like *fall* and *rise* – pitch accents, in the analysis subsequently developed in Bolinger 1958. More importantly for the issue under discussion here, Bolinger also claimed that the three putative variants 21, 31, and 41 are just arbitrarily selected steps on a gradient continuum of emphasis or finality. Pitch range, he said, can vary gradiently to reflect gradients of meaning; different "pitch levels" are simply the result of gradient variation of range on different pitch accents.

Bolinger's insistence on the primacy of pitch configurations and the irrelevance of levels now appears overstated: Bruce (1977) and Pierrehumbert (1980), and several others since them, have provided clear evidence of remarkable invariance of pitch level at certain points in contours. Moreover, Pierrehumbert (1980) showed that Bolinger's theoretical objections to levels can be met, so long as pitch accents are recognized as units at some level of analysis, and if the number of phonologically distinct levels is reduced from four to two (H and L). But Bolinger's views on gradient variability have been incorporated more or less intact into the theoretical consensus that has been built on the foundation of Bruce's and Pierrehumbert's pioneering work. Once pitch accents are analyzed as sequences of H and L tones, then the actual F_0 values in a given pitch accent can be analyzed in terms of the realization of the Hs and Ls on a vertical scale, specified in a separate, essentially orthogonal part of the phonological description. In the new theoretical consensus, the parameters that are manipulated in this orthogonal part of the description are gradient.

As I said at the beginning of the paper, it cannot be denied that certain vertical scale effects – at least those that affect whole utterances – are gradiently variable in essentially the way that Bolinger and the new theoretical consensus presuppose. In my view, however, most of the factors that govern the relative height of accents *within* a phrase or utterance are phonological, and hence categorical rather than gradient. Where I disagree with the new consensus, in other words, is in positing distinctions of relative pitch range that – like downstep – are orthogonal to the basic tone distinctions *but not gradient*. Among these distinctions is the one proposed here between normal High and Overhigh tone.

The proposal for Overhigh tone was foreshadowed in my early critique of Pierrehumbert's intonational phonology (Ladd 1983), in which I proposed that nuclear accents might display a categorical feature "raised peak." As I noted at the time, the raised-peak proposal was essentially a restatement of what was involved in the distinction between pitch levels 3 and 4 in the four-level analyses. As such it was incompatible with the FGV hypothesis, and it was simply dismissed by Beckman and Pierrehumbert (1986: 307), who reiterated their belief that all such differences of vertical scale are gradient, and suggested that my proposal was based on a "misinterpretation" of the experimental findings discussed in section 4.2.2 above. However, the data and theoretical considerations presented here suggest that the notion of raised peak or Overhigh tone is at least as plausible as unrestricted FGV.

Overhigh tone fits into my relational analysis of downstep (see section 4.2.1 above) as follows. The basic claim of that analysis is that there are only two distinct phonological relations between a prenuclear and a nuclear accent, namely downstepped and nondownstepped:

(3)

h   l   l   h

One of the difficulties with this view, however, is that it provides no distinct representation for what appear to be two subcases of nondownstepped – one in which the nuclear accent is approximately at the same level as the prenuclear accent, and one in which the nuclear accent is clearly upstepped. I would now suggest that in the nondownstepped case, it is possible for the H tone of the nuclear accent to be replaced by an Overhigh (H +) tone, yielding a distinct upstep. This means that relative to a prenuclear accent peak, the peak of a nuclear falling accent can be distinctively lower, roughly the same height, or higher. Graphically:

(4)

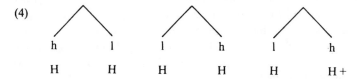

h	l	l	h	l	h
H	H	H	H	H	H +

I believe this three-way distinction is the basis for the three types of nuclear fall – 21, 31, and 41 – posited in the original Pikean analyses of English intonation. Perhaps, in other words, pitch level 4 lives.[4]

While I have framed the discussion here at least in part as a critique of Pierrehumbert's intonational phonology, it should be noted that in Pierrehumbert's original observations (quoted at length above) we can find the seeds of the analysis just proposed. Recall that Pierrehumbert sees the prominence of an accent as "the aggregate of metrical strength and emphasis"; she specifically notes that "the prominence of a metrically stronger accent is at least as great as that of a weaker accent, though not necessarily greater." We might say that Pierrehumbert is implicitly distinguishing only two kinds of cases: those where the metrically stronger accent is *not* more prominent than the weaker one (the "level 3" cases), and those where it is (the "level 4" cases). (The level 2 cases are of course downstepped and treated entirely differently by Pierrehumbert.) If we remove the large facultative element of gradient emphasis from this view, we are left with a distinction very much like the one proposed here between normal High and Overhigh tone.

4.5 Conclusion

In revising this paper for publication I have deliberately refrained from modifying the proposal for Overhigh tone, in order not to pull the rug out from under Hayes's excellent critique (chapter 5). However, I should note that I find his interpretation of Overhigh as "gesturally reinforced High" quite plausible and intuitively appealing; more generally, I think we may draw considerable insight from his suggestion that "the beast knows the grammar." On the whole I think our analyses differ little in their practical consequences for the proposed explanation of the experimental data discussed here.

However, I think there remains an issue between us, namely whether the distinction between normal and "gesturally reinforced" is categorical. Hayes appears to suggest that it is not: in his view, as in Bolinger's, the beast is always active in the production of pitch accents, and the phonetic variability of pitch accents results from the extent of the beast's activity. I incline to an alternative view, namely that the presence or absence of "gestural reinforcement" is an all-or-none matter, though of course if gestural reinforcement is present its extent is gradient. In effect, the beast may simply sleep through certain pitch accents, and reinforce only those in which it has some special involvement. At this point I see little basis for determining which of these views is correct.

In any case, the central point of the descriptive proposals I have made here and elsewhere is that the Bruce–Pierrehumbert approach to intonational phonology must be enriched with a notion of categorical distinctions of pitch range. We need to get rid of the idea that any distinction that is orthogonal to the basic opposition between High and Low tones is *ipso facto* gradient: both gradient factors and categorical ones play a role in the vertical scaling of any given tone. Once this idea is accepted, I believe that we will be in a much better position to understand downstep, emphasis, and intonational cues to textual organization generally. Perhaps more importantly, a great many conceptual problems with pitch range will effectively disappear.

Notes

The experiment by Verhoeven, Jacobs and myself reported in section 4.3.3 forms part of the research program of the Human Communication Research Centre (HCRC). The support of the UK Economic and Social Research Council (ESRC), which provides funding for HCRC, is gratefully acknowledged.

1 The most egregious example of this known to me comes from Cooper and Sorenson (1981). One of the sentences on which they tested their model of the declining F_0 "topline" is *The CAT in the GARAGE ran SWIFTLY UNDERNEATH the CAR* (where the capitalized words are the ones in which F_0 values constituting the "topline" were measured); in the experimental data, the measured peaks on *garage* and *underneath* were significantly lower than predicted, and that on *swiftly* substantially higher. They explain these deviations away as follows:

> It seems likely that... *swiftly* was responsible for the perturbation.... Since this word is an Adverb, it probably received more stress than a non-Adverb at the same sentence location [references omitted]. In addition, it seems reasonable that the extra focus given to the Adverb might cause a defocusing of the neighboring key words.... In short, the focused Adverb pulls up on the topline; to compensate, a lowering of the topline occurs just after the focus, creating the observed zigzag pattern. The present rationale is admittedly ad hoc, but such proposals seem useful at this rudimentary

stage of F_0 research in sentence contexts, in order to suggest directions for independent further testing. (1981: 70–71)

2 This proposal is broadly consistent with the findings recently reported by Terken (1991), though Terken's procedures (and his theoretical assumptions) are so different from Gussenhoven and Rietveld's that it is difficult to compare their findings in detail.

3 By and large we followed procedures similar to Gussenhoven and Rietveld's. Perhaps the biggest difference was that, instead of a reiterant nonsense utterance, we used a natural utterance of the sentence *The melon was yellow*, resynthesized with different F_0 contours. Listeners were asked to rate the prominence on the word *yellow*. Full details of this experiment and the follow-up are reported in Ladd, Verhoeven, and Jacobs (forthcoming).

4 It would appear that it is also possible to have Overhigh tone on the prenuclear accent in a downstepping phrase; in line with the Gussenhoven–Rietveld effect, this seems to add finality to the entire phrase rather than adding emphasis to the prenuclear accent, as in:

(5)

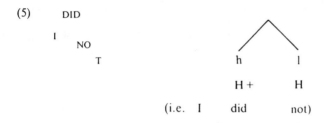

References

Beckman, M. and J. Pierrehumbert. 1986. Intonational structure in Japanese and English. *Phonology Yearbook* 3: 255–309.

1992. Comments on chapters 14 and 15. In G. J. Docherty and D.R. Ladd (eds.) *Papers in Laboratory Phonology II: Gesture, Segment, Prosody*. Cambridge: University Press; 387–397.

Van den Berg, R., C. Gussenhoven and T. Rietveld. 1992. Downstep in Dutch: Implications for a model. In G.J. Docherty and D. R. Ladd (eds.) *Papers in Laboratory Phonology II: Gesture, Segment, Prosody*. Cambridge University Press, 335–359.

Bolinger, D. 1951 Intonation: Levels versus configurations. *Word* 7: 199–210.

1958. A theory of pitch accent in English. *Word* 14: 109–149.

Bruce, G. 1977. *Swedish Word Accents in Sentence Perspective*. Lund: Gleerup.

1982. Developing the Swedish intonation model. *Working Papers 22, Department of Linguistics, Lund University*: 51–116.

Cooper, W. and J. Sorensen. 1981. *Fundamental frequency in sentence production.* Heidelberg: Springer-Verlag.

Gussenhoven, C. and T. Rietveld. 1988. Fundamental frequency declination in Dutch: testing three hypotheses. *Journal of Phonetics* 16: 355–369.

Jacobs, K. 1990. On the relationship between fundamental frequency of the initial accent peak and perceived prominence of the second accent peak, in two-peak utterances. Undergraduate Honours dissertation, University of Edinburgh.

Ladd, D.R. 1983. Phonological features of intonational peaks. *Language* 59: 721–759.

1987. A phonological model of intonation for use in speech synthesis by rule. In *Proceedings of the European Conference on Speech Technology.* Edinburgh: CEP Associates, 21–24.

1988. Declination "reset" and the hierarchical organization of utterances. *Journal of the Acoustical Society of America* 84: 530–544.

1990. Metrical representation of pitch register. In J. Kingston and M. Beckman (eds.) *Papers in Laboratory Phonology I: Between the Grammar and the Physics of Speech.* Cambridge: University Press, 35–37.

1993. In defense of a metrical theory of intonational downstep. In H. van der Hulst and K. Snider (eds.) *The Phonology of Tone: The Representation of Tonal Register.* Berlin, New York: Mouton de Gruyter, 109–132.

Ladd, D. R, J. Verhoeven, and K. Jacobs (forthcoming). Influence of adjacent pitch accents on each other's perceived prominence: Two contradictory effects. To appear in *Journal of Phonetics.*

Liberman, M. and J. Pierrehumbert. 1984. Intonational invariance under changes in pitch range and length. In M. Aronoff and R. Oehrle (eds.) *Language Sound Structure.* Cambridge, MA: MIT Press, 157–233.

McHugh, B.D. 1990. The phrasal cycle in Kivunjo Chaga tonology. In S. Inkelas and D. Zec (eds.) *The Phonology–Syntax Connection.* Chicago: University of Chicago Press, 217–242.

Monaghan, A.I.C. 1988. Generating intonation in the absence of essential information. In W. Ainsworth and J. Holmes (eds.) *Speech 88: Proceedings of the 7th FASE Symposium.* Edinburgh: Institute of Acoustics, 1249–1256.

1991. Intonation in a text-to-speech conversion system. Ph.D dissertation, Edinburgh University.

Pierrehumbert, J. 1980. The phonology and phonetics of English intonation. Ph.D dissertation, MIT.

1981. Synthesizing intonation. *Journal of the Acoustical Society of America* 70: 985–995.

Pierrehumbert, J. and M. Beckman. 1988. *Japanese Tone Structure.* Cambridge, MA: MIT Press.

Pike, K.L. 1945. *The Intonation of American English.* Ann Arbor: University of Michigan Press.

Terken, J. 1991. Fundamental frequency and perceived prominence of accented syllables. *Journal of the Acoustical Society of America* 89(4): 1768–1776.

Trager, G.L. and H.L. Smith. 1951. *An Outline of English Structure*. Norman, OK: Battenburg Press. (Reprinted 1957 by American Council of Learned Societies, Washington.)
Wells, R. 1945. The pitch phonemes of English. *Language* 21: 27–40.

5

"Gesture" in prosody: comments on the paper by Ladd

BRUCE HAYES

Ladd's paper is a beautiful example of how experimental work can, with serious thought, be made to bear on the abstract system of phonetic rules and representations. In the case at hand, he has shown how the Gussenhoven–Rietveld effect, initially just a minor data puzzle, bears importantly on a much larger issue, that of how pitch is scaled by the system of phonetic rules.

5.1 Ladd's arguments

Ladd takes on the claim that pitch range is subject to "Free Gradient Variability"; i.e. that over a window no larger than pitch-accent size, the speaker is free to select a local pitch range. We might characterize this as positing a "beast within"; this creature monitors our speech constantly, assessing how much it cares about what we are saying at that instant, and adjusts the pitch range of our voices accordingly.

The beast metaphor should not be dismissed as absurd. For example, Bolinger (1986, 1989) has suggested quite explicit analogies between intonation and more primitive forms of vocal expression.

Ladd subjects Free Gradient Variability to three criticisms:

1. It fails to explain the Gussenhoven–Rietveld effect. When the effect occurs, listeners must interpret increases in the pitch of the first of two peaks as increases in the prominence attached to the second peak. Under Free Gradient Variability, listeners surely would interpret increases in the pitch of the first peak more directly; i.e. as increases in the prominence of the first peak.

   As a corollary, Ladd notes that the *overriding* of the Gussenhoven–Rietveld effect when the second peak is especially high implies the existence of a H + * accent, i.e. an Overhigh which is interpreted by listeners as especially prominent no matter what the context.

2. Ladd and others (4.2.1) have found quite subtle hierarchical effects relating the pitch levels of H* accents to syntactic and discourse grouping. It is hard to see how such effects could be discerned by listeners if the beast were constantly adjusting pitch up and down at the same time.

3. If pitch range is freely variable, it is unlikely that pitch-scaling experiments (e.g. the "Anna came with Manny" experiment of Pierrehumbert 1980, Liberman and Pierrehumbert 1984) could produce such beautifully clean mathematical relations between pitch targets. Presumably, the random variations of Free Gradient Variability would overwhelm such patterns in noise.

Arguments (1) and (2) seem particularly compelling; we return to (3) later. I also agree with Ladd's point concerning research strategies: we are better off doing without Free Gradient Variability unless it is firmly shown to be necessary. A theory lacking it makes more precise predictions, and forswearing Free Gradient Variability serves as inducement to explain apparently "random" variation in the height of pitch peaks.

5.2 Objections to H +

My disagreement with Ladd centers on his proposal that English intonation should involve a *phonological* category H + , found in the "Overhigh" pitch accent H + *. I think this proposal has a number of drawbacks, to be outlined below. Moreover, I will suggest later that there is a plausible alternative to H + that retains Ladd's insights while permitting a simpler phonological system.

5.2.1 Phonemic opposition or continuum?

To begin, it seems likely that in setting up the category H + , Ladd is phonemicizing a continuum. Consider figure 5.1, which shows pitch tracks of myself pronouncing "The melon was yellow", with four different degrees of special emphasis on *yellow*. It is possible that there is an identifiable line on this continuum, but this is certainly not proven at this stage. Note that the pitch of *melon* does not vary much, suggesting that what was being varied was not the *overall* pitch range of the utterance.

The problem becomes worse if we consider *monosyllables* pronounced with the putative H + * versus H*: here, it becomes even harder to imagine

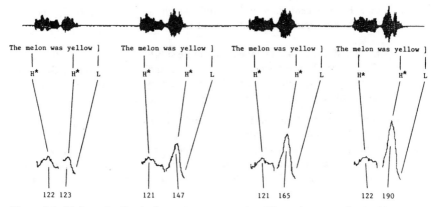

Figure 5.1. Pitch track of a single speaker pronouncing 'The melon was yellow' with tonal sequence shown and four different degrees of special emphasis on *yellow*.

that a phonological opposition is present; cf. the continuum of pronunciations presented by Liberman and Pierrehumbert (1984: 159).

True phonological contrasts can be supported by their effect on the perceptions of native speakers: phonetic differences tend to be far more perceptible when they cross phonemic boundaries (Werker and Tees 1984, and references cited there). In fact, experiments of the appropriate type have been carried out for intonation, with positive results (Pierrehumbert and Steele 1987; Kohler 1987). I believe the existence of H+ could be best defended with perceptual evidence of this sort.

5.2.2 The mix-and-match problem

H+ amplifies what I will call the *mix-and-match* problem: if we set up a number of basic primitives (pitch accents, boundary tones) as the elements of the intonational system, to what extent can they be freely combined in actually occurring intonations? A striking aspect of the two-height system of Pierrehumbert (1980) is that *every* logically possible tonal sequence is a possible intonation, at least as far as nuclei (in the sense of Ladd 1980) are concerned. My estimate is that if we add H+ to the basic inventory of H and L, the logical possibilities will be less fully instantiated. (This is a point made in a similar connection by Beckman and Pierrehumbert 1986.)

For example, I believe there is no H + analogue of the so-called "calling contour" of Ladd (1978). Such an analogue would resemble (1a), but with a higher starting point.

(1)   = *[dʒɑːːː

a. Johnny!   b. *Johnny!

   | | =   [dʒɑːːː | |
  H* ʼH   niːːː]   **H+*** ʼH   niːːː]

(In these examples and below, downstep is transcribed ʼH for convenience; no claims are intended concerning the controversy over how downstep is to be represented; cf. Ladd 1983, Beckman and Pierrehumbert 1986).

It also appears that H + does not occur as a boundary tone. The boundary tones of English are limited to the binary contrast of L versus H, and variation in the pitch scaling is determined by pragmatics (Pierrehumbert and Hirschberg 1990: 279).[1]

In general, it appears that adopting H + would force us to add to the grammar various rules that sharply limit its distribution. This would wipe out much of the progress that has been made on the mix-and-match problem.

5.2.3 Undergeneralization

A third problem for H + is *undergeneralization*. Reverting briefly to the beast metaphor, it seems that the beast makes his views clear by exaggerating the prosodic contrasts that are already present. Consider, for instance, the natural way of emphasizing the word *yellow* when *The melon was yellow* is pronounced as a question. Figure 5.2 shows four tokens from my own speech; tonal representations are schematic. Note that: (a) the pitch of the L* accent doesn't vary much. This accords with previous observations (Liberman and Pierrehumbert 1984; 218–219). (b) The H boundary tone varies greatly with degree of emphasis.

The point is that H + will not solve the problem of expressing extra emphasis in this intonation, since there is no high accent in nuclear position. The tone that gets shifted up is a boundary tone. But the semantics of final boundary tones (Pierrehumbert and Hirschberg 1990) are characteristically not affiliated with individual words, but with whole phrases. In essence, the H boundary tones in figure 5.2 are raised "accidentally," to accommodate emphasis on the word *yellow*.

When we turn to downstepped contours, illustrated in figure 5.3, the situation looks worse. It appears that a speaker cannot vary the height

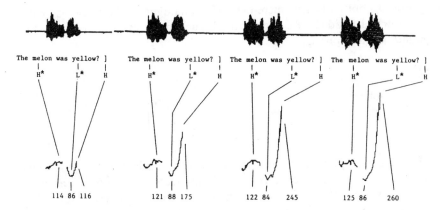

Figure 5.2. Pitch track of a single speaker pronouncing 'The melon was yellow' with tonal sequence shown and four different degrees of emphasis on *yellow*.

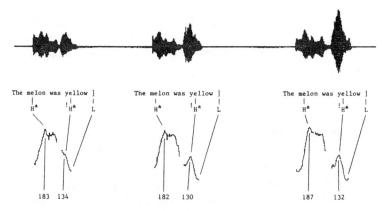

Figure 5.3. Pitch track of a single speaker pronouncing 'The melon was yellow' with tonal sequence shown and three different degrees of special emphasis on *yellow*.

of $^!$H* very much, given the existence in the system of both higher (H*) and lower (L*) targets, a point made by Ladd (1990a: 39). Therefore, the beast can only adjust amplitude and perhaps duration to mark special emphasis. This is probably why it is harder to produce as many degrees of emphasis in this contour, and I only produced three examples here instead of four.[2]

In general, it seems that positing an H + * accent only addresses part of the problem of how individual words or phrases are emphasized.

To summarize, the H + hypothesis suffers from the lack of evidence for a true phonological contrast, from loss of system symmetry, and from insufficient generality as an account of emphasis.

Bruce Hayes

5.3 A paralinguistic alternative

What is needed is an analysis that preserves Ladd's insights about the Gussenhoven–Rietveld effect without causing problems with the phonology. Such an account is possible if we consider more seriously the nature of the "beast" alluded to above. Suppose that systematic behavior in pronunciation can be the result of either regularities in the linguistic system or regularities in what I will call the *gestural system*. Within the linguistic system I include the word sequence and its phonemic, syntactic and semantic structure, the stress pattern, phonological phrasing, and the intonational tune. Within the gestural system I would include the communicative elements that accompany spoken language: gesture as conventionally construed, body movements not ordinarily considered to be gesture, facial configuration, gaze, and so on.

Suppose also that certain *vocal* elements are part of the gestural system. Crucially, these include pitch range, though I would also include expressive adjustments of duration, amplitude and voice quality. This basic distinction between language and paralanguage is a long-standing one; see for instance Ladd's quotation (this volume, pp. 43–44) from Trager and Smith (1951), or Stockwell *et al.* (1956).

Kendon (1975, 1980) has made intensive studies of gesture in the more conventional sense of body movement. His method was to record conversations on motion pictures along with a sound track. The film is then examined one frame at a time, with all body motions, down to the smallest finger movements, recorded according to the frames during which they begin and end.

An article resulting from this work that is of great interest to intonational phonologists is Kendon (1972). Here, Kendon focused on the alignment in time between body movements and the linguistic structure of the speakers' utterances. Although Kendon's results include various complexities, the overall picture can be summarized as follows. Body movements during speech are not aligned haphazardly, but coincide with crucial landmarks in the linguistic signal. In particular, they can be aligned with (a) stressed syllables (typically the ending point of the movement falls on or just before the stress); (b) the boundaries of linguistic units. In addition, a phenomenon we might refer to as "spreading" is widely found: a body part will take on a particular configuration, and change it synchronously with a linguistic boundary.

Students of modern intonational theory (as developed by Liberman 1975; Bruce 1977; Pierrehumbert 1980; Ladd 1983, and others) should find this a strikingly familiar pattern. Intonational tones are characteristically divided into pitch accents, which align with stressed syllables, and boundary tones, which align with the edges of linguistic units. Moreover, the spreading of boundary tones has also been observed. Even the loose "semantics" of body gestures is reminiscent of the semantics of intonational tones, as comparison of Kendon's paper with Pierrehumbert and Hirschenberg (1990) shows.

Kendon (1975) provides additional evidence for the alignment of body gestures with linguistic structure: listeners can synchronize their gestures without seeing each other, provided they are both listening to the same speaker.

The upshot is this: the gestural "beast" is more sophisticated than we might have thought, in that it *knows the grammar*. Kendon's work suggests that the boundary between language and paralanguage can sometimes be startlingly thin.

Now, if we extend the notion of gesture to include vocal gestures like pitch-range expansion, another point emerges: the beast characteristically respects grammatical contrasts. For example, in Finnish, with phonemic vowel length, gestural lengthening of short vowels is avoided (Prince 1980, citing L. Carlson). Similarly, the absence of pitch-range expansion during the production of downstepped pitch accents (figure 5.3 above) plausibly reflects the need to preserve the phonological contrast of L^* versus $^!H^*$ versus H^*.

In light of the apparent linguistic sophistication of paralanguage, it seems plausible to write paralinguistic *rules*, of a rough and gradient nature, which can refer in their structural descriptions to linguistic information. Here is a conjectured rule for the part of the gestural system controlling pitch range:

(2)   *Vocal Emphasis*

To emphasize a constituent, exaggerate (to the desired degree) the phonetic correlates of stress within that constituent. Conditions:

a. Do not override the stress contour of the utterance.
b. Do not override the H^* ∼ $!H^*$ contrast.

By "phonetic correlates of stress" I mean anything available, including amplitude, duration, and pitch range. Increases in pitch range will make themselves felt not just on pitch accents, but on boundary tones, as in figure 5.2.

It should be pointed out that (2) is a gradient rule; one can provide as little extra emphasis to a word as one likes. Hence exaggerated H^* is not a different category from H^*; i.e. there is no phonemic contrast. It is in this sense that our proposal is not the same thing as introducing a H + tone.

Provision (2a) is the crucial part of the hypothesis. Following Chomsky and Halle (1968), Selkirk (1984), and others, I assume a set of rules which assigns a stress contour to an utterance, based on focus, old versus new information, linear order, and constituency. The output of these rules, i.e. a set of relative-prominence relations among syllables, is assumed to be one of the phonological configurations that is treated as inviolate by the gestural system. The upshot is that only words bearing the main, nuclear stress are eligible for gestural enhancement, since enhancement elsewhere would perturb the realization of stress.

Within his system, Ladd says basically the same thing (4.3.4): "Gradient pitch-range variability can be a property of an individual accent only when the accent is both (a) nuclear, and (b) overhigh [= H+]." We modify this statement in two ways: the hypothesis doesn't need phonemic H+ in order to work, and the limitation to *nuclear* accents is a natural consequence of a more general principle, namely that gestural vocalizations tend not to override phonological distinctions. With these changes, Ladd's scenario for interpreting the experiments (4.3.2) still goes through.

5.4 Against going overboard: Is all intonation gestural?

A potentially disturbing aspect of our effort to write rules for gesture is a blurring of the distinction between language and paralanguage: is perhaps *all* of intonation gestural?

While this issue does not seem settled, I presently believe that the language/paralanguage boundary is real, and that intonation falls on the side of language. Intonation systems are amenable to phonemic analysis using a small number of contrasting categories. It seems unlikely that this is true of gesture, where the number of entities is enormous, and the notion of contrasting categories seems less useful. Moreover, intonation systems incorporate a clear and fairly rigid criterion of well-formedness. For example, (3) (modeled after Pierrehumbert 1980: 2.36C) strikes me as a clearly ill-formed English intonation:

(3)

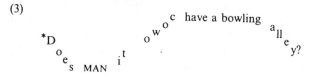

Such well-formedness judgments are language-specific, as Ladd (1990b) has argued. Thus (4) is bizarre in English, but fine in Bengali, where this shape is the normal one for yes/no questions (Hayes and Lahiri 1991).

(4)

While gestural systems may be culture-specific, it seems unlikely that the notion of well-formedness can be defined with such clarity as it can in language (Kendon 1980: 223).

5.5 Pitch–height experiments

Ladd raises question (3) above (p. 65): how is it that pitch-scaling experiments such as Liberman and Pierrehumbert (1984) can produce such clean results? His own explanation is very simple: there is no Free Gradient Variability, so such experiments access linguistically defined pitch-scaling relations, unperturbed by local emphasis. In the view presented here, the answer cannot be so simple: we have proposed to exclude gestural emphasis on nonnuclear accents, but since nuclear accents can vary freely, and are included in most pitch-scaling experiments, we still need an explanation.

The suggestion here is again based on attributing some sophistication to the gestural beast: on request, people can control gestural behavior precisely. For example, in repeating the sentence *Anna came with Manny* several dozen times, they have no reason to give varying emphasis to the nuclear accent on different occasions; and unless they do so as a way of combatting boredom, they will not. What emerges directly reflects the phonological scaling.

There is anecdotal evidence that at least some speakers possess exquisite control over their vocal gestural patterns. This comes from Liberman and Pierrehumbert's (1984) important research on the pitch-scaling system of English. Given a particular pitch-scaling model, Liberman and Pierrehumbert's experiments might be thought of as a means of searching for the "fundamental constants" of English intonation, much as constants are determined by experiment in the physical sciences. The intonational constants investigated were: (a) the downstep constant, which scales a downstepped tone with respect to the preceding tone; (b) the final lowering coefficient, which lowers pitch range at the end of a phrase; and (c) the answer/background ratio, which scales focused new information.

The values for the constants that were found differed from subject to subject (see example 5).

(5)

	MYL	JBP	DWS	KXG
Downstep constant	**0.59**	**0.62**	0.68	(not measured)
Final lowering coefficient	**0.68**	**0.68**	0.77	0.59
Answer–background ratio	**1.66**	**1.63**	1.33	1.59

What is striking is the close resemblance between MYL and JBP (the authors of the study) versus their divergence from DWS and KXG. I bring this out not to claim any problem with the results; rather, I believe that the "constants" are in fact under gestural control. For example, the variable nature of final lowering, and its use to convey discourse structure, is discussed by Hirschberg and Pierrehumbert (1986) and Pierrehumbert and Hirschberg (1990). The answer/background ratio is probably determined by the value employed in the Vocal-Emphasis rule (2).

If these "constants" vary gesturally, then subjects must choose arbitrarily which values to use in an experiment. It should not surprise us if two authors, accustomed to enacting intonation contours in each other's presence, should have arrived at a tacit agreement on the values to use in making the recordings. The Liberman/Pierrehumbert results are well supported by their *qualitative* agreement with the data; we should not expect the quantitative values to agree, since the subjects choose them.

This example suggests an answer to Ladd's original question: in the arbitrary context of an experiment, speakers can exercise close control over their gestural systems, yielding clean experimental results.

5.6 Conclusion

In the study of phonological rules, paralanguage can usually be ignored, as it impinges little on the categorial entities with which phonologists deal. But in the study of phonetic rules, paralanguage often interacts closely with the linguistic system. In these comments, I have argued for dealing explicitly with paralanguage, as a rule system distinct from but closely connected to the linguistic system. A potential benefit is that our conception of the linguistic system can be more tightly constrained. In particular, Ladd's striking interpretation of the Gussenhoven–Rietveld effect is more persuasive, I think, when recast in a theory that distinguishes linguistic and paralinguistic rules.

Notes

1 There is one other case: Ladd's footnote 4 proposes the existence of H+ as a nonnuclear pitch accent. For discussion and an alternative account, see Hayes (1992).

2 The downstepped nuclear accents in the more emphatic versions of figure 5.3 have a peak shape, rather than the smooth shoulder of the least emphatic version. The pitch rises in the peaks are not especially audible, and I believe the peaks are in fact the acoustic result of heightened subglottal pressure on the nuclear-stressed syllable, rather than being phonologically specified.

References

Beckman, M. and J. Pierrehumbert. 1986. Intonational structure in Japanese and English. *Phonology Yearbook* 3: 255–309.

Bolinger, D.L. 1986. *Intonation and its Parts*. Stanford, CA: Stanford University Press.

1989. *Intonation and its Uses*. Stanford, CA: Stanford University Press.

Bruce, G. 1977. *Swedish Word Accents in Sentence Perspective*. Lund: Gleerup.

Chomsky, N. and M. Halle. 1968. *The Sound Pattern of English*. New York: Harper & Row.

Hayes, B. 1992. "Gesture" in prosody. Ms. UCLA, Los Angeles, CA. (Distributed, together wtih Ladd's chapter, as an Occasional Paper of the Linguistics Department, University of Edinburgh.)

Hayes, B. and A. Lahiri. 1991. Bengali intonational phonology. *Natural Language and Linguistic Theory* 9: 47–99.

Hirschberg, J. and J. Pierrehumbert. 1986. The intonational structuring of discourse. In *Proceedings of the Twenty-fourth Annual Meeting*. New York: Association for Computational Linguistics.

Kendon, A. 1972. Some relationships between body motion and speech: An analysis of an example. In Aron Siegman and Benjamin Pope (eds.) *Studies in Dyadic Communication*. New York: Pergamon Press.

1975. *Studies in the Behavior of Social Interaction*. Bloomington: Indiana University and Lisse: Peter de Ridder Press.

1980. Gesticulation and speech: Two aspects of the process of utterance. In M.R. Key (ed.) *The Relationship of Verbal and Nonverbal Communication*, 207–227.

Kohler, K. 1987. Categorical pitch perception. *Proceedings of the Eleventh International Congress of Phonetic Sciences*, 5: 331–333. Tallinn: Academy of Sciences of the Estonian SSR.

Ladd, D.R. 1978. Stylized intonation. *Language* 54: 517–540.

1980. *The Structure of Intonational Meaning: Evidence from English*. Bloomington: Indiana University Press.

1983. Phonological features of intonational peaks. *Language* 59: 721–759.

1990a. Metrical representation of pitch register. In J. Kingston and M. Beckman (eds.) *Papers in Laboratory Phonology I: Between the Grammar and Physics of Speech*. Cambridge: University Press, 35–57.

1990b. Intonation: emotion vs. grammar. *Language* 66: 806–816.

Liberman, M. 1975. The intonational system of English. Ph.D. dissertation, MIT.

Liberman, M. and J. Pierrehumbert. 1984. Intonational invariance under changes in pitch range and length. In M. Aronoff and R. Oehrle (eds.) *Language Sound*

Structure: Studies Presented to Morris Halle by his Teacher and Students. Cambridge, MA: MIT Press, 157–233.

Pierrehumbert, J. 1980. The phonology and phonetics of English intonation. Ph.D. dissertation, MIT.

Pierrehumbert, J. and J. Hirschberg. 1990. The meaning of intonational contours in the interpretation of discourse. In P. Cohen, J. Morgan and M. Pollock (eds.) *Intentions in Communication*. Cambridge, MA: MIT Press, 271–312.

Pierrehumbert, J. and S. Steele. 1987. How many rise–fall–rise contours? *Proceedings of the Eleventh International Congress of Phonetic Sciences*, 3: 145–148. Tallinn: Academy of Sciences of the Estonian SSR.

Prince, A. 1980. A metrical theory for Estonian quantity. *Linguistic Inquiry* 11: 511–562.

Selkirk, E.O. 1984. *Phonology and Syntax: The Relation between Sound and Structure*. Cambridge, MA: MIT Press.

Stockwell, R.P., J.D. Bowen and I. Silva-Fuenzalida. 1956. Spanish juncture and intonation. *Language* 32: 641–645.

Trager, G.L. and H.L. Smith. 1951. *An Outline of English Structure*. Norman, OK: Battenburg Press.

Werker, J. and R.C. Tees. 1984. Phonemic and phonetic factors in adult cross-language speech perception. *Journal of the Acoustical Society of America* 75: 1866–1878.

6

What is the smallest prosodic domain?

VINCENT J. VAN HEUVEN

It is widely held that the syllable is the smallest prosodic domain. Notions such as stress, accent, and preboundary lengthening are typically defined as properties of an entire syllable. This paper considers another possibility: that single segments may also function as prosodic domains below the syllable. Within a syllable, if any of the segments is placed in narrow (contrastive) focus, is it prosodically marked by the speaker, e.g. by melodic and/or temporal means? If so, then accent must be a property of the segment, not the syllable, and each segment must be a prosodic domain. And if that is the case, then the question arises which of the segments is the head of the larger prosodic domain, the syllable. These questions can be addressed through acoustic and perceptual studies.

6.1 Theoretical considerations

6.1.1 Integrative focus, narrow focus, and accent position

Accent is defined here as prosodic prominence of a syllable (or part thereof, see below) brought about mainly by melodic means (cf. Bolinger 1958). In Dutch, for instance, it is a sufficient condition for the perception of accent that one of four different fast pitch movements is executed in an appropriate position within the syllable (cf. 't Hart *et al.* 1990).

The function of a (pitch) accent is to place a linguistic unit in focus, i.e. present the unit as expressing important information to the listener (cf. Ladd 1980; Gussenhoven 1984; Baart 1987; Nooteboom and Kruyt 1987). For example, an appropriate answer to question (1a) would be (1b):

(1)   a. WHO wrote that NOVEL?

        b. The DEAN of our FACulty wrote that silly book.

In the answer both *The dean* and *of our faculty* are presented in focus by pitch accents (indicated by capitalized stressed syllables). The second part of the answer (*wrote that silly book*) contains no accent(s) and is therefore out of focus, since it is a mere repetition of material mentioned earlier in the question.

Although it would be possible to mark every (content) word in a larger focus domain by a separate pitch accent, this is not normally done. Speakers typically present several words in focus together in a coherent word group by marking only one word within the larger constituent with a pitch accent. This word is called the "exponent" (Fuchs 1984) or "prosodic head" of the constituent. Consequently, (1c) with an accent only on *faculty* would be an alternative answer to question (1a) expressing essentially the same focus distribution, i.e. presenting the entire constituent *The dean of our faculty* in focus:

(1)   c. The dean of our FAculty wrote that silly book.

When a word such as *dean* in (1c) has no pitch accent, it may therefore either be out of focus (i.e. presented as less important to the listener), or be in focus as part of a larger constituent with an accent on the prosodic head elsewhere in the constituent. More generally, an accent on the prosodic head of a larger constituent is ambiguous, signifying that either the entire constituent is meant to be in focus, or only the head. Consequently, we would expect (1c) to be an appropriate answer to both questions (1a) and – with implicit negation – (1d):

(1)   d. Did the dean of your CHURCH write that novel?
        c. (No,) the dean of our FAculty wrote that silly book.

If a pitch accent occurs on a word other than the prosodic head of the larger domain, all other words in the larger domain are out of focus, and the accented word is presented with narrow focus, typically expressing a contrast. For instance, (1f) can only express a contrast with another faculty official, as in (1e):

(1)   e. Did the SEcretary of your faculty write that novel?
        f. (No,) The DEAN of our faculty wrote that silly book.

To sum up, accenting the head of a prosodic constituent yields an ambiguous focus distribution: it may signal either integrative focus on the entire domain, or narrow focus (with implicit contrast) on the accented unit only.

6.1.2 Lexical stress and pitch accent

So far we have described accent as if it were a property of an entire word. However, we can generalize the mechanism of integrative focus to situations at the word level if we define the (lexically) stressed syllable as the exponent of the word domain. Clearly, an accent on the lexically stressed syllable suffices to mark the entire word for focus, as in (2a):

(2)   a. I said diGEST, not EAT.

Here the entire word *digest* is contrasted with *eat*; yet, one accent on the lexically stressed second syllable is needed to put both the stressed and the unstressed syllable in focus.

This also accounts for the fact that accent on the lexically stressed syllable is ambiguous, since it may also express narrow focus on just the lexically stressed syllable, as in (2b), in which the realization of *digest* is indiscriminable from that in (2a); for Dutch data bearing this out see Sluijter (1992).

(2)   b. I said diGEST, not diVERT.

Here only the lexically stressed (final) syllables of *digest* and *divert* are in focus, since the identical initial syllables *di-* are not contrasted.

It is, of course, quite possible to place the accent on a syllable that does not bear the lexical stress (Bolinger 1961). Accent on a lexically nonstressed syllable would then be a case of narrow focus, expressing a contrast below the word at the level of the syllable, as in (2c):

(2)   c. I said DIgest, not SUGgest.

Here the contrast is made only for the initial lexically nonstressed syllables *di* versus *sug*, whilst the lexically stressed second syllables *gest* are identical and therefore out of focus. That only the nonstressed syllables are in focus is clear from the incorrect expressions (2d–e) in which the accent is not on the exponent of the word, even though entire words rather than individual syllables are contrasted:

(2)   d. *I said DIgest, not EAT.
          e. *I said SUGgest, not CLAIM.

We therefore claim that accent is a property of a syllable rather than of an entire word. Whole words are presented in focus by widening the scope of the accent on the vowel in the lexically stressed syllable.

Vincent J. van Heuven

6.1.3 Accent as a segmental property

The question that I wish to address is if, by an extension of the argument above, the focus domain can be narrowed further to a subsyllable level: for instance, to the level of the segment.

Segments within a syllable are hierarchically organized: the vocalic nucleus is more basic to the syllable than the other, consonant-like elements. A single vowel may quite well constitute a syllable on its own; even single-vowel words do occur (English: *eye*, *a*; Dutch *u* [y] "you," *ei* [ei] "egg," *ui* [ʌy] "onion"). Consonantal elements, on the other hand, can often be omitted without yielding an illegal structure, and are generally incapable of constituting syllables by themselves. Clearly, then, if the segments within the syllable are hierarchically ordered, the vowel should be the head or exponent, and the consonants the satellites.

Generally, accent is defined as a property of a constituent of at least the size of a syllable. The notable exception would be Chomsky and Halle (1968) who proposed that vowels (rather than consonants) be marked for stress (stress and accent were not differentiated). Although this proposal was primarily motivated by the circumstance that phonological theory at the time did not incorporate syllables, we have taken our cue from it: we shall work from the assumption that individual segments can be given narrow focus, and hence can be marked by an accent. Moreover, we claim that the vowel is the exponent of the syllable, so that accenting the vowel creates an ambiguity: either the vowel is in narrow focus, or the entire syllable is in broader focus through integration.

We approached the problem by examining the production and perception of identical (monosyllabic) words containing narrow focus contrasts, involving individual segments, and broader focus involving the entire word, as in (3a–d):

(3)   a. I said p̲it, not b̲it [contrasted element: C1]
       b. I said pi̲t, not pa̲t [contrasted element: V]
       c. I said pi̲t̲, not pic̲k̲ [contrasted element: C2]
       d. I said p̲i̲t̲, not b̲a̲c̲k̲ [contrasted element: entire syllable]

If the syllable is truly the smallest prosodic domain, the phonetic structure of the word *pit* in (3a–d) should be the same, irrespective of the position or scope of the contrasted unit. However, if there are systematic differences in the four realizations of *pit* due to variation in focus (here: contrast), the segment rather than the syllable is the minimal prosodic domain. Moreover, if (3a–c) differ from each other, but (3b) does not differ from (3d), the ambiguity between (3b) and (3d) is evidence that the vowel is the prosodic head of the syllable.

If segmental contrasts are prosodically coded, and if the vowel can be shown to be the exponent of the syllable, the most elegant account of accent is that it is basically a property of the vowel, with the option of marking ever larger domains for focus (syllable, word, constituent, phrase, etc.) through the mechanism of integrative focus.

The perception experiment and subsequent stimulus analysis to be described in the following sections were designed to explore these possibilities.

6.2 Perception of subsyllable contrasts

6.2.1 Introduction

Speakers were asked to read out materials with target words of the CVC type placed in contexts that suggested a narrow focus contrast on either C1, V, or C2, or with the entire syllable contrasted (relatively broad focus). The primary purpose of the experiment was to establish to what extent listeners would be able to retrieve the focus distribution intended by the speaker, when the target words were presented after having been isolated from their original, spoken context. If listeners could correctly decode the intended focus distribution from the spoken stimulus, or at least perform this task well above chance, this would mean that prosody is used to focus linguistic units below the level of the syllable, i.e. individual segments.

Secondly, we were interested in testing the consequences of the status of the vowel as the exponent (Fuchs 1984), or prosodic head, of the syllable. As explained in section 6.1.1, marking the head of a prosodic unit for focus is always ambiguous for the listener, since it can be construed either as narrow focus on the exponent itself, or as broader focus on the larger constituent which is headed by the exponent through so called integrative focus. If listeners can differentiate between intended narrow focus on C1, V and C2, but not between narrow focus on V and broader focus on the entire target syllable, this would be independent support for the claim that the vowel is the prosodic head of the syllable.

6.2.2 Method

Three Dutch target words were selected, each a CVC monosyllable with a phonologically long vowel and voiced consonants throughout: *boon* [bo:n] "bean," *vaar* [va:r] "sail" and *zeem* [ze:m] "sponge." Each target was embedded in a fixed carrier sentence in prefinal position, in which it was contrasted with an earlier word, e.g.:

(4)   Ik heb niet been maar boon gezegd
        ɪk hɛp niːt beːn maːr boːn ɣəzɛχt]
        (I have not leg but bean said)

In the above example the contrasted element is the vowel. Likewise, the contrasted elements could be C1, C2, or the entire syllable.

(5)   Ik heb niet woon maar boon gezegd [contrasted element C1]
        Ik heb niet boom maar boon gezegd [contrasted element C2]
        Ik heb niet veer maar boon gezegd [entire syllable contrasted]

Five native Dutch speakers (two males, three females), fully naive to the purpose of the experiment, read out the twelve utterances. Speakers were seated in a sound-insulated recording booth, and were recorded on audio tape using semi-professional equipment (Sennheiser MKH-416 condenser microphone, Studer-Revox B77 recorder).

The recordings were analog-to-digital (A/D) converted (10 kHz, 12 bits, 0.3–4.5 kHz BP) and stored on computer disk. This filter band was chosen to prevent aliasing and to de-emphasize the strong energy concentration in the region of the fundamental. The last three words of each sentence (. . . *maar boon/zeem/vaar gezegd*) were excised from their spoken context using a high resolution waveform editor. These fragments were D/A converted and recorded back on to audiotape in quasi-random order (excluding immediate succession of the same lexical target word). Each stimulus was recorded three times in a row with three-second intervals (offset to onset). Triplets were separated by a seven second interval. The stimulus set proper was preceded by five practice triplets using similar, but not identical, CVC words.

The tape was presented over loudspeakers in a quiet lecture room to nine native Dutch listeners (staff and/or students at the Department of Linguistics/Phonetics Laboratory of Leiden University). Listeners indicated what they thought would be the most likely context for each stimulus, with forced choice from among four alternatives. The answer sheets listed the stimulus words in the order in which they appeared on the tape. Each target word was printed in four alternative sentences with C1, V, C2, or the entire target syllable in contrast, as exemplified above.

6.2.3 Results

The dataset nominally comprised 540 responses (9 listeners * 5 speakers * 12 stimulus types). In nine cases (1.7%) listeners failed to respond, so that the actual number of responses was 531. The data analysis will proceed in two stages. We shall first examine the results for all responses. This analysis will reveal a number of tendencies, not all of which can be shown to be statistically significant. In a further analysis, however, we shall select the more task-proficient speakers and listeners. After this selection, the trends that are visible in the aggregate data can easily be shown to reach statistical significance.

6.2.3.1 First analysis: all data

Table 6.2.1 presents a confusion matrix with the four intended focus distributions vertically and the listeners' reconstruction of the speakers' intention horizontally. Generally, the effects of intended focus distribution are small. Nevertheless the response distributions deviate highly significantly from chance for each of the four stimulus conditions by a simple chi-square test. Moreover, the overall number of correct responses (the main diagonal cell frequencies taken together) is significantly better than chance ($p = 0.001$, binomial test). When the speaker intended to contrast C1, C1 is the most frequent response category (37%). When V is the contrasted element, V is the most frequently chosen option (38%). When C2 is focused, it is the second most frequent option in its row (30%). However, there appears a rather strong bias throughout the matrix against C2 (and favoring V); when considered column-wise, the C2 cell on the main diagonal contains about as many responses as the rest of the column taken together. Finally,

Table 6.2.1. *Confusion matrix of focus distribution as intended by speakers (C1 contrasted, V contrasted, C2 contrasted, whole word contrasted) and as perceived by listeners. Absolute numbers and row percentages are indicated.*

Intended contrast	Perceived focus distribution			
	C1	V	C2	Word
C1	49	44	19	21
	37%	33%	14%	16%
V	39	51	11	32
	29%	38%	8%	24%
C2	22	44	40	26
	17%	33%	30%	20%
Word	30	56	14	33
	23%	42%	11%	25%

Table 6.2.2. *Pairwise chi-square comparisons of focus conditions (rows in table 6.2.1). Df = 3 for all comparisons.*

Focus conditions compared	Chi-square	p-value
C1 vs. V	6.1	0.108
C1 vs. C2	18.3	<0.001
C1 vs. Word	9.4	0.024
V vs. C2	22.4	<0.001
V vs. Word	1.8	0.619
C2 vs. Word	16.0	0.001

when the intended contrast is on the whole word, focus is predominantly perceived on V (42%), with the whole-word option in second place (25%).

The data show that the response distributions generally differ significantly for all intended focus conditions, except for the pair "V in focus" versus "whole word in focus." This can be observed in table 6.2.2, which lists the results of six pairwise comparisons between rows in the confusion matrix, using chi-square tests (df = 3). Although the first comparison (C1 versus V) does not yield a truly significant difference (but see below), this difference is a trend at least. However, the difference between V and whole word in focus is absolutely insignificant. In sum, the results indicate a weak, but significant, effect of intended focus distribution. Listeners are able to some extent, and above chance level, to reconstruct the speaker's intention from the acoustic make-up of the stimulus. The response distributions for "focus on C1" and "focus on C2" differ considerably, and in the predicted direction. Both these types differ from either "focus on V" or from "focus on whole word," but these latter two do not differ from each other.

6.2.3.2 Second analysis: selection of data
Speakers and listeners may well differ in their abilities to encode and decode subtle differences in focus distribution. Let us therefore examine the individual performance of speakers and listeners. For the sake of conciseness, we shall present only the percentage of correctly transmitted focus distributions, broken down by speaker (table 6.2.3a) and by listener (table 6.2.3b), rather than presenting complete confusion matrices. We observe that four listeners (#1, #4, #6 and #9) performed their task better than the others. Only two speakers (#4 and #5) were able to more or less successfully encode differences in focus distribution. Let us go through the data twice more, once after selecting only the four most able listeners (but across all speakers), and once after selecting only the two best speakers (but

Table 6.2.3. *Percentage of correct responses broken down by individual listeners (panel a) and by individual speakers (panel b)*

(a)	Listener #	Mean	Cases
	1	0.3667	60
	2	0.2667	60
	3	0.3462	52
	4	0.3667	60
	5	0.2833	60
	6	0.3667	60
	7	0.3220	59
	8	0.2500	60
	9	0.3667	60
(b)	Speaker #	Mean	Cases
	1	0.2547	106
	2	0.2308	104
	3	0.2500	108
	4	0.5185	108
	5	0.3714	105
For entire population		0.3258	531

Table 6.2.4. *Like table 6.2.1; only the results for the four best listeners have been included.*

Intended contrast	Perceived focus distribution			
	C1	V	C2	Word
C1	23	17	10	10
	38%	28%	17%	17%
V	15	22	4	19
	25%	37%	7%	32%
C2	7	15	21	17
	12%	25%	35%	28%
Word	14	15	9	22
	23%	25%	15%	37%

Table 6.2.5. *Pairwise chi-square comparisons of focus conditions (rows in table 6.2.4). Df = 3 for all comparisons.*

Focus conditions compared	chi-square	p-value
C1 vs. V	7.7	0.053
C1 vs. C2	14.4	0.002
C1 vs. Word	6.9	0.076
V vs. C2	15.9	0.001
V vs. Word	3.5	0.321
C2 vs. Word	7.8	0.051

across all listeners). The confusion matrices and associated statistics resulting after this selection are presented in tables 6.2.4 and 6.2.5 (listener selection), and tables 6.2.6 and 6.2.7 (speaker selection). Concentrating on percent correct (main diagonal cells) we observe – predictably – that the intended focus distribution has been transmitted more effectively than in table 6.2.1. Also, the selected listeners suffer less from bias. The intended contrast has been retrieved at 12% above chance level, with clear differences between the response distributions for C1, V, and C2, but, again, with no

Table 6.2.6. *Like table 6.2.1; only the results for the two most successful speakers have been included.*

Intended contrast	Percieved focus distribution			
	C1	V	C2	Word
C1	30	13	7	4
	56%	24%	13%	7%
V	17	23	3	11
	32%	43%	6%	20%
C2	5	17	23	7
	10%	33%	44%	14%
Word	11	21	2	19
	21%	40%	4%	36%

Table 6.2.7. *Pairwise chi-square comparisons of focus conditions (rows in table 6.2.6). Df = 3 for all comparisons.*

Focus conditions compared	chi-square	p-value
Cl vs. V	11.2	0.011
Cl vs. C2	27.7	<0.001
l vs. Word	23.2	<0.001
V vs. C2	23.7	<0.001
V vs. Word	3.7	0.296
C2 vs. Word	25.8	<0.001

clear distinction between "focus on V" and "focus on the whole word." Pairwise comparisons of focus conditions bear this out (table 6.2.5). More pairwise contrasts reach statistical significance after than before listener selection, including the contrast Cl versus V that could not be shown to be significant in table 6.2.2. Unfortunately, the contrast "focus on Cl versus Word" that was significant in table 6.2.1 now just falls short of reaching significance. The crucial point, of course, is that only one contrast remains absolutely insignificant, viz. "focus on V versus Word."

The confusion matrix for the two best speakers is presented in table 6.2.6 with pairwise contrasts in table 6.2.7. After the two most task-proficient speakers have been selected, all pairwise comparisons yield significant differences, with one exception: "focus on V versus whole word," which difference remains totally insignificant.

6.2.4 Conclusion

Clearly then, some speakers are much more proficient in encoding differences in focus distribution at the level of the segment than others. Also, certain listeners are better attuned to these cues than others. However, especially when the better performers have been picked out, the results show that contrasts (narrow focusing) on linguistic units below the level of syllable, i.e. individual segments, can be made with some measure of success, and certainly above chance. Moreover, given that differences could nowhere be established between "focus on V" versus "focus on whole word," these data independently support the status of the vowel as the exponent or prosodic head of the syllable.

6.3 Acoustic analysis of subsyllable contrasts

6.3.1 Introduction

What cue or cues do speakers use to convey subsyllable contrasts? To answer this question we acoustically analyzed the speech material used in the perception experiment. We had originally assumed that our speakers would use rather trivial tricks to express narrow focus on individual segments, such as making the contrasted segment unnaturally long or loud. One part of the stimulus analysis is therefore concentrated on measures of absolute and relative segment duration and intensity. However, we have also looked for more subtle, and less trivial, cues in the position and shape of the accent-lending pitch movements on the syllables that contained the various contrasts. In the next section (6.3.2) we shall outline the types of acoustic analysis that were performed; the results and preliminary conclusions will be presented in sections 6.3.3 and 6.3.4, respectively.

6.3.2 Analysis

After A/D-conversion (see p. 81 above) the target phrases were submitted to a pitch-extraction and tracking algorithm using the method of subharmonic summation (Hermes 1988) which calculated F_0 for time frames of 10 ms. Remaining errors (typically octave jumps) were corrected by hand.

For each target phrase acoustic properties were measured in six domains: (i) segment duration, (ii) duration of pitch movements, (iii) excursion size of pitch movements, (iv) synchronization of pitch movements relative to segment boundaries, (v) segment intensity, and (vi) spectral distribution. In the next sections we shall discuss the various measurements per domain.

6.3.2.1 Segment durations

Segment durations were measured by hand (eye) using a high-resolution waveform editor. Segment boundaries were determined by visual criteria only, i.e. abrupt changes in the amplitude and shape of successive glottal periods. In order to define valid relative duration measures some additional time intervals were determined, yielding the following set of duration measurements:

> duration of entire sentence
> duration of sentence until target CVC word
> duration of target segments:
>> initial consonant C1
>> medial vowel V
>> final consonant C2

6.3.2.2 Duration of pitch movements

We started from the assumption that each contrastive accent would be realized as a so-called pointed-hat pitch configuration (configuration 1&A in the intonation grammar of Dutch, cf.'t Hart *et al.* 1990). However, we anticipated that the rise and the fall constituting this configuration could be separated by a plateau. The pitch contour of each target was therefore reduced to three straight lines (in a log frequency by linear time display), whose durations were measured with a precision of 10 ms:

> duration of pitch rise
> duration of pitch plateau
> duration of pitch fall.

6.3.2.3 Excursion size of pitch movements

The F_0 intervals between the onset and offset moments of pitch rises and falls were measured in semitones. Semitone conversion abstracts away from actual pitch levels, enabling better comparison between speakers. The following excursion sizes were determined:

> excursion size of pitch rise
> excursion size of pitch fall.

6.3.2.4 Synchronization of pitch movements relative to segment boundaries

We determined the moments of onset and offset of the accent-lending rise and fall for each target word, expressed in milliseconds relative to the vowel onset. When a pitch-movement onset or offset was located before the vowel onset, a negative value resulted. The following set of synchronization measures was determined:

> onset of (virtual) pitch rise
> offset of pitch rise
> onset of fall
> offset of fall.

6.3.2.5 Segment intensity

The peak intensity of each target segment was measured in decibels (25.6 ms integration time). Since there is no guarantee that our speakers observed a constant distance to the microphone, the segment intensities were expressed as differences (in dB) relative to a reference vowel that occurred outside the target word in the spoken context: [ε] in the final word *gezegd* [ɣəzɛχt] (this is the last nonreduced vowel within the same phonological phrase as the target). If the reference has a lower intensity than the target segment, the difference was given a negative value. The following intensities were entered in the database:

> relative peak intensity of initial consonant C1
> relative peak intensity of medial vowel V
> relative peak intensity of final consonant C2.

The intensity of the initial voiced stop [b] of the target word *boon* could not be measured, so the number of observations for this parameter is limited to 10 rather than 15.

6.3.2.6 Spectral distribution

At the intensity maximum of each target vowel the center frequencies and bandwidths of the lowest five formants (F_1 through F_5, B_1 through B_5) were estimated by the split-Levinson LPC-based robust formant tracking method (Willems 1986; analysis window 25.6 ms, time-shift 10.0 ms). Only F_1 and F_2 were used for further analysis.

6.3.3 Results

6.3.3.1 Segment durations

It would seem a reasonable assumption that narrow focus on one segment would prompt the speaker to lengthen this segment relative to its competitors in the same syllable.

Table 6.3.1 presents the absolute segment durations of the initial consonant (C1), the vowel (V), the final consonant (C2), and the duration of the entire target word (W), broken down by intended contrast condition

Table 6.3.1. *Absolute (in ms) and relative (in percent) duration of initial consonant (C1), medial vowel (V), final consonant (C2), and of entire word, broken down by focus condition: "focus on initial consonant" (C1), "focus on medial vowel" (V), "focus on final consonant" (C2), and "focus on entire word" (Word). Data have been accumulated over lexical items and speakers; each mean is based on 15 measurements.*

Focus on	Absolute duration of				Relative duration of			
	C1	V	C2	Word	C1	V	C2	Word
C1	100	176	100	375	26	47	27	16
V	97	166	106	369	26	45	29	16
C2	95	180	106	382	25	48	27	16
Word	100	166	99	366	27	46	27	16

("C1 in focus," "V in focus," "C2 in focus," "whole word in focus"). The data have been accumulated over speakers and over lexical items. Table 6.3.1 further contains relative segment durations that express the duration of individual segments as a percentage of the duration of the entire word, and the duration of the word as a percentage relative to the duration of the entire utterance. None of the segment durations, whether absolute or relative, is influenced by a difference in focus condition. Classical two-way analyses of variation (ANOVAS), performed separately for each of the acoustic measures with focus condition and speaker as fixed factors, show that all effects of focus distribution are completely insignificant, $F_{(3,56)} < 1$.

6.3.3.2 Duration of pitch movements

The duration of the three components of the accent-lending pitch movement (rise, high plateau, fall) is presented in table 6.3.2, accumulated over speakers and lexical items, but broken down by focus condition.

We reasoned that narrow focus contrasts might be pointed out to the listener when the speaker makes the rise–fall combination more compact in time, i.e. with shorter (and steeper) rises and falls, and centered over the contrasted segment. So we expected that pitch configurations would be shifted along the time axis depending on the position of the contrasted segment (see below under synchronization measures), and that a narrow focus contrast would be characterized by a more compact shape of the pitch configuration. Whether this is true can be examined in table 6.3.2. The pitch rise lasts longer as the focused segment is closer to the left word edge, i.e. the pitch rise is long when C1 is in focus, average when either V or the whole word is in focus, and shortest when C2 is focused, $F_{(3,56)} = 4.2$, p = 0.011.

The duration of the high plateau is quite short throughout, and differences between the focus conditions cannot possibly reach perceptual

Table 6.3.2. *Duration (in ms) of pitch rise, high plateau, and pitch fall on target word, broken down by focus condition (as in table 6.3.1).*

Focus on	Duration of pitch movement		
	rise	plateau	fall
C1	254	21	166
V	213	31	160
C2	187	25	183
Word	203	43	145

relevance, even though ANOVA shows significant effects for this parameter, $F_{(3,56)} = 3.1$, $p = 0.039$.

The duration of the pitch fall is about 20 ms longer than average when C2 is in focus, and some 20 ms shorter than average when the whole word is in focus. This effect, however, fails to reach statistical significance, $F_{3,56} = 1.5$, n.s.

Thus it would appear that the pointed-hat configuration is more distributed in time when the subsyllable contrast is towards the end of the target syllable, and more compact when the contrast is towards the beginning of the syllable.

6.3.3.3 Excursion size

We expected that accenting a constituent that does not normally receive accent, i.e. that is not the exponent of its larger domain, would prompt speakers to give extra prominence to this accent. For instance, it would seem plausible that accents on syllables that are not lexically stressed (as in the phrase *putting the emPHAsis on the wrong sylLABle*) are given extra prominence by increasing the magnitude of the pitch excursions. If this reasoning· is correct, we should observe larger pitch excursions in our material when the narrow-focus contrast does not involve the exponent of the syllable, i.e. involves the consonant segments (C1 or C2), than when it is on the exponent, i.e. on the vowel or on the whole word.

Table 6.3.3 presents mean excursion size of pitch rise and fall on the target word, across speakers and lexical items, but broken down by focus condition. Here we shall consider the results for all speakers; the results for

Table 6.3.3. *Excursion size of pitch rise and of pitch fall (in semitones) on target word, broken down by focus condition (as in table 6.3.1). In the rightmost two columns, the breakdown is repeated for the two most successful speakers (means are now based on 6 measurements).*

Focus on	Excursion size of pitch movements			
	all speakers		two best speakers	
	rise	fall	rise	fall
C1	6.6	9.0	9.0	10.9
V	5.3	8.0	7.0	8.5
C2	6.4	9.4	7.1	10.0
Word	6.0	7.6	8.2	8.3

the two most successful speakers have been included separately for the sake of the general discussion only (section 6.4.1). The excursion size of the rise is larger when there is narrow focus on either C1 or C2 than when focus is on either the vowel (1 semitone difference) or the whole word (0.5 semitone difference). Unfortunately, this effect of focus on excursion size of the rise just falls short of statistical significance, $F_{(3,56)} = 2.6$, $p = 0.067$. There is a similar effect of focus condition on the excursion size of the fall: 1 to 2 semitone larger falls are observed for focus on consonants than for focus on vowel or whole word. Here the effect is just significant, $F_{(3,56)} = 2.8$, $p = 0.051$ (with lexical word as a second factor and after removing differences between speakers through normalization by Z-transformation).

Still, to us these findings suggest that focusing on the consonants of the syllable is "marked" by a more conspicuous pitch movement than in the normal situation, when focus is on the head of the syllable, i.e. the vowel.

6.3.3.4 Synchronization of pitch movements relative to segments

We expected our speakers to center the rise–fall configuration over the specific segment they wished to put in focus position. Accordingly we predicted that the pivot points of the pitch contour, especially the middle two (end of rise, beginning of fall) that are associated with the pitch peak, would shift along the time axis with the position of the focused segment.

Table 6.3.4 presents the relative positions of onset and offset of the accent-lending pitch rise and fall, expressed in ms relative to the vowel onset of the target word.

We observe a tendency especially for the middle two pivot points in the F_0 contour (i.e. the culmen or pitch peak) to be shifted along the time axis into the direction that is opposite to the position of the focused segment within

Table 6.3.4. *Synchronization of pitch movements (rise onset, rise offset, fall onset, fall offset), in ms relative to vowel onset broken down by focus condition (as in table 6.3.1).*

Focus on	Synchronization point of pitch movement			
	rise onset	rise offset	fall onset	fall offset
C1	−163	91	112	278
V	−163	51	82	241
C2	−147	39	64	247
Word	−145	58	101	246

the syllable. When C1 is in focus, the pitch peak is shifted towards the end of the syllable; when the final consonant C2 is in focus, the culmen is advanced towards the beginning of the target syllable. The pitch contour assumes a middle position when either V or the entire word is in focus. The effect is most regular for the fall onset, i.e. the position along the time axis where the culmen of the pitch contour is located. For this parameter the effect of focus position reaches significance by a classical two-way ANOVA with focus condition and lexical word as fixed factors, but only when the two best speakers are selected, and after speaker normalization through Z-transformation, $F_{(3,20)} = 3.8$, $p = 0.054$.

6.3.3.5 Intensity

An easy way for the speaker to mark an individual segment for contrast would be to increase its intensity. Table 6.3.5 contains the peak intensities of C1, V, and C2 expressed in decibels above the peak intensity of the reference vowel (see p. 88 above). As before, data have been accumulated across speakers and lexical items, but are broken down by focus condition. When the initial consonant is in focus, its relative intensity is slightly stronger than in other focus conditions. Similarly, when the vowel is in focus, it is somewhat more intense than when it is not. However, the effects are minute, and this tendency is reversed in the case of focus on the final segment, so that there is no general effect of focus position on the intensity of individual segments, $F_{(3,56)} < 1$ for all intensity parameters.

Table 6.3.5. *Intensity of initial consonant (C1), medial vowel (V), and final consonant (C2), expressed in decibels relative to the intensity of the last vowel in the utterance, broken down by focus condition (as in table 6.3.1). Means for the two rightmost columns are based on 15 measurements, the mean for the leftmost column is based on 10 measurements.*

Focus on	Relative intensity of		
	C1	V	C2
C1	6.2	11.6	2.8
V	5.1	12.1	2.9
C2	3.7	10.1	0.9
Word	4.5	11.8	2.2

Table 6.3.6. *Center frequency of first and second formants (in Hz) broken down by word and by focus condition (as in table 6.3.1). Each mean is based on five measurements.*

Focus on	First formant of:			Second formant of:		
	/boːn	vaːr	zeːm/	/boːn	vaːr	zeːm/
C1	480	741	447	957	1235	1719
V	495	682	423	974	1202	1549
C2	497	688	449	985	1198	1486
Word	501	731	416	975	1224	1554

6.3.3.6 Spectral distribution

Unaccented segments are generally articulated less carefully, which leads to temporal (see p. 89 above) and spectral reduction, so that peripheral vowels tend to gravitate towards the center of the F_1/F_2 plane. Table 6.3.6 therefore presents the center frequencies of F_1 and F_2 broken down by word and by focus condition. Separate two-way analyses of variance on all formants (only F_1 and F_2 are shown) with vowel type (/eː, oː, aː/) and focus condition (C1, V, C2, Word) showed complete insignificance of focus shifts, $F_{(3,56)} < 1$ for all parameters, as well as utter insignificance of any vowel by focus interaction, $F_{(6,48)} < 1$ for all formants. Clearly, spectral differences do not cue our subsyllable contrasts.

6.3.4 Conclusions

Virtually none of the large number of acoustic parameters measured or derived proved susceptible to effects of narrowing and/or shifting focus on individual segments within a syllable. Focusing on individual segments has no effect on either the duration, intensity, or spectral characteristics of segments, even though these would be the most likely candidates for focus cues on the segmental level.

However, there are systematic effects of subsyllable focus shifts on the position and shape of the accent-lending pitch contour on the target word. Typically the position of the pitch peak moves away from the center of the syllable in such a way that it assumes a position that is opposite that of the focused segment, i.e. late when C1 is in focus, intermediate when V or the whole word is focused and early when C2 is in focus. We shall come back to this in the general discussion (section 6.4). Also, it seems that the rise is shorter (and steeper) when the pitch peak occurs early in the syllable (C2 in focus), and longer and more gradual when the peak occurs late (C1 in focus). Finally, the rise has a larger excursion when a consonant is in focus than when the vowel (or the whole word) is in focus.

6.4 General discussion

6.4.1 Summary of main findings

The purpose of this study was to find experimental support for the hypothesis that the segment rather than the syllable is the smallest, and basic, domain of a (pitch) accent. We approached this issue by examining the production and perception of relatively unusual speech utterances containing contrastive elements at the level of individual segments. Although at first sight this may seem a highly contrived communicative situation, I must stress that there is no other way if we want to get at the true nature of accent. The fact that the crucial events only occur in exceptional communicative situations may well be the reason why no one has pursued the possibility of accent as a segmental property before.

Our experiment demonstrates that at least some speakers have the means to express narrow focus on linguistic units below the level of the syllable. Crucially, such speakers do this by purely prosodic means, viz. by changing properties of the accent-lending pitch contour (its shape and location) on the syllable that contains the contrasted segment, rather than by changing acoustic properties of the individual contrasted segment. Moreover, both the results of the perception experiment and of the stimulus analysis clearly bear out that narrow focus on the vowel is brought about by the same means as broader focus on the entire syllable, which supports the status of the vowel as the prosodic head of the syllable.

The effects of focus distribution within the syllable are subtle. It takes a highly proficient speaker to produce them, but if he does, at least certain listeners are able to reconstruct the speaker's intended focus distribution much better than by chance. It appears that the best speakers exploit intonational means more fully than ordinary speakers do. As a case in point, table 6.3.3 shows that the optimal speakers used larger F_0 excursions to mark accents than ordinary speakers. Note, incidentally, that neither speakers nor listeners were trained, or given much time to develop an ad-hoc strategy for marking subsyllable contrasts. We are therefore convinced that we have studied phenomena with linguistic significance, rather than experimental artifact.

Our general conclusion is therefore that accent is best regarded as a property of the segment. Stress, of course, will remain what it has always been: an abstract property of a word specifying the syllable that has the integrative accent position within the word domain.

The true nature of accent will only come to light in exceptional communicative situations, such as those used in the present experiment, in which a speaker wishes to focus on one specific consonant within a syllable. Normally, however, the accent will be on the head of the syllable, i.e. the vocalic nucleus, so that the entire syllable will be highlighted through integrative focus. Since, again, it takes unusual circumstances for the accent not to occur on the lexically stressed syllable, an accent on the vowel generally marks the whole (polysyllabic) word for focus, and so on for larger domains above the word level.

6.4.2 Pitch-peak location and perceived duration

We were both amazed and puzzled by the finding that the pitch peak of the accent marking a segmental contrast should tend to move away from the middle of the syllable in a direction opposite to the location of the contrasted segment, rather than coincide with it. On second thoughts, however, this behavior may not be so odd as it seems. Normally, the pitch peak coincides with the vocalic nucleus, i.e. is located roughly halfway through the syllable. By postponing the pitch peak (either by moving the entire rise–fall configuration towards the end of the syllable or by making the rise longer as well) the speaker creates the impression that the segment(s) preceding the pitch peak last longer, and those following it are shorter. When the pitch peak is advanced towards the syllable onset the listener is tricked into believing that the first half of the syllable is short and the second half long. If this hypothesis is correct, shifting the pitch peak is used by speakers as an alternative to manipulating segment durations within the syllable.

There is circumstantial evidence for the correctness of this account. Van Dommelen (1980) made a contrastive study of production and perception of vowel duration in Dutch and German. The impressionistic and pedagogic literature claims that German high vowels are longer than their Dutch counterparts, and suggests that Dutch learners of German should be taught to double the duration of these vowels. Van Dommelen's measurements, however, brought to light the fact that German high vowels were not longer than their Dutch counterparts, and that the difference in perceived duration could not be explained by production duration. Adriaens (1991) showed that there are systematic intonation differences between Dutch and German, not only in the excursion size of the pitch movements, but also in the timing of the accent-lending rise. Crucially, the German accent-lending rise starts very late in the syllable, whereas the

Dutch rises occur early. Now, if it is true that a late accent-lending rise makes the preceding part of the syllable sound long, Van Dommelen's paradox is solved.

6.4.3 Final remarks

Our experiment is a small-scale exploration that leaves room for improvements and extensions. Its findings will have to be replicated with larger groups of speakers and listeners. The stimulus analysis will have to be submitted to more sophisticated statistical procedures. So far only gross relations have been established between perception of intended focus distribution and acoustic differences. Rather we should try to correlate the production and perception of subsyllable focus differences on a token-individual basis. And ultimately, we shall have to check whether the acoustic differences in shape and position of the pitch configuration, rather than other differences, are indeed the perceptual cues that listeners use to reconstruct the intended subsyllable focus distribution. This will necessarily involve systematic manipulation of selected acoustic parameters through speech synthesis or resynthesis techniques, and testing the perceptual effects of such manipulations.

Acknowledgment

The experiment and stimulus analysis described in this paper were run by my student Jacqueline de Leeuwe as part of a class assignment. I thank my colleagues Anneke Neijt (Department of Dutch, Leiden University), Tom Cook (Department of African Linguistics, Leiden University), and Reneé van Bezooijen (Department of Linguistics, Nijmegen University) for ideas and discussion.

References

Adriaens, L. 1991. Ein Modell deutscher Intonation, eine experimentell-phonetische Untersuchung nach den perzeptiv relevanten Grundfrequenzänderungen in vorgelesenem Text. Ph.D. dissertation, Eindhoven University of Technology.

Baart, J.L.G. 1987. Focus, syntax and accent placement. Ph.D. dissertation, Leiden University.

Bolinger, D.L. 1958. A theory of pitch accent in English. *Word* 14: 109–149.

    1961. Contrastive accent and contrastive stress. *Language* 37: 83–96.

Chomsky, N. and M. Halle. 1968. *The Sound Pattern of English*. New York: Harper & Row.

Dommelen, W.A. van. 1980. Temporale Faktoren bei ausländischem Akzent, eine kontrastive deutsch-niederländische Untersuchung zur Produktion und Perzeption von Segmentdauerwerten. Ph.D. dissertation, Leiden University.

Fuchs, A. 1984. "Deaccenting" and "default accent". In Gibbon, D. and H. Richter (eds.) *Intonation, Accent and Rhythm*. Berlin: de Gruyter 134–164.

Gussenhoven, C. 1984. *On the Grammar and Semantics of Sentence Accents*. Dordrecht: Foris.

Hart, J.'t, R. Collier and A. Cohen. 1990. *A Perceptual Study of Intonation*. Cambridge: University Press.

Hermes, D.J. 1988. Measurement of pitch by subharmonic summation. *Journal of the Acoustical Society of America* 83: 257–264.

Ladd, D.R. 1980. *The Structure of Intonational Meaning: Evidence from English*. Bloomington: Indiana University Press.

Nooteboom, S.G. and J.G. Kruyt. 1987. Accents, focus distribution, and the perceived distribution of given and new information. *Journal of the Acoustical Society of America* 82: 1512–1524.

Sluijter, A. 1992. Lexical stress and focus distribution as determinants of temporal structure. In R. Bok-Bennema and R. van Hout (eds.) *Linguistics in the Netherlands*. Amsterdam: John Benjamins, 247–259.

Willems, L.F. 1986. Robust formant analysis. *IPO Annual Progress Report* 21. Eindhoven: Institute for Perception Research, 34–40.

7

The segment as smallest prosodic element: a curious hypothesis

ALLARD JONGMAN

In his original contribution, Van Heuven challenges the traditional view that accent is a property of the syllable or word. He suggests instead that accent is a *segmental* property. In a perception experiment, words produced under different focus conditions were played back to determine if listeners could tell under which focus condition a particular word had been produced. Narrow focus was placed on an individual segment of the target word. The results of the perception experiment constitute a significant finding in that listeners performed this task at better than chance level. However, when it comes to determining the kind of acoustic information on which listeners base their decision, the situation becomes more complex.

In a subsequent production study, the acoustic characteristics of segments of target words were analyzed. Surprisingly, the cues that are often thought to indicate accent or focus, such as duration and intensity, did *not* play a significant role. Instead, it turned out that pitch was the only cue to segmental contrast. Specifically, there seemed to be an inverse relation between the position of the pitch peak and the position of the focused segment. For a CVC word, the pitch peak occurred relatively late when the initial consonant was in focus, at an intermediate position when the vowel was in focus, and relatively early when the final consonant was in focus.

Evidence for the claim that accent is a segmental property is entangled in suprasegmental variables. Acoustically, segmental contrast as studied in this experiment is signaled by properties of the pitch contour over the *entire word* containing the segment, not by a property restricted to that segment. In my original discussion of Van Heuven's paper, I suggested that it might be worthwhile to look at spectral properties of individual segments in an attempt to find a segmental cue. A recent study by Koopmans-van Beinum and Van Bergem (1989) showed that vowels occurring in "old" and "new" Dutch words (old words are words previously introduced in the discourse) differed in the extent to which they were spectrally reduced. That is, vowels in new words were spectrally less reduced than those in old words. In terms of the present study, in a sentence such as "Ik heb niet w̲oon maar b̲oon gezegd", one might argue that the initial consonant of the target word ("boon") is new, while the rest of the word is old. In contrast, in the sentence "Ik heb niet be̲e̲n maar bo̲o̲n gezegd," it is the vowel which is new and the consonants that are old. Comparing the spectral characteristics of consonants and vowels across these conditions might reveal some interesting differences which would be truly segmental in nature. One could, for example, look at vowel reduction, target undershoot, or degree of coarticulation.

I am pleased to see that Van Heuven has followed up some of those suggestions. Formant measurements of the vowels in focus and nonfocus position are now provided. These measurements do not reveal any differences between vowels in the two conditions. However, the possibility that spectral characteristics of the consonants might vary as a function of focus is still open.

As a second point, I should mention a possible discrepancy between the perception and production studies. In the perception study, the last three words of the original utterance were presented to listeners. Listeners would hear, for example, "maar boon gezegd," where the target word "boon" occurs in phrase-medial position. The listeners' task was to determine which segment in "boon" was in focus. However, in the production study, all measurements (with the exception of duration) were restricted to the target word. Potential cues in the preceding and following words were not analyzed. This leaves open the possibility that listeners made judgements on the basis of properties other than the ones analyzed in the production study. For example, cues present in the words preceding and following the target word (e.g. pause and segment durations, pitch movement, as well as spectral information) could have helped listeners to determine which segment was carrying focus.

A complicating factor also involving the context of the target word has to do with the measurement of pitch and duration. Since target words were embedded in a clause, it may be the case that measurements of pitch and duration did not coincide. If Van Heuven measured the pitch rise from [r] (if sonorous), or from the vowel [a] in "*maar* boon gezegd," a longer pitch rise may simply have been the result of a longer silence between "maar" and "boon." If the silence between "maar" and "boon" was relatively long this would result in a longer pitch rise with a relatively late location of the pitch peak. There may be a confound, then, of duration of pitch rise with silence duration. The reason this did not come out in the segment durations is that for segment duration Van Heuven started measuring from the onset of voicing. If this is true, the important cue would *not* be location of pitch peak but duration of preceding silence, and this could possibly explain Van Heuven's somewhat counterintuitive finding of a later pitch peak when narrow focus is on the initial consonant and an earlier pitch peak when narrow focus is on the final consonant.

Finally, a comment about the interpretation of the results seems in order. Van Heuven's reasoning is as follows: in a sentence such as "Ik heb niet woon maar boon gezegd" there is a narrow-focus contrast involving a single segment. Since listeners are sensitive to subtle differences in focus distribution at the level of the segment, Van Heuven's claim is that narrow focus or accent is a segmental property. In the Dutch examples given in the paper, all segment distinctions are differentiated by a single feature, as in "woon–boon." This raises the question why one should stop at the segment. One could say that in the sentence "Ik heb niet woon maar boon gezegd" there is a narrow–focus constraint involving a single *feature*. By the same logic, would Van Heuven be willing to claim that accent is a featural property? It seems to me that either option – accent as a segmental or featural property – is an unlikely and unattractive solution. Analogously, simply because the past tense of "sit" is "sat," one would not want to argue that past tense is a property of the vowel![1]

A second finding of this study is that listeners could not tell whether a word had been produced with narrow focus on the vowel or with broader focus on the entire word. Acoustic measurements revealed that narrow focus on the vowel was brought about in the same way as broader focus on the entire monosyllabic word. These findings lead to the fairly uncontroversial conclusion that accent, when there is broad focus on the word, is a property of the vowel, the vowel being the prosodic head of the syllable.

At the end of his paper, Van Heuven suggests how his claims might be verified, for example, by manipulating pitch contours to determine if these are really the cues that listeners use to reconstruct the intended focus. What is the possible role of focus in lexical access and word recognition? Assuming that a goal of speech perception is to parse the acoustic signal and comprehend individual words, it is well known from the psycholinguistic literature that listeners use prosodic structure to direct their attention to the location of sentence accents. For example, Shields *et al.* (1974) found that reaction times to target segments in stressed syllables are faster than reaction times to target segments in unstressed syllables. Moreover, Cutler (1976) showed that this was not due to the acoustic correlates of stress (i.e. fundamental frequency, duration, intensity, or degree of spectral reduction). Rather, the intonation contour imposed on the sequence preceding the target word was the determining factor. An acoustically identical word was spliced into two prosodically different (high-stress or reduced-stress) sentence contexts. Results showed that listeners responded faster to words spliced into high-stress positions than into reduced stress positions. This finding indicates that information in the preceding prosody had enabled listeners to direct attention to the location of accent or focus.

Van Heuven's results, on the other hand, suggest that the prosody of the target word itself tells listeners whether the word has been produced with focus. One could then investigate whether listeners are faster at recognizing an excised word carrying focus compared to the same word without focus. It would also be interesting to look for differences in accessing a word with focus on the initial consonant as compared to the final consonant. One of the most influential models of spoken-word recognition, Marslen-Wilson's Cohort model (Marslen-Wilson and Welsh 1978; Marslen-Wilson 1987), assigns word-initial segments more weight or importance in word recognition than later-occurring segments. The Cohort model might then predict that access of lexical entries with narrow focus on the initial segment would be faster. Paradoxically, however, Van Heuven's results indicate that acoustic information signaling that the initial segment carries focus occurs *later* in the word. Recall that the pitch peak occurs relatively late in a word with focus on the initial consonant. It would be interesting to see if this later-occurring information would help listeners to recognize the word faster.

In sum, I think that Van Heuven has provided a promising paradigm to study the effects of focus in terms of both production and perception. One can think of many extensions of the present study, ranging from perception experiments with manipulated synthetic pitch contours to higher-level word-recognition tasks. As interesting as this area of research may be, I hesitate to conclude that the segment, or indeed the feature, is the smallest prosodic domain.

Note

1 I thank Carlos Gussenhoven for suggesting the analogy.

References

Cutler, A. 1976. Phoneme-monitoring reaction times as a function of preceding intonation contour. *Perception and Psychophysics* 20: 55–60.

Heuven, V.J. van. This volume. What is the smallest prosodic domain?

Koopmans-van Beinum, F.J. and D.R. van Bergem. 1989. The role of 'given' and 'new' in the production and perception of vowel contrasts in read text and in spontaneous speech. In J.P. Tubach and J.J. Mariani (eds.) *Proceedings of the*

Allard Jongman

European Conference on Speech Communication and Technology, Paris 1989; 113–116.

Marslen-Wilson, W.D. 1987. Functional parallelism in spoken word recognition. In U.H. Frauenfelder and L.K. Tyler (eds.) *Spoken Word Recognition*. Cambridge, MA: MIT Press, 71–102.

Marslen-Wilson, W.D. and A. Welsh. 1978. Processing interactions during word-recognition in continuous speech. *Cognitive Psychology* 10: 29–63.

Shields, J. L., A. McHugh, and J.G. Martin. 1974. Reaction time to phoneme targets as a function of rhythmic cues in continuous speech. *Journal of Experimental Psychology* 102: 250–255.

Part II
Syllables

8

Articulatory phonetic clues to syllable affiliation: gestural characteristics of bilabial stops

ALICE TURK

8.1 Introduction

While it is widely assumed that word-initial and word-final consonants are syllable-initial and syllable-final respectively, the syllable affiliation of word-medial intervocalic consonants is less clear. In American English, word-medial intervocalic consonants preceding stressed vowels (as in *repáir*) are argued to be syllable-initial because they pattern phonologically with syllable-initial consonants: voiceless stops in this position exhibit the aspiration characteristic of word-initial voiceless stops. However, the syllable affiliation of word-medial intervocalic consonants preceding unstressed vowels (as in *léper* and *cáliper*) is much debated in the phonological literature. Kahn (1976) argues that these intervocalic consonants are ambisyllabic (they are linked to both the preceding and the following syllable at the same time) while Selkirk (1982) argues that they are simply syllable-final. Since many phonological phenomena in American English appear to be driven by the prosodic affiliation of the segments which undergo them (Kahn 1976), it is important to have an accurate description of the structural representation of the segments. The purpose of this paper is to clarify the nature of consonantal syllable affiliation in American English by providing articulatory phonetic evidence in the form of a comparison of the characteristics of upper-lip movement of consonants whose syllable affiliation is equivocal with consonants with known syllable affiliations (either syllable-initial or syllable-final). Assuming a direct phonology-to-phonetics mapping, intervocalic consonants which precede unstressed vowels are predicted to pattern phonetically with syllable-initial consonants if they are phonologically syllable-initial. Similarly, they should pattern with syllable-final consonants if they are phonologically syllable-final. Ambisyllabic consonants are predicted to share the phonetic characteristics of both syllable-initial and syllable-final consonants.

The structure of the paper is as follows: First, the phonological process of syllabification is discussed, followed by phonological and psycholinguistic evidence for the resyllabification of consonants preceding unstressed vowels. Previous work on the phonetic realizations of syllable-level distinctions is then presented, followed by the details of the present experiment, results, and a discussion of the results' implications for phonological theory.

8.2 Background

8.2.1 Syllabification

Theories which have a rule-based approach to the assignment of syllable structure generally posit a series of core-syllabification rules which syllabify consonants and vowels (Kahn 1976; Steriade 1982; Clements and Keyser 1983; Clements 1990; among others; but see Milliken 1988 for an alternative account).

As stated in Clements and Keyser (1983: 38)

1. (a) V-elements are prelinked to syllables.
    (b) C-elements to the left are adjoined one by one as long as the configuration resulting at each step satisfies all relevant syllable structure constraints.
    (c) Subsequently, C-elements to the right are adjoined in the manner described in (b) above.

For example, the words *repair* and *leper* would be syllabified in the following way:

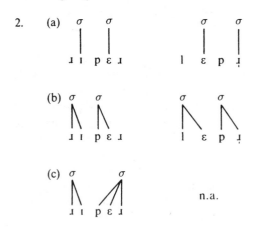

108

As shown above, the core-syllabification rules syllabify intervocalic consonants in the environments V—v (as in *léper*) and v—V (as in *repáir*) in the same way. However, there is both phonological and psycholinguistic evidence that intervocalic consonants which precede unstressed vowels do not behave like syllable-initial consonants which precede stressed vowels. Such evidence has led phonologists to posit resyllabification rules that make the consonants in question either exclusively syllable-final (Selkirk 1982):

or ambisyllabic (Kahn 1976):

8.2.2 Resyllabification

Although a wide variety of phenomena has been explained by the resyllabification of intervocalic consonants (see Kahn 1976; Selkirk 1982; Myers 1987; Gussenhoven 1986; Milliken 1988), the most widely cited phonological evidence for resyllabification is the distribution of the allophones of alveolar stops. Kahn (1976) and Selkirk (1982) note that word-medial /t/s and /d/s which follow [− cons] segments and which precede stressless vowels are realized as flaps (very short prevoiced alveolars with little or no sign of a release burst, Zue and Laferriere 1979) as in the words *city*, *butter* and *Ida*. Also, /t/ and /d/ are optionally flapped word-finally between [− cons] segments and either stressed or unstressed vowels (e.g. *not I*). In contrast, /t/s and /d/s which occur either word-medially before stressed vowels (e.g. *attack*) or word-initially before vowels, stressed or unstressed (e.g. *tomorrow*), are realized with clearly defined closures and releases: /t/'s are aspirated, as are voiceless stops of other places of articulation in the same environments. Among other things, the authors also discuss glottalized /t/, which occurs in words such as *cats* and *atlas*.

Both Kahn (1976) and Selkirk (1982) argue that the distribution of alveolar stop allophones is syllable conditioned. However, their accounts differ crucially in their description of the flapping phenomenon. In Kahn's (1976) account consonants in the flapping environment are resyllabified and become ambisyllabic (simultaneously syllable-initial and syllable-final) by the following resyllabification rules, as stated in Kahn (1976: 55, 56):

Rule III (normal-rate and faster speech only)

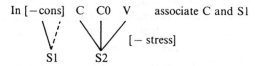

By this rule, a word such as *leper* would be syllabified as follows:

In his account, the alveolar-stop allophones are distributed as follows: stops are aspirated if they are syllable-initial and nonsyllable-final, /t/ is glottalized following a nonconsonant, and /t/ is flapped when it is ambisyllabic and occurs between a nonconsonant and a vowel.

Selkirk (1982), on the other hand, argues that the phonological phenomena can be accounted for in a more principled way without ambisyllabicity. She proposes that consonants in the flapping environments are in fact syllable-final in surface representation. Following rules of basic syllable composition and stress assignment, they are resyllabified by the following rule, as stated in Selkirk (1982: 365):

Resyllabification I:

$$+syl$$

$$X \quad [-cons] \quad [-syl] \quad -stress \quad Y$$

$$1 \quad 2 \qquad 3 \qquad 4 \qquad 5 \quad \rightarrow \quad 1, 2 + 3, 0, 4, 5$$

By this rule, *leper* would be syllabified as follows:

According to her account, the /t/ in *butter*, realized as a flap [ɾ], and the /t/ in *atlas*, realized as a glottalized /t/ [t'], are both syllable-final; the different allophones of /t/ and /d/ are predicted by whether or not the consonant is released. Consonants are [+release] "if immediately following the articulation and not during or after the articulation of a following segment the closure is reopened" (Selkirk 1982: 373). She takes [+release] to be the default value of the feature, and describes the environments for nonrelease. Consonants which occur after [−cons] and before [−syl], as in the words *atkins* and *rapt*, are obligatory [−release]. After [−cons] and before pause, as in the phrase *Watch the cat*, consonants are optionally [−release]. Selkirk also describes the contexts in which stops following other consonants are [−release] (see Selkirk 1982: 373–376). Her rules for flapping (Tap) and glottalization are given below.

Tap:

t,d → ɾ/ σ([−cons] _____)σ
+ release

Glottalization:

p,t,k → p̓,t̓,k̓/ _____
− release

By positing a feature which distinguishes the two environments for flapping and glottalization, she is able to account for the distribution of flaps and glottalized stops without making reference to ambisyllabicity (Selkirk, 1982: 373).

Thus, Kahn and Selkirk propose to account for the same phonological phenomena by positing different syllable affiliations in surface representation for stops following [−cons] segments and preceding unstressed vowels. In Kahn's theory, they are ambisyllabic; in Selkirk's they are syllable-final. Selkirk acknowledges that ambisyllabicity has an intuitive appeal (she cites the impressions of Kenyon 1950; Pike 1967; and Smalley 1977). However, she hypothesizes that these impressions can be attributed to the combined effect of perceiving the consonants as syllable-final in surface representation and of the knowledge that the consonants are underlyingly syllable-initial, or to "a conflict between the perceived syllable-final character of the consonant in phonetic representation and the universal tendency to assign pre-vocalic consonants to the following syllable, in phonological as well as phonetic representation" (Selkirk, 1982: 379).

8.2.3 An alternative foot-based account

As an alternative to resyllabification accounts of the distribution of alveolar-stop allophones, Kiparsky (1979) proposes that these phenomena are instead predicted by foot structure. In his account, consonants become [+lax] after a nonconsonantal segment in the same foot (Kiparsky 1979: 437):

C → [+lax]/ɸ[...[−cons] ___ ...]ɸ

Then, postcyclic rules voice syllable-initial lax /t/s (which are then realized as flaps), aspirate nonlax voiceless stops, and optionally glottalize lax voiceless stops.

Because the primary concern of this paper is to present phonetic evidence for the above three views, the reader is referred to Gussenhoven (1986), Milliken (1988), and Inouye (1989) for more systematic discussions of other aspects of Kahn's, Selkirk's and Kiparsky's analyses.

8.2.4 Psycholinguistic evidence

Another type of evidence for the syllable affiliation of intervocalic consonants preceding unstressed vowels can be found in Treiman and Danis (1988). They conducted a psycholinguistic experiment in which subjects were asked to reverse the syllables of 84 spoken words which contained intervocalic consonants and which varied in stress. The subjects first practiced by reversing *grandfather* as *father grand*. They were then asked to reverse words with single intervocalic consonants. For example, the word *lemon* could be reversed as *monlem, monle,* or *onlem*. A *monlem* type result was interpreted to mean that the /m/ was ambisyllabic; a *monle* type result was interpreted to mean that the /m/ was syllable-initial; and an *onlem* response indicated that the /m/ was syllable-final.

When the intervocalic consonant was spelled with one letter, subjects gave a high proportion of syllable-initial responses for words with stress on the second syllable. When the stress was on the first syllable, however, subjects gave all three types of responses: syllable-initial, syllable-final and a few ambisyllabic responses. Consonant type had an effect on response type: it was only when the medial consonant was a liquid or a nasal that there was a significant difference between the number of syllable-final and the number of syllable-initial responses (syllable-final > syllable-initial). Also, ambisyllabic responses were significantly greater than other responses (responses which were neither syllable-initial nor syllable-final) only when the medial consonant was a liquid or a nasal. Subsequent work by Treiman and Zukowski (1990) suggests that the length of the vowel also has an effect on subjects' responses.

As discussed in Treiman and Danis (1988), Kahn's (1976) theory provides a possible explanation for the small number of ambisyllabic responses they found. However, they propose Selkirk's (1982) theory as an alternative account: at the level of basic syllable composition, intervocalic consonants preceding unstressed vowels are syllable-initial; after resyllabification, they are syllable-final. The subjects' inconsistencies in choosing between syllable-initial, syllable-final, and ambisyllabic responses can be explained if subjects have knowledge of both underlying and surface representations, as hypothesized in Selkirk (1982). However, both theories are inadequate in explaining different effects of consonant type.

8.2.5 The phonetics of position-in-syllable

As described above, there is considerable disagreement in the phonological literature about the syllable affiliation of intervocalic consonants that precede unstressed vowels. Psycholinguistic experiments have also yielded ambiguous results. The present experiment was designed to clarify these issues by presenting phonetic evidence for the syllable affiliation of equivocal stops by comparing them with unequivocally syllable-initial and syllable-final stops.

Syllable-initial and syllable-final consonants have been shown to differ phonetically in several previous studies. Lehiste (1960) found that word-initial stops were longer in acoustic closure duration than word-final stops. Fromkin (1965) showed that word-initial /b/ had a greater amplitude and duration of muscle activity than word-final /b/, and word-initial /p/ had a great duration of muscular tension, although there was no significant difference in amplitude across conditions. Coker and Umeda (1975) found that the voiced murmurs of initial stops have energy predominantly at the first and second harmonics, whereas final stops have a broader spectrum. Different allophones of /l/ and /ɹ/ are found in word-initial and word-final positions (Nakatani and Dukes 1977). Fujimura and Lovins (1978) report that velum height is greater for syllable-initial nasals than for syllable-final nasals. In a study of labial and velic gestures during the production of /m/, Krakow (1989) found that labial gestures were enhanced in initial position (they had larger and longer movements along with a higher maximum position), whereas velic gestures were enhanced in final position (they had larger displacement amplitudes of velum lowering and raising, a lower spatial minimum, and the velum was in a low position for a longer time). Furthermore, studies of inter-articulator timing have shown that there are different patterns of coordination for syllable-initial versus syllable-final stops (Nittrouer *et al.* 1988; Krakow 1989).

There is one study that compares the phonetic characteristics of syllable-initial and syllable-final stops with intervocalic consonants preceding unstressed vowels (labeled as ambisyllabic by Kahn 1976). Krakow (1989) compared the intervocalic /m/s in *homey, seamy, helmet, pomade,* and *Seymour* with the syllable-final /m/s in *Home E, Seam E, helm it, palm ade,* and *seem ore* as well as with the syllable-initial /m/s in *hoe me, see me, hell mitt, pa made,* and *see more.* She based her comparisons on measures of velum height at the middle of the vowel preceding the nasal consonant and at the onset of bilabial contact for the /m/, of the duration of the low velic plateau, and of the interval between the end of velum lowering and onset of lip raising. She found slightly different results for the two subjects in .her study. The first subject's tokens of *homey, seamy* and *helmet* patterned with the corresponding syllable-final stops; *pomade* and *Seymour* patterned with syllable-initial stops. The other subject was similar to the first subject in that both *homey* and *seamy* patterned with syllable-final /m/s, and *pomade* patterned with the syllable-initial /m/ in *pa made*. However, the second subject was different in that some of her tokens of *helmet* were syllable-final while others were syllable-initial. The /m/ in *Seymour* had combined characteristics of syllable-initial and syllable-final /m/s. Stress played a significant role in the behavior of both speakers: when primary or secondary stress followed the /m/ (as in *pomade* and *Seymour*), the /m/s exhibited syllable-initial characteristics for the most part. When the second syllable was unstressed, /m/s were syllable-final, except for the /m/s in some of the second subject's *helmet* tokens, which patterned as though they were syllable-initial. Krakow (1989) hypothesizes that the *helmet* results might indicate that in some cases the /1m/ cluster was divided between the two syllables, whereas in the other cases, the word was syllabified according to its stress pattern.

8.3 The experiment

The present experiment was designed in the same spirit as the study in Krakow (1989) described above. Its purpose is to determine the syllable affiliation of intervocalic stops before unstressed vowels by comparing them with both syllable-initial and syllable-final stops. It builds on the previous work not only by presenting additional data from three speakers, but also by presenting evidence from different kinematic parameters (vertical displacement and peak velocity) of a different articulator (the upper lip) during the production of different consonants (/p/ and /b/).

8.3.1 Hypotheses

The following hypotheses about intervocalic consonants preceding unstressed syllables are tested by comparing them with unequivocally syllable-initial and syllable-final consonants. A direct phonology-to-phonetics mapping is assumed in all cases.

1. They are syllable-initial; resyllabification has not occurred. In this case, both closing and opening gestures of the equivocal stops should pattern with the closing and opening gestures of syllable-initial stops.
2. They are syllable-final (Selkirk 1982). Both closing and opening gestures of the equivocal stops are predicted to pattern with both the closing and opening gestures of syllable-final stops.
3. They are ambisyllabic (Kahn 1976). Kahn's theory predicts that the consonants would share features of both syllable-initial and syllable-final

stops, a physical definition tentatively proposed by Fujimura and Lovins (1978). Two possibilities present themselves here for the realization of both syllable-initial and syllable-final characteristics. Either the closing gesture patterns with syllable-final closing gestures and the opening gesture patterns with syllable-initial closing gestures, or vice versa. The former is intuitively more plausible.

4. The fourth possibility is that the phonological evidence for which both Kahn and Selkirk posit resyllabification rules (the American English flapping rule, for example), is not syllable conditioned at all, but is instead foot conditioned (Kiparsky 1979). Recall that under this theory, alveolar stops are laxed nonfoot-initially. Kiparsky's theory predicts that there should at least be phonetic differences between foot-initial and nonfoot-initial consonants. Therefore, consonants preceding unstressed vowels (being nonfoot-initial) should pattern with other nonfoot-initial consonants, in both their closing and opening gestures.

8.3.2 Data collection

The data were collected at the X-Ray Microbeam facility in Madison, Wisconsin, and included movement trackings of a small gold pellet attached to the vermilion border of the upper lip.

Vertical movement (as well as horizontal movement) was tracked with reference to the occlusal plane and to the upper incisor, at a sampling rate of 45 samples per second. Sampled points thus occur every 22.2 ms, which is adequate for the relatively slow movements of the upper lip. Movement trajectories shown in figures below have points interpolated between samples at 5-ms intervals. The data were corrected for head movement.

8.3.3 Stimuli

The stimuli used in the experiment contain /p/s and /b/s in different stress environments in different syllabic positions. They are listed in table 8.1. The tokens came from a data set collected for a different experiment. For this reason, it was impossible to analyze a balanced set of tokens whose vowel context was held constant. However, the validity of the statistical technique used in the analysis is not diminished by unbalanced data sets. Furthermore, vowel context is not expected to have much effect on the vertical positioning of the upper lip with respect to the occlusal plane. Because the other experiment tested rate effects, the words were repeated at two self-selected rates: three to five times at a slower rate and two to five times at a faster rate (appendix 8.A lists the exact number of repetitions of each token for each speaker). The number of repetitions varied because of mistrackings and

Table 8.1. *The stimuli classified according to position in syllable and stress environment.* V = *stressed vowel;* v = *unstressed vowel.*

1. Syllable-initial stops:	
$vC_0\_C_0V$	$VC_0\_C_0v$
the parable	looked pyramidal
repair	
rebel (the verb)	
2. Syllable-final stops:	
$vC_0\_C_0V$	$VC_0\_C_0v$
observed	microscope
	captor
	object (the noun)
3. Syllable affiliation unknown:	
$VC_0\_C_0v$	$vC_0\_C_0v$
rabble	parable
leper	caliper

because of limitations on radiation exposure time for each subject. The words were spoken in meaningful sentences (see appendix 8.B for the list).

8.3.4 Subjects

The author and two other female native speakers of American English served as subjects. The three subjects are treated as replicate experiments.

8.3.5 The choice of kinematic characteristics

The kinematic characteristics used to describe both closing and opening gestures during the production of /p/ and /b/ are vertical displacement and peak velocity. Articulator displacement and peak velocity were chosen because they are known to vary with both position in syllable and stress (Kent and Netsell 1971; Kuehn and Moll 1976; Ostry *et al.* 1983; Munhall *et al.* 1985; Krakow 1989; de Jong 1991). Syllable-initial consonants and consonants in stressed syllables tend to have greater articulator displacements than their syllable-final and unstressed counterparts (Kent and Netsell 1971; Krakow 1989; de Jong 1991). Peak velocity is known to increase with greater displacement (Kuehn and Moll 1976); however, the peak velocity/displacement ratio is also known to vary with stress: stressed syllables tend to have greater peak velocity/displacement ratios (Ostry *et al.* 1983; Munhall *et al.* 1985).

Vertical movement of the upper lip with respect to the occlusal plane was chosen since the upper lip moves relatively little in the vertical dimension during the production of vowels or nonlabial consonants (except /r/). Figures 8.1, 8.2 and 8.3 show a comparison of vertical movement trajectories of the upper lip during the production of the phrases *to the salad* and *cigar* (with no labial consonants) with the upper-lip trajectory during the production of *leper*. During the production of /p/ and /b/, the upper lip moves an average of 2.7 mm during closing gestures and 3.1 mm during opening gestures for Speaker 1; 4.4 mm during closing and 4.5 mm during opening for Speaker 2, and 2.1 mm during closing and 2.3 mm during opening for Speaker 3. Movement in the vertical dimension was chosen since it contributes most to achieving closure.[1]

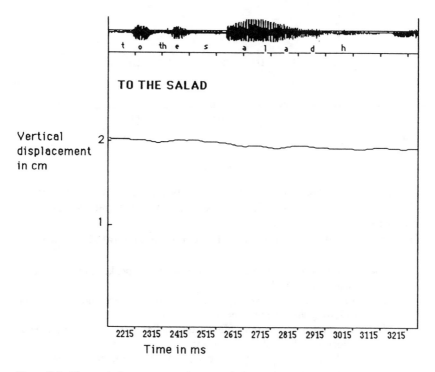

Figure 8.1. The vertical movement trajectory, relative to the upper incisor and the occlusal plane, of a pellet attached to the upper lip during the production of the phrase *to the salad*.

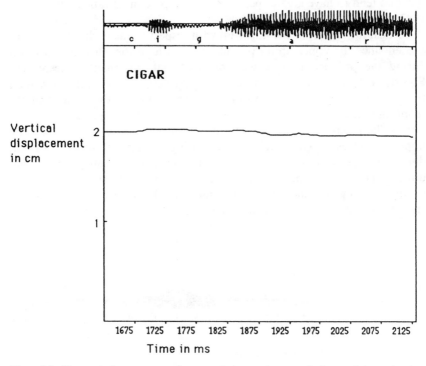

Figure 8.2. The vertical movement trajectory relative to the upper incisor and the occlusal plane, of a pellet attached to the upper lip during the production of the word *cigar*.

8.3.6 Measurements

The measurements were made using ACE analysis software (including an implementation of a peak-picking algorithm) developed at Haskins Laboratories.

The measurements are defined as follows, and are illustrated in figure 8.3.

The closing gesture begins at a displacement peak, and ends at a displacement valley.

The opening gesture begins at the displacement valley and ends at the following displacement peak.

Peak velocity (in the vertical dimension) is the maximum instantaneous velocity of the gesture, in cm/sec.

Vertical displacement is defined as the absolute difference between the *displacement peak and displacement valley* in cm for both closing and opening gestures.

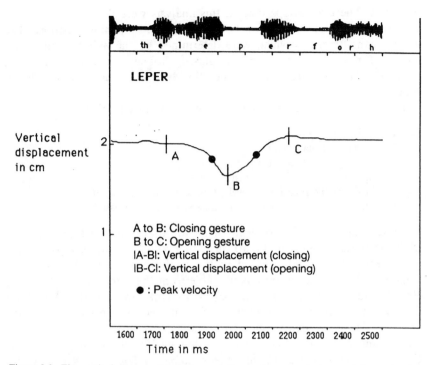

Figure 8.3. The vertical movement trajectory relative to the upper incisor and the occlusal plane, of a pellet attached to the upper lip during the production of the word *leper*

8.3.7 Analysis

The data were statistically analyzed by means of discriminant analysis (Klecka 1980 is a recommended reference) using SAS statistical software on a VAX/VMS 8530 computer. Discriminant analysis can be used to discriminate tokens from two different groups. The analysis derives a set of discriminant functions (linear combinations of the variables used to describe each token) which can best distinguish the two groups. These functions can then be used to classify any token into the group that it most closely resembles, and the probability of correct classification can be calculated. Even though some misclassifications are possible, the largest possible probability of correct classification can be achieved under regular assumptions. The main goal of the analysis is to classify new cases whose group affiliation is unknown, based on the previously derived discriminant functions. The two groups used in this analysis were the groups Syllable-Initial and Syllable-Final, for both closing and opening gestures. The discriminant functions which were determined by the Syllable-Initial and Syllable-Final data were used to classify tokens from the Unknown Syllable Affiliation group into either the Syllable-Initial or the Syllable-Final group.

The variables used to describe each token are listed below:

1. Peak velocity
2. Vertical displacement
3. Voicing (/b/ versus /p/)
4. Speech rate (slow versus fast)
5. Stress of the preceding vowel (stressed versus unstressed)
6. Stress of the following vowel (stressed versus unstressed)

Because the stress environment of all the tokens in the known groups (Syllable-Initial or Syllable-Final) was either $VC_0\_C_0v$ or $vC_0\_C_0V$, only one stress factor could be used in the analysis, since the Stress of the Following Vowel was entirely predictable from the Stress of the Preceding Vowel, and vice versa. Since the tokens of Unknown Syllable Affiliation did include stops which occurred between two unstressed vowels, the analysis was done twice: once with the factor Stress of the Preceding Vowel, and once with Stress of the Following Vowel. When Stress of the Preceding Vowel was used, the tokens *caliper* and *parable* were put into the same Stress category as consonants in the environment $vC_0\_C_0V$; when Stress of the Following Vowel was used, the tokens *caliper* and *parable* were put into the same Stress category as consonants in the environment $VC_0\_C_0v$.

Using the variables described above, discriminant functions were derived to discriminate between the Syllable-Initial and Syllable-Final groups. These functions were used to classify tokens from the Unknown Syllable Affiliation group into either the Syllable-Initial or the Syllable-Final group. The probability of membership in the Syllable-Initial and the Syllable-Final category was computed for each token for both closing and opening gestures. Tokens with a probability of 0.5 or more of membership in a particular category were classified in that category.

8.3.8 Results

Results from discriminant analyses are given in tables 8.2, 8.3, and 8.4. Kinematic properties of Syllable-Initial, Syllable-Final, and Unknown stops are shown in figures 8.4, 8.5, and 8.6. Figure 8.4 compares peak-velocity/vertical-displacement ratios (peak velocity normalized for vertical displacement) for *leper*, a member of the Unknown category and for *captor*, a member of the Syllable-Final category with the same stress environment. Figure 8.5 compares the peak-velocity/displacement ratios for two Syllable-Final token types with the same stress environment. Figure 8.6 is a three-way comparison of peak-velocity/displacement ratios for Syllable-Initial, Syllable-Final and Unknown exemplars with the same stress environment.

8.4 Discussion

Table 8.2 shows that, as expected, the discriminant analysis classified the majority of Syllable-Initial tokens as Syllable-Initial (for both opening and closing gestures for all speakers), and also classified the majority of Syllable-Final tokens as Syllable-Final. Misclassifications are listed in appendix 8.C.

With regard to the consonants whose syllable affiliation is unknown, both the closing and opening gestures patterned with both the closing and opening gestures of syllable-final stops. Although this pattern is robust for Speaker 1 (78% of closing gestures and 81% of opening gestures were classified as syllable-final), Speakers 2 and 3 showed quite a few Unknown cases being classified as Syllable-Initial (closing gestures, Speaker 2: 38%, Speaker 3: 25%; opening gestures, Speaker 2: 45%, Speaker 3: 41%). Table 8.3 shows how each token type was classified for all three speakers.

It can be seen in table 8.3 that, except for six tokens of *parable* for Speaker 2 and five tokens of *parable* for Speaker 3, it is *not* the case that the closing gestures are classified as syllable-final and opening gestures are classified as syllable-initial, which would be a possible interpretation of ambisyllabicity (see Coleman, this volume). Furthermore, for most cases it is also not the case that closing gestures are Syllable-Initial and opening gestures are syllable-final (except for three tokens of *leper* and one token of *parable* for Speaker 2, and one token of *caliper* for Speaker 1). In most instances, both the closing and opening components of the tokens are classified as either syllable-final or syllable-initial stops. For all speakers, consonants that occur after a stressed vowel and before an unstressed vowel were classified as Syllable-Final, except for three consonants for Speaker 2. However, many of the tokens which include consonants between two unstressed syllables were classified as syllable-initial (*caliper* for Speaker 1, *caliper* and *parable* for Speaker 2, and *caliper* for Speaker 3). To see whether this result is an artifact of which stress factor was included in the specifications for the Syllable-Initial and Syllable-Final tokens an analysis was performed that included Stress of the Following Vowel instead of Stress of the Preceding Vowel. Results are shown in table 8.4. When the data from the categories were coded with the Stress of the Following Vowel instead of the Stress of the Preceding Vowel, all except three tokens in the Unknown category were

Table 8.2. *Results of a discriminant analysis when the stress environment of the consonants was described using the Stress of the Preceding Vowel.*

Speaker 1:
Closing gestures

	Number classified as	
	Syllable-Initial	Syllable-Final
Coded as:		
Unknown	6 (22%)	21 **(78%)**
Syl-Initial	18 **(72%)**	7 (28%)
Syl.-Final	3 (12%)	23 **(88%)**

Opening gestures

	Number classified as	
	Syllable-Initial	Syllable-Final
Coded as		
Unknown	5 (19%)	22 **(81%)**
Syl.-Initial	21 **(84%)**	4 (16%)
Syl.-Final	1 (4%)	25 **(96%)**

Speaker 2:
Closing gestures

	Number classified as	
	Syllable-Initial	Syllable-Final
Coded as:		
Unknown	12 (38%)	20 **(63%)**
Syl.-Initial	23 **(74%)**	8 (26%)
Syl.-Final	4 (13%)	27 **(87%)**

Opening gestures

	Number classifed as	
	Syllable-Initial	Syllable-Final
Coded as:		
Unknown	15 (45%)	18 **(55%)**
Syl.-Initial	31 **(100%)**	0 (0%)
Syl.-Final	10 (32%)	21 **(68%)**

Speaker 3:
Closing gestures

	Number classified as	
	Syllable-Initial	Syllable-Final
Coded as:		
Unknown	8 (25%)	24 **(75%)**
Syl.-Initial	21 **(70%)**	9 (30%)
Syl.-Final	4 (14%)	25 **(86%)**

Opening gestures

	Number classified as	
	Syllable-Initial	Syllable-Final
Coded as:		
Unknown	13 (41%)	19 **(59%)**
Syl.-Initial	23 **(77%)**	7 (23%)
Syl.-Final	6 (21%)	23 **(79%)**

Table 8.3. *Classification of closing and opening gestures of the Unknown stops into Syllable-Initial and Syllable-Final categories by token type.*

Speaker 1:

Closing		Opening	
Syl-Initial	*Syl-Final*	*Syl-Initial*	*Syl-Final*
caliper 6 (100%)	leper 7 (100%)	caliper 5 (83%)	leper 7 (100%)
	rabble 8 (100%)		rabble 8 (100%)
	parable 6 (100%)		parable 6 (100%)
			caliper 1 (17%)

Speaker 2:

Closing		Opening	
Syl.-Initial	*Syl-Final*	*Syl.-Initial*	*Syl.-Final*
leper 3 (38%)	leper 5 (63%)	caliper 7 (100%)	leper 8 (100%)
caliper 7 (100%)	rabble 9 (100%)	parable 7 (88%)	rabble 9 (100%)
parable 2 (25%)	parable 6 (75%)		parable 1 (13%)

Speaker 3:

Closing		Opening	
Syl.-Initial	*Syl.-Final*	*Syl.-Initial*	*Syl.-Final*
caliper 8 (100%)	leper 8 (100%)	caliper 8 (100%)	leper 8 (100%)
	parable 7 (100%)	parable 5 (71%)	rabble 9 (100%)
	rabble 9 (100%)		parable 2 (29%)

Table 8.4. *Results of a discriminant analysis done when the stress environment of the consonants was described using the Stress of the Following Vowel. Only the classifications of the Unknown tokens are shown here since the classifications of the Syllable-Initial and Syllable-Final tokens are listed in Table 8.2.*

	Number classified as	
	Syllable-Initial	Syllable-Final
Speaker 1:		
Closing	0 (0%)	27 (**100%**)
Opening	0 (0%)	27 (**100%**)
Speaker 2:		
Closing	3 (9%)	30 (**91%**)
Opening	0 (0%)	33 (**100%**)
Speaker 3:		
Closing	0 (0%)	32 (**100%**)
Opening	0 (0%)	32 (**100%**)

classified as Syllable-Final, for both opening and closing gestures. The three exceptions were the closing gestures of three tokens of *leper* for Speaker 2. None of the consonants that occurred between two unstressed vowels were classified as Syllable-Initial, as they had been when Stress of the Preceding Vowel was used as a factor. This change, which is particularly apparent for Speakers 2 and 3, indicates that for those speakers, stress is an extremely influential variable. Since there are no Syllable-Initial or Syllable-Final tokens that have consonants which occur between two unstressed syllables, it is difficult to assess the results for consonants which occur between two unstressed syllables for those speakers.

In short, two things can be concluded from the discriminant analyses:

1. Syllable affiliation is greatly influenced by stress;
2. Consonants in the environment VC_0—C_0v pattern with Syllable-Final stops.

In order to support the results of the discriminant analyses which showed that consonants in the environment VC_0—C_0v pattern with syllable-final stops, analyses of variance (ANOVAs) were performed on the peak-velocity/vertical-displacement ratios (peak velocity normalized for vertical displacement) for the pairs *leper-captor* (figure 8.4) and *rabble–object* (figure 8.5). The stress environment was held constant. Since the discriminant analysis classified all of those stops as syllable-final, we would expect no significant differences in either their opening or closing gestures. In fact this is true for all except for the closing gestures of Speaker 1 for *rabble* and *object*, and for both the closing and opening gestures of Speaker 2's *rabble* and *object* ($p < 0.05$).

In a similar vein, we would expect there to be a significant difference between syllable-initial stops and syllable-final stops that have the same stress pattern, as well as between syllable-initial stops and intervocalic stops preceding unstressed vowels. To test this prediction, ANOVAs were performed on the triplet *pyramidal–captor–leper* for all speakers. Results are shown in figure 8.6. For the opening gestures, there is a significant difference between *pyramidal* and both *captor* and *leper*, and, as shown in figure 8.4, no significant differences between *leper* and *captor*. For the closing gestures, on the other hand, none of the words was significantly different. These results suggest that differences in syllable position are more robust for the opening gestures.

The results from the comparisons shown in figure 8.4, 8.5, and 8.6 support the results from the discriminant analyses: that kinematic characteristics of /p/ and /b/ in the environment VC_0—C_0v pattern with those of syllable-final /p/ and /b/ in both closing and opening gestures, although syllable-affiliation differences show up more clearly in the opening gestures. These results for the upper lip are consistent with those of Krakow (1989) for the velum.

It seems, therefore, that if we assume a direct phonology-to-phonetics mapping, Kahn's theory of ambisyllabicity is not supported by the present experiment. Consonants did not share properties of syllable-initial and syllable-final consonants, as ambisyllabicity would predict. The results are consistent with the predictions made by the theory of Selkirk (1982) in which intervocalic consonants preceding unstressed vowels are syllable-final. However, the foot-based theory of Kiparsky (1979) cannot be ruled out, either: the syllable-final tokens with which the Unknown tokens patterned were also nonfoot initial; there were no nonfoot-initial consonants that were also syllable-initial. Experiments that include nonfoot-initial syllable-initial consonants will be able to distinguish between the two theories.

Yet another possibility is that the labial consonants in *rabble* and *leper* patterned with the syllable-final consonants not because of their prosodic status, but instead because they all precede [+cons] segments. The point is well taken, but the similar results of Krakow (1989) for velar gestures during the production of /m/ in *seamy* and *homey* suggest that it is the absence of stress on the second syllable in *rabble* and *leper*, rather than the presence of the liquids, that account for the patterns observed here. Also, since the structures tested here are derived surface representations, it seems unlikely that abstract consonantal properties would be the basis for surface similarities.

8.5 Conclusion

The results from the present experiment on vertical movements of the upper lip show that the consonants which Kahn (1976) classifies as ambisyllabic do not share combined characteristics of both syllable-initial and syllable-final stops. Instead, stops which follow stressed vowels and precede unstressed vowels pattern in both their closing and opening components with syllable-final stops. Furthermore, stress was shown to have a great influence on syllable affiliation, which is not surprising, since in the phonology of American English, it is the absence of stress on a following vowel which triggers consonantal resyllabification. The results are consistent with those of Krakow (1989) for velum movement. However, the results from the present experiment cannot distinguish between the theory of Selkirk (1982), in which intervocalic consonants preceding unstressed vowels are syllable-final in surface representation, and the theory of Kiparsky (1979), in which they are similar to syllable-final consonants in that they are both nonfoot-initial. Further research is needed to decide this issue as well as the issue of

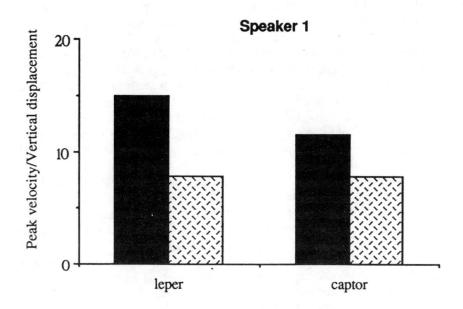

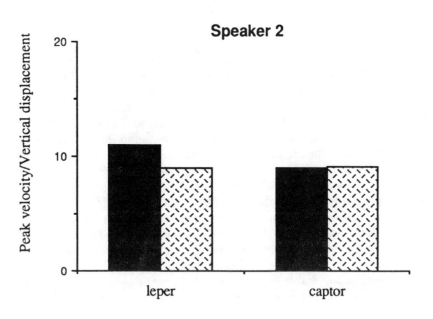

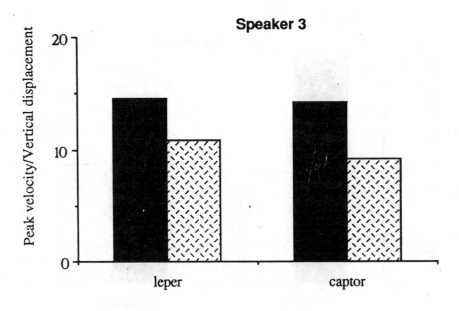

Figure 8.4. Peak-velocity/vertical-displacement ratios for upper-lip vertical movement during the production of the /p/s in *leper* and *captor* for all speakers. Dark bars indicate peak-velocity/vertical-displacement ratios for closing gestures; light bars indicate peak-velocity/vertical-displacement ratios for opening gestures. The unit along the vertical axis is $\frac{1}{10}$ second.

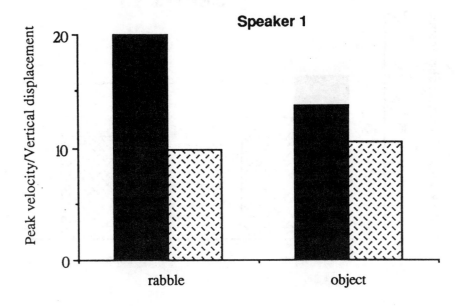

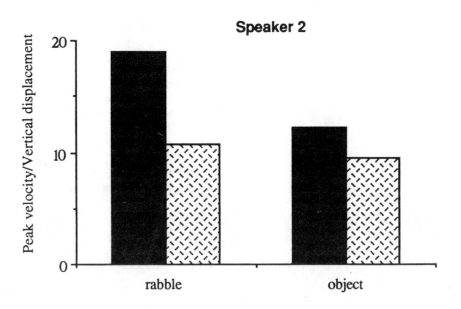

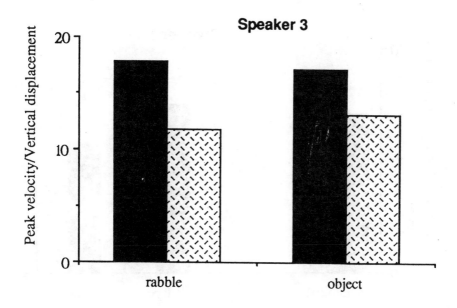

Figure 8.5. Peak-velocity/vertical-displacement ratios for upper-lip vertical movement during the production of the /b/'s in *rabble* and *object* for all speakers. Dark bars indicate peak-velocity/vertical-displacement ratios for closing gestures; light bars indicate peak-velocity/ vertical-displacement ratios for opening gestures. The unit along the vertical axis is $\frac{1}{10}$ second.

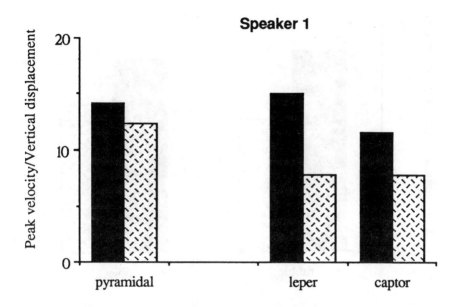

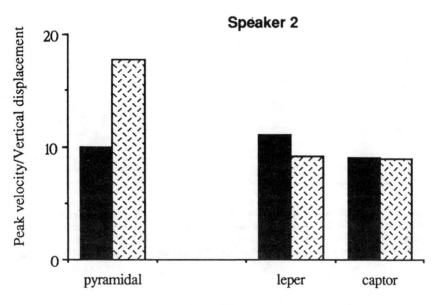

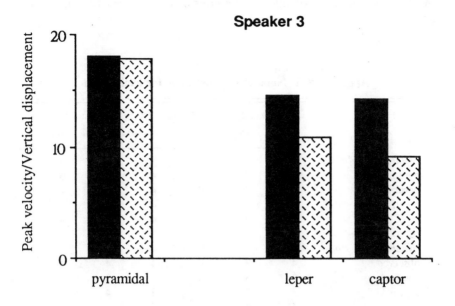

Figure 8.6. Peak-velocity/vertical-displacement ratios for upper-lip vertical movement during the production of the /p/s in *pyramidal, leper,* and *captor* for all speakers. Dark bars indicate peak-velocity/vertical-displacement ratios for closing gestures; light bars indicate peak-velocity/vertical-displacement ratios for opening gestures. The unit along the vertical axis is $\frac{1}{10}$ second.

the syllable affiliation of intervocalic consonants between two unstressed syllables.

Appendix 8.A: Number of repetitions for each token

	Speaker 1		Speaker 2		Speaker 3	
	Slow	Fast	Slow	Fast	Slow	Fast
1. Syllable-Initial stops:						
pyramidal	4	3	4	4	4	3
parable	4	3	4	4	4	4
repair	3	3	4	4	4	4
rebel	3	3	4	4	4	4
2. Syllable-Final stops:						
observed	4	3	4	4	4	4
microscope	3	3	4	3	3	3
captor	3	3	4	3	4	2
object	4	4	5	4	4	5
3. Syllable Affiliation unknown:						
rabble	3	5	5	4	5	4
parable	3	3	4	4	4	4
leper	4	3	4	4	4	4
caliper	3	3	4	4	4	4

Appendix 8.B: Test sentences

1. She studied the *parable* in religion class.
2. He avoided the *leper* for health reasons.
3. We watched the *rabble* from the tower.
4. She decided to *rebel* against her captors.
5. She *observed* the follicle under the *microscope*.
6. The *object* looked *pyramidal* in shape.
7. He decided to *repair* the green car.
8. He misplaced the *caliper* on his workbench.

Alice Turk

Appendix 8.C: Misclassifications for the tokens from known categories

Misclassifications of Speaker 1's tokens

Closing		Opening	
Initial as Final	Final as Initial	Initial as Final	Final as Initial
pyramidal 7 (100%)	captor 1 (17%) microscope 2 (33%)	pyramidal 4 (57%)	microscope 1 (17%)

Misclassifications of Speaker 2's tokens:

Closing		Opening	
Initial as Final	Final as Initial	Initial as Final	Final as Initial
pyramidal 8 (100%)	captor 4 (57%)		observed 7 (88%) microscope 3 (43%)

Misclassifications of Speaker 3's tokens:

Closing		Opening	
Initial as Final	Final as Initial	Initial as Final	Final as Initial
rebel 2 (25%) pyramidal 7 (100%)	observed 4 (50%) pyramidal 3 (43%)	rebel 4 (50%)	observed 6 (75%)

Note

I am indebted to Cathe Browman, Louis Goldstein, and Caroline Smith for help with data measurement; to George Casella, Tim Dorcey, Nae Yuh Wang, and especially to Naisyin Wang, for statistical help. It was Naisyin Wang who suggested that I use discriminant analysis for this data set. My thanks go to Nick Clements, Abby Cohn, Jim Flege, Allard Jongman, Pat Keating, John Kingston, Francis Nolan, Donca Steriade, Dan Turk, Bruce Wootton, and an anonymous reviewer for comments on this and previous versions of this paper. Any mistakes are mine. Data collection was supported by a Sigma Xi Grant in Aid of Research.

1 Vertical movement was analyzed for this study. However, the horizontal-movement component is currently being investigated (Turk, in preparation).

References

Clements, G.N. 1990. The role of the sonority cycle in core syllabification. In J. Kingston and M. Beckman (eds.) *Papers in Laboratory Phonology I: Between the Grammar and Physics of Speech.* Cambridge: University Press, 283–333.

Clements, G.N. and S.J. Keyser. 1983. *CV Phonology: a Generative Theory of the Syllable.* Linguistic Inquiry Monograph 9. Cambridge, MA: MIT Press.

Coker, C.H. and N. Umeda. 1975. The importance of spectral detail in initial-final contrasts of voiced stops. *Journal of Phonetics* 3: 63–68.

de Jong, K. 1991. The oral articulation of English stress accent. Ph.D. dissertation, Ohio State University.

Fromkin, V. 1965. Some phonetic specifications of linguistic units: an electromyographic investigation. Ph.D. dissertation, University of California at Los Angeles. *UCLA Working Papers in Phonetics* 3.

Fujimura, O. and J. Lovins. 1978. Syllables as concatenative phonetic units. In A. Bell and J.B. Hooper (eds.) *Syllables and Segments.* New York: North Holland, 107–120.

Gussenhoven, C. 1986. English plosive allophones and ambisyllabicity. *Gramma* 10.2. University of Nijmegen, Instituut Nederlands, 119–141.

Inouye, Susan B. 1989. Flap as a contour segment. *UCLA Working Papers in Phonetics* 72: 40–81.

Kahn, D. 1976. Syllable-based generalizations in English phonology. Ph.D. dissertation, MIT. (Distributed by Indiana University Linguistics Club.)

Kent, R.D. and R. Netsell. 1971. The effects of stress on certain articulatory parameters. *Journal of Phonetics* 24: 23–44

Kenyon, J.S. 1950. *American Pronunciation,* 10th edition. Ann Arbor, MI: George Wahr Publishing Company.

Kiparsky, P. 1979. Metrical structure assignment is cyclic. *Linguistic Inquiry* 10(3): 421–441.

Klecka, W. 1980. Discriminant analysis. *Sage University Paper Series: Quantitative Applications in the Social Sciences* .07–.019. Beverly Hills and London: Sage Publications.

Krakow, R.A. 1989. The articulatory organization of syllables: a kinematic analysis of labial and velic gestures. Ph.D. dissertation, Yale University.

Kuehn, D. and K. Moll. 1976. A cineradiographic study of VC and CV articulatory velocities. *Journal of Phonetics* 4: 303–320.

Lehiste, I. 1960. An acoustic–phonetic study of internal open juncture. *Phonetics* 5 (Suppl.): 1–54.

Milliken, S. 1988. Protosyllables: syllable and morpheme structure in the lexical phonology of English. Ph.D dissertation, Cornell University.

Munhall, K.G., D.J. Ostry, and A. Parush. 1985. Characteristics of velocity profiles of speech movements. *Journal of Experimental Psychology* 4: 457–474.

Myers, S. 1987. Vowel shortening in English. *Natural Language and Linguistic Theory* 5: 485–518.

Nakatani, L.H. and K.D. Dukes. 1977. Locus of segmental cues for word juncture. *Journal of the Acoustical Society of America* 62: 714–719.

Nittrouer, S., K. Munhall, J.A.S. Kelso, B. Tuller, and K.S. Harris. 1988. Patterns of interarticulator phasing and their relation to linguistic structure. *Journal of the Acoustical Society of America* 84: 1653–1661.

Ostry, D.J., E. Keller, and A. Parush. 1983. Similarities in the control of the speech articulators and the limbs: Kinematics of tongue dorsum movement in speech. *Journal of Experimental Psychology: Human Perception and Performance* 83: 622–636.

Pike, K.L. 1967. *Language in Relation to a Unified Theory of the Structure of Human Behavior*, 2nd edition. The Hague: Mouton.

Selkirk, E.O. 1982. The syllable. In H. van der Hulst and N. Smith (eds.) *The Structure of Phonological Representations*. Dordrecht: Foris, 337–383.

Smalley, W.A. 1977. *Manual of Articulatory Phonetics*. South Pasadena, CA: William Carey Library.

Steriade, D. 1982. Greek prosodies and the nature of syllabification. Ph.D. dissertation, MIT.

Treiman, R. and C. Danis. 1988. Syllabification of intervocalic consonants. *Journal of Memory and Language* 27: 87–104.

Treiman, R. and A. Zukowski. 1990. Toward an understanding of English syllabification. *Journal of Memory and Language* 29: 66–85.

Umeda, N. 1977. Consonant duration in American English. *Journal of the Acoustical Society of America* 61: 846–858.

Zue, V. and M. Laferriere. 1979. Acoustic study of medial /t,d/ in American English. *Journal of the Acoustical Society of America* 66: 1039–1050.

9
The phonology and phonetics of extrasyllabicity in French

ANNIE RIALLAND

A central goal of Laboratory Phonology is to improve our understanding of
the relationship between phonological representations and their phonetic
interpretation. From this point of view, extrasyllabicity presents an
interesting case. An extrasyllabic consonant is not part of any syllable.
This notion was introduced by Clements and Keyser in *CV Phonology*
(1983) and is now widely used among phonologists. However, no systematic
study has yet been carried out of the phonetic implementation of this notion
or of its correlate, core syllabification. This question has been raised in
regard to English data in recent work, but not as a central concern (see
Browman and Goldstein 1988, as well as Fujimura and Lovins 1978 for a
related perspective).

The case of French is a particularly interesting one. Unlike English,
French has phonological rules sensitive to extrasyllabicity. While many of
these rules are lexical, some of them, including a rule involving a constraint
on geminates to be discussed below, are postlexical. If phonological rules
can refer to extrasyllabicity, we would expect to find phonetic correlates of
this notion as well. Among other things, we will see that extrasyllabic
consonants do not exhibit the high degree of coarticulation with following
segments that is typical of onset consonants. Other processes, such as
voicing assimilation and cluster timing, will be seen to depend not only on
syllable organization, but also on the way extrasyllabic consonants are
affiliated to larger constituents such as the word and phrase, allowing a
better understanding of the nature of extrasyllabicity.

This paper focuses mainly on word-initial consonants. In section 9.1, we
consider the status of word-initial consonants, and offer phonological
evidence in favor of extrasyllabicity. Section 9.2 is devoted to the distinction
between core syllabification and extrasyllabicity. Core-syllabification rules
are studied, as well as the main characteristics of extrasyllabic consonants.

136

The phonetics of extrasyllabic consonants and of core-onset consonants are also considered. Section 9.3 is devoted to word-final consonants and consonant clusters. In sections 9.4 and 9.5, we examine postlexical processes sensitive to extrasyllabicity: schwa drop and geminate formation on the one hand, and the prosodic status of consonants after schwa drop on the other.

9.1 The status of word-initial consonants

Strings of consonants may occur at the beginning of French words that do not form an indivisible constituent, i.e. an onset. Certain phonological processes shed light on the structure of these sequences and offer arguments in favor of an analysis in terms of extrasyllabicity. Most of the relevant processes apply at the lexical level, but some of them apply postlexically. In this section we will examine processes belonging to the lexical level, leaving the examination of postlexical processes to later sections (9.4 and 9.5).

9.1.1 Phonological processes sensitive to extrasyllabicity at the lexical level

The most familiar of the rules sensitive to extrasyllabicity at the lexical level is that of glide formation. Let us consider this rule first.

Glide formation can optionally apply to the first of two vowels if the syllable onset has only one consonant, yielding variants like the following:

lier	[lje]	or	[lije]	"to bind"
nouer	[nwe]	or	[nue]	"to tie"
suer	[sɥe]	or	[sye]	"to sweat"

It cannot apply if the onset consists of a Cr or Cl cluster:

trouer	[tʁue]	not	*[tʁwe]	"to make a hole in"
plier	[plije]	not	*[plje]	"to fold"
cruel	[kʁɥɛl]	not	*[kʁɥɛl]	"cruel"

Thus, the following structure is not acceptable (σ = syllable, O = Onset, N = Nucleus, C = Consonant, L = Liquid, G = Glide, V = Vowel):

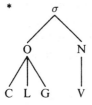

Glide formation was used by Kaye (1989) to support the idea that the syllable onset cannot have more than two consonants. This rule also shows that not every sequence of two consonants forms an onset. Indeed, glide formation applies in words such as:

skier   [skje]   or   [skije]   "to ski"
skiable   [skjabl] or   [skijabl] "skiable"

or in the following less frequent words:

psiadie   [psjadi] or   [psijadi] "psiadie"
ptyaline [ptjalin] or   [ptijalin] "ptyalin"

In these examples, the first consonant does not block the rule. These words behave like words beginning with one consonant. Consequently, the first consonant can be considered extrasyllabic, and the following structure may be proposed for *skier*:

Here, [s] is extrasyllabic and [kj] forms an onset.

As glide formation is blocked after CL and CG clusters but not after others, we conclude that the only permissible two-member onsets are CL and CG clusters. The other clusters are composed of an extrasyllabic consonant followed by an onset consonant.

However, let us now look at CLG clusters, which appear at first sight to be counter-examples to this claim.

9.1.2 Diphthongs

Words such as *trois* [tʁwa] appear to begin with a three-consonant onset of the form CLG. However, an alternative analysis can be proposed in which the glide is considered part of an underlying diphthong (see Hyman 1985 among others). In such an analysis, the representation of *trois* is the following:

There are only three underlying diphthongs: /wa, ɥi, wɛ̃/. Some examples follow:

wa:	proie	[pʁwa]	"prey"
	croissant	[kʁwasã]	"crescent"
ɥi:	ébruiter	[ebʁɥite]	"to disclose"
	truite	[tʁɥit]	"trout"
wɛ̃:	groin	[gʁwɛ̃]	"snout" (only example)

These glide + vowel sequences cannot be analyzed in the same way as others, since they are the only ones that can occur after CL clusters. Other glide + vowel sequences are avoided after CL clusters even if they are directly suggested by the orthography, as in:

dryade	[dʁijad]	not:	*[dʁjad]	"dryad"
amphitryon	[...tʁij5̃]	not:	*[...tʁj5̃]	"host"

But the glide + vowel sequences which are rejected after CL clusters can be found after other types of consonant clusters:

squeezer	[skwize]	"to cheat"
skiable	[skjabl]	"skiable"
squaw	[skwo]	"squaw"
ptyaline	[ptjalin]	"ptyalin"
psiadie	[psjadi]	"psiadie"

The sequence at the beginning of the word *squeezer* can be represented as follows, where the glide is part of the onset and the first consonant is extrasyllabic:

Thus, the distribution of diphthongs is consistent with our analysis.

9.2 Core syllabification and extrasyllabicity

Core syllabification can be understood as the set of basic syllabification processes used in a language in the deepest layers of its phonology (Clements and Keyser 1983). We apply this term to French to refer to the syllabification processes occurring during the formation of the stem (a unit consisting of the word with its suffixes but excluding any prefixes). The stem forms the domain of various rules sensitive to syllable structure, in particular the well-known *règles de position* which forbid [e] and [ə] in a closed syllable, transforming [e] and [ə] into [ɛ] in this context (see Dell 1985 and Selkirk 1972 for discussion of various aspects of these rules). These rules are important for our purposes because they create phonological cues to syllable structure: [e] and [ə] occur only in open syllables, and any following consonant belongs to the next syllable.

9.2.1 Core syllabification of medial clusters

In the domain of core syllabification as defined above, a syllable nucleus can consist of a single vowel or one of the diphthongs /wa, ɥi, wɛ̃/. The core-syllabification rules for medial clusters are the following:

any CL cluster forms an onset:
étriqué	[e-tʁi-ke]	"tight"
ébriété	[e-bʁi-je-te]	"intoxication"
écrémé	[e-kʁe-me]	"skimmed"

where CL clusters are:
stop + liquid
fricative + liquid (but only [vʁ, fʁ, fl])

all other CC clusters are split between two syllables:
sermon	[sɛʁ-mɔ̃]	"sermon"
Alexandre	[a-lɛk-sãdʁ]	"Alexander"
espérer	[ɛs-pe-ʁe]	"to hope"
estimer	[ɛs-ti-me]	"to value"
restituer	[ʁɛs-ti-tɥe]	"to return"
espiègle	[ɛs-pjɛgl]	"mischievous"
estuaire	[ɛs-tɥɛʁ]	"estuary"

It will be observed that permissible onset clusters are a subset of those permitted by the sonority hierarchy given below:

obstruents	nasals	liquids	glides	vowels

We will see that this hierarchy plays a further role in determining admissible consonant sequences in the later discussion.

Note also that the syllabification required by the *règles de position* is consistent with the glide-formation rule, as shown by the last two examples. This agreement offers further support for the extrasyllabic analysis.

the medial consonant in a CCC or CCCL cluster is always extrasyllabic:
expert	[ɛk-s-pɛʁ]	"expert"
exprimer	[ɛk-s-pʁi-me]	"to express"
expier	[ɛk-s-pje]	"to expiate"

As a result of this cluster splitting, there is only one consonant in the coda. (N.B. syllable codas and word-final clusters will be examined later.)

The application of glide formation in *expier* shows that [s] does not belong to the following onset. In the later discussion, we argue that it should not be syllabified with the coda of the preceding syllable, and must therefore remain extrasyllabic.

9.2.2 Word-initial extrasyllabic consonants

Let us now consider the extrasyllabic consonants themselves. We find the following sequences of extrasyllabic consonants and clusters in initial position:

(1)   fricative + obstruent/nasal/liquid:

s/z:	sbire [zb] "henchman"
	spleen [sp] "spleen," splash [sp] "splash"
	smash [sm] "smash," SMIC [sm] (abbr.) "minimum wage"
	sphère [sf] "sphere," sphincter [sf] "sphincter"
	svelte [zv] "svelte"
	stade [st] "stadium," stèle [st] "stele," stopper [st] "to stop,"
	strophe [st] "verse," strict [st] "strict," stylo [st] "pen"
	slave [sl] "Slavic," slow [sl] "slow dance"
	snobisme [sn] "snobbery," snuggli [sn] (type of baby pouch)
	ski [sk] "ski," squatter [sk] "squatter," squelette [sk] "skeleton,"
	sclérose [sk] "sclerosis," scribe [sk] "scribe"
	(N.B. (s/z is much less common before a voiced obstruent.)

f/v:	vlan [vl] "wham!", Wladimir [vl] "Vladimir"
	FNAC [fn] (name of retail chain)
	phtisie [ft] "phthisis," phtaléine [ft] "phtalein"

ʃ:	shtroumpf [ʃt] (comic-strip character)
	schlinguer [ʃl] "to stink," schlague [ʃl] "drubbing"
	schnock [ʃn] "blockhead," schnouff [ʃn] "dope, junk"

(2)   stop + obstruent/nasal

stop + coronal obstruent:

p + t:	ptérodactyle [pt] "pterodactyl," ptose [pt] "ptosis,"
	Ptolémée [pt] "Ptolemy"
k + t:	chtonien [kt] "Chtonic"
C + s/z:	psaume [ps] "psalm," pseudonyme [ps] "pseudonym,"
	psychique [ps] "psychic"
	tsar [ts] or [dz] "czar," tsigane [ts] or [dz] "gipsy,"
	xylophone [ks] or [gz] "xylophone," xérès [gz] "sherry,"
	Xavier [gz] "Xavier," xénophobe [gz] "xenophobe"
C + ʃ:	tchèque [tʃ] "Czech," Tcherkess [tʃ] "Tcherkess,"

Tchad [tʃ] "Chad"
(No labial fricatives occur in second position.)

C + nasal: pneu [pn] "tire," pneumatique [pn] "pneumatic"
tmèse [tm] "tmesis"
knout [kn] "leather scourge," CNET [kn] (research center).
CNIT [kn] (trade-fair center), khmer [km] "Khmer"

m + n: mnémotechnique [mn] "mnemonic"

From this list, it appears that no more than one extrasyllabic consonant occurs word-initially, and that only obstruents can be extrasyllabic (with the exception of the group [mn]).

It is interesting to find that word-initial sequences of consonants are constrained by the sonority scale given earlier, even in cases where the initial consonant is extrasyllabic. Thus we find that an extrasyllabic consonant may have the same degree of sonority as the following onset consonant, but no more. As a result, an onset obstruent cannot be preceded by an extrasyllabic nasal, nor a nasal by a liquid. Moreover, the most sonorous consonants – i.e., the liquids and the glides – are totally excluded from extrasyllabic position. Thus the sonority profile at the beginning of a word must be level or rising, and the extrasyllabic consonant never introduces a sonority reversal.

9.2.3 Phonetics of extrasyllabic and core-onset consonants

We will now consider the phonetic realization of word-initial consonants to determine how it relates to the phonological analysis given above. Focusing first on the various realizations of [k] in the context of different following vowels, we will show that an extrasyllabic [k] does not have the same relationship with the nucleus as an onset [k]. Secondly, looking at the way voicing assimilation affects the extrasyllabic consonant, we will see that the extrasyllabic consonant does not behave like a completely independent or extraprosodic consonant, but like one which belongs to the phonological word. The timing of the sequence of consonants will also be considered.

9.2.3.1 Assimilation triggered by vowels: the velar consonants

We have chosen to study velar consonants because they are more influenced by the following vowel than other stops, and because they may occur either as the only member of an onset, as the first member of an onset cluster, or as an extrasyllabic consonant.

9.2.3.1.1 Realizations of the velar stop as an onset of a CV syllable The syllable affiliation of consonants has been examined recently on the basis of

the relative timing of articulatory gestures (see e.g. Krakow 1989 and Turk, this volume, among others). Here, we will consider the relationship between the velar stops and some vocalic gestures, referring to the analysis published by Zerling (1981).

On the basis of articulatory evidence, Zerling shows interesting asymmetries between [gV] transitions and [Vg] ones studied in a [əgVg] context. In [gV] transitions, during the velar closure, the tongue anticipates the movement of the following vowel, and at the release of the consonant the tongue shape clearly varies according to the quality of the following vowel. On the contrary, in [Vg] transitions, the apex movement tends to be identical regardless of the vowel quality. Figure 9.1 illustrates this dissymmetry. The figure gives a comparison of vocal-tract shapes for the pronunciation of [g] in [Vg] and [gV] sequences just before and just after the closure. We see that in the [Vg] transition, the position of the tongue tip is relatively uninfluenced by the preceding vowel, and is determined mainly by the consonant movement which pulls the tongue towards the velum. In the [gV] transition, in contrast, the position of the tip of the tongue is strongly influenced by the identity of the following vowel. Thus the vocalic movement executed by the tongue tip appears to be initiated during the consonant closure. Moreover, the point of articulation of the velars is influenced by the following vowel (see Zerling 1981, figure 3). As a consequence, there are important cues to the identity of the vowel at the

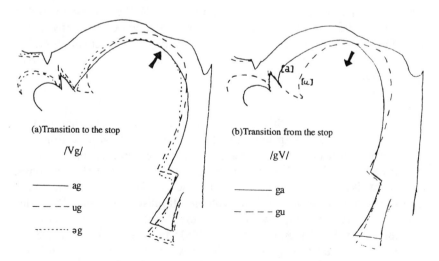

(a)Transition to the stop

/Vg/

——— ag

– – – – ug

·········· əg

(b)Transition from the stop

/gV/

——— ga

– – – – gu

Figure 9.1. Comparison of vocal-tract shapes for the pronunciation of [g] in [Vg] and [gV] sequences: (a) just before the closure, (b) just after the closure. (After Zerling 1981.)

consonant release, which is an important acoustic as well as articulatory landmark.

These facts show an orientation of consonants towards the following vowel. Let us now look at velar + liquid groups.

9.2.3.1.2 [kl]/[kʁ] clusters and their relationship with the following vowel As [kl] and [kʁ] clusters form an onset, we could expect these clusters as a whole to bear close ties with the nucleus. To see whether this is so, let us look at representative spectrograms of [ukʁi] and [ikʁu], shown in figure 9.2. In [ukʁi], the F_2 value at the [k] release has a value of 1700 Hz, while in [ikʁu] it has a value of 1100 Hz. We see that the F_2 value at the [k] release is strongly influenced by the following vowel, even when it is separated from it by a liquid [ʁ]. (Similar results were obtained for [l], not shown here.) Thus the articulation of [k] as a member of a syllable onset is closely dependent on the nature of the following vowel, even in [kL] clusters. (For other studies giving similar results, see Vaissière *et al.* 1988).

9.2.3.1.3 Extrasyllabic [k] Now, let us consider the realization of the extrasyllabic [k] in words such as *knout* [knut], *CNET* [knɛt], and *CNIT [knit]*. Representative spectrograms are given in figure 9.3. Here we see that the F_2 onset at the [k] release (marked with an "x") shows only a small amount of variation, especially compared to the variation of [k] before [ʁV] and [lV]. This means that there is little anticipation of the following vowel at the release of [k]. A part of the observed variation might be attributed to the anticipation of lip protrusion which may spread onto segments unspecified for roundness, which shows considerable variability across different speakers (see for example Bonnot *et al.* 1985).

9.2.3.1.4 Conclusion In this section, we have brought together various data showing a strong coarticulation of onset consonants with the following vowel, even when there are two consonants in the onset. A main acoustic manifestation of this coarticulation occurs at the release of the first onset consonant ([k] in our examples). This release corresponds to an important acoustic landmark (cf. Stevens, this volume). It must also be noted that this landmark corresponds closely to the p-center, as this has been determined for English by Fowler and Tassinary (1981) in an experiment where the subjects were asked to align monosyllabic words on a regular metronome beat. (As far as we know, no similar experiment has been conducted for French.) When we examine postlexical rules sensitive to extrasyllabicity in

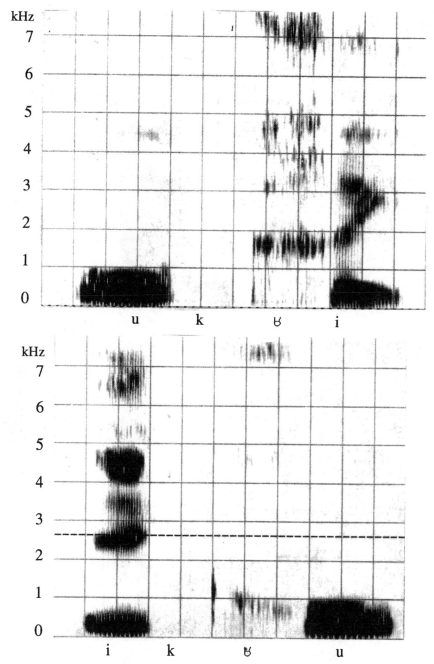

Figure 9.2. Spectrograms of [ukʁi] and [ikʁu].

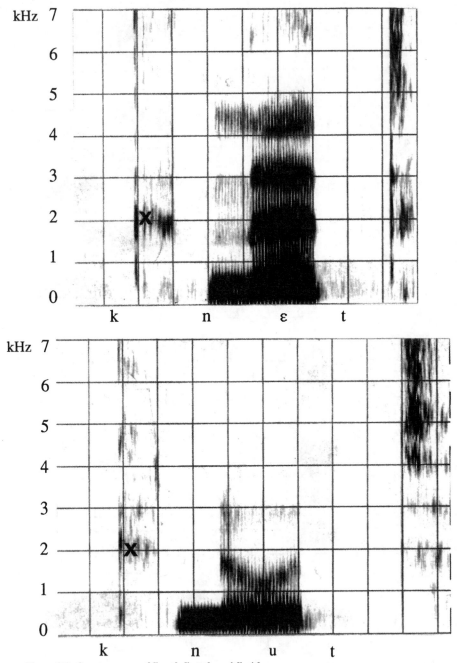

Figure 9.3. Spectrograms of [knɛt], [knut], and [knit].

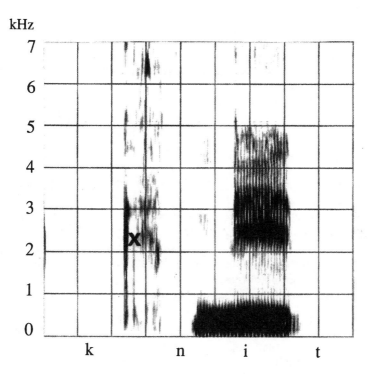

Figure 9.3. (*continued*)

section 9.3, we will again find that this landmark plays a crucial role in cueing syllable structure.

9.2.3.2 Timing

There are two detailed studies of cluster shortening in French, O'Shaughnessy (1981) and Bartkova and Sorin (1987). In general, their results show that cluster shortening is a compression-type phenomenon which depends on the number of elements in a given constituent. Cluster shortening affects any sequence of consonants in a word, and usually applies across word boundaries. According to O'Shaughnessy (1981), vowels are lengthened after stops as opposed to continuants (by 51% for a high vowel and 23% for a low vowel), but vowels are "not influenced by the number of preceding consonants."

Thus, unlike the coarticulation phenomena discussed above, cluster shortening does not appear to be related to syllable organization or extrasyllabicity.

9.2.4 Voicing assimilation

In initial clusters such as [sk] or [skl], consisting of two obstruents possibly followed by a liquid or glide, the second obstruent triggers both regressive and progressive voicing assimilation as schematized below:

Voicing assimilation is triggered by obstruents and not by sonorants, whose voicing is specified by default. *Regressive* assimilation involves complete voicing agreement, and affects the extrasyllabic obstruent. *Progressive* assimilation involves partial and optional devoicing, affecting a following liquid or glide. Regressive assimilation is a phonological process, while the progressive assimilation is a phonetic one. We will be concerned with regressive assimilation here.

Regressive assimilation affects any sequence of obstruents in the word:

accès	[aksɛ]	"access"
abcès	[apsɛ]	"abscess"
razzia	[ʁadzia]	"raid"
axe	[aks]	"axis"

However, it does not apply across words:

il s(e) baisse	[i s bɛs]	"he bends down"
laisse voler	[lɛs vole]	"let fly"
il ne pèse pas	[i n pɛz pa]	"it doesn't weigh"

These facts suggest that the rule is not restricted to the domain of the syllable, but is restricted to a larger domain, the word. Notice, however, that it is not triggered by a liaison consonant, which belongs morphologically to the first word but phonologically to the second:

| fortes amies | [fɔʁt zami] | "good friends" |
| pèsent-ils | [pɛz til] | "do they weigh?" |

Since liaison consonants are syllabified postlexically after the formation of phrases (Clements and Keyser 1983; Encrevé 1988), this suggests that voicing assimilation may be postlexical, and restricted to the phonological word.

We see, then, that regressive voicing assimilation applies on the domain of the word, not the syllable. The extrasyllabic consonant undergoes the rule by virtue of the fact that it belongs to the same phonological word as the following obstruent. Thus while extrasyllabic consonants lie outside the core syllable, they still constitute an element of the phonological word. We can express this fact by linking them directly to the word in prosodic structure, as follows:

A similar treatment of extrasyllabic consonants has been proposed by Milliken (1988) and Rubach and Booij (1990).

9.3 The status of word-final consonants

This section completes our review of extrasyllabicity by considering the analysis of word-final consonants.

9.3.1 Liquid drop

As far as word-final clusters are concerned, only the rule of liquid drop appears to be related to extrasyllabic status. This rule has been studied in detail by Dell (1985), who shows that it applies differently depending upon the nature of the syntactic boundaries and the lexical item in question. What is important for us is the fact that a word such as *arbre* can be pronounced [aʁbʁ] before a vowel or a pause, [aʁb] before a consonant or a pause and [aʁbʁə], with schwa insertion, before a consonant or a pause:

un arbre	"a tree"	[aʁbʁ] or [aʁb] or [aʁbʁə]
un arbre de Noël	"Christmas tree"	[aʁb] or [aʁbʁə]
un arbre à pain	"breadfruit tree"	[aʁbʁ]

An extrasyllabic consonant is more "fragile" than a syllabified consonant, as it is not associated to a syllable. Except in utterance-final position, it is deleted unless it can be syllabified to a following vowel.

Liquid drop demonstrates that extrasyllabic consonants must be recognized in word-final as well as in word-initial position. At the same time, other rules demonstrate that some final consonants must belong to the coda. Thus, the *règles de position* mentioned earlier (section 9.2.1) apply to vowels in closed syllables in the core-syllabification domain. These rules apply in word-final syllables as well as medial ones, as is shown by the fact that [e] and [ə] are replaced by [ɛ] before a word-final consonant. We now examine the structure of word-final consonants more closely.

9.3.2 Possible word-final consonant sequences

After a vowel, at the end of a word, there may be up to four consonants. The various possibilities are the following:

(1)   One consonant: no restrictions
        sac [sak] "bag," bague [bag] "ring," chatte [ʃat] "cat (fem.),"
        port [pɔʁ] "harbor," pâle [pal] "pale," paye [pɛj] "pay"

(2)   Two consonants
        liquid + nasal/obstruent/liquid:
        arme [aʁm(ə)] "weapon," Marne [maʁn(ə)] (river), harpe [aʁp(ə)]
        "harp,"
        large [laʁʒ(ə)] "wide," "large," Arles [aʁl(ə)] (city)
        obstruent + liquid
        sobre [sɔbʁ(ə)] "sober," souple [supl(ə)] "supple"
        obstruent + obstruent
        apte [apt(ə)] "capable," acte [akt(ə)] "act," Metz [mɛtz(ə)] (city),
        axe [aks(ə)] "axis," reste [ʁɛst(ə)] "stay"

(3)   Three consonants
        liquid + obstruent + liquid
        arbre [aʁbʁ(ə)] "tree," sépulcre [sepylkʁ(ə)] "sepulchre"
        liquid + obstruent + obstruent
        hertz [ɛʁtz(ə)] "hertz," Marx [maʁks(ə)], bortsch [bɔʁtʃ(ə)] "borscht"
        (very few examples)
        obstruent + obstruent + liquid
        astre [astʁ(ə)] "star," spectre [spɛktʁ(ə)] "phantom," sceptre [sɛptʁ(ə)]
        "scepter"
        obstruent + obstruent + obstruent
        mixte [mikst (ə)] "mixed" (very few examples)

(4)   Four consonants
        obstruent + obstruent + obstruent + liquid
        dextre [dɛkstʁ(ə)] "right hand," cepstre [sɛpstʁ(ə)] "cepstrum" (very few
        examples)

We observe that these word-final consonants can all be mapped onto the following maximal template, where parentheses enclose a possible, but not necessarily actual, syllabification:

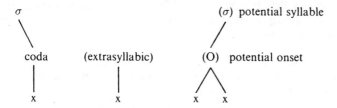

The coda position has only one slot, as proposed by many authors (Dell 1984; Encrevé 1988). Following the coda position, the structure of the remaining part of the cluster is the same as the one we find in word-initial position. To account for this similarity, we posit the same constituents in the template, that is, an extrasyllabic position preceding a potential onset which can itself contain two positions. In this structure, the extrasyllabic position is filled only if there is a potential onset with which it cannot be potentially syllabified. Moreover, the potential syllable becomes a full syllable when the schwa is pronounced. These consonants in postcoda position can be considered as a special type of extrasyllabic consonants, since they are only potentially syllabified.

9.3.3 Phonetic characteristics of word-final consonants

9.3.3.1 Coarticulation with the preceding vowel
In section 9.2.3.1, we compared [Vg] and [gV] transitions, focusing on the latter. Let us now return to [Vg] transitions. We saw that the tongue tip tends to stay in a neutral position as the tongue body approaches closure, and when the closure occurs the differences conditioned by the various vowels have been considerably reduced. Thus the "landmark" which corresponds to the closure of the coda consonant is not in the same close relationship with the vowel as the one which corresponds to the release.

9.3.3.2 Durational effects
The coda consonant – especially in word-final position – triggers specific durational effects on the preceding vowel. The effects of single-code consonants are well known: voiceless obstruents have the greatest shortening effect (40%, estimated from O'Shaughnessy 1981), while [ʁ] and the voiced fricatives have the greatest lengthening effect (40% and 70%).

If an extrasyllabic consonant is added, the effects vary as follows (Delattre 1940):

> If an extrasyllabic consonant occurs after [ʁ] in coda position, the vowel is much shorter than it is before word-final [ʁ], with differences depending upon the identity of the extrasyllabic consonant (voiceless obstruents having the main effects, as in coda position).

> An extrasyllabic [ʁ] has a slight lengthening effect, with differences depending upon the voicing of the coda consonant (but not on the fricative versus stop distinction).

> If the extrasyllabic consonant is an obstruent after another obstruent in coda position, it has no influence, or causes a slight further shortening.

As we have seen, the second consonant in two-member clusters is a potential onset. Its main effect – particularly in liquid + obstruent clusters – is to reduce the lengthening influence of the coda consonant on the preceding vowel. This is comparable to the shortening effect obtained by the addition of a second syllable (except in magnitude, since the presence of a full second syllable, bearing accent, is associated with a prosodic reorganization). However, in the case of extrasyllabic consonants this effect cannot be directly related to an actual syllable but only to the presence of the extrasyllabic consonant, which prevents the coda consonant from appearing at the end of the word.

9.3.4 Voicing assimilation

Voicing assimilation in final clusters is the same as in word-initial clusters: it is triggered by the last obstruent, and it is progressive and regressive in the same way:

> axe [aks] "axis," rostre [ʁɔstʁ] "rostrum," Dresde [dʁɛzd] "Dresden,"
> arbre [aʁbʁ] "tree"

Word-final extrasyllabic consonants can therefore be linked directly to the word node, just like word-initial ones:

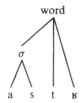

9.3.5 Conclusion

In this section, we have seen that extrasyllabic consonants occur at the end of word-final clusters. In core-syllable structure, only one consonant can belong to the coda; following this, extrasyllabic consonants are permitted up to the limits defined by the prosodic template. Phonetically, a coda consonant coarticulates less closely with the nuclear vowel than does an onset consonant, and extrasyllabic consonants diminish the durational effect of the coda consonant on the vowel of the preceding syllable. Voicing assimilation applies word-finally in the same way it does word-initially, giving evidence that final extrasyllabic consonants form part of the phonological word.

9.4 Extrasyllabicity, geminates and schwa drop

Rules of schwa drop and geminate (or identical-consonant) formation provide a further source of evidence for extrasyllabicity. Schwa drop has been well studied in the previous literature (see especially Dell 1985). We will be concerned here with an interesting restriction on schwa drop motivated by the avoidance of geminates, which has not been previously studied. A detailed study of this phenomenon is in progress by M. Plénat, who first encouraged me to look at it.

First, let us look at the formation of geminates due to schwa drop. In the following contexts, a schwa can drop even if it leaves two identical consonants in contact:

before CV (where V is a vowel or diphthong):
Il viendra c(e) soir. [...sswaʁ] "He will come this evening."
C(e) soir, tout ira mieux, [sswaʁ...] "This evening, everything will go better."

before a CL or CG cluster:
[Ça t(e) tracasse? [sattʁa...] "Does that bother you?"
Il n'y a pas d(e) drap. [...paddʁa] "There is no sheet."

However, schwa cannot drop before an extrasyllabic consonant:

*Il ne connait pas c(e) speaker. *[...sspi...] "He doesn't know this speaker."
*Il n'a jamais pratiqué c(e) sport. *[...sspɔʁ] "He never played this sport."

Therefore, this rule is sensitive to the status of the initial consonant of the word.

These facts are to be related to more general rules concerning the occurrence of geminates across word boundaries. Geminates are created by identical consonants across word boundaries in the following contexts:

> before a vowel:
> laisse s'établir [lɛsse...] "let become established"
> which contrasts with:
> laisse établir [lɛse...] "let establish"
> before a CL or CG cluster:
> un bac crevé [...bakkʁə...] "a punctured tub"
> which contrasts with:
> un bas crevé [...bakʁə...] "a punctured stocking"

However, extrasyllabic consonants do not form geminates with a preceding consonant:

> laisse strier "let striate"

which does not contrast with *laisse trier* "let sort," unless a schwa is inserted between the two [s]s. This constraint shows a certain amount of speaker-dependent variation, some speakers believing that they can make such a difference. In contrast, judgments are unanimous concerning the impossibility of schwa drop before an identical extrasyllabic consonant.

Some contrasts seem easier to make: thus

> un pape psychologue [...pappsi...] "a psychologist pope"
> un pas psychologue [...papsi...] "a non-psychologist"

are distinguished by some speakers, even when there is no release of the final [p] of *pape*. However, in such examples, there are also cues indicating that the first part of the geminate consonant closes the preceding syllable and ends the word. Thus, a [p] at the end of a syllable, especially when word-final, shortens the preceding vowel which is then produced with articulatory "undershoot."

In any case, a dissymmetry is clear: geminate consonants involving an extrasyllabic consonant seem difficult to produce and are most often – if not completely – avoided, while other types of geminates are produced quite regularly. These facts point to the same conclusions as the constraints on schwa drop.

We may now ask: what is the phonetic motivation for such facts? Why is a geminate whose second part is an onset preferred both in production and recognition to a geminate consonant whose second part is an extrasyllabic consonant? If we reason in terms of landmarks, we could suggest that recognition of the first type of geminate is easier because it is based on a major landmark: its release into the following vowel, liquid or glide. Indeed, following Stevens's hierarchy of landmarks, this landmark is more important than one corresponding to the release of a consonant before another consonant. The release of the geminate closure or constriction may be perceptually more salient if it coincides with a more important acoustic event. Moreover, such a landmark might make a better contribution to the recognition of the vocalic and consonantal phases involved in geminate formation and recognition (for an acoustic study of phase variations involving geminate consonants and the preceding vowel in French, see Abry *et al.* 1990).

9.5 The status of consonants after schwa drop

In a previous paper (Rialland 1986), we examined the phonological and phonetic behavior of consonants following schwa drop. We showed that consonants after schwa drop (occurring mainly in monosyllabic words) are not resyllabified, and we explained this by an analysis in which the deleted schwa leaves a "trace' in the form of an empty nucleus. We will here re-examine some of these data and show how they could be reinterpreted in term of extrasyllabicity. The advantage of such a reanalysis would be to permit a more unified approach.

In the phonological literature on French, consonants following a deleted schwa have sometimes been considered to be resyllabified with the preceding syllable (Anderson 1982). However, this analysis runs into certain problems. First, the schwa can be deleted in a sentence-initial syllable, where no resyllabification of the stranded consonant is possible:

R(e)commence pas   [ʁkɔmãs pa]   "Don't start again"

Second, even if deletion takes place sentence-internally, there are phonetic and phonological cues showing that the stranded consonant remains unsyllabified. Thus, the [ʁ] of *r(e)commencer* may occur internally in sentences such as:

On r(e)commence?   [ɔ̃ʁkɔmãs]   "Shall we start again?"

In such examples /ʁ/ can be pronounced as an uvular trill. This is not a possible realization for syllable-final /ʁ/s, which tend to be realized as glides (Simon 1967). (For fuller discussion of these and related facts, see Rialland 1986.) Thus, an uvular trill cannot occur in a coda, and it cannot be syllabified into the onset of the following syllable. As in the case of the extrasyllabic consonants we saw before, this independent [ʁ] remains outside syllable structure, and can be attached directly to the word node as follows:

r(e)commencer:

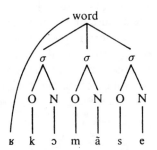

A similar analysis can be proposed for the [t] of *t(e)renverser* "overturn you," whose realization suggests that it does not form a cluster with [ʁ] (cf. its different timing and longer transitions; see Rialland 1986 for a more detailed study). However, there is a slight difference between this case and the last. When schwa drop strands a consonant in the same word as the following consonant, voicing assimilation may apply to it: *s(e)cond* [zgõ] "second." In contrast, when the stranded consonant is in a different word, it does not undergo voicing assimilation: *il va t(e) gronder* "he's going to scold you" [...tg...], not *[...dg...]. Since voicing assimilation only applies within the domain of the phonological word, we may account for this difference by attaching the [t] to the phrase node, as shown below:

t(e) renverser:

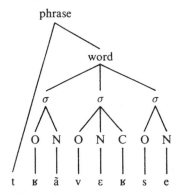

This analysis predicts that at the phonetic level, a consonant stranded by schwa drop should have the same phonetic realization as an underlying extrasyllabic consonant in the same context. We cannot test this by comparing the [ʁ] of *r(e)commencer* with an extrasyllabic [ʁ] at the beginning of a word, because extrasyllabic [ʁ] does not occur in this position. Nor can we compare the *t(e)renverser* with an extrasyllabic [t] followed by a [ʁ], as this sequence is also impossible. However, when both types of sequence are possible, we notice that they are similar. Thus, [s] in *ski* and *s(e)couer* appear to be identical. The [m] which is extrasyllabic in *MRAP* (abbreviation of "Mouvement contre le Racisme et pour l'Amitié des Peuples") [mʁap] and the *m* due to schwa drop in *m(e)ringue* [mʁɛ̃g] also seem identical. It is possible that the current proliferation of extrasyllabic consonants in French is facilitated by the fact that consonants stranded by schwa drop provide a model for it.

9.6 Conclusion

This paper has proposed a survey of extrasyllabicity in French in both word-initial and word-final position. The notion of extrasyllabicity allows for a unified explanation of a variety of phonological phenomena in French such as glide formation, liquid drop, constraints on geminate formation, and the status of consonants after schwa drop. We have seen that while only one extrasyllabic consonant is possible at the beginning of a word, longer sequences of extrasyllabic consonants can occur word-finally if they can be parsed by a prosodic template having the form of a word-initial cluster. We have also presented evidence that extrasyllabic consonants in French are not totally extraprosodic, but are linked to higher-level nodes in prosodic organization such as the (phonological) word and the phrase.

This analysis is consistent with (and to some degree supported by) the facts of phonetic interpretation. Thus, we have seen some evidence that a word-initial extrasyllabic consonant is coarticulated less closely with the following vowel than is/are the onset consonant(s), and that its release constitutes a minor landmark, less effective in perception – for example in the recognition of geminates – than the major landmark occurring at the release of the onset consonant.

More studies have to be carried out to test some of the implications of this analysis at the phonetic level, for example:

> the relation between the characteristics of extrasyllabicity and the perception of geminates
>
> durational properties of extrasyllabic consonants at different speech rates.

We hope to undertake studies of these questions in the future.

References

Abry, C., J.P. Orliaguet and R. Sock. 1990. Patterns of speech phasing. Their robustness in the production of a timed linguistic task: single vs. double (abutted) consonants in French. *Cahiers de Psychologie Cognitive, European Bulletin of Cognitive Psychology* 10-3: 269–288.

Anderson, S. 1982. The analysis of French schwa: or, how to get something for nothing. *Language* 58(3): 534–573.

Bartkova, K. and C. Sorin. 1987. A model of segmental duration for speech synthesis in French. *Speech Communication* 6: 245–260.

Bonnot, J-F., C. Chevrie-Muller, B. Maton, C. Arabia-Guidet, and G.F. Greiner. 1985. Incidence des facteurs physiologiques et structuraux sur la coarticulation de la labialité et de la nasalité en chaîne parlée. *Travaux de l'institut de Phonétique de Strasbourg* 17: 141–171.

Browman, C.P. and L. Goldstein. 1988. Some notes on syllable structure in articulatory phonology. *Phonetica* 45: 140–155.

Clements, G.N. and S.J. Keyser. 1983. *CV Phonology: A Generative Theory of the Syllable.* Linguistic Inquiry Monograph 9. Cambridge, MA: MIT Press.

Delattre, P. 1940. Anticipation in the sequence vowel and consonant group. *The French Review*: 13.4. Reprinted in *Studies in French and Comparative Phonetics* 1966. The Hague: Mouton, 122–127.

Dell, F. 1984. Consonant clusters and syllable structure in French. Unpublished paper. Paris: C.N.R.S.

1985. *Les règles et les sons: introduction à la phonologie générative.* Paris: Hermann.

Encrevé, P. 1988. *La liaison avec et sans enchaînement: phonologie tridimensionelle et usages du français.* Paris: Editions du Seuil.

Fowler, C.A. and L. Tassinary. 1981. Natural measurement criteria for speech: the anisochrony illusion. In J. Long and A. Baddeley (eds.) *Attention and Performance* 9. Hillsdale, NJ and London: Lawrence Erlbaum Associates, 521–535.

Fujimura, O. and J. Lovins. 1978. Syllables as concatenative phonetic units. In A. Bell and J. Hooper (eds.) *Syllables and Segments.* Amsterdam: North-Holland.

Hyman, L. 1985. *A Theory of Phonological Weight.* Dordrecht: Foris.

Kaye, J. 1989. *Phonology: A Cognitive View.* Hillsdale, NJ and London: Lawrence Erlbaum Associates.

Krakow, R.A. 1989. The articulatory organization of syllables: a kinematic analysis of labial and velar gestures. Ph.D. dissertation, Yale University.

Milliken, S. 1988. Protosyllables: A theory of underlying syllable structure in nonlinear phonology. Ph.D. dissertation, Cornell University.

O'Shaughnessy, D. 1981. A study of French vowel and consonant durations. *Journal of Phonetics* 9: 385–406.

Rialland, A. 1986. Schwa et syllabes en français. In E. Sezer and L. Wetzels (eds.) *Studies in Compensatory Lengthening.* Dordrecht: Foris.

Rubach, J. and G.E. Booij. 1990. Edge of constituent effects in Polish. *Natural Language and Linguistic Theory* 8(3): 427–464.

Selkirk, E.O. 1972. The phrase phonology of English and French. Ph.D. dissertation, MIT. (Published in 1980 by Garland Publishing, New York.)

Simon, P. 1967. *Les consonnes du français. Mouvements et positions articulatoires à la lumière de la radiocinématographie.* Paris: Klincksieck.

Annie Rialland

Stevens, K.N. (This volume). Phonetic evidence for hierarchies of features.
Turk, A. (This volume). Articulatory phonetic clues to syllable affiliation: gestural characteristics of bilabial stops.
Vaissière, J., M. Eskenazi and F. Lonchamp. 1988. Cours sur les indices acoustiques du français. GRECO (unpublished).
Zerling, J.-P. 1981. Particularités articulatoires et acoustiques de l'occlusive [g]. *12 èmes Journées d'Etude sur la Parole* (proceedings of a workshop). Université de Montréal, 328–338.

10

Phonetic correlates of syllable affiliation

FRANCIS NOLAN

In this commentary I intend to focus on the issue of deciding whether a consonant belongs to a particular syllable or not. This issue is dealt with in detail in Turk's paper, and is touched on more briefly by Rialland where she considers acoustic arguments for extrasyllabicity.

Turk uses x-ray microbeam data to demonstrate that medial labial stops in an English word like *leper* have closing and opening gestures more similar to those of phonologically unambiguously syllable-final labials (e.g. *captor*) than to those of syllable-initial labials (e.g. *repair*). The discriminant analysis of the articulatory data points pretty clearly to the conclusion that a medial stop following a stressed syllable belongs in that syllable.

Rialland, in her section 9.2.3.1.1, argues briefly from acoustic data for the conclusion that the initial velar in a French sequence such as /knɛt/ is extrasyllabic. Specifically, the burst frequency of the velar does not vary across a range of vowel environments in the way that it would if the velar immediately preceded the vowel or an intervening liquid. There are good phonological arguments for an extrasyllabic treatment, which Rialland also presents, and the acoustic data appears to provide useful confirmation of the phonological analysis.

However, a number of interesting questions are raised by work of these kinds, such as

(a)   Do other similar sounds pattern in the same way as the stops examined?

(b)   Which of the many phonetic dimensions, both articulatory and acoustic, are of relevance for the matter of syllable affiliation?

(c)   If different phonetic dimensions point to conflicting syllable divisions, how could the conflict be resolved?

(d)   Should we expect to find phonetic cues to syllable structure at all?
(e)   Might the relevant phonological structure be more complex than a uniquely syllabified string?

In what follows, I don't attempt to resolve such questions, but merely to articulate them.

As a speaker of English and a phonetician who (perhaps because I learned phonology in the aftermath of 1968) finds it very difficult to have clear intuitions about syllables, I nevertheless spent some considerable time thinking about Turk's results for labials, and searching for counter-examples. In the spirit of question (a) above, I explored my intuitions for the other stop series, and came to the conclusion that in the case of velars, a medial stop coarticulates more with the following vowel than with the preceding one. The reader may find useful for this thought-experiment words such as *talkie*, where I felt the /k/ to be fairly fronted, and *decoy* (noun), where my impression was of a back velar. The fact that I took any interest in such examples meant that I had implicitly answered question (b) with a reply such as "one dimension relevant to syllable affiliation is coarticulation" – an idea with a pedigree stretching back at least to Kozhevnikov and Chistovich (1965) – even if I had not sorted out exactly what I meant by coarticulation, and in particular whether I was thinking in terms of articulation or its acoustic consequences.

Coincidentally, Rialland's paper mentions work by Zerling (1981) which indicates that in the context [əgVg] in French the configuration of the tongue for the first [g] during release reflects the following vowel, whereas the transition into the second [g] is relatively constant and uninfluenced by the preceding vowel. Rialland's discussion may be slightly misleading in that she refers, in discussing tracings of vocal-tract shapes taken from Zerling (1981), to the position of the tongue "apex" and "tip," which are probably not of great significance in velars; but it is nonetheless clear that the position of the dorsum of the tongue in these tracings supports her interpretation that the velars show "an orientation towards the following vowel." The phonological conclusion is that the velars should be regarded as constituting the onset of a syllable.

To check my introspection for English, I devised materials of the form /-'VkV-/, where V ranged over two vowels. In doing this I exploited the fact that in my own British, but non-RP, English proununciation, stressed /ʌ/ is realized with much the same quality as unstressed schwa (/ə/); also the fact that my pronunciation (in common with RP) has /r/ only pre-vocalically. The phonetic environments in the words below are therefore as nearly symmetrical as possible:

['ɪkɪ]   *ticking*
['ɪkə]   *ticker*
['əkɪ]   *tucking*
['əkə]   *Tucker*

I recorded each word ten times, along with other disyllables with the same vowels and stress on the second syllable. I made simultaneous (but not synchronized) acoustic and electro-palatographic (EPG) recordings.

To assess coarticulation from the EPG records I measured the area of palate contacted by the tongue at the start and end of the velar closure. The start was identified as the first EPG frame with a complete row of electrodes contacted, and the end as the last frame with a complete row contacted (on the Reading EPG system used, rows run from side to side of the palate). The area of contact was estimated simply as the total of electrodes contacted. The higher, and further front, the tongue is, the greater the area of contact. The outcome of this procedure, in each case averaged over the ten tokens, is shown in figure 10.1.

Imagine my dismay on discovering that the EPG evidence seemed to show that my intuitions were wrong. At the start of closure, the words *ticking* and *ticker* (open symbols), which have [ɪ] before the velar, exhibit greater palatal contact than the other two words; and this greater contact persists through to the end of the closure. *Tucking*, it is true, shows a considerable movement during closure towards a fronter contact pattern, but it is still possible to draw a line on the graph separating the ['ɪkV] words at the top of the graph from the ['əkV] words below. It is thus the preceding vowel which has the

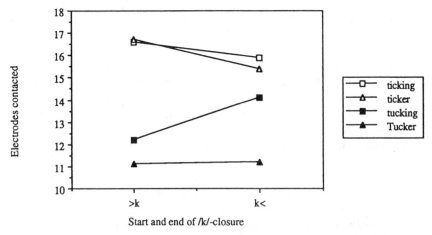

Figure 10.1. Electro-palatographic contact patterns for medial /k/ at start and end of stop closure. Each point represents the mean of ten tokens spoken by one speaker.

greater influence on the overall configuration of the velar, and we may therefore take this as evidence that the velar "belongs" in the first syllable. This, of course, is in accord with Turk's findings for labials; and, it is worth mentioning, with Wells's (1990: 80) main principle of syllabification that "consonants are syllabified with the more strongly stressed of two flanking syllables."

So why were my intuitions about my own performance at variance with this finding? To find an explanation it is necessary to look in the acoustic domain. From the simultaneous acoustic recordings I analyzed the spectrum of the velar burst, and of the aspiration phase. For the burst I used a short (approximately 9 ms) time window placed to include the burst. In some cases velars exhibit more than one pulse of energy at release, and in such cases I normally analyzed the last pulse. For the aspiration, I used a longer (approximately 20 ms) window placed centrally within the aspiration phase. In each case I tried to locate the lowest major spectral prominence in the region 1–3 kHz. This was reasonably easy to do in the case of the burst. The spectrum of the aspiration tended to be more variable, particularly in the context of a following [ɪ]. Clear trends emerged, however, for both events, as shown in figure 10.2.

At the release of closure the consistently fronted and raised tongue-body configuration for *ticking* gives rise to a high frequency burst (around 2200 Hz). This is mainly due to the relatively small cavity in front of the tongue. Conversely, in *Tucker*, where both vowels are mid-central, a

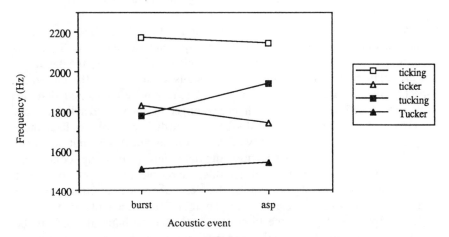

Figure 10.2. Frequency of the lowest major spectral prominence in the region 1–3 kHz for the burst and aspiration of medial /k/. Each point represents the mean of ten tokens spoken by one speaker.

presumably mid-velar stop closure gives the lowest burst. The other two words have almost identical bursts. (The fact that the overall patterning for the acoustic bursts is different from that of the EPG end-of-closure pattern in figure 10.1, which relates to virtually the same point in time, is probably the result of factors such as lip position, and overall configuration of the tongue body.) Since *ticker* and *tucking* have virtually identical bursts, it is not possible on this dimension to argue that the velar "belongs" more with the first or the second syllable.

When we examine in figure 10.2 the dominant frequency in the aspiration, however, the patterning at last turns out to be in line with my auditory impression. The two words with [ɪ] in the second syllable (square symbols on the graph) exhibit a higher frequency than the two words with [ə]. It is quite possible that the aspiration, which is a relatively long, nearly steady-state element (often upwards of 35 ms in these tokens), and which before [ɪ] is effectively a retracted palatal fricative, is of more importance in determining the perceptual impression of the frontness of the /k/ realization than the short-lived transient of the burst, or of course the silence of the stop closure. The aspiration spectra might explain, and to an extent justify, my original impression that *ticking* and *tucking* share a fronter velar in my speech.

This is not, of course, a full-scale experiment, since it consists of data from only one speaker producing limited material, and so any conclusions must be treated tentatively. But this pilot experiment does exemplify a problem which might well emerge from a full-scale version, or from similar attempts to determine syllable affiliation from phonetic data. The problem is the one anticipated in question (c) at the beginning, and its particular instantiation here is as follows.

Using only EPG, we would have concluded that the medial post-stress velars belonged to the first syllable. This approach is similar to Turk's in focusing on articulation, though hers more effectively captures the dynamics of articulatory gestures. Using only an acoustic measure of the dominant spectral region after release, we would probably have concluded that the velar was adjusting most to, and hence belonged in, the second syllable. This approach is similar, in that it looks at acoustic evidence, to Rialland's arguments for the extrasyllabicity of /k/ in (for instance) /kn-/ but not /kr-/, /kl-/. A combined approach, unfortunately, has thrown up conflicting evidence in a particular case. Put like this, the problem appears to be one of not having a theory of the relation between phonological structures and phonetic data which is specific enough to tell us which phenomena are relevant to phonological questions. In particular, perhaps, it needs to be explicit on whether production or perception is the more relevant to syllabification, since it is not always the case that the information in these two domains is equivalent.

On the other hand, we could step back from phonological issues, and state what is phonetically evident from figure 10.1 and 10.2, namely that in mixed-vowel disyllables the whole velar plosive (including aspiration) reflects a continuous transition from the first vowel to the second. From this perspective, it is then tempting to suggest that efforts to determine syllable affiliation from phonetic performance are misguided, since they are attempting to draw boundaries in a physical event which is continuous. After all, an analysis involving phoneme-sized segments (whether of the traditional kind, or merely "timing slots") for the word *worrier* is useful, even though the physical event fails to provide cues which unambiguously allocate a given transitional portion of the event to the preceding or following segment. If there are no compelling arguments from phonological processes that the /k/ of *ticker* must be in one syllable or the other, shouldn't we just accept that it is phonologically between two syllables, free to be phonetically realized as a transitional segment, constituting an articulatory "transit destination" between two syllable nuclei, but equally independent of either? Might not the task of the phonetic mechanism be to realize a sequence of sound specifications, some of which may owe their shape to syllable affiliation at one or more phonological levels, but which from the point of view of the phonetic mechanism are simply a linear sequence, on which can be imposed whatever organizational structures – probably not syllabic – facilitate production? If syllabic structures are reflected in speech production, why did the extensive research effort stimulated by Kozhevnikov and Chistovich (1965) fail to find clear coarticulatory evidence for the syllable?

In this spirit, one could also question Rialland's inference of extrasyllabicity. When she finds that in sequences such as [kn-] and [ks-] the frequency of the stop burst does not vary according to the following vowel, whereas in sequences such as [kl-] and [kʀ-] it does, is this perhaps explained not by the extrasyllabicity of the velar in the former sequences, but instead by a purely segmental "blocking" of coarticulation by [n] and [s] – which perhaps suffer a greater degree of constraint on lingual configuration than [l] and [ʀ] because of the need to achieve an airtight seal laterally around the sides of the palate in the former pair?

Thus pleads the devil's advocate, the unbeliever in the relevance of syllable structure to the phonetic event who answers "no" to question (d) at the start of this commentary. I think such pleading is answerable. On the specific points cited, there are straightforward answers. Turk's research goes beyond the traditional kind of coarticulation research exemplified by my pilot experiment. Such coarticulation studies generally merely ask where a given articulator is at a particular time. Turk examines instead the dynamics of gestures. From such data, it is possible that a more coherent picture of the phonetic correlates of syllables may emerge than from coarticulation. If all consonant gestures do turn out to be consistently different depending on position in the syllable, this will be a striking confirmation of the relevance of the syllable to phonetic performance. The route is certainly worth exploring further. Rialland could probably have presented evidence that the [n] and [s] of [kn-] and [ks-] sequences do coarticulate with the following vowel, thus undermining the "blocking" explanation.

More generally, phonological processes often have their roots in phonetic detail. Systematic vowel harmony develops out of vowel–vowel coarticulation, tonal contrasts emerge from pitch perturbations associated with classes of consonants, and so on. If there are reliable phonetic correlates of syllable position, for instance residing in gestural dynamics, their clarification will open the way to understanding many phonological processes which are sensitive to syllable position.

But it may be necessary to free our thinking from the view that there is a single phonological syllabification of an utterance which will be reflected in phonetic correlates. Perhaps, instead, successive stages in a phonological derivation can leave imprints of alternative syllabifications on the phonetic event. Harris (1990: 97) provides some interesting data. In some varieties of London English, *feel, fill* and *pool, pull* lose the final lateral and neutralize to [fɪʊ] and [pʊu] respectively (I assume, for the following argument, varieties where the alveolar lateral is consistently absent prepausally and preconsonantally). However, according to Harris "when the lateral constitutes the onset of the following syllable" the vowel distinctions are maintained – hence [fiilɪn – fɪlɪn], [pʊulɪn – pʊlɪn] for *feeling filling, pooling pulling*. In parallel fashion, *roll* is realized as [ɹɒʊ]; but with this vowel, there is a sensitivity to morphological structure which gives rise to what Harris terms a "derived contrast." *Roland* and *rolling* are differentiated as [ʁɐʊlənd – rɒʊlɪn], with a retracted diphthong in *rolling*. According to Harris's Lexical Phonological account, the retracted diphthong of *rolling* is produced by a rule "sensitive to class-II boundaries" which applies at Stratum 2 and affects vowels before a tauto-syllabic /l/. Phonotactic considerations suggest that the [l] of *rolling* must be in the second syllable, and though I have no acoustic data, it is plausible that its duration would be like that of other syllable-initial sonorants. On the other hand the diphthong allophone preceding it signals an earlier "claim" on the affiliation of the lateral by the first syllable.

It seems then that the answer to question (e) is "yes – the relevant phonological structure may be more complex than a uniquely syllabified string." With this in mind, we might usefully seek parallel, but phonetically less salient examples. Could morphology affect the syllable affiliation of medial stops? Will the monomorphemic structure of *bicker, flicker, wicker* allow the /k/ to behave more as an onset to the second syllable than in dimorphemic *thick-er*, *sick-er*, and *kick-er*, *pick-er*, where morphologically it belongs in the first syllable? Even if not, there may still be other cases where different phonetic cues to syllable affiliation apparently conflict, but each faithfully reflects an aspect of the linguistic structure underlying the phonetic sequence.

References

Harris, J. 1990. Derived phonological contrasts. In S. Ramsaran (ed.) *Studies in the Pronunciation of English*. London: Routledge, 87–105.

Kozhevnikov, V.A. and L.A. Chistovich, 1965. *Speech: Articulation and Perception.* Translation: Joint Publications Research Service, 30–543. U.S. Department of Commerce.

Wells, J.C. 1990. Syllabification and allophony. In S. Ramsaran (ed.) *Studies in the Pronunciation of English*. London: Routledge, 76–86.

Zerling, J.-P. 1981. Particularités articulatoires et acoustiques de l'occlusive [g]. *Journées d'Etude de la Parole*, Montréal.

II

Syllable structure and word structure: a study of triconsonantal clusters in English

JANET PIERREHUMBERT

11.1 Introduction

Current phonological theory maximizes the responsibility of the syllable for explaining co-occurrence restrictions on consonants. The inventory of word-initial consonant clusters is chiefly explained by the constraints on the syllable onset. The syllable coda also plays a central role in explaining which word-final consonants are permissible. The word node comes into play only by picking up extra peripheral elements, most notably the coronal appendices of English, and by defining the domain for any co-occurrence restrictions which cross syllable boundaries. (See Fudge 1969; Fujimura and Lovins 1978; Selkirk 1982; Clements and Keyser 1983.) With the phonotactic responsibility of the syllable thus maximized, the cross-product of codas and onsets is the starting point for any description of medial clusters. That is, in the absence of additional provisos, any concatenation of a well-formed coda and a well-formed onset is predicted to be possible medially in a word.

The present project evaluated the extent to which syllable structure explains the inventory of long medial clusters – the clusters of three or more consonants – in English. It was motivated by the observation that word-internally such clusters are extremely restricted in comparison with the set defined by the cross-product of codas and onsets. The basic model obviously requires modification, and a detailed examination of the occurring and missing clusters reveals what type of modification is needed.

Two methods were applied in the study. The pronunciation fields of the on-line Collins English Dictionary (distributed through the ACL Data Collection Initiative) were used to make an inventory of onsets, codas, and their frequencies, and to establish which medial clusters occur at all. Then, a follow-up experimental study showed that members of the critical set of missing clusters represent systematic rather than accidental gaps.

The study deals only with clusters found medially in morphemes. That is, it deals with the triconsonantal clusters found intervocalically in words such as "vanquish," "lobster," "doldrums," "palfrey," and "orchestra," excluding those found in words such as "exactly," "vastness," "width-wise," and "marksman." Clusters found medially in bound morphemes were included, e.g. "anthro," "andro." However, the study does not deal with clusters occurring morpheme peripherally, such as /ntl/ in "gentl + er," arising from /gentler/. Such cases present additional complications which we hope to investigate in a future study.

In the dictionary, 675 distinct clusters of three or more consonants are found. However, only fifty are found morpheme-medially (in a sense of "found" to be made more precise below). Compound words are by far the biggest source of long consonant clusters. The listing of compounds in the dictionary is of course spotty, and many more clusters would no doubt be found in a study of productively formed compounds.

In order to grasp the force of the number fifty, consider the number of different clusters which are taken to be well-formed according to the hypothesis that morphemes are arbitrary concatenations of syllables. The dictionary has 147 different consonantal sequences at the end of words and 129 at the beginning. (Words beginning or ending in a vowel are taken to represent a single case, that of no consonants.) Taking all possible combinations yields 18,963 possible medial sequences. This number is of course reduced by stripping appendices off final clusters and by enforcing a widely noted constraint against morpheme-initial geminates. Geminates are found only in compounds or across a word boundary, e.g. "subbasement." Taking these generalizations into account only reduces the number of viable candidates to 8708. It's a long way from 8708 to 50.

The assumption that the syllable grammar is stochastic was found to make the single greatest contribution towards addressing this discrepancy. The combination of a low-frequency coda and a low-frequency onset is expected to be a low-frequency occurrence. In fact, if the coda and following onset are statistically independent, then the probability of the combination is the product of the two low frequencies, and therefore far lower than that of either part. This means that many combinations are not expected to be found in a vocabulary of realistic size, even if both parts are found. It turned out that almost all occurring triconsonantal clusters were among the 200 most likely combinations, and that a stochastic interpretation of syllable grammar effectively ruled out a huge number of possible clusters, eliminating the need for many idiosyncratic constraints in the grammar.

However, it is still necessary to address the finding that only 50 of the 200 most likely combinations actually occur. Additional constraints, enforced at the morpheme or word level, are needed to rule out clusters which were likely a *priori*, but were not found. The experimental study established that these constraints represent part of the tacit knowledge of native speakers, rather than reflecting accidental gaps. The implications of the constraints for phonological theory are examined in section 11.6.

11.2 Methods I. Study of the dictionary

All arguments for hierarchical structure in linguistics have implicit statistical assumptions. We argue for constituents by showing that they serve as a domain for dependencies among elements. To defend a hierarchical structure, we must also show that elements which are equally close in the terminal string, but not claimed to be in the same constituent, do not exhibit such dependencies. If an equal degree of statistical dependence were found among all *n* adjacent elements, then no hierarchical structure would usefully distill the dependencies, and the data would suggest a quite different mathematical characterization, namely an *n*th-order Markov process.

The statistical viewpoint is particularly important in studies of the lexicon. The adult mental lexicon may be viewed as quasi-finite, with new forms added only slowly, and any given dictionary is certainly finite. Thus if a particular phonological combination is absent from the lexicon, it is necessary to establish whether its probability of occurrence is actually high enough that we would expect to find it in a sample the size of the lexicon or dictionary.

In order to address this issue, a method was adopted which was crude but nonetheless instructive. A pronouncing dictionary was extracted from the main dictionary by combining entries sharing both spelling and pronunciation, even if they differed in meaning. This was done because the dictionary uses polysemy to convey breadth of meaning; there are, for example, nine entries for "brother." Predicted probabilities for medial clusters of any length were then estimated by taking the cross-product, with frequencies, of all occurring word onsets and word-final syllable codas in the pronouncing dictionary. The medial clusters were then rank-ordered by predicted probability, from most to least likely. The remainder of the study then used the predicted probability rank (or the relative predicted probability), not the predicted probability itself.

The predicted probabilities were computed without regard to the morphological or etymological status of the words, for the sake both of economy of effort (there are approximately 70,000 phonologically distinct entries in the dictionary) and of replicability. For example, no subjective judgment was made about which foreign borrowings are fully assimilated and which are not; it was assumed that the frequency of the consonant clusters in such words adequately represents their linguistic and cognitive status, with high-frequency combinations being fully acceptable even if they all came from the same donor language. Similarly, compounds were included on the grounds that all compounds have a good word beginning and a good word ending. The inclusion of compounds of course tends to inflate the contribution of words which are phonologically unusual but form part of many compounds. On this point, the crudeness of the approach may perhaps be excused by the results.

To tabulate coda frequencies, it is necessary to make a specific assumption about which word-final coronals are in the appendix and which are in the coda. For the present study, the conservative assumption is the one which maximizes the role of the appendix, thus minimizing the coda and accordingly minimizing the predicted number of medial clusters. The most conservative possible assumption would thus be the following:

(1)   Any word-final sequence of coronal obstruents is analyzed as being in the appendix.

According to this assumption, the appendix would cover not only the final /s/ in "pasts," but the entire /sts/ cluster. Indeed, it would cover the /t/ in "cat."

However, this extreme assumption cannot be maintained. It would make it impossible to syllabify the words in (2) (or whatever subset of these words the reader may judge to lack a word boundary within the cluster). The difficulty arises because word-final codas are being used as evidence about word-internal codas. Since (1) puts all coronals into an appendix rather than into a coda, it incorrectly implies that no word-internal coronal codas are permitted.

(2)   vodka   jodhpurs
        Atlanta   pizza
        atlas   Nazi
        badminton   bedlam
        chitling   Presbyterian
        jitney   Aztec
        litmus   husband
        nutmeg   witness
        ordnance   Frisbee
        apartment   antler

Therefore, a simple weakening of (1) was sought which would permit word-internal coronal codas. It was noted that in all the words in (2), the coronal follows a vowel, offglide, or nasal, never an obstruent or /l/. As a result, it was decided to count as codas only coronal obstruents which directly followed a vowel, offglide or nasal; those following any other phoneme were taken to be appendices. This means that the coronal in "cat" is put in the coda rather than in the appendix, and that in "vodka," etc., the coronal can also go in the coda. In "weft" the /t/ is in the appendix and the /f/ counted towards the tally for /f/ in coda position. This treatment of the appendix still yields a rather conservative estimate of the number of possible medial clusters.[1]

The constraint against geminates was not enforced in constructing the list of possible clusters. There was no reason to do so since the treatment of geminates does not affect the way in which nongeminate clusters rank with respect to each other in expected probability. Including clusters with geminates in the list provides an opportunity to compare the statistical behaviour of a known constraint to the behavior of constraints emerging from the study.

Once the rank-ordered list of properly syllabifiable clusters of three or more elements was constructed, it was then compared to a list of clusters of three or more consonants which actually occur morpheme-medially. The latter list was constructed by extracting all words in the dictionary with three or more consonants in a row in the pronunciation field and sorting by the cluster exemplified. The set of entries for each cluster was then read to determine if it included any in which the cluster was morpheme-medial.

A few comments are in order about this determination, clearly the most subjective step in the entire process. A cluster was taken to occur if it occurred morpheme-medially in at least two reasonably familiar words. No effort was made to establish or interpret rates of occurrence, which indeed varied widely and not always as predicted. The class of "reasonably familiar" words was taken to include words such as: "pancreas," "extirpate," "palfry," "doldrums," "velcro," "imbroglio," "eclampsia," "wainscot." Examples of words in the dictionary which were not taken to be "reasonably familiar" include: "Melanchthon," "rigsdaler," "hoactzin," "anschluss," "pozzuolana." "Monomorphemic words" were taken to include a number of Greco-Latinate words which are historically polymorphemic, but which, it was felt, were probably not decomposed by most present day speakers. Examples include: "complete," "extreme," "inspect," "obtuse." Words such as "exhusband" and "Transsiberian" were of course taken to be polymorphemic, as were words in which the meaning of an affix was discernible even if the meaning of the entire word could not be determined compositionally. Examples of the latter type include "excavate," "exclude," "excrete," and "excursion" (all sharing a meaning of "ex" as "out") and "transparent," "transform," and "transfer" (sharing the use of "trans" to indicate change of location or state).

Many generative linguists would decompose "complete," "extreme," "inspect," and "obtuse," following principles laid out in Nida (1949). These principles permit the isolation of meaningless morphemes, or formatives, provided that they form the residue when an independently meaningful part is taken away. For example, "con" in "condense" can be isolated because "dense" is independently found with the appropriate meaning. Then, a principle of transitive closure on isolatability permits the isolation of "con" in "condense" to support the isolation of e.g. "flict" in "conflict," "trol" in "control," and so on. When these principles are applied in a literal fashion, they lead to ludicrous overdecomposition. For example, by isolating "con," we get "con + quer," leading to "bi + cker," "han + ker" and "pu + cker"; similarly the noun "con + tra" supports the decomposition "Char + tres" (according to the British pronunciation listed in the dictionary) and the decompositions "king + dom" and "con + dom" support "a + dam," "ma + dam" and "maca + dam." The fact that such decompositions have not been proposed in practice suggests that scholars have implicitly applied their knowledge of semantics, spelling, and historical development. There's no reason to suppose that the intuitions of people with so much linguistic sophistication and training would be shared by the ideal naive speaker-listener. Psycholinguists have in general been far more conservative about assuming that forms involving semantically opaque and nonproductive derivational morphology are synchronically decomposed; see, for example Bradley (1979), Bybee (1988), Nagy and Anderson (1984). As a result, I am inclined to agree with the position expressed in Bybee (1988), according to which the identification of a meaningful subpart of a word does not imply that the residue is also a morpheme.

A number of possibly interesting points were not addressed in the study. Since the dictionary has British pronunciations, there are no postvocalic /r/s and any questions concerning their behavior in American English cannot be addressed. The palatal onglide (as in "tune") was not treated as a consonant. The possible role of stress in conditioning medial clusters was not investigated. Due to the large number of noun–verb pairs differing only in stress (e.g. "'conflict," "con'flict") it was judged that stress would not be a primary influence on the form of medial clusters. However, the possible role of stress deserves further attention, in particular the relation of stress to homorganicity requirements for nasals.

11.3 Results of the dictionary study

The assumption that the syllable grammar is stochastic, with the likelihood of medial clusters derived from the independent likelihoods of the component codas and onsets, made an extremely successful contribution to the characterization of medial clusters. This success is displayed in figure 11.1. To construct this figure, the triconsonantal clusters as ordered by likelihood were arbitrarily grouped in twenties: "1" on the x-axis represents the group of the most likely twenty, "2" represents the group of the next most likely twenty (that is, clusters ranked 21–40), and so on. The y-axis shows how many in each group are actually found.

The top ten groups (or the 200 most likely clusters) include practically all those found; a single group of exceptions will be discussed below. The predicted rate of occurrence for the 200th cluster is approximately 1 in 10,000. Though the method used did not actually provide a count of the number of polysyllabic monomorphemic words, it may be noted that the dictionary had about 70,000 distinct entries, with a very large number of these words being polymorphemic or monosyllabic. Thus, the cutoff has a realistic relationship to the size of the dictionary. The figure also shows that the rate of occurrence decreases as the predicted likelihood goes down.

Figure 11.1 also shows that a stochastic syllable grammar is not the whole story. It reduces the number of candidates to 200, but (as already noted)

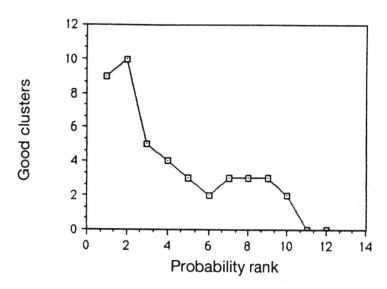

Figure 11.1. Occurring clusters per twenty candidates.

only about fifty are found. Even for the forty most likely candidates (all with expected rates of occurrence above 1 in 1842), just fewer than half are found.

Examination of the occurring and nonoccurring clusters in the top 200 candidates revealed the following generalizations:

First, nasal-stop sequences agree in labiality: either both phonemes are labial, or neither. This generalization covers eleven clusters which would otherwise be sufficiently probable that one would expect to find examples of them in the dictionary. Of these eleven, four involve /n/ before a labial; five have /m/ before a velar; and two have /m/ before a coronal. None of these in fact occurs. However, agreement in labiality is not enforced before fricatives, or at least not as strictly. /mst/ and /msp/ are marginally attested: /n/ does occur before /f/.

Second, clusters with a coronal obstruent in the coda do not occur.[2] A total of 79 cases are covered by this generalization (excluding clusters with geminates). This is by far the strongest generalization observed. Thirty-seven cases covered involve /t/ or /d/ in the second coda position following a nasal. 42 involve /t/, /d/, or /s/ preceding a biconsonantal onset. Triconsonantal clusters such as /str/ which comprise a well-formed onset are of course allowed.

Reference to the biconsonantal clusters found in the study of the appendix suggests a way to understand this generalization. As noted above, coronal obstruents must be permissible in coda position in order to syllabify occurring biconsonantal sequences. However, cases of biconsonantal medial clusters with a coronal obstruent in coda position are obviously rare compared to what one would expect from the overall phoneme frequencies for /t/, /s/, and /d/. This pattern is partly explained by the fact that final coronals in Latinate prefixes have assimilated in place of articulation to following obstruents. (See e.g. Nesfield 1898: §570). In fact such assimilation of coronals is very common and probably has occurred in some of the many other languages which have contributed to the English vocabulary. Speaking synchronically rather than diachronically, the observation is that the coronal obstruents have a lowered probability internally as opposed to word-finally. If the probabilities for the triconsonantal clusters were estimated using the internal rather than the word-final frequencies, then triconsonantal clusters with coronal coda obstruents would fall below the threshold for occurrence. The linguistic problem thus reduces to that of enforcing position-dependent probabilities.

Third, velar obstruents occurred only before coronals in the clusters studied, never before labials or other velars. This generalization covers 14 clusters which would otherwise be expected to occur. Seven of the clusters ruled out involve a /k/ before a labial. Five involve /k/ before another velar.

Of these, three are independently covered by antigemination, and the remaining two would be covered if antigemination were to disregard voicing. Two involve the velar nasal before a labial. The velar nasal (having been tabulated word-finally) is interpreted phonologically as /ng/ before a labial, where it could not have arisen from assimilation. It is interesting to note that /ng/ is actually more common as a coda than /g/ alone. No clusters beginning with /g/ were sufficiently likely to be in the running.

It may be noted that velar obstruents do occur before labials in biconsonantal clusters: "rigmarole," "pigmy," "dogma," "Egbert," "rugby," "tacmahack," "acme," "Micmac," "Achmed." Furthermore, in the word "angma" (not in the dictionary), an underlying /g/ is presumed to precede a labial in a triconsonantal cluster, although this /g/ does not appear as an obstruent on the surface. However, velars before noncoronals appear unexpectedly rare. This fact could be described in terms of position-dependent effects on probability, just as the shortage of coda coronal obstruents was.

Fourth, as expected, there were no clusters involving geminates. This generalization covers seventeen cases; however, of these, twelve also had unacceptable coronal obstruents in coda position.

Fifth, in addition to the lack of geminates, a lack of clusters with identical first and third elements was also observed. Clusters of this form falling in the most likely 200 are:

(3)   /lfl/   /lkl/   /lpl/   /lbl/   /lgl/   /lsl/
       /tst/   /ntn/   /ndn/   /tstr/   /nsn/
       /ksk/

Of these, four are also excluded by the restriction against coronal-obstruent codas. /nsn/ can be syllabified with /s/ in the onset. All but two involve /l/, already observed by Clements and Keyser (1983) to be subject to a dissimilarity requirement between the onset and the coda. Therefore the status of /nsn/ and /ksk/ is of particular interest. /ksk/ actually occurs in a number of words beginning with "ex." Of these, quite a number are viewed here as decomposable because they contain the meaning element usually associated with "ex"; in many cases the decomposition is further supported by related forms. Such cases include "excommunicate" (cf. communicate), "exculpate" (cf. culpable), "exclaim" (cf. claim, disclaim, declaim), "excavate" (cf. cavity), "excruciate" (cf. crucifix). However in three cases ("excuse," "Excaliber," and "exquisite"), the support for decomposition is less apparent. The unclear status of these examples led to /ksk/ being included in the experimental study, so the issue will be taken up again below.

Enforcing these five generalizations leaves us with the following unexplained gaps:

(4)   /lpr/ /nsm/ /lbr/ /nsw/ /lsp/ /lkw/ /kdr/ /ngtr/ /ndw/ /ksl/
         /vpr/ /ksw/ /ngks/ /ptr/ /nspr/ /lstr/ /pst/ /vtr/ /vst/ /pkr/ /mstr/

Of these clusters, the following occur marginally in single examples, partially unassimilated borrowings, or proper names which may be decomposed:

(5)   /lpr/   culprit
         /lbr/   Galbraith, Albrecht
         /nsw/   mansuetude, consuetude
         /lsp/   felspar
         /lkw/   Alcuin
         /ngtr/   Langtry
         /ndw/   Gondwana
         /ksl/   Bexley, Huxley
         /ksw/   Maxwell
         /ngks/   Yangtze; common word-finally, e.g. Bronx
         /ptr/   calyptra
         /lstr/   maelstrom
         /pst/   capstan, Epstein
         /mstr/   Armstrong

The reader is left to his or her own conclusions about the status of these examples. /nsm/ and /nspr/ occur only in compounds and across word boundaries (advancement, mainspring, etc.).

The following are completely absent from the dictionary.

(6)   /kdr/, /vpr/, /vtr/, /vst/, /pkr/

Since no clusters beginning in /v/ are good, one might propose a frequency dependence on position for /v/ as for /t/. However, with only three relevant examples, all of which are already none too likely, it is difficult to say whether this gap is accidental or systematic.

Study of the dictionary also revealed a group of examples which are found in defiance of their unlikelihood. These are clusters beginning in /b/ followed by an /s/ or /t/, almost all historically originating from the prefixes "sub-," "ob-," and "ab-." Examples are:

(7)   /btr/   subtract, obtrude
         /bst/   abstain, substance, lobster, obstetric, obstinate, substitute
         /bsk/   obscure
         /bskr/   subscribe
         /bstr/   abstruse, abstract, obstruent, obstruct, obstreperous

The expected frequencies for these combinations are in the range of 1/20,000 to 1/80,000.

Any mechanism which can decrease the likelihood of /t/ morpheme-internally can also be applied to increasing the likelihood of /b/. In this sense, the examples are not problematic. However, they raise the issue of the extent to which these clusters are acceptable in other phonemic contexts than they usually appear in. Is "tibstance" a possible word of English? How about "chabtry"? If the acceptability of the clusters depends on their broader phonological form, this would tend to support the idea that the degree of overall similarity between a word and the others in the lexicon determines how good it is phonotactically. Suggestions of this sort have been made by Greenberg and Jenkins (1964) and Ohala and Ohala (1986).

11.4 Methods II: experiment

In order to verify that a number of the observed constraints actually represent aspects of the tacit knowledge of native speakers, a small experiment was carried out.

Sixteen actually occurring clusters were selected which had a range of predicted frequencies and which are found in at least two reasonably familiar disyllabic words. These clusters were:

(8)   /str/ /spr/ /skr/
        /ntr/ /nst/ /nkr/ /ngr/ /nkw/ /nkl/ /ndr/
        /mpr/ /mbr/ /mpl/
        /lst/ /lkr/
        /kst/

Note that the set of occurring clusters is highly unbalanced phonologically, and thus it was impossible to select a phonologically balanced experimental set. An effort was made for a reasonable degree of diversity. However, the possibility of artifactual effects due to phoneme imbalance within the experiment (as opposed to within the English language) cannot be excluded.

Sixteen bad clusters were also selected. They all had predicted frequencies within the range for good clusters, and violated one of the above observations. The bad clusters used were:

(9)   /lfl/   /lkl/ /ksk/ /nsn/   (duplicate consonants)
        /tkl/ /dbr/ /dgr/ /tpr/ /tfl/ (coronal coda)
        /ʃp/   /ʃk/   /ʃm/   (coronal coda)
        /mkr/ /mgr/ /mtr/   (/m/ before a nonlabial stop)
        /mst/   (/m/ before a nonlabial obstruent)

Clusters with /ʃ/ were included to provide examples in which a coronal obstruent was clearly not a morphologically separate appendix. They were the only biconsonantal clusters in the experiment; triconsonantal clusters with /ʃ/ had predicted frequencies too low to be included. /mst/ was included as an example of a cluster which is only weakly unacceptable. It provides a baseline for the results for the other clusters.

Forty-eight existing disyllabic words (actually containing one of the good clusters) were used to create 48 "good" or simplex nonsense words and 48 "bad" or compound nonsense words. The nonsense words were created by substituting at random a different medial cluster for the one that actually occurred. After this random substitution, further switches were made to remove substrings corresponding to actual words as actually spelled. Particularly recalcitrant examples which made it impossible to remove actual words while maintaining the balance of the set were resolved by altering a consonant in the base word to create a new base form. This new base was used for both the "good" and the "bad" versions.

This procedure resulted in a "good" word and a "bad" word formed from each base, e.g.

(10) BASE   GOOD   BAD
      bistro   bimplo   bilflo
      constant cosprant   comkrant

Each good cluster was found in three different words, paired with a variety of bad clusters. Similarly, each bad cluster was found in three words, paired with a variety of good clusters.

Words were presented in ordinary English spelling to an undergraduate linguistics class. Nasals preceding a velar were written "n," even if presumed to be homorganic, e.g.:

(11) tancrum, pongrete

/kw/ was spelled with a "qu":

(12) fonquess, inquigue

/ks/ was spelled with an "x":

(13) traxtil, uxkage

The palato-alveolar fricative was written "sh," somewhat disguising its anomalous status in the experiment.

Ordinary spelling was used because many of the undergraduates had a poor grasp of transcription. The course in question was an introductory class satisfying a distribution requirement and covering only basic concepts of phonology and phonetics. As a result, the subjects can be assumed to have had at most a very general understanding of the aims of the experiment.

The students were told that the words were candidates for the vocabulary of a science-fiction novel. Half were asked to judge which word of a matched pair was "most like a compound." The other half were asked to judge which seemed "most suitable to be part of the vocabulary of an English speaker of the 21st century." All subjects were instructed to work quickly, giving their first impression, and to answer all questions even if they had to guess. There were twelve sets of responses for each set of instructions. Subjects working under one set of instructions were not aware that others had a different set of instructions.

The presentation randomized the position (first or second) of the "good" cluster of each pair. The different pairs were also randomized with each other. Matched pairs (e.g. "cosprant," "comkrant") were presented rather than unmatched pairs (e.g. "bimplo," "comkrant") in order to facilitate the comparison. Calling attention in this way to the contrast under investigation obviously maximizes the chance of finding a difference. It was felt that success with this format of presentation would lay the groundwork for a more elaborate experiment disguising the contrast under study. That is, if the present design failed to produce results there would be no point in continuing. However, the present experiment must be viewed as a pilot and a full-scale study should also be carried out.

11.5 Results of the experiment

The responses to both sets of instructions show that subjects had tacit knowledge of the regularities in triconsonantal clusters and could apply this knowledge in evaluating novel forms.

For the instruction "which is a compound," 40 out of 48 possible word comparisons went in the direction predicted (that is, more than six subjects selected the intended compound as a compound.) There were three ties and five comparisons were contrary to prediction. Scores were tabulated for each cluster by combining scores for all three pairs in which it occurred. Of the 16 clusters predicted to occur only in compounds, 15 were judged to occur in compounds more than half the time. There was a tie for /mst/, the cluster which had been included as only marginally problematic.

For the instruction "which is more suitable," 42 word comparisons came out as predicted with three ties and two contrary to prediction. All 16 bad clusters were judged to be "more suitable" less than half the time.

Tabulating by groups yields the following results. Numbers represent percents of judgments pooled across subjects and words.

(14)

	Compound	Suitable
Coronal in coda:	71	22
/ʃ/ in coda:	76	19
/t/ or /d/:	68	23
Duplicate consonants:	66	20
/ksk/ alone	75	17
Nonhormorganic /m/:	58	26
excluding /mst/:	61	19

It is interesting to note that the constraints against coronals in the coda and against duplicate consonants are both stronger than the tendency to avoid non-homorganic nasals, which has been previously noted in the literature. This result was obtained even using the nonhomorganic clusters of clearest status, those involving /m/ before a nonhomorganic stop. It may also be noted that /ksk/ was the least acceptable of the clusters involving duplicate consonants, and the most likely to be viewed as arising from a compound. This result tends to support the claim that the constraint is not idiosyncratic to /l/. However, further work is needed to rule out the possibility that this result is an artifactual result of spelling with an "x."

In interpreting the results, it is necessary to rule out the possibility that they are adequately explained by differences in predicted frequency between the good and bad clusters. This possibility must be evaluated, because the experimental design did not actually control for predicted frequency. No bad cluster had a predicted frequency as high as the most likely good clusters. The materials were designed in this way because the aims in designing the materials were to some extent at odds with each other. These aims were: to use several different clusters to evaluate each proposed constraint; to control for predicted frequency; and to include some clusters which were unequivocally acceptable, in view of the actual rarity of some occurring clusters. Because of imbalance in predicted frequencies for good and bad clusters, pooled data would be expected to exhibit some tendencies in the direction noted even under the null hypothesis. If subjects simply selected the most probable cluster of each pair, the judgments would on the average favor the "good" clusters.

A subset of the "compound" data was extracted in order to eliminate this possibility. The ten pairs in which the predicted frequency of the "bad" cluster strictly exceeded the predicted frequency of the "good" cluster were extracted. Out of 120 individual judgments, 81 were nonetheless as predicted. This is highly significant by a binomial test. Pooled data for eight word pairs were as predicted, with one tie and one contrary to prediction. It may be concluded that subjects do have phonotactic knowledge of the triconsonantal clusters, apart from that implied by a stochastic syllable grammar.

11.6 Discussion and conclusions

A stochastic model of syllable structure goes far towards explaining which triconsonantal clusters are found. The extent to which the clusters can be generated as statistically independent selections of a coda and a following onset confirms the existence of the syllable as a unit of hierarchical structure. It provides evidence against the view that the form of medial clusters is determined entirely by sequential constraints. The form of the evidence is brought out by considering the alternative, that sequential constraints in the form of a finite state model define the allowable medial clusters. Under this approach, a separate model is needed for medial clusters since many occur neither initially nor finally. The fact that the statistics of initial and final clusters so effectively circumscribe the medial alternatives is treated as accidental under this approach.

Statistical knowledge of phonological structure has also been demonstrated in two other areas. Experiments described in Kelly (1988) show that English speakers are able to apply statistical knowledge of the rhythmic contexts for nouns and verbs. Cassidy and Kelly (1991) show that English speakers are aware that nouns are typically longer than verbs.

One of the observed constraints above the syllable level can be adequately described in current phonological theory using marking conditions. Condition (15) prevents a nasal from preceding a stop which does not agree in the feature [labial]:

(15)

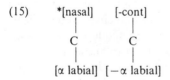

If [labial] is viewed as a privative feature, then it becomes difficult to collapse the cases of e.g. */mk/ and */np/.

A reviewer suggests that the generalization stated in (15) be attributed to failure of the coda to license a place of articulation for nasals. Place of articulation would either be acquired by a spreading rule from the following stop, or default to coronal. The marginal existence of a contrast between /m/ and /n/ before fricatives provides equally marginal counterevidence to this suggestion. In addition, under this approach it is unclear how to cope with the fair number of English words containing coda /m/ before onset /n/.

Let us now turn to the cases which do have implications for autosegmental theory. Consider first the distribution of coronal obstruents in coda position. Such obstruents are found to be far more frequent in word-final position than medially; that is, word and syllable position interact to determine frequency. This frequency difference (which is supported by a study of biconsonantal clusters) effectively predicts the absence of triconsonantal clusters beginning with coronal obstruents. Similarly, velars are found to be unexpectedly infrequent in coda position preceding noncoronals. Their infrequency in this position, as revealed by their sporadic occurrence in biconsonantal clusters, effectively precludes them from appearing in the triconsonantal clusters.

The central idea of current licensing theory is that structural nodes (such as the syllable, the onset, or the coda) support phonological contrasts by supporting segmental features. If a particular structural position – for example the coda – does not display the full set of contrasts which are available in the language, this is because that particular structural position does not license all the features in the language. Licensing theory provides two examples of how nodes can interact to control segmental content. The first is the treatment of the appendix. The syllable coda can license a single stop, which can have any place of articulation. The word node licenses additional segments following the coda (that is, the appendix), which must be coronal. These segments might be direct structural dependents of the word node. Or else they could be structural dependents of the coda which are only permissible when this coda is word final, as argued in Scobbie (1991). But in either case, the syllable licenses all the different place features but the word node doesn't. The interaction between the syllable and the word is seen from the fact that the segments licensed by the word node come after those licensed by the syllable.

It is also possible for two nodes to jointly control different aspects of the same segment. This is the case of parasitic licensing, as studied in Itô (1986). In a number of languages, including Japanese, a consonant is only permitted in the coda if it agrees in place with the onset of the next syllable. That is, the only distinctive feature in this position is [nasal], with the outcome being either a nasal homorganic cluster or a geminate. This situation is described by permitting the coda to license only [nasal], with the place features formally originating with the following syllable onset. Itô's treatment relies on the use of negative marking conditions with links interpreted exhaustively; however, the same idea can be carried out using positive conditions, as described in Goldsmith (1990) and Scobbie (1991).

In cases of parasitic licensing studied to date, the two nodes controlling features of a segment are adjacent syllable nodes. However, nothing in principle prevents hierarchically related nodes from behaving in the same way. Note however, that the pattern found here for coronals and velars in coda position involves two nodes jointly controlling the same set of features, not merely different features of the same phoneme. The situation thus requires a straightforward formal extension of the present formalism, permitting hierarchically superior nodes to readjust or load probabilities assigned lower down in the hierarchy. In the case of the velars, this readjustment must also refer to the onset of the following syllable whose place of articulation is relevant. In general, this type of interaction among nodes is only brought out in a statistical treatment of phonotactics.

It is interesting that a statistical effect operating above the syllable level is found to effectively describe two absolute patterns in the triconsonantal clusters. It would of course be possible to formulate a purely qualitative marking condition which prohibited e.g. coronal codas in triconsonantal clusters only. However, this description would fail to relate the situation in triconsonantal clusters to that in biconsonantal clusters and would thus be less succinct and general than the description proposed here. These two cases thus raise an important issue, namely to what extent the notion of an "ill-formed" word can be reduced to that of a "statistically improbable" word.

The required dissimilarity between the first and third consonants in a cluster is also interesting. There are two relevant precedents in the literature, but neither of them can account for this dissimilarity.

To prevent the occurrence of morpheme internal geminates, English is taken to have a marking condition of the following form:

(16)   * C   C
          \   /
         [root]

(That is, two adjacent consonants cannot share all features). However, this condition does not preclude identity of the first and third consonants of a cluster, because they are not adjacent; the second consonant intervenes.

There is also by now a substantial literature on dissimilarity requirements which affect nonadjacent as well as adjacent consonants. Effects on nonadjacent consonants are described using the combined assumptions of autosegmental projection, the Obligatory Contour Principle (OCP), and underspecification theory. The OCP says that two adjacent like elements are prohibited. This idea, introduced in work on tone by Leben (1973) and christened in Goldsmith (1976), was then applied in McCarthy (1986) to problems in segmental morphophonology in Arabic and other languages.

By applying the OCP only to some particular featural projection, it is possible to rule out sequences of segments which are similar in some particular respect without being completely identical. For example, disallowing two identical specifications on the nasal tier would make it impossible to have two nasals of any type in a row. (It would also rule out sequences which agreed in being nonnasal, without the further understanding that nonnasal segments are unspecified for nasality rather than being [−nasal].) Analyses of this sort are Yip's (1988) treatment of voicing restrictions in Japanese, Steriade's (1987) treatment of /r/ – /l/ alternation in Latin, and McCarthy's description (this volume) of cooccurrence restrictions in the verbal roots of Arabic. These analyses all exploit underspecification and/or privativity to make certain segments transparent to OCP effects. That is, if a segment is not specified for some feature, then it will be invisible on the tier for that feature, and otherwise nonadjacent segments will be rendered effectively adjacent. In combination, then, the OCP and underspecification or privativity can effectively prevent even nonadjacent phonemes from sharing some phonological properties.

In attempting to apply this approach to the present problem, the absence of clusters /ksk/, /nsn/, /lfl/, /lpl/, and /lbl/ turns out to be particularly important. The first two undercut the otherwise plausible suggestion that the gaps are explained by an OCP effect on the [lateral] tier, since the first and third consonants are not lateral. The last three, involving a medial labial, show that underspecification for coronals, as advocated in Paradis and Prunet (1991), cannot be exploited to render the first and third consonants effectively adjacent (either on the place tier or with respect to one of the place features). Furthermore, if coronals were unspecified for place, then not only /s/ but also /n/ would be unspecified. As a result, /nsn/ could not represent an OCP violation with respect to place, but only with respect to [nasal] or [continuant]. However, these features cannot be the domain for the constraint because of the contrast between acceptable and nonacceptable clusters which are entirely nonnasal, and because of the contrast between */nsn/ and /nst/, /nsk/, /nsp/.

In general, it is impossible for the OCP to prevent total identity across arbitrary intervening material, if its operation is restricted to features which are strictly adjacent on a tier. This is impossible because checking for total identity requires examination of all the tiers. But some of these tiers will be tiers on which the features of intervening material appear. If two segments are not adjacent, then there is some tier on which their features are not adjacent, for some choice of intervening material.

In view of this difficulty, the present study was followed up with a statistical study of the verbal roots of Arabic (Pierrehumbert 1993). These roots consist of three consonants, with dissimilarity requirements affecting nonadjacent as well as adjacent consonants (see McCarthy, this volume). They thus provide a very relevant comparison to the medial clusters of English; but because they are so much more numerous and varied, they provide more detailed evidence about the formal character of dissimilarity requirements. The study, completed just as the present article goes to press, demonstrates that even in Arabic the dissimilarity constraints must be permitted to refer to nonadjacent feature specifications. The constraint against total identity is shown to be more persistent (better able to cross intervening material) than the constraint against mere homorganicity, and a model derived from the psychological literature which exhibits this behavior is laid out.

The lack of clusters in English with identical first and third consonants is thus consistent with a more extensive pattern in Arabic, the now classic example of a language with OCP effects on segments. We conclude, therefore, that English provides a further example of a dissimilarity requirement operating across, intervening material. This conclusion is already anticipated by Clements and Keyser (1983), who note the absence of words like "flill," and Davis (1989), who established the systematic absence of sequences such as "spep." Future work will need to establish why words in which one of two identical consonants is word-initial (such as "lilt" and "cake") are apparently exempted from such a constraint.

Notes

1 With hindsight, the author would suggest that postnasal coronals (as in /pænt/) probably actually count as appendices. The main consequence of this treatment would have been to raise the already high frequency tally for coda /n/, and to absolutely preclude internal clusters in which /n/ precedes a coronal obstruent that cannot be syllabified in the following onset. In short, "antler" and "handsome" would necessarily be polymorphemic under this view. We also observe that the possibility of a long nucleus before a coronal obstruent coda hangs by the thread of the word "ordnance" (pronounced with a long vowel in British English and a rhotic offglide in many American dialects).

2 In making this generalization /ntl/ is taken to be nonoccurring even though it is actually found in "antler." This is because the word is the sole exemplar of this cluster, once having set aside words in which the entire cluster is morpheme-final. The acceptability of "antler" may be related to the large number of such words in which a morpheme-final /l/ is syllabified with the following suffix.

References

Bradley, D.C. 1979. Lexical representation of derivational relations. In M. Aronoff and M.L. Kean (eds.) *Juncture*. Cambridge, MA: MIT Press, 37–55.

Bybee, J. 1988. Morphology as lexical organization. In M. Hammond and M. Noon (eds.) *Theoretical Morphology*. New York: Academic Press, 119–142.

Cassidy, K.W. and M.H. Kelly. 1991. Phonological information for grammatical category assignments. *Journal of Memory and Language* 30: 348–369.

Clements, G.N. and S.J. Keyser. 1983. *CV Phonology: A Generative Theory of the Syllable*. Cambridge, MA: MIT Press.

Davis, Stuart. 1989. Cross-vowel phonotactic constraints. *Computational Linguistics* 15(2): 109–111.

Fudge, E.C. 1969. Syllables. *Journal of Linguistics* 5: 253–286.

Fujimura, O. 1990. Demisyllables as sets of features. In J. Kingston and M. Beckman (eds.) *Papers in Laboratory Phonology I. Between the Grammar and Physics of Speech*. Cambridge: University Press.

Fujimura, O. and J. Lovins. 1978. Syllables as concatenative phonetic units. In Bell and Hooper (eds.) *Syllables and Segments*. Amsterdam: North-Holland.

Goldsmith, J. 1976. Autosegmental phonology. Ph.D. dissertation, MIT. Published by Garland Press, New York, 1979.

1990. *Autosegmental and Metrical Phonology*. Oxford: Blackwell.

Greenberg, J. H. and J. J. Jenkins. 1964. Studies in the psychological correlates of the sound system of American English. *Word* 20: 157–177.

Itô, J. 1986. Syllable theory in prosodic phonology. Ph.D dissertation, University of Massachusetts at Amherst. Published by Garland Press, New York, 1988.

Kelly, M. H. 1988. Rhythmic alternation and lexical stress differences in English. *Cognition* 30: 107–137.

Leben, W. R. 1973. Suprasegmental phonology. Ph.D. dissertation, MIT. Published by Garland Press, New York.

McCarthy, J. 1986. OCP Effects: gemination and antigemination. *Linguistic Inquiry* 17: 207–265.

Nagy, W. and R. Anderson. 1984. How many words are there in printed school English? *Reading Research Quarterly* 19: 304–330.

Nesfield, J. C. 1898. *English Grammar Past and Present*. New York and London: Macmillan and Co.

Nida, E. 1949. *Morphology: The Descriptive Analysis of Words*. Ann Arbor: The University of Michigan Press.

Ohala, J. J. and M. Ohala. 1986. Testing hypotheses regarding the psychological manifestation of morpheme structure constraints. In J. J. Ohala and J. J. Jaeger (eds.) *Experimental Phonology*. Orlando: Academic Press, 239–252.

Paradis, C. and J-F. Prunet. 1991. *The Special Status of Coronals: Internal and External Evidence*. San Diego: Academic Press.

Pierrehumbert, J. 1993. Dissimilarity in the Arabic verbal roots. In NELS 23. Amherst, MA: University of Massachusetts at Amherst, GLSA Publications.

Scobbie, J.M. 1991. Attribute value phonology. Ph.D dissertation, University of Edinburgh.

Selkirk, E.O. 1982. The syllable. In H. van der Hulst and N. Smith (eds.) *The Structure of Phonological Representations*, Parts I and II. Dordrecht: Foris.

Steriade, D. 1987. Redundant values. In A. Bosch, B. Need, and E. Schiller (eds.) *Papers from the Parasession on Metrical and Autosegmental Phonology (23rd Regional Meeting of the Chicago Linguistic Society)*, 339–362.

Yip, Moira. 1988. The obligatory contour principle: a loss of identity. *Linguistic Inquiry* 19: 65–100.

Part III
Feature Theory

The phonetics and phonology of Semitic pharyngeals[1]

JOHN J. McCARTHY

12.1 Introduction

An adequate theory of phonological distinctive features must meet four criteria: (i) it must have a relatively consistent and direct relation to the phonetic properties of speech sounds; (ii) it must be able to describe all and only the distinctions made by the sound systems of any of the world's languages; (iii) it must be able to characterize all and only the natural classes of sounds that recur in the phonological phenomena of different languages; and (iv) it must correctly characterize the subgrouping of features by recurrent phonological phenomena. The third criterion is the most important one and probably the hardest to achieve. The fourth has assumed greater importance in the last five years or so in the context of work on feature geometry (Clements 1985; Sagey 1986; and others).

The Semitic languages have many consonants produced with a primary constriction in the posterior regions of the vocal tract. Traditional grammars refer to these consonants as "gutturals." Standard Arabic and most modern Arabic dialects have retained the full set of gutturals usually reconstructed for Proto-Semitic: laryngeals ʔ and h̰; pharyngeals ħ and ʕ; and uvulars χ and ʁ. Other Semitic languages, as well as several other branches of the larger Afro-Asiatic family, have similar or smaller inventories of gutturals.

The phonology of the various Semitic languages provides a remarkable range of evidence that the gutturals are treated as a natural class by phonological rules. This can be shown through independent developments in the various languages at different historical periods and in different areas of the phonology. Reference to the guttural class is not limited to just underlying or just surface level, but rather pervades the phonological structure of these languages. From these observations, it follows that the gutturals must constitute a robust natural class that is directly represented within distinctive feature theory.

By detailed examination of the acoustic and articulatory properties of the Semitic gutturals, I show that they constitute a class in terms of a traditional means of classifying consonants, point of articulation. Specifically, I argue that the natural class of gutturals is defined by their place of articulation, [pharyngeal]. The [pharyngeal] consonants are produced with a constriction anywhere in the entire region that encompasses the larynx through the oropharynx, a constriction locus that correlates acoustically with a relatively high F_1. I then go on to relate this idea to a proposal by Perkell (1980) that distinctive features are *orosensory targets*, and I suggest that the difference between [pharyngeal] and other place-of-articulation features lies in the varying distribution of sensory feedback mechanisms in different regions of the vocal tract. Ultimately, the thesis I develop is not unlike the earliest classification of these sounds by the Arab grammarian Sibawayh. In his terms, the gutturals are all "throat consonants," produced at "the back of the throat" (laryngeals), "the middle of the throat" (pharyngeals), and "the part of the throat nearest the mouth" (uvulars). It is also quite similar to Hayward and Hayward's (1989) independent proposal that there is a feature [guttural] characterizing a "zone" rather than a place of articulation, justified mostly on the basis of Cushitic rather than Semitic evidence.

Having established the properties of the feature [pharyngeal] and the evidence for it, I then turn to the issue of how it relates to other distinctive features. First, I sketch some of the phonetic and phonological properties of the emphatics, the coronal and uvular pharyngealized consonants, contrasting them with the gutturals. Second, I briefly indicate how [pharyngeal] fits into a model of feature geometry, a subject examined in depth in McCarthy (forthcoming). Third, I return to take a closer look at the laryngeal consonants, which are not always members of the guttural class.

There are also very rich systems of uvular, pharyngeal, and laryngeal consonants in the Northwest Caucasian languages as documented by Catford (1983) and Colarusso (1988). Unfortunately, relatively little is known about the phonological systems of these languages apart from phoneme lists, whereas virtually all of the conclusions about Semitic are based on phonological processes and constraints. In the absence of evidence from phonological processes, conclusions about featural representation are almost entirely speculative. There is, however, good phonological evidence concerning the uvulars and pharyngeals in some of the languages of the Pacific Northwest. Nevertheless, to keep the survey to manageable proportions, I have deliberately confined my attention to the Semitic languages with occasional excursions into broader Afro-Asiatic.[2]

12.2 Gutturals within distinctive feature theory

12.2.1 The articulatory and acoustic properties of gutturals

To provide a secure basis for the subsequent discussion, I will begin by reviewing the abundant phonetic evidence for the properties of gutturals in Arabic, a language with the full suite of six. This review takes each of the three types of gutturals (laryngeal, pharyngeal, and uvular) in turn, examining first their articulatory and then their acoustic properties. This section concludes with a summary of the characteristics of gutturals, taking special note of the properties common to all of them.

There is no body of articulatory data that specifically deals with the production of the laryngeals ʔ and ḥ in Arabic (but see section 12.5). Al-Ani (1970) reports that he made cineradiograms of the Arabic laryngeals but was unable to interpret them usefully. Acoustically, the laryngeals are characterized by a complete lack of formant transitions or other effects on adjacent vowels (Klatt and Stevens 1969; also see Younes 1982 on the "neutral environment"), as is typical of laryngeals in other languages (Stevens and House 1963: 116). During the production of ḥ, the resonances of the vocalic context are weakly excited by fricative-like noise (voiced intervocalically) (Al-Ani 1970, Klatt and Stevens 1969). The ʔ is realized sometimes by an obvious stop, sometimes only by creaky voice quality.

Interpreting the acoustic evidence in articulatory terms, we would have to say that ʔ and ḥ, although they involve an obvious laryngeal gesture, do not have any constriction higher in the vocal tract (discounting coarticulatory effects from surrounding vowels). In particular, there is no evidence for a pharyngeal or uvular constriction accompanying the glottal gesture. Even raising of the larynx during production of the consonant (a conspicuous property of the pharyngeals) should produce a falling transition of the second format in a following vowel as the larynx returns to its normal position. Therefore the entire burden of producing the laryngeal consonants falls on the larynx.

Ghazeli (1977) describes in some detail the results of a cineradiographic investigation of the pharyngeals ʕ and ḥ. (There are similar studies by Delattre, 1971, on Lebanese and Bukshaisha, 1985, on Qatari; their results do not appear to differ significantly from Ghazeli's.) The main gesture in the production of the pharyngeals is an approximation of the posterior wall of the laryngopharynx and the tongue root from the epiglottis down to the larynx. Both the posterior pharyngeal wall and the tongue root are moved inward from their rest positions. Concomitantly, the larynx itself and adjoining structures are raised considerably. The constriction is significantly narrower for ħ than for ʕ. (Delattre points to a perceptual basis for this; the increased friction in the voiceless approximant compensates for its otherwise lower amplitude.) Apparently for mechanical reasons, the tongue dorsum is concave during the production of ħ.

The place of articulation of ʕ and ħ, then, is the lower pharynx. The active articulator is some combination of the tongue root and the epiglottis. Laufer and Condax (1979) observed the epiglottis with a fiberscope during the production of pharyngeals by Sephardic Hebrew speakers and concluded that the epiglottis was retracting independently of the tongue root. Against this, Boff Dkhissi (1983, cited by Butcher and Ahmad 1987) concluded on the basis of a cinefluorographic investigation of Moroccan Arabic that both tongue root and epiglottis were involved. El-Halees (1985) has published a xeroradiogram of an Iraqi Arabic speaker producing ʕ as an epiglottal stop made with considerable retraction of the tongue root. Thus, it seems likely that both the tongue root and the epiglottis are being actively recruited to make the pharyngeal constriction.

Neither Delattre nor Ghazeli made films of pharyngeals in different vocalic contexts. Thus, although we see some raising of the anterior portion of the tongue body during the pharyngeals, we cannot know whether this is the influence of the vowel or an additional requirement of the pharyngeal consonants. In the actual tokens that Ghazeli examined, the vowel following the pharyngeal is [æ]. In Delattre's data, the tongue-body position also looks fairly [æ]-like.

Acoustically, we expect to find a high F_1 in pharyngeals (Klatt and Stevens 1969), and that is what the literature shows (Al-Ani 1970, 1978; Ghazeli 1977; Klatt and Stevens 1969; Alwan 1986; Butcher and Ahmad 1987). Butcher and Ahmad present particularly detailed information. The ħ has pseudo-formants at around 700–900 Hz, 1600–2200 Hz, and 2200–3000 Hz. At the consonant/vowel boundary of ʕ, F_2 is relatively low, in the 1200–1400 Hz range. F_1 is high – 900–1000 Hz – although it is somewhat lower before the round vowels u: and o:. The spectrum of ħ is roughly the same, although F_1 is not quite as high. The major effect of the pharyngeals on the steady-state portions of the adjoining vowels is signficant raising of F_1, by about 100 Hz relative to a neutral (glottal) environment.

The voiceless pharyngeal ħ is some kind of fricative or approximant (or perhaps even a glide). The realizations of ʕ vary dialectally or even individually between a stop (presumably epiglottal) and an approximant or fricative. Al-Ani (1970) found that he and three Iraqi informants produced ʕ as a stop (cf. El-Halees 1985). In contrast, Ghazeli (1977) did not find stopped ʕ with any of his informants, including one Iraqi. In Ghazeli's spectrograms the ʕ looks very much like a glide in intervocalic position. Butcher and Ahmad (1987) had three Iraqi informants, and found stop bursts at the release of ʕ about 60% of the time. (These were initial and final; they did not look at medial pharyngeals.) There are no phonological consequences of the superficial dialectal distinction between stop and continuant ʕs in Arabic. But, according to Catford (1983: 347), there is a Caucasian language ("the Burkikhan dialect of the Dagestanian language Agul") which does have distinct stop and continuant ʕ phonemes. Another possibility of phonemic contrast is that between plain and glottalized ʕ, found in Columbian Salish (Kinkade 1967).

Further properties of ʕ and ħ involve the larynx. I have already noted that the larynx is considerably raised during the production of the pharyngeals (Ghazeli 1977), and ʕ is often accompanied by creaky voice. This phenomenon is probably not unique to Arabic; Hayward and Hayward (1989), citing Sasse (1979) and Hayward (1989), note that ʕ is frequently "glottalized" in Ethiopian (Semitic and Cushitic) languages.

Could laryngeal involvement in the production of pharyngeals explain the class of gutturals? Both types of laryngeal effects in pharyngeals, larynx raising and creaky voice, have plausible mechanical explanations. The raising of the larynx in pharyngeals is probably a side-effect of the gestures involved in narrowing the pharynx. Ladefoged (1975: 143) has speculated that the creakiness of ʕ comes about "because the necessary constriction in the pharynx also causes a constriction in the larynx." Furthermore, Laufer and Condax (1979: 52) point out that the creakiness is consistent with compression of the top of the arytenoids by the retracted epiglottis (as in swallowing). If laryngeal involvement in pharyngeals is a superficial mechanical effect, then it is unsuitable as an explanation for a truly *phonological* property like the guttural class, with effects throughout the phonology.[3]

Finally, we turn to the uvular gutturals ʁ and χ. Again, Ghazeli (1977) presents x-ray data that differs only slightly from the data in Delattre (1971). The uvulars are produced with a much higher and slightly narrower constriction than the pharyngeals. This constriction is obtained by raising and retracting the dorsum of the tongue toward the posterior wall of the oropharynx. In ʁ, the uvula is curved downward and anteriorly to produce a trill. The constriction in χ is narrower than that in ʁ, and this is associated with a slight raising of the larynx (supporting the earlier claim that larynx raising in pharyngeals is purely a mechanical effect).

Acoustically, χ is characterized by very low frequency noise, below 1200 Hz. The consonant ʁ has formants at 500–600 Hz and 1200–1300 Hz – in other words, F_1 is high, but not as high as in the pharyngeals. F_2 is as low as in the pharyngeals. The lower F_1 of the uvulars compared to the pharyngeals is consistent with the fact that they are produced quite close to the midpoint of the vocal tract. The χ is a voiceless fricative or approximant; the usual realization of ʁ̱ is a voiced trill.

This completes the review, and we can now sum up the observations about the phonetic properties of gutturals:

   (i)   *Active articulator.* The gutturals are produced by three distinct gestures: a purely glottal one in the laryngeals; retraction of the tongue root and epiglottis and advancement of the posterior wall of the laryngopharynx in the pharyngeals; and a superior-posterior movement of the tongue dorsum in the uvulars.

   (ii) *Place of articulation.* The gutturals are all produced in the posterior region of the vocal tract.

   (iii) *Spectrum.* The gutturals all have relatively high F_1. F_1 is at the theoretical maximum in the case of laryngeals, close to the maximum for the pharyngeals, and higher than any orally articulated consonants in the case of uvulars.

   (iv) *Stricture.* All gutturals except ʔ̱ meet Catford's (1977: 122) definition of *approximant*: "*non-turbulent* flow when voiced; but the flow becomes *turbulent* when they are made voiceless." Clements (1990) modifies this definition to require oral stricture in non-approximants. With this modification, even ʔ̱ is included in the class of approximants.[4]

Crucially, the gutturals share posterior place of articulation, high F_1, and stricture (see section 12.4); the gutturals do not share active articulator.

12.2.2 Previous featural treatments of gutturals

There are many ways to organize a system of distinctive features. The *Preliminaries* feature system (Jakobson *et al.* 1963) classifies sounds in acoustic terms, even if they are articulatorily quite dissimilar (like [+ grave] ḵ and p̱). The *SPE* feature system (Chomsky and Halle 1968) is primarily oriented toward the active articulator, effecting a major four-way classification of consonants by the features [coronal] and [anterior], with finer distinctions supplied by features like [distributed], [high], [low], and [back]. Ladefoged (1975) and Williamson (1977) propose a many-valued place feature that essentially measures distance from the glottis, taking values like [[pharyngeal]Place] or [1Place].

The acoustically based *Preliminaries* system, applied to Arabic by Jakobson (1957), maps low F_2 onto the single feature [flat]. The [+ flat] consonants of Arabic are the uvulars and the emphatics (see section 12.4). Stretching the point a bit, Jakobson classifies the pharyngeals as [+ flat] as well. Since F_2 is not low in the laryngeals, though, there can be no natural class of the gutturals defined by the feature [flat]. Additional problems arise from the identification of [flat] with rounding, which is independent of uvular or pharyngeal place of articulation.

Problems with the *SPE* treatment of gutturals have been previously noted by Kenstowicz and Kisseberth (1979: 250) and Keating (1988: 7–8). The chart (example 1) gives the values of the relevant features for the gutturals and for other places of articulation found in Semitic, according to Chomsky and Halle (1968: 307).

(1)	Anterior	Coronal	High	Low	Back
Labial	+	−	−	−	−
Alveolar	+	+	−	−	−
Palato-alveolar	−	+	+	−	−
Velar	−	−	+	−	+
Uvular	−	−	−	−	+
Pharyngeal	−	−	−	+	+
Laryngeal	−	−	−	+	−

Here, it appears that the gutturals really can be singled out by featural specifications: they are [−anterior, −high]. Within that set, the features [low] and [back] distinguish the uvulars, pharyngeals, and laryngeals from one another.

The real problem is not with this chart, which gives the desired classification, but with the fact that the chart is inconsistent with the definitions of the features in *SPE* and the phonetic properties of the gutturals described above. The features [high], [low], and [back] refer to movements of the tongue body from its theoretical "neutral position" (at about the location of the vowel in English *bed*). Uvulars are said to be [−high], but we have seen that the Arabic uvulars are actually produced with a high tongue body. Pharyngeals are [+low, +back], but the distinctive gesture in pharyngeals is with the tongue root/epiglottis and posterior pharyngeal wall, not the tongue body. In fact, the tongue body is not back but front with the Arabic pharyngeals, as we can see by the adjacent front allophone of the low vowel: compare pharyngeal [ħææl] "condition" with uvular [χɑɑl] "maternal uncle." Finally, the tongue body cannot be implicated in the production of the laryngeals at all; thus, the assignment of [+low] to laryngeals is simply inconsistent with the definition of [low] as a feature referring to tongue height.

Even if these problems with the *SPE* system could be set aside, there would be good reason to reject the [−anterior, −high] characterization of the gutturals. As Sagey (1986) and McCarthy (1988) show, this sort of cross-classificatory use of [anterior] presents major difficulties in the context of feature theory as a whole.

The multi-valued [place] feature of Ladefoged (1975) and Williamson (1977) does provide a natural classification of the gutturals: they are the three places of articulation closest to the glottis. Formally, in a theory with numerical feature coefficients, the gutturals are the class [0–2Place]. The problem is that, as a theory of consonantal place classifications, this is far too weak. Although the gutturals are clearly a natural class in Semitic, this theory permits classifications of contiguous places that are rare or nonexistent: labial, labiodental, and dental; labiodental, dental, and alveolar; velar, uvular, and pharyngeal; and so on. Although certain sets of contiguous places of articulation do indeed constitute natural classes, contiguity alone is not enough to make a class natural.

Recent phonological research on distinctive features (beginning with Anderson 1971 and taken up by Halle 1983; Sagey 1986; Halle 1988; McCarthy 1988; Maddieson and Ladefoged 1988, and others) has developed a model that places very rigid restrictions on reference to "place of articulation" in consonant systems. In this theory, speech sounds are principally classified by active articulator. The fruit of this work is a set of three features that refer to the active articulator. The [labial] sounds are produced by raising or protruding the lower lip (and possibly the upper one as well). Thus, they include true labials, labiodentals, and, as a secondary articulation, lip rounding. The [coronal] sounds are produced by raising the tongue tip or blade. They include the dentals, alveolars, palato-alveolars, retroflexes, and, as a secondary articulation, apicalization. Finally, the [dorsal] sounds, made by moving the tongue body from its neutral position, include the vowels, the palatals, velars, and uvulars, and, as a secondary articulation, velarization and perhaps palatalization. The obvious extension of this approach to pharyngeals posits a fourth active articulator, [tongue root] or [radical] (McCarthy 1985; Cole 1987; Maddieson and Ladefoged 1988).

But even adding [radical] to the set of candidate features does not solve the problem. Gutturals are produced by three distinct active articulators, the larynx, the tongue root and epiglottis (that is, [radical]), and the tongue body (that is, [dorsal]). Thus, a natural class of gutturals is incompatible with the fundamental assumption of articulator-based feature theory.

12.2.3 The [pharyngeal] place

Since the gutturals do not share a single major articulator, we should instead ask what they do have in common. All gutturals are produced by a constriction in the same region of the vocal tract. "Region" here must be broadly defined, to encompass the area from the larynx to the oropharynx inclusive. Three different articulators have access to that region – the larynx, the tongue root, and the tongue body. The defining characteristic of the gutturals is not the major articulator, but the place of articulation, characterized by the feature [pharyngeal].

This account, though, leads to a major asymmetry. The anterior part of the vocal tract is organized in terms of active articulator, but the posterior part is organized in terms of place of articulation. More strikingly, the three active articulator features [labial], [coronal], and [dorsal] divide up a region of the vocal tract approximately equal in length to the region subtended by the single feature [pharyngeal]. In other words, the asymmetry is that finer distinctions of place are made in the front of the vocal tract than in the back.

An explanation for this asymmetry comes from examining the relation between phonological features and speech production. In the articulator-based theory, each of the features [labial], [coronal], and [dorsal] can be thought of as "driving" the corresponding active articulator (Halle 1983). In contrast, Perkell (1980) has proposed that distinctive features are

orosensory patterns corresponding to distinctive sound producing states. These 'orosensory' patterns consist of proprioceptive, tactile and more complicated air-pressure and airflow information from the entire vocal tract. . . . As examples, the orosensory goals for the features 'high' and 'back' might consist of specific patterns of contact of the sides of the tongue body with the teeth and the pharyngeal wall. The orosensory goal for the feature 'coronal' might be contact of the sides of the tongue blade with the teeth or alveolar ridge . . . . (Perkell 1980: 338)

The vocal tract can report its state through feedback mechanisms like touch or proprioception. Distinctive features are defined as particular patterns of feedback from the vocal tract (which have consistent acoustic consequences).

The proposed feature [pharyngeal], then, would be defined as the orosensory pattern of constriction anywhere in the broad region of the pharynx. The corresponding "distinctive sound producing state" of [pharyngeal] is high F_1, a property that the gutturals share.[5]

If features are defined as orosensory goals rather than articulatory instructions, we expect that differences in the acuity of orosensation at different points in the vocal tract will be reflected in the phonological organization imposed on those regions. In particular, the large [pharyngeal] region should be rather poorly differentiated compared to the smaller [labial], [coronal], and [dorsal] regions.

There are three sources of evidence for differences in sensory acuity in the vocal tract. All of these do indeed support the model proposed here, where the wide [pharyngeal] region is treated as equivalent to the narrower [labial], [coronal], and [dorsal] regions. None of the evidence is perfect, though, so the argument at this point becomes somewhat speculative.

First, the actual distribution of sensory neurons in the vocal tract corresponds quite well to our expectations. In a comprehensive survey of the histological literature, Grossman (1964) concludes:

> This review of the reported oral sensory nerve elements reveals a progressive decrease in the frequency of sensory endings from the front to the rear of the mouth in humans . . . These findings are compatible with the author's initial experimental evidence which indicates that tactile discriminations are most acute in the anterior mucosal surfaces of the mouth. It is probably not coincidental that many important speech articulatory phenomena occur in the same oral region. (Grossman 1964: 132)

Second, direct measurements of sensory acuity can be obtained from experiments determining the minimal distance for two-point discrimination, in which subjects are asked to report whether they feel two points rather than one from a caliper-like device. Ringel (1970) performed such an experiment on four regions of the vocal tract at the midline and right and left sides. The results (means of 25 subjects, in millimeters, followed by standard deviations) are shown in example 2.

(2)		Left	Middle	Right
	Upper lip	2.47 (0.84)	2.31 (0.72)	2.49 (0.69)
	Tongue tip	1.82 (0.41)	1.70 (0.46)	1.72 (0.47)
	Alveolar ridge	3.21 (1.39)	2.66 (1.09)	3.20 (1.29)
	Soft palate	2.95 (1.17)	2.64 (1.10)	3.06 (1.26)

Unfortunately, there are no measurements of two-point discrimination for the tongue body or the pharynx. (The apparatus is rather large and would probably excite the faucal gagging reflex.) Certainly, what we do see are differences in sensory acuity among different regions of the vocal tract. Furthermore, the tongue tip, an articulator that is associated with several phonological features ([coronal], [distributed], and [anterior]), is unusually sensitive.

Third, another kind of evidence for the relative lack of pharyngeal sensory differentiation comes from the observation that the size of the cortical projection of a body part corresponds to its sensory acuity. Penfield and Rasmussen's (1950) sensory homunculus, deduced from experiments involving low-voltage stimulation of the cortex in conscious patients undergoing brain surgery, shows that the whole pharynx is about half the size, sensorily speaking, of the tongue, which includes two articulators. There may also be a similar equivalence for the lips.[6]

The available evidence on differential sensitivity within the oral vocal tract is not wonderfully detailed, but it is sufficient to provide at least some support for the following speculation. With respect to orosensation, the regions of the vocal tract covered by each of the features [labial], [coronal], [dorsal], and [pharyngeal] may be equal in subjective size. To be more precise, imagine determining a subjective unit of measurement for each region of the vocal tract based on the minimum distance of two-point discrimination in that region. The objective size of this subjective unit will vary at different points in the vocal tract, being much greater in the more poorly innervated posterior regions. Measured in these "cognitive units," the different regions of the vocal tract might be of approximately equal size. Moreover, the regions themselves can be defined as areas where the objective size of the cognitive unit of measure is roughly constant. In this way, orosensation provides a kind of quantization of the vocal tract into featural regions, as Perkell (1980) suggests. Since the anterior active articulators contribute significantly to orosensation (the lower lip and the tongue tip being particularly sensitive), the correspondence between active articulators and the place features [labial], [coronal], and [dorsal] is not so unexpected.

The orosensory target model is not the only possible approach to the problem posed by the feature [pharyngeal]. One obvious alternative is that the pharynx has a uniform characterization in motoric terms. Clearly this is not true at the lowest level: the uvular constriction is presumably made primarily by a gesture of the styloglossus, while the true pharyngeals ʕ and ħ are formed by the pharyngeal constrictors and the glottals are made by the intrinsic muscles of the larynx. But it is certainly possible that these consonants form a motoric unity at some much higher level.[7]

Another approach to [pharyngeal] place is provided by Hess's (1990) work. Hess presents a factor analysis (see Jackson 1988) based on x-ray tracings from two speakers of Damascene Arabic and one speaker of Tunisian. The segments with pharyngeal articulation include the pharyngeal consonants ʕ and ħ, the emphatics S̲ and T̲, the vocalic near-phonemes a̲ and æ, and the vocalic allophones I̲ and U̲. Nonpharyngeals in the data set are k̲, t̲, s̲, i̲, and u̲. (Throughout this chapter "emphatic" or "pharyngealized" segments are transcribed with capital letters, e.g. S̲ – as the counterpart of s̲.)

One factor that she obtains corresponds to retraction of the tongue root along a horizontal axis through the epiglottis, accompanied by raising of the larynx and posterior movement of the upper pharyngeal wall. This factor basically distinguishes pharyngeal articulation from nonpharyngeal, and Hess characterizes it by the feature [radical]. The other factor involves lowering the tongue dorsum, retracting the tongue root, and raising the larynx. This factor distinguishes the low pharyngeals ħ, ʕ, a, and æ from the others, and Hess characterizes this factor as [low].[8]

The most relevant aspect of Hess's study is the conclusion that the same factor is responsible for the pharyngeal constriction in both pharyngealized coronals like S̱ and Ṯ and primary pharyngeals like ʕ and ħ, despite the fact that these pharyngeal constrictions are widely separated from one another. As Hess (1990: 13) observes, "Factor analysis has ascribed the difference to the influence of the tongue blade in the pharyngealized segments and given us one factor for retraction." The uvulars ʁ, χ, and q have a constriction in the upper pharynx very similar to that of S̱ or Ṯ, so it is important to know whether the same factor could produce upper pharyngeal retraction for them. Unfortunately, Hess did not include the uvulars in her study, so this approach must remain speculative for now.

To sum up, the guttural class is defined by the place of articulation feature [pharyngeal]. I have suggested that the basis for such a broad class, encompassing about half the length of the vocal tract, can be found in Perkell's (1980) notion of distinctive features as correlations of distinctive acoustic events and orosensory targets. Differences between [pharyngeal] and other place or articulator features plausibly follow from the large differences between the pharynx and the oral vocal tract in sensory innervation.

12.3 Evidence for the natural class of gutturals

We now turn to the phonology, considering a number of arguments for the gutturals as a natural class. Evidence comes primarily from the synchronic phonology of Semitic languages, with occasional forays into the Cushitic material adduced by Hayward and Hayward (1989). The material is classified according to the phonological role of the guttural class: co-occurrence restrictions, vowel lowering, avoidance of syllable-final position, and degemination. We shall also look at some historical changes affecting gutturals in Semitic.

The chart in example 3 gives the consonant system of Standard Arabic; all of the consonants in the columns labeled Emphatic, Uvular, Pharyngeal, and Laryngeal have [pharyngeal] components in their articulation. Original g is realized by many speakers as the palatoalveolar affricate d͡ʒ; nevertheless, it patterns as a velar with respect to the root co-occurrence restrictions (section 12.3.1) and assimilation of the definite article in Standard Arabic. The consonants with a [pharyngeal] constriction include the gutturals χ, ʁ, ħ, ʕ, ʔ, and h, the uvular stop q, and the pharyngealized coronals or "emphatics" Ṯ, Ḏ, S̱, and Ẕ. The phenomena I will be analyzing throughout this section affect only the gutturals proper, not the pharyngealized coronals or the uvular stop q. The similarities and differences between gutturals and other consonants with [pharyngeal] constriction are discussed in section 12.4.

(3)

	Labial	Coronal	Emphatic	Velar	Uvular	Pharyngeal	Laryngeal
		t	T	k	q		ʔ
	b	d	D	g			
	f	θ, s	S		χ	ħ	h
		ð, z	Z		ʁ	ʕ	
		ʃ					
		l, r					
	m	n					

w, j

Since the evidence comes mostly from a single language family, Semitic, an objection naturally comes to mind. Could the natural class of gutturals be an idiosyncratic property of this language family, with no bearing on a universal feature theory? The notion "idiosyncratic property of a language family" makes sense only as a claim about language history. But a phonological rule referring to gutturals that is an innovation in a particular Semitic language cannot be inherited from the proto-language; in this case, appeal to a Semitic idiosyncrasy is purely mystical, since there is no mechanism by which language learners might discover this idiosyncrasy and apply it in a novel rule. The only sensible account is that the natural class of gutturals is already available to language learners from linguistic theory; they could not discover it from their Semitic heritage.

12.3.1 Root-consonant cooccurrence restrictions on gutturals

The lexicon of the Semitic languages is organized around a sequence of two, three, or four consonants called the root. It has long been known that certain combinations of consonants in the same root are avoided, although this matter was not investigated systematically until Greenberg (1950). Since then, other studies (McCarthy 1985, Mrayati 1987) have looked at the evidence with different lexical material and different statistical methods and have extended the results to other languages: Amharic (Bender and Fulass 1978), Hebrew (Koskinen 1964), Qafar (Hayward and Hayward 1989).

The basic observation is that consonants within the same root cannot be homorganic (with certain qualifications). In Arabic, roots rarely or never contain adjacent consonants from any of the following sets:

(4)   a. Labials = {f, b, m}
        b. Coronal sonorants = {l, r, n}
        c. Coronal stops = {t, d, T, D}
        d. Coronal fricatives = {θ, ð, s, z, S, Z, ʃ}
        e. Velars = {g, k, q}
        f. Gutturals = {χ, ʁ, ħ, ʕ, h, ʔ}

In addition to the classes in (4), there is considerable avoidance of roots that combine coronal stops and fricatives (Greenberg 1950, cf. Yip 1989) and, as we will see later (section 12.4), a significant patterning of the uvulars χ and ʁ with the velars as well as with the gutturals. The high glides w and j may also be subject to cooccurrence restrictions, but for other reasons this is difficult to establish.

Evidence in support of (4) is statistical rather than categorical. The table in figure 12.1 shows the number of roots combining adjacent consonants in

	bfm	td	TD	θδ	sz	SZ	ʃ	gk	q	χʁ	ʕħ	ʔh	lr	n	wj
bfm	0	76	57	24	68	28	32	43	43	31	79	44	180	40	91
td	68	4	0	2	9	0	6	17	11	10	32	21	69	20	51
TD	61	4	0	0	5	0	5	4	5	9	25	11	59	14	38
θδ	29	0	0	0	0	0	0	6	7	4	5	9	44	3	24
sz	87	17	7	0	0	0	0	31	20	19	40	24	75	21	65
SZ	52	15	0	0	0	0	0	1	5	4	16	7	38	5	24
ʃ	41	14	10	3	1	2	X	19	9	11	24	10	33	8	37
gk	75	33	2	16	46	4	11	1	0	1	29	24	90	29	47
q	51	19	19	7	11	15	10	0	X	0	22	6	45	12	31
χʁ	70	18	31	13	23	13	11	2	1	0	2	0	63	13	42
ʕħ	91	42	29	17	35	27	18	34	22	0	0	2	83	28	60
ʔh	67	32	10	10	29	4	8	25	6	3	2	2	65	16	54
lr	149	51	36	15	58	20	20	66	48	29	74	42	0	14	91
n	55	23	19	7	26	12	14	31	26	16	28	21	2	X	51
wj	83	44	31	14	44	14	18	34	33	20	49	29	89	26	21

Figure 12.1. Roots combining adjacent consonants.

the order row–column. For example, the root <u>ktb</u> is counted twice, in row <u>gk</u>, column <u>td</u>, and in row <u>td</u>, column <u>bfm</u>. Outlining and shading highlight cells with frequencies significantly lower than expected (shaded: $p < 0.05$; outlined: $p < 0.005$; χ^2 on 1 degree of freedom). Since Arabic independently disallows adjacent identical root consonants (McCarthy 1981, 1986), these combinations were not included in the computation of expected frequencies. Cells containing X have 0 frequency because of this prohibition on adjacent identical consonants. Similar observations can be made about nonadjacent root consonants (*k* and *b* in the root *ktb*), but the effects are not as robust.

Our particular concern, of course, is with the gutturals. Roots combining two gutturals are significantly infrequent. If gutturals freely combined in roots, we would expect to have 114 roots containing adjacent nonidentical gutturals, but in fact there are just 11. (For nonadjacent gutturals, the expected frequency is 79 and the observed frequency is 36.) Inspection of figure 12.1 shows that the whole guttural class defines a block of cells with 0 frequency, significantly low frequency, or both. Thus, this phenomenon requires reference to the gutturals as a natural class.

Formal accounts of the Semitic root cooccurrence restrictions and similar dissimilatory constraints begin with McCarthy (1985) and continue with Mester (1986), Yip (1989), Selkirk (1988), Dresher (1989), and Padgett (1991). The last three studies have most strongly influenced the refinements I offer here.

In the simplest case, that of the prohibition against a root containing two labials, we need to rule out hypothetical representations of a nonoccurring root like *<u>fbt</u>:

(5)

   a.   *[labial]   [coronal]

            f   b   t

   b. *[labial] [labial] [coronal]

            f   b   t

It is reasonable to suggest that the branching configuration in (5a) is ruled out universally from underlying representations; it can arise only in derived representations, through the application of Place Assimilation. This principle can be formulated as follows:

(6)   No-branching Condition

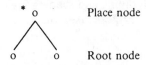

* o   Place node

o   o   Root node

The No-Branching Condition prohibits representations that contain a single Place node branching to two Root nodes. This constraint holds of underlying representation but is explicitly overridden by rules of Place Assimilation in Arabic and elsewhere.[9]

The other way to represent a prohibited root like f̱ḇt is (5b), with two instances of the feature [labial]. The impossibility of (5b) is determined by the Obligatory Contour Principle (Leben 1973; Goldsmith 1976; McCarthy 1981, 1986), formulated most generally as in (7):

(7)   Obligatory Contour Principle (OCP)
        Adjacent identical elements are prohibited.

The OCP functions categorically in Arabic phonology to exclude adjacent identical consonants within a root: thus, applied to entire segments, it absolutely prohibits roots like Cʕʕ or ʕʕC (McCarthy 1981, 1986).

Dresher (1989), Selkirk (1991), and Padgett (1991) have suggested that the scope or domain of the OCP can be limited by statements restricting its applicability to a particular feature in a particular context. Specifically, in the phonology of Arabic, the features [continuant] and [sonorant] define separate domains of cooccurrence for [coronal]:

(8)   Domain of the OCP

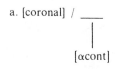

a. [coronal] / ____
   |
   [αcont]

b. [coronal] / ____
   |
   [αson]

The first restriction on the scope of the OCP is not absolute, since there is a weaker prohibition on roots containing two coronals that differ in [continuant].[10]

Subject to these qualifications, the system described will mark as ill-formed any root containing two homorganic consonants. The system, via the OCP and (6), refers to [pharyngeal] as well as the familiar Place features [labial], [coronal], and [dorsal]. In this respect, the feature defining the guttural class functions like all other features characterizing a place of articulation or active articulator.

12.3.2 Vowel lowering in guttural context

In the basic derivational class of the Arabic verb, perfect and imperfect verbs alternate in the quality of the thematic vowel, the last vowel of the stem: *katab* "wrote," *jaktub* "writes." Roots are assigned to one of five Ablaut classes according to which thematic vowels they have in the perfect and imperfect. The chart in example 9 gives the frequency of the five types, based on all relevant verbs (including doublets) occurring in Wehr (1971). Membership in the u/u class is semantically determined; all u/u verbs are statives. The i/a class is often intransitive or stative, but not invariably so. Membership in classes a/u or a/i is entirely unpredictable – that is, it must be specified for each lexical item.[11]

(9)

Ablaut class	Example		Frequency
a/u	katab/jaktub	"write"	1029
a/i	Darab/jaDrib	"beat"	842
i/a	ʃarib/jaʃrab	"drink"	518
a/a	faʕal/jafʕal	"do"	436
u/u	balud/jablud	"be stupid"	191

Membership in the a/a Ablaut class, though, is phonologically conditioned. Of the 436 a/a verbs, 411 contain a guttural consonant adjacent to the imperfect thematic vowel a. Examples include verbs like *faʕal/jafʕal* "do" with the guttural preceding the ablauting vowel and verbs like *radaʕ/jardaʕ* "prevent" with the guttural following the ablauting vowel. The thematic vowel a replaces u or i, which are not usually found in the imperfect of guttural roots.

The lowering of the thematic vowel under adjacency to a guttural is paralleled by raising triggered by a high glide w or j. An examination of roots containing both a guttural and a high glide shows that the high glide prevails in case of conflict. There is, then, a rule raising vowels near high glides that undoes the effect of lowering next to a guttural.

Besides this pattern, there is a significant residue of 118 guttural verbs that do not evidence lowering, although about half (55) have lowering as a variant pronunciation. Curiously, the uvular gutturals are represented disproportionately among these exceptions: see example 10. That is, there are about twice as many exceptions to Guttural Lowering among the uvulars as there are among the pharyngeals, though the laryngeals and pharyngeals clearly pattern alike. This is perhaps related to the fact that the uvular gutturals have some of the characteristics of complex segments, with simultaneous [pharyngeal] and [dorsal] specifications (see section 12.4).

(10)	Guttural	Frequency in root II/III	Number of exceptions	Ratio
	ʔ	114	6	0.05
	h	138	21	0.15
	ʕ	234	30	0.13
	ħ	183	30	0.16
	ʁ	66	20	0.30
	χ	85	31	0.36

We have now established an accurate descriptive generalization and so we can consider how to formulate the rule. The central question is why gutturals have a lowering effect on vowels. There is abundant phonetic evidence that low vowels involve some pharyngeal constriction (Delattre 1971; Perkell 1971; Wood 1979), with concomitant acoustic similarities between a and the gutturals (high F_1). Clearly, this requires that [pharyngeal] be assigned to low vowels as well as guttural consonants. This is close to the position in Chomsky and Halle (1968), where low vowels, phayngeals, and laryngeals are all [+low]. It is also the view taken by Perkell (1971), based on Halle and Stevens (1969), where low vowels and pharyngeal consonants are marked [Constricted Pharynx] (cf. Kiparsky 1974). Recent work by Van der Hulst (1988), Hayward and Hayward (1989), Gorecka (1989), Lowenstamm and Prunet (1989), Prunet (1990), Herzallah (1990), and Selkirk (1991) further pursues this and related ideas.

Within this theory, the rule of Guttural Lowering will be formulated as follows (I use "C" and "V" to stand for the Root nodes of consonants and vowels):

(11)   Arabic Guttural Lowering (final version)

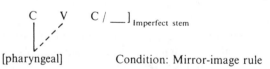

[pharyngeal]   Condition: Mirror-image rule

That is, [pharyngeal] spreads from any guttural to the adjacent thematic vowel, changing it to a. This is essentially the form of Guttural Lowering in Herzallah (1990), who further develops the analysis of this phenomenon in McCarthy (1989). This account raises further questions about the nature of vowel-height distinctions, but we cannot pursue those here.

Two other examples of guttural lowering come from Tiberian Hebrew, one of the pronunciation traditions for Biblical Hebrew. There is a considerable literature on Hebrew phonology, including in particular Prince

(1975), Malone (1984), and McCarthy (1979). The overall structure of the analysis is drawn from these works without special attribution; when a particular insight is important, though, I have attempted to note its source.[12]

One of the central problems in Hebrew phonology is the treatment of schwa. The Tiberian vocalization system represents four types of schwa: a-colored ǎ, e-colored ĕ, o-colored ŏ, and neutral or plain ə. The colored schwas are often associated with guttural contexts, and so they will be our focus below.

The rule of Vowel Reduction, which affects short unstressed vowels in open syllables, is a major source of schwas in the language. One of many places where Vowel Reduction occurs is the initial syllable of the plural nouns in (12a); compare the same syllable in the guttural-initial nouns of (12b).

(12)   *Singular*   *Plural*
       a. Plain-initial nouns
       melek   məla:ki:m   "king"
       qeber   qəba:ri:m   "grave"
       se:per   səpa:ri:m   "book"
       qo:deʃ   qŏda:ʃi:m   "holiness"

       b. Guttural-initial nouns
       ʔeben   ʔǎba:ni:m   "stone"
       hebel   hǎba:li:m   "vapor"
       ħeder   ħǎda:ri:m   "room"
       ʕe:der   ʕǎda:ri:m   "flock"
       ħo:deʃ   ħŏda:ʃi:m   "month"

Rounding of the stem vowel *o* persists under reduction, usually with an initial guttural and less regularly otherwise. Apart from that, the consistent picture is one where gutturals are followed by a-colored schwa, while nongutturals are followed by plain schwa. This is a pervasive regularity of the language, so much so that plain schwa is never found after a guttural (in a search of the whole Pentateuch). Schwa *before* a guttural is not affected: compare the singular/plural pair *baʕal/bəʕa:li:m* "master".[13]

A second source of schwas in Hebrew is epenthesis into unsyllabifiable consonant clusters. Hebrew has many surface CVCVC nouns with penult stress. Since penult stress is otherwise impossible in consonant-final words, these nouns are analyzed as underlying /CVCC/ with stress and epenthesis applied in that order. The epenthesis rule is responsible for alternations like those in (13). The underlined vowel in (13) is epenthetic, and from (13b) it is clear that this vowel is lowered by a preceding guttural.

(13)   *Underlying*   *Singular*

a. Plain roots

/malk/	melek	"king/my king"
/sipr/	se:per	"book"
/qudʃ/	qo:deʃ	"holiness"

b. Medial guttural roots

/baʕl/	baʕal	"master"
/kaħʃ/	kaħaʃ	"lying"
/lahb/	lahab	"flame"
/tuʔr/	toʔar	"form/his form"

Prince (1975) and Garr (1989) argue that the epenthetic vowel in (13) is actually schwa, so (13b) evidences the same guttural lowering rule as (12). The argument for epenthesis of ə rests on a central distributional fact of Hebrew: the reduced vowels ə, ă, ĕ, and ŏ never occur in closed syllables. This distributional evidence is supported by the alternation in (14a).

(14)   a. /dabar/ da:ba:r dəbar   dibre: "word/word of/words of"
         b. /ħakam/ ħa:ka:m ħăkam   ħakme: "wise/wise of/wise (pl.) of"

The intermediate representation *dəbəre:* loses the second of two adjacent schwas by a separate rule, yielding *dəbre*: The realization of schwa in this nonfinal closed syllable is i. The choice between the e realization of schwa in *melek* and i realization of schwa in *dibre*: reflects another general distributional fact of the language: i never occurs in closed final syllables and e never occurs in closed medial syllables.[14]

We can now return to the behavior of medial guttural roots in (13b). We know from the previous discussion that Hebrew has a rule lowering schwa to ă after a guttural (12b). The epenthetic schwa of medial guttural roots like *baʔal* (from /baʔəl/) behaves in exactly that way. Its realization is the full vowel a rather than a the reduced vowel ă for prosodic reasons – because the syllable is closed (compare (14b)). The rule of Guttural Lowering in Hebrew affects only a guttural + schwa sequence in that order:

(15)   Hebrew Guttural Lowering I

[pharyngeal]   Condition: Feature-filling

The intent of the condition restricting (15) to feature-filling applications is to block the rule from lowering any vowel other than the featureless vowel schwa.

Hebrew has another rule of vowel lowering induced by gutturals, but in this case the guttural must follow the affected vowel. Nouns of the same type as (13) but with final gutturals are exemplified in (16):

(16) /zarʕ/ zera̱ʕ zarʕi: "seed/my seed"
     /miSħ/ me:Sa̱ħ miSħo: "brow/his brow"
     /ʔurħ/ ʔo:ra̱ħ ʔorħi: "way"
     /gubh/ go:ba̱h gobho: "height"

The underlined vowel in (16) has been lowered under the influence of the following guttural. Final ʔ deletes after triggering epenthesis but before lowering: /palʔ/ → pele "wonder."

Is this phenomenon an indication that (15) should be a mirror-image rule or is it the result of a distinct process? There are two arguments for the latter. First, lowering in final guttural words like zeraʕ must apply later in the derivation than lowering in medial guttural words like baʕal. The reason has to do with the vowel of the first syllable, in both cases derived from underlying /a/. In zeraʔ, this vowel has umlauted to e, like melek, but unlike baʕal. Therefore lowering in baʕal must precede umlauting, but lowering in zeraʕ must follow umlauting (Malone 1984).

Besides this difference in ordering, a more significant indication that preguttural lowering is a distinct rule from (15) is that preguttural lowering affects not only schwa, but any vowel before a tautosyllabic root-final guttural (Malone 1978); see (17).

(17)   *Underlying*   *Surface*   *Compare*
     a.

| /ʃameʕ/ | ʃa:maʕ | ʃa:me:ʕu: | "he heard/they heard" |
| /gaboh/ | gəbah | gəbo:hi:m | "high of/high (pl.)" |

     b.

/mo:ħ/	moaħ		"marrow"
/no:h/	noah		"eminency"
/ru:ħ/	ruaħ	ru:ħi:	"spirit/my spirit"
/ʃu:ʕ/	ʃuaʕ		"cry"
/Ti:ħ/	Tiaħ		"coating"
/s'ameħ/	s'a:meaħ	s'əme:ħi:m	"glad/pl."

There are sporadic examples of (17a) with etymologic *r as the trigger. Accepting Malone's interpretation of the orthography for (17b), we can see that any short vowel and the second mora of a long vowel are lowered by a following tautosyllabic guttural (stem-finally). This feature-changing process is clearly distinct from the feature-filling guttural assimilation rule (15), and so it requires a different formulation:

(18)   Hebrew Guttural Lowering II

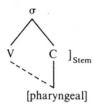

[pharyngeal]

This rule affects an entire short vowel (17a) but only the second mora of a long vowel (17b).

In a completely separate historical development, Bedouin Arabic also has a fully productive rule lowering a vowel after a guttural consonant. This process is documented in treatments of various Bedouin dialects, including Johnstone (1967), Abboud (1979), Al-Mozainy (1981), Prochazka (1988), Irshied and Kenstowicz (1984), and Irshied (1984). The data here come from the 'Anaiza (Saudi Arabia) dialect described by Johnstone, who provides the most extensive exemplification.

This language has a pervasive rule of vowel raising, which applies to any short a̲ in an open syllable:

(19)   Raising

$$a \rightarrow i \ / \ C \_\_]_\sigma$$

Raising is responsible for alternations in paradigms like (20).

(20)   a. /katab/   ki̲tab   "he wrote"
          /katabat/   kti̲bat   "she wrote"
        b. /samiʕ/   si̲miʕ   "he heard"
          /samiʕat/   samʕat   "she heard"
        c. /dʒamal/   dʒi̲mal   "camel"
          /dʒamaluh/   dʒmi̲luh   "his camel"
        d. /bagar/   bi̲gar   "cows"
          /bagarah/   bgi̲rih   "a cow"

Since Bedouin Arabic has only a very limited distinction between short i̲ and u̲, the output of Raising is quite variable and dependent on consonantal context, ranging from u̲ or ʉ in some labial contexts to i̲ in emphatic contexts to i̲ elsewhere.

There are, however, various circumstances where Raising is systematically blocked or undone, so that a short a̲ does occur in an open syllable. Of these, the relevant one is after a guttural (21). Vowels before short *i* are raised even when a guttural precedes (*ʁi̲ðib* "he got angry," *ʕiTiʃ* "he became thirsty"), but this is caused by a different rule that is not our concern here. There is striking support for Raising and Guttural Lowering

(21) ?akal   "he ate"   habaT   "It became flat (hair)"
                                   had3iin   type of camel
      ʕazam   "he invited"   ħamal   "he carried"
      ʕasiib   "palm leaf"   ʕariim   "women"
      baaʕatuh "she sold it"   ħasuud   "envious"
      ʁaSab   "he forced"   χazan   "he stored"
      ʁariib   "strange"   χasiis   "bad (person)"
      bʁatuh   "she wanted him" taχχatuh   "she hit him"
      ʁayuur   "jealous"   χaluuf   type of she-camel
      ʁabuug   "evening milk"

from a secret language that permutes the root consonants (Al-Mozainy 1981). In this secret language, Raising applies or not, exactly as expected:

(22) *Normal form*   *Secret-language forms*
      difaʕ "he pushed"   fidaʕ
                           ʕadaf

Raising and Guttural Lowering are productive rules of the lexical phonology of Bedouin Arabic, applicable in secret-language forms and in loans.

These various rules do not exhaust the Semitic evidence of a strong preference for low vowels in guttural contexts. For example, the epenthetic vowel in Lebanese Arabic (Haddad 1984: 46), normally i̱, is realized as a̱ when adjacent to a guttural: *bala̱ʕ* "swallowing," *ʃi̱ʕar* "poetry," *dʒara̱ħ* "wounding." Hayward and Hayward (1989) observe that in many Ethiopian Semitic languages (Tigrinya, Harari, Gafat, Amharic) the opposition between mid and low central vowel phonemes is neutralized to low when tautosyllabic with a guttural. Outside Semitic, a connection between low vowels and laryngeal or other guttural consonants has been observed in the Cushitic language D'opaasunte (Hayward and Hayward 1989), the Chadic language Kera (Odden 1988), the Athabaskan language Carrier (Prunet 1990), and the Tsimshian language Nisgha (Shaw 1987).

In sum, the material shows that, with respect to vowel lowering, all three guttural types – uvular, pharyngeal, and laryngeal – behave alike. The core result, of course, is that all these generalizations require that we identify the gutturals as a natural class.

12.3.3 Avoidance of syllable-final gutturals

An equally robust but somewhat more puzzling phenomenon is a prohibition on guttural codas. In a typical case, a CVGCV sequence, where G is a guttural, becomes a CVGVCV by epenthesis, so that the guttural becomes the onset of a new syllable and is shifted out of coda position.

One case of this sort is found in various Bedouin Arabic dialects (Mitchell 1960; Johnstone 1967; Blanc 1970; Abboud 1979; Al-Mozainy 1981; Irshied 1984). Blanc dubs it the *gaháwah* syndrome after the word "coffee," an example of the phenomenon.

In Negev Bedouin Arabic (Blanc 1970), CaGCVC, where G is a guttural, becomes CaGaCVC. Compare the plain and guttural roots in (23).

(23)

	Plain roots		Guttural roots
jaʃrab	"he drinks"	jahard3	"he speaks"
aʃrab	"I drink"	aħalam	"I dream"
		aʕarf	"I know"
		aχabar	"I know"
taʃrab	"you drink"	taħalam	"you dream"
		taʕarf	"you know"
		taχabar	"you know"
bnaʃrab	"we drink"	bnaʁazil	"we spin"

Apparently this dialect has lost ʔ altogether, though other Bedouin dialects have retained ʔ in some contexts (but not syllable-finally). As in Hebrew, there is no epenthesis after word-final or stem-final gutturals: *rawwaħ/rawwaħna* "he/we went home"; *balaħ* "dates," *manaʕ* "he prohibits," *difaʕna* "we pushed." This follows if stem-final consonants are extrasyllabic and so not subject to a requirement imposed on codas.[15]

In Al-Mozainy's (1981) Bedouin Hijazi dialect, words like *gaháwah* undergo a further transformation to emerge as *gháwa* (24).

(24)

Plain root	Guttural roots
Color adjectives	
sawda 'black'	bʁaθa "gray"
	dhama "dark red"
Verb form X	
ʔistaslam "he surrendered"	ʔistʕazal "he got in a hurry"
	ʔisʁafar "he asked forgiveness"
Form I passive participle	
maktuub "written"	mχaSuur "neglected"
	mʕazuum "invited"
	mħazuum "tied"
	mʕaðuur "excused"
Form I imperfect	
jaʃrab "he drinks"	jχadim "he serves"
	jħakim "he governs"

The Hijazi forms in (24) undergo an additional rule (called Elision by Irshied and Kenstowicz, 1984, who provide a convincing rationale for it) that deletes a̲ in a ＿CVCV context. Elision applies to the output of postguttural epenthesis (Abboud 1979: 471; Al-Mozainy 1981: 172), so the derivation proceeds: /jaχdim/ → /jaχadim/ → *jχadim* "he serves."[16]

Postguttural epenthesis is restricted to syllables containing the vowel a̲. With syllables containing a high vowel preceding the guttural, there is no epenthesis: *tiħtirim/tiħtarmih* "she respects/she respects him" (Al-Mozainy 1981: 238). Thus, the descriptive generalization is that syllable-final gutturals are prohibited just in case the preceding vowel is a̲. Formally, we require a well-formedness condition something like the following:

(25)   Bedouin Arabic Syllabic Co-occurrence Condition

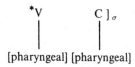

The condition on the preceding vowel is a kind of OCP-triggered dissimilation, prohibiting two [pharyngeal]s within the rhyme domain of the syllable. Like guttural lowering, this phenomenon shows both the need for a guttural class and a similarity between gutturals and low vowels.

Hebrew, though, prohibits guttural codas regardless of the preceding vowel, also resolving them by epenthesis (26). In some words ʔ is lost syllable-finally, so epenthesis does not happen. The process is subject to exceptions and some other complications (cf. Malone 1984: 94).

(26) *a. Plain roots*
     jikto:b   "he will write"
     hiʃmi:d   "he annihilated"
     huʃlak   "he was thrown"

    b. Guttural roots
     jaʕămo:d   "he will stand"
     jeħĕzaq   "he is strong"
     jahăpo:k   "he will turn"
     jeʔĕso:p   "he will gather"
     heʕĕmi:d   "he made stand"
     heħĕzi:q   "he strengthened"
     joʕŏmad   "he is made to stand"

The quality of the inserted schwa in (26b) is obviously determined by the quality of the preceding vowel; I deal with this matter elsewhere (McCarthy forthcoming). The fact that a schwa rather than a full vowel is inserted is typical of Hebrew (see section 12.3.2). Therefore, the only real issue is that of prohibiting syllable-final gutturals, which we can accomplish by the following coda condition (cf. Itô 1986, 1989):

(27)   Hebrew Coda Condition

[pharyngeal]

This constraint simply marks as ill-formed any syllable with a guttural coda. Epenthesis repairs violations of the Coda Condition (27) by inserting schwa, which then harmonizes with the preceding vowel across the intervening guttural. The Coda Condition does not affect word-final or even stem-final gutturals: *ʃaːmaʕ* "he heard," *ʃaːlaħtiː* "I sent," *jədaʕtem* "you knew," *jədaʕtiːka* "I knew you" (but 1st pl. *jədaʕănuːka* "we know you"). This follows, as in Bedouin Arabic, if we suppose that stem-final consonants are extrasyllabic and hence not subject to the Coda Condition.

An examination of Tigre (Ethiopian Semitic) verb paradigms shows virtually the same rule in that language (28). The Tigre gutturals are the same as those of Hebrew (but see section 12.5). In the published material on Tigre (Leslau 1945; Palmer 1956, 1962; Raz 1983), I have not located a plain statement of the generality of this phenomenon or the further deletion in the second two examples. Nevertheless, it seems quite clear that there is a process inserting a copy of the preceding vowel after any syllable-final (but not word-final) guttural.

(28)   *Plain roots*   *Guttural roots*
       təqnaʃ   "you get up"   təħəsab   "you wash"
       qanʃa   "he got up"   ʃaʕana   "he loaded"
       qanaʃko   "I got up"   balʕako   "I ate"
       ləqanʃo   "they get up"   ləʃʕano   "they load"

To sum up, the class of gutturals, defined by the feature [pharyngeal], is required to characterize the consonants prohibited in stem-medial coda position in Hebrew and Tigre. Bedouin Arabic also prohibits gutturals in the coda, but only after a low vowel, perhaps as a kind of dissimilation.

12.3.4. Guttural degemination

Hebrew and Tigre also exhibit a prohibition on geminate gutturals, a phenomenon that is perhaps to be related to (27). In Hebrew, geminate gutturals are simplified without exception. This is clear from a comparison of plain and guttural roots in examples like (29). Discussions of this phenomenon appear in Prince (1975: 219–220), Malone (1978, 1984: 79), and Lowenstamm and Kaye (1986). Guttural degemination itself is straightforward, though the compensatory lengthening seen in the cited examples does not always occur (cf. Prince 1975).[17]

(29)

	Plain root		Guttural roots	
	dibbe:r	"he said"	me:ʔe:n	"he refused"
	/jinte:/→jitte:n	"he gives"	/jinħat/→je:ħat	"he marches down"
	dalli:m	"weak ones"	ra:ʕi:m	"evil ones"

Likewise in Tigre (Leslau 1945, Palmer 1956, 1962, Raz 1983), gutturals are degeminated. Compare the following plain and guttural roots:

(30)

	təqarraʧa	"he was cut off"	təbaʔasa	"he quarreled"
	ləqannəS	"he gets up"	ləSʕən	"he loads"

Raz and Leslau describe dialects where the high glides w̲ and j̲ are also degeminated, but this is not true in Palmer's material. Thus, it seems appropriate to see the degemination of gutturals and of high glides as two separate generalizations.

It is straightforward to write a rule simplifying geminate gutturals or prohibiting their creation. Something like the following would do and would accord with the fact that languages frequently impose conditions on which geminates are licit.

(31)   Guttural Degemination

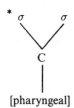

[pharyngeal]

Violations of this constraint are repaired in the most straightforward way, by delinking and compensatory lengthening.

Guttural Degemination may be related to the Coda Condition in both Hebrew and Tigre. If gutturals are prohibited in syllable codas, then they cannot be geminated either, since the left branch of a geminate is necessarily a coda. Although this move is appealing, it does lead to a significant conflict with Itô's (1986) results about the applicability of the Linking Condition (Hayes 1986) to coda conditions like (27). Itô shows that geminates constitute a systematic exception to coda conditions in other languages. Until this conflict is resolved, Guttural Degemination and the Coda

Condition should be regarded as separate pieces of evidence for the natural class of gutturals.

12.3.5 Interim summary

The evidence presented establishes the existence of a natural class of gutturals and thus provides direct support for the claims about the feature [pharyngeal]. The evidence meets the various criteria established at the outset. First, it involves robust, well-attested phenomena that come from historically independent innovations of different languages within the Semitic family. Second, the evidence is entirely synchronic rather than historical. Third, the evidence comes from several different types of processes: root co-occurrence restrictions, vowel lowering, and conditions on syllable position and gemination. Fourth, the evidence comes from all levels of representation, not just deep morphophonemics and not just the surface.

12.4 Pharyngeals and pharyngealization

Thus far we have discussed only the guttural consonants. The goal of this section is to provide some initial suggestions about how to integrate the pharyngealized sounds – the coronal emphatics and q – into the analysis. The phonetic and phonological evidence shows that the pharyngealized consonants share the feature [pharyngeal] with gutturals, although they also have a primary oral articulation.

In addition to the gutturals, the Semitic languages have a class of sounds called emphatics, with what is traditionally regarded as a secondary pharyngeal constriction. In Standard Arabic, the emphatics include the coronal fricatives S̱ and Ẕ (the latter often interdental), the coronal stops Ṯ and Ḏ, and the uvular stop q. The coronals contrast with corresponding nonemphatics s̱, ẕ/ð, ṯ, and ḏ, while q contrasts with the velar stop ḵ. Other Semitic languages have a subset of the Standard Arabic emphatics, and in South Semitic languages like Tigre the emphatics are realized phonetically as ejectives.

Ghazeli's (1977) x-ray study deals with the emphatics of Tunisian Arabic in great detail. His observations about the coronal emphatics are confirmed elsewhere in the literature (by Ali and Daniloff 1972; Al-Ani 1970; and Bukshaisha 1985), and his observations about the uvular stop q are confirmed by Delattre (1971). Despite differences in details, the overall picture is consistent: the emphatics and q have a constriction in the upper pharynx similar to that of the uvular gutturals χ and ʁ. Although there are suggestions (Keating 1988) that Arabic dialects differ in the location of the secondary constriction of emphatics (with some showing a low, ʕ-like constriction), this does not seem to be true; all studies, now encompassing several different dialect areas, find that the emphatics have a constriction in the upper pharynx. The so-called pharyngealized consonants of Arabic should really be called uvularized.

The phonetic evidence establishes important points of similarity between the gutturals and the emphatics. Broadly, the gutturals and the emphatics share constriction in the pharynx, and narrowly, the uvular gutturals share with *q* and the coronal emphatics a constriction in the oropharynx produced by raising and retracting the tongue body. We expect to find two principal types of phonological patterning corresponding to these phonetic resemblances: a class of primary and secondary [pharyngeal] sounds, including gutturals, q̱, and emphatics; and a class of sounds with [pharyngeal] constriction produced by the [dorsal] articulator, including uvular gutturals, q̱, and emphatics.

A striking example of the first type of phonological patterning comes from Herzallah's (1990) analysis of *'imāla* (raising/fronting) of the feminine suffix. In many Eastern Arabic dialects, the feminine suffix, historically -a̱, appears as -e̱ or -i̱ except when preceded by a [pharyngeal] consonant. The data in (32) come from Syrian Arabic (Cowell 1964: 138; Grotzfeld 1965: 45).

(32) *a.* daraže   "step"   kbi:re   "large"
          madrase   "school"   ʃərke   "society"
          χafi:fe   "light"

      b. ʔəSSa   "story"   ʕari:Da   "broad"
          χayya:Ta "seamstress"   ba:jZa   "foul"
          Tabχa   "cooking"   dagga:ʁa "tanning"
          mni:ħa   "good"   wa:žha   "display"
          Sanʕa   "handwork"   χərʔa   "rag"

In dialects that have retained q̱, it too patterns with the consonants in (32b), as does ṟ when it is emphatic. Some dialects distribute the allomorphs of this suffix according to different principles and some have *'imāla* everywhere, but the pattern in (32) is probably the most widespread.

The synchronic underlying representation of the feminine suffix is a non-low vowel e̱ or i̱, with the examples in (32b) derived by lowering this vowel to a̱ after any [pharyngeal] consonant. This lowering rule can be stated as follows, essentially following Herzallah (1990: 138):

(33)   Feminine Suffix Lowering

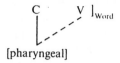

[pharyngeal]

This process is similar to Guttural Lowering (section 12.3.2), but it is triggered by any [pharyngeal] consonant, not just a guttural.

Other evidence of the emphatic/guttural connection comes from historical changes in which an emphatic lost its primary place of articulation to become a guttural. Two independent historical changes of this sort have occurred in Semitic (Blake 1946: 214). First, some Ugaritic words have ʁ for original Z̲: compare Arabic *nZr* with Ugaritic *nʁr* "guard." Second, original D̲ became ʕ in Aramaic; compare Arabic *ʔarD* with Aramaic *ʔăraʕ* "earth." In these cases, then, the primary [coronal] articulation is lost, thereby promoting the secondary [pharyngeal] one. The parallel to sound changes like $^*k^w > p$ in the history of Greek is obvious.[18]

The other phonological class expected on phonetic grounds is defined by oropharyngeal constriction – that is, consonants that are both [dorsal] and [pharyngeal], including the emphatics (S̲, Z̲, T̲, and D̲) and the uvulars (q, χ, and ʁ). Since the definition of this class requires reference to the redundant [dorsal] specification of the coronal emphatics, it should only be relevant in relatively late rules, after default [dorsal] has been filled in. That seems to be the case.

This class plays a role in the complex phenomenon of backing or emphasis spread in Arabic. Perhaps the earliest description of this comes from Sibawayh (quoted in Younes 1982: 82): "The back variant [of a̲] occurs, that is the low vowel is not fronted, when it derives from underlying w̲ (or u̲u̲) and when immediately preceded or followed by one of the following consonants: S̲, Z̲, T̲, D̲, ʁ, χ, q, and r̲." Since r̲ is contextually emphatic, in our terms this is the class of dorso-pharyngeals. Herzallah (1990: 181) describes a similar process in Palestinian Arabic, which derives the imperfect theme vowel u̲ from i̲ adjacent to a coronal emphatic or uvular, as spreading of [dorsal]. But there are many additional complications, and a full discussion of emphasis spread in Arabic dialects would require a monograph rather than these few lines.

Another phonological class we would expect to find on phonetic grounds is the set of underlying [dorsal] consonants: the velars and uvulars k̲, g̲, q̲, χ, and ʁ. In Moroccan Arabic (Ahmed Alaoui p.c.; Heath 1987: 254), consonant labialization, realized as rounding on a following schwa, is restricted to the dorsals. The following imperative verbs exemplify this:

(34)   Moroccan Labialization

dχ^wəl   "come in!"
nʁ^wəZ   "prick!"
nq^wəZ   "copy down!"
rg^wəd   "sleep"
nk^wər   "deny!"

Labialization is not permitted with other consonants, oral or guttural: *ktəb* "write!", *nʕəs* "sleep!." Formally, this means that the marking conditions that describe the Moroccan Arabic consonants system must contain a statement like [+ round] → [dorsal].

Even more striking evidence for the underlying [dorsal] class comes from an additional property of the system of root-co-occurrence restrictions in Arabic. Recall from section 12.3.1 that Arabic prohibits (with exceptions) roots containing two consonants from the set (g, k, q) and roots containing two consonants from the set (χ, ʁ, ħ, ʕ, h, ʔ). The first set is actually incomplete, though; it should include the uvular gutturals χ and ʁ as well. This patterning of the uvular continuants with both the gutturals and the dorsals is apparent from the statistical evidence in figure 12.1.

This final observation about the dual patterning of χ and ʁ in the system of root co-occurrence restrictions provides the strongest indication that the uvular gutturals are complex segments, bearing simultaneous specifications for [dorsal] and [pharyngeal]. The coronal emphatics and q are also complex segments, with both oral and pharyngeal articulations. Under standard feature-geometry assumptions (Clements 1985; Sagey 1986; McCarthy 1988), the various types of consonants are represented approximately as follows:

(35)   a. Low gutturals ʔhħʕ   b. Uvular gutturals χʁ

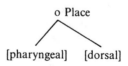

    c. Coronal emphatics TDSZ   d. Uvular stop q

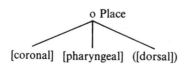   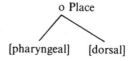

Here, the redundant [dorsal] specification of the coronal emphatics is parenthesized to indicate that it is not present in underlying representation.

This proposal resolves the issue of phonetic and phonological connections between emphatics and gutturals, but it raises another question of how to tell them apart phonologically. In particular, how is the true guttural class referred to in the rules developed in section 12.3, and how are the uvular gutturals distinguished from the uvular stop?[19]

Although more elaborate accounts based on the distinction between primary and secondary articulations are possible and may be correct (McCarthy 1991b; Herzallah 1990), the most straightforward answer to these questions relies on the observation, noted originally in section 12.2.1, that the gutturals are approximants but the emphatics and q are not. Thus, the guttural class is defined by the conjunction of the place feature [pharyngeal] and the major class feature [approximant]. This makes good sense of the evidence for the guttural class: the root co-occurrence restrictions are known independently to refer to another major class feature, [sonorant], to distinguish between the coronal sonorants and obstruents; guttural lowering is typical of the robust effect that approximants have on the quality of adjacent vowels; and rules specifying possible codas or geminates must often refer to major class features. The proposal in (35), then, makes the necessary distinctions while also defining the right natural classes of guttural and pharyngealized consonants.

12.5 Conclusion

The major observation of this paper is that the gutturals of Semitic constitute a natural class. The major thesis is that sounds are classified by place of articulation as well as articulator. In particular, there is a [pharyngeal] place of articulation, referring to the region from oropharynx to larynx inclusive. Furthermore, I have argued that this region in the articulatory space makes sense under Perkell's (1980) characterization of features as "orosensory targets," given what is known about the different distribution of sensory nerves in the vocal tract.

The principal source of evidence for this claim is the synchronic phonology of the Semitic languages, with occasional forays into diachrony and Afro-Asiatic. I have comprehensively treated the recurrent phonological phenomena of Semitic involving the gutturals. I have also extended the results in a less comprehensive way to the pharyngealized consonants.

It is customary to conclude a work like this by raising questions for further research. There are many, but two are particularly pressing. The first involves the locus of [pharyngeal] in an overall model of feature geometry along the lines of Clements (1985), Sagey (1986), and McCarthy (1988).

Because of space limitations, I can only sketch the answer to that question here. In McCarthy (forthcoming), I argue that there is a division between Oral and [pharyngeal] place-of-articulation features:

(36)

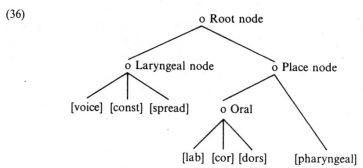

The claim is that [pharyngeal] can, but need not, pattern phonologically with the other place features [labial], [coronal], and [dorsal].

From a phonetic point of view, this model is quite plausible. The feature [pharyngeal] is defined in terms of a region of the vocal tract (the pharynx) and a particular spectral property (high F_1), two characteristics that are basically what we expect of Place features. At the same time, this model makes sense of the asymmetry (noted in section 12.2.3) between the anterior part of the vocal tract, which is organized in terms of active articulator, and the posterior part, which is organized in terms of place of articulation.

Phonological evidence for (36) comes principally from two partly conflicting descriptive requirements. On the one hand, the system of root co-occurrence restrictions in Semitic (section 12.3.1), which is based on prohibiting two homorganic consonants within a root, treats [pharyngeal] exactly on a par with the other Place features [labial], [coronal], and [dorsal]. On the other hand, there is a class of vowel–vowel assimilation rules, documented in McCarthy (forthcoming), to which Oral consonants are opaque and [pharyngeal] ones are transparent. In connection with other assumptions about transparency effects (Steriade 1987), this evidence shows the need for a separation between [pharyngeal] and the oral place features.

A very different sort of question concerns the laryngeals ʔ and ḥ. Although their behavior as part of the guttural class securely establishes that they have a place of articulation in many Semitic languages, the laryngeals have usually been regarded as placeless within recent phonological work (Clements 1985; Sagey 1986; Hayes 1986; Steriade 1987). This ambiguity in the treatment of laryngeal consonants is not a special problem of Semitic. Hayward and Hayward (1989: 186) comment on it, and witness Catford (1977: 104) in a discussion of glottal stops: "complete closure of the glottis has either an initiatory or an articulatory function: the former in phonationless glottalic initiation and the latter in glottal stop as an articulatory type functionally parallel in languages to other kinds of stop articulation." Merlingen (1977: 205–206) finds even more types of *h* based on phonological patterning, though not all of the evidence is persuasive.

Even within Semitic, there is one compelling case where the laryngeals ʔ and ħ do not pattern as gutturals. In Tigre (Leslau 1945: 155–157; Raz 1983:5), ʔ and ʕ are in free variation in words that contain an emphatic (T, Tʃ, S, q) or pharyngeal (ħ, ʕ): *ʔaddəħa* ~ *ʕaddəħa* "noon," *ʔarqaj* ~ *ʕarqaj* "bed," *ʔaTaːl* ~ *ʕaTaːl* "goats." In other words, the ʔ/ʕ distinction is neutralized in a context that includes true pharyngeals and emphatics but not laryngeals. (Tigre has no uvular gutturals.) The most natural interpretation of this process is spreading of [pharyngeal] to ʔ, changing it to ʕ. But of course this requires that ʔ not be [pharyngeal] to start with.[20]

Further evidence from Tigre supports this view. The vowels ɐ and a are in complementary distribution: a is always followed or immediately preceded by an emphatic or a true pharyngeal (but not a laryngeal), while ɐ never occurs in that context (Palmer 1956: 569; Lowenstamm and Prunet 1989):

(37) a. ʃənaT   "haversack"
         warəq   "gold"
         faraʕ   "clan"
         warəħ   "month"

      b. fɐrɐs   "horse"
         dʒɐhɐt   "direction"

Lowenstamm and Prunet analyze this as a case of vowel lowering in the context of a [pharyngeal] consonant (therefore comparable to (33) above). But this analysis presupposes that Tigre ʔ and ħ are not [pharyngeal] (cf. *dʒɐhɐt* in (37b)). Moreover, the rules referring to the guttural class in Tigre – prohibitions on syllable-final and geminate gutturals (sections 12.3.3 and 12.3.4) – can be recast as positive conditions requiring codas and geminates to have the Oral node of (36) rather than as negative conditions referring to the class of gutturals.

It seems, then, that the laryngeal consonants of Arabic and Tigre are different phonologically: in the former, but not the latter, the laryngeals are specified as [pharyngeal] and so belong to the guttural class. It is, of course, easy to set up such a phonological distinction but quite hard to find a phonetic basis for it. The most attractive proposal is Hess's (1990) suggestion that Arabic ʔ is actually not a true glottal stop at all, but an aryepiglottic one. Hess finds support for this conjecture in one x-ray of ʔ (from Boff Dkhissi 1983) which shows an apparently protruding epiglottis. But there are several problems with this claim. First, as Hess notes, the position of the epiglottis in this token of ʔ might just be its resting state for this particular speaker. Second, the context (saʔala "he asked," evidently a Standard Arabic word being read by a Moroccan Arabic speaker) could show pharyngeal constriction simply because of coarticulatory influence from the adjoining low vowels. Third, aryepiglottic place should perturb the formants of adjacent vowels, but no such perturbation by ʔ has been observed. So we as yet have no evidence for a special phonetic treatment of Arabic ʔ.

We have seen evidence for the class of guttural consonants and how that class can be accounted for phonetically. We have also seen some of the phonological connections between the gutturals and emphatics and how those connections find phonetic support. These observations encourage us in the view that phonological classes always have a phonetic basis. But the difference between Arabic and Tigre laryngeals, phonologically important but phonetically invisible, may have shown us a limit in our understanding of the relation between phonetic events and phonological features.

Notes

1 Portions of this paper have been circulated as McCarthy (1989, 1991a, 1991b). Additional related material will appear in McCarthy (forthcoming). During the long gestation and mitosis of this paper I have received helpful comments from Nick Clements, Elan Dresher, Louis Goldstein, Rukayyah Herzallah, Morris Halle, John Kingston, Linda Lombardi, Ian Maddieson, Paul Newman, Jaye Padgett, Janet Pierrehumbert, Ken Stevens, Alison Taub, and Loren Trigo. I am particularly grateful for extensive and detailed comments from Ellen Broselow, Lisa Selkirk, and an anonymous reviewer. Remaining errors are my fault.

2 Evidence from non-Semitic languages is comprehensively reviewed by Elorrieta (1991) within a framework related to the one proposed here.

3 Based on a study of vowel-register phenomena. Trigo (1991) concludes that tongue-root advancement/retraction and larynx raising/lowering are different features that are phonetically (but apparently not phonologically) independent.

4 I disregard the stopped realization of ʕ of Iraqi Arabic, since it is apparently a relatively superficial characteristic with no known phonological consequences.

5 But high F_1 alone does not define the class of gutturals. El-Halees (1985) has found that speakers use the relatively higher F_1 of true pharyngeals to distinguish them from uvulars, so F_1 actually functions perceptually to differentiate among gutturals.

6 There are very substantial problems with the interpretation and use of the Penfield sensory homunculus, but I know of no better alternative.

7 Michael Kenstowicz has directed my attention to Kuriyagawa et al. (1988), an EMG study of the geniohyoid and posterior genioglossus (GGP) during the production of Arabic emphatic consonants (coronals with secondary upper pharynx constriction). The experimental materials contain two words with ḥ as

well. Kuriyagawa *et al.* find that plain s̲ and t̲ have activity in the GGP but emphatic S̲ and T̲ do not. The pharyngeal ħ is like the emphatics in this respect. This might be a slight indication of a motoric connection between the emphatics (which are similar to the uvulars) and the pharyngeals, but there is another explanation. As Ghazeli (1977) notes, plain s̲ and t̲ in Arabic are considerably fronted (they are dental, with a forward tongue body, enhancing their dissimilarity from S̲ and T̲), and the GGP activity is consistent with that.

 8 The allophonically pharyngealized vowel I̲ has a negative value for the first factor, but its value is much higher than for i̲. The vowel æ̲ is positive for the first factor, but less than the value of ɑ̲, so Hess interprets it as [−radical].

 9 The evidence for Place-linked structures at underlying representation in Itô (1986) can equally well be understood as evidence for placeless consonants in coda position, as noted by Yip (1991). This removes the only obvious counterexample to the universality of (6) as a condition on underlying representations.

10 The split between coronal sonorants and coronal obstruents is a very different matter: it is absolute and it is repeated in unrelated languages. It therefore demands a more principled explanation than (8b), though I do not know of one.

11 I have looked for phonological regularities concerning membership in classes a̲/u̲ or a̲/i̲ in Standard Arabic, but there are none (contra Gorecka 1989). For instance, sorting roots according to the consonants adjacent to the thematic vowel, we get ratios of a̲/i̲ verbs to a̲/u̲ verbs ranging from 1.03 (labials) to 0.93 (coronals) to 0.62 (dorsals). None differs strikingly from the overall ratio of 0.82. The a̲/u̲ versus a̲/i̲ distinction is, however, largely predictable in many modern dialects (Haddad 1984; Herzallah 1990).

12 Several penetrating questions from Alicja Gorecka led me to reconsider an earlier version of this analysis. Her account of some of the same data can be found in Gorecka 1989: 98–99.

13 Gesenius-Kautzsch (1910: 78) suggests that ĕ̲ rather than ă̲ is the preferred coloring of schwa after the guttural ʔ̲. A search of all initial guttural + schwa sequences in the Pentateuch shows that this is not generally true, though the very high frequency of the single word ʔĕlo:hi:m "God" may create this false impression.

14 Systematic exceptions involve adjacent j̲, which requires i̲, and e̲ in forms suffixed with -ka̲:. There are perhaps 50 other apparent exceptions scattered through the Bible.

15 Geminate integrity (Steriade 1982; Hayes 1986; Schein and Steriade 1986) blocks epenthesis into geminate gutturals (Al-Mozainy 1981: 187–188): ʔaχχaS "he dressed up," ʃaʁʁal "he made something work," laħħaam "butcher," naħħaas "blacksmith."

16 In this and other Bedouin dialects, certain morphological formations (varying slightly from dialect to dialect) are not affected by post-guttural epenthesis. Abboud (1979: 471) and Al-Mozainy (1981: 187) have particularly comprehensive lists.

17 Like the gutturals, etymologic r̲ degeminates in Hebrew, though there are

exceptions. Recall too that etymologic r̲ sporadically triggers the preguttural lowering rule of section 12.3.2. There are several possible explanations for this, none of which directly bear on the issue of gutturals as [pharyngeal].

18 In the earliest attestations of Aramaic, the Proto-Semitic reflex of Arabic D̲ is written as q̲: *ʔằraq* "earth" (Jer. 10: 11). It evidently did not merge with original q̲, since the subsequent change to ʕ did not affect original q̲. It may be that the q̲ writing of original D̲ was intended for the intermediate stage ʁ, giving the sequence of steps *D̲ > *ʁ > ʕ, with the first step paralleling Ugaritic.

19 There is in any case some reason to think that the sounds called "uvular" are actually somewhat inhomogeneous. Keating (1988: 8) has noted that this label is applied to fairly diverse consonants in different languages, and Elorrieta (1991) and Trigo (1991) have demonstrated that, on phonological grounds, there are at least two types of "uvulars" in some languages (back dorsals, Chomsky and Halle 1968, versus complex pharyngealized dorsals: Cole 1987: 93; McCarthy 1989).

20 There are some unresolved inconsistencies in the descriptions of Tigre that could prove problematic. Tigre emphatics are actually realized as ejectives, as in other Ethiopian Semitic languages.

A similar example comes from Hoberman's (1985) analysis of the historical phonology of Neo-Aramaic in Northern Iraq. Hoberman reconstructs a stage of this language, called Proto-Azerbaijan-Koy Sanjaq, in which ʔ̲ and ʕ were in complementary distribution: ʕ occurs in words containing an emphatic consonant, while ʔ̲ occurs in all other words. Compare, for example, reconstructed *ʔizla with *ʕaqla. (For independent reasons, it is difficult to show the same complementarity for ḥ and h̲.)

A different phenomenon that requires the same classification comes from Kurdish, a non-Semitic language of northern Iraq in close contact with two branches of Semitic (Arabic and Neo-Aramaic). In Kurdish (Kahn 1976; Hoberman 1989), no word can contain more than one consonant from the set {ʕ, ḥ, q, S, T, Z, Tʃ, P} – that is, the primary pharyngeals ʕ and ḥ and the emphatics. Arabic loans like *Suḥbat* "conversation" or *quuTijja* "box," which contain two [pharyngeal] segments, are restructured as *sɪbḥæt* and *qoti* in Kurdish. Hoberman analyzes this cooccurrence restriction in essentially the same way as the Arabic phenomena of section 12.3.1, but again the analysis makes sense only if the laryngeal consonants are not [pharyngeal].

References

Abboud, P. 1979. The verb in Northern Najdi Arabic. *Bulletin of the School of Oriental and African Studies. University of London* 42: 467–499.

Al-Ani, S. 1970. *Arabic Phonology*. The Hague: Mouton.

1978. An acoustical and physiological investigation on the Arabic /ʕ/. In S. Al-Ani (ed.) *Readings in Arabic Linguistics*. Bloomington: Indiana University Lingustics Club, 89–101.

Al-Mozainy, H.Q. 1981. Vowel alternations in a Bedouin Hijazi Arabic dialect; abstractness and stress. Ph.D dissertation, University of Texas, Austin.

Ali, L. and R.G. Daniloff. 1972 A contrastive cinefluorographic investigation of the articulation of emphatic–nonemphatic cognate consonants. *Studia Linguistica* 26: 81–105.

Alwan, A. 1986. Acoustic and perceptual correlates of uvular and pharyngeal consonants. MA thesis, MIT Department of Electrical Engineering and Computer Science.

Anderson, S. 1971. On the description of 'apicalized' consonants. *Linguistics Inquiry* 2: 103–107.

Bender, M.L. and H. Fulass. 1978. *Amharic Verb Morphology*. East Lansing, Michigan: African Studies Centre, Michigan State University.

Blake, F.R. 1946. Studies in Semitic grammar IV. *Journal of the American Oriental Society* 66: 212–218.

Blanc, H. 1970. The Arabic dialect of the Negev Bedouins. *Proceedings of the Israel Academy of Sciences and Humanities* 4: 112–150.

Boff Dkhissi, M.-C, 1983. Contribution à l'étude expérimentale des consonnes d'arrière de l'arabe classique (locuteurs marocains). *Travaux de l'Institut Phonétique de Strasbourg* 15: 1–363. [Not seen. Cited in Butcher and Ahmad 1987.]

Bukshaisha, F. 1985. An experimental study of some aspects of Qatari Arabic. Ph.D. dissertation, University of Edinburgh.

Butcher, A. and K. Ahmad 1987. Some acoustic and aerodynamic characteristics of pharyngeal in Iraqi Arabic. *Phonetica* 44: 156–172.

Catford, J.C. 1977. *Fundamental Problems in Phonetics*. Edinburgh: University Press.
1983. Pharyngeal and laryngeal sounds in Caucasian languages. In D.M. Bless and J.H. Abbs (eds.) *Vocal Fold Physiology: Contemporary Research and Clinical Issues*. San Diego: College-Hill Press.

Chomsky, N. and M. Halle. 1968. *The Sound Pattern of English*. New York: Harper and Row.

Clements, G.N. 1985. The geometry of phonological features. *Phonology Yearbook* 2: 223–250.
1990. The role of the sonority cycle in core syllabification. In J. Kingston and M. Beckman (eds.) *Papers in Laboratory Phonology I: Between the Grammar and the Physics of Speech*. Cambridge: University Press, 283–333.

Colarusso, J. 1988. *The Northwest Caucasian Languages, a Phonological Survey*. New York: Garland.

Cole, J. 1987. Planar phonology and morphology. Ph.D dissertation, MIT.

Cowell, M.W. 1964. *A Reference Grammar of Syrian Arabic*. Washington, DC: Georgetown University Press.

Delattre, P. 1971. Pharyngeal features in the consonants of Arabic, German, Spanish, French, and American English. *Phonetica* 23: 129–155.

Dresher, B.E. 1989. Comments on "Guttural Phonology" [McCarthy (1989)]. Paper presented at MIT Conference on Feature Geometry.

El-Halees, Y. 1985. The Role of F₁ in the place-of-articulation distinction in Arabic. *Phonetica* 13: 287–298.

Elorrieta, J. 1991. The feature specification of uvulars. ms., University of Texas, Austin.

Garr, W.R. 1989. The *seghol* and segholation in Hebrew. *Journal of Near Eastern Studies* 48: 109–116.

Ghazeli, S. 1977. Back consonants and backing coarticulation in Arabic. Ph.D. dissertation, University of Texas, Austin.

Gesenius-Kautzsch, W. 1910. *Gesenius' Hebrew Grammar as Edited and Enlarged by the Late E. Kautzsch*. Oxford: University Press.

Goldsmith, J. 1976. Autosegmental phonology. Ph.D. dissertation, MIT.

Gorecka, A. 1989. Phonology of articulation. Ph.D. dissertation, MIT.

Greenberg, J. 1950. The Patterning of Root Morphemes in Semitic. *Word* 6: 162–181.

Grossman, R.C. 1964. Sensory innervation of the oral mucosae. *Journal of the Southern California State Dental Association* 32: 128–133.

Grotzfeld, H. 1965. *Syrisch-Arabische Grammatik*. Wiesbaden: Otto Harrassowitz.

Haddad, G.F. 1984. Epenthesis and sonority in Lebanese Arabic. *Studies in the Linguistic Sciences* 14: 57–88.

Halle, M. 1983. On distinctive features and their articulatory implementation. *Natural Language and Linguistic Theory* 1: 91–106.

  1988. The immanent form of phonemes. In W. Hurst (ed.) *The Making of Cognitive Science: Essays in Honor of George A. Miller*. Cambridge: University Press, 167–183.

Halle, M. and K.N. Stevens 1969. On the feature "Advanced Tongue Root". *MIT Research Laboratory of Electronics Quarterly Progress Report* 94: 209–215.

Hayes, B. 1986. Inalterability in CV phonology. *Language* 62: 321–352.

Hayward, K.M and Hayward, R.J. 1989. "Guttural": arguments for a new distinctive feature. *Transactions of the Philiological Society* 87: 179–193.

Hayward, R. J. 1989. Comparative notes on the language of the S'aamakko. *Journal of Afroasiatic Languages* 2: 1–53.

Heath, J. 1987. *Ablaut and Ambiguity: Phonology of a Moroccan Arabic Dialect*. Albany, NY: State University of New York Press.

Herzallah, R. 1990. Aspects of Palestinian Arabic phonology: a non-linear approach. Ph.D. dissertation, Cornell University.

Hess, S. 1990. Pharyngeal articulations in Akan and Arabic. ms., University of California, Los Angeles.

Hoberman, R. 1985. The phonology of pharyngeals and pharyngealization in pre-modern Aramaic. *Journal of the American Oriental Society* 105: 221–231.

  1989. Parameters of emphasis: autosegmental analyses of pharyngealization in four languages. *Journal of Afroasiatic Languages* 2: 73–97.

van der Hulst, H. 1988. The geometry of vocalic features. In H. van der Hulst and N. Smith (eds.) *Features, Segmental Structure, and Harmony Processes*. Dordrecht: Foris, 77–126.

Irshied, O. 1984. The phonology of Bani-Hassan Arabic, a Bedouin dialect. Ph.D. dissertation, University of Illinois, Champaign-Urbana.

Irshied, O. and M. Kenstowicz. 1984. Some phonological rules of Bani-Hassan Arabic: a Bedouin dialect. *Studies in the Linguistic Sciences* 14: 109–147.

Itô, J. 1986. Syllable theory in prosodic phonology. Ph.D. dissertation, University of Massachusetts, Amherst.

1989. A prosodic theory of epenthesis. *Natural Language and Linguistics Theory* 7: 217–260.

Jackson, M. 1988. Analysis of tongue positions: language-specific and cross-linguistic models. *Journal of the Acoustical Society of America* 84: 124–143.

Jakobson, R. 1957. Mufaxxama, the 'emphatic' phonemes of Arabic. In E. Pulgram (ed.) *Studies Presented to Joshua Whatmough on his 60th Birthday*. The Hague: Mouton, 105–115.

Jakobson, R., C.G.M. Fant and M. Halle. 1963. *Preliminaries to Speech Analysis*. Cambridge, MA: MIT Press.

Johnstone, T.M. 1967. *Eastern Arabian Dialect Studies*. Oxford: University Press.

Kahn, M. 1976. How abstract is pharyngology: evidence from Kurmanji. *Papers from the Twelfth Regional Meeting Chicago Linguistic Society*. Chicago: Chicago Linguistic Society.

Keating, P.A. 1988. *A Survey of Phonological Features*. Bloomington: Indiana University Linguistics Club.

Kenstowicz, M. and C. Kisseberth. 1979. *Generative Phonology*. New York: Academic Press.

Kinkade, M.D. 1967. Uvular-pharyngeal resonants in Interior Salish. *International Journal of American Linguistics* 33: 228–234.

Kiparsky, P. 1974. A note on the vowel features. In E. Kaisse and J. Hankamer (eds.) *Papers from the Fifth Annual Meeting, North Eastern Linguistics Society*. Cambridge, MA: Dept. of Linguistics, Harvard University, 162–171.

Klatt, D.H. and K.N. Stevens. 1969. Pharyngeal consonants. *MIT Research Laboratory of Electronics Quarterly Progress Report* 93: 208–216.

Koskinen, K. 1964. Kompatibilität in den dreikonsonantigen hebräischen Wurzeln. *Zeitschrift der Deutschen Morgenländischen Gesellschaft* 114: 16–58.

Kuriyagwa, F., M. Sawashima, S. Niimi and H. Hirose. 1988. Electromyographic study of emphatic consonants in Standard Jordanian Arabic. *Folia Phoniatrica* 40: 117–122.

Ladefoged, P. 1975. *A Course in Phonetics*. New York: Harcourt Brace Jovanovich.

Laufer, A. and I.D. Condax. 1979. The epiglottis as an articulator. *Journal of the International Phonetic Association* 9: 50–56.

Leben, W. 1973. Suprasegmental phonology. Ph.D. dissertation, MIT.

Leslau, W. 1945. *Short Grammar of Tigre*. New Haven, CT: American Oriental Society.

Lowenstamm, J. and J. Kaye. 1986. Compensatory lengthening in Tiberian Hebrew. In Leo Wetzels and Engin Sezer (eds.) *Studies in Compensatory Lengthening*. Dordrecht: Foris, 97–132.

Lowenstamm, J. and J.-F. Prunet. 1989. Tigre vowel harmonies. ms., Université du Québec à Montréal and University of British Columbia.

Maddieson, I. and P. Ladefoged. 1988. Multiply articulated segments and the feature hierarchy. Paper presented at 1988 Annual Meeting of the Linguistic Society of America.

Malone, J. 1978. "Heavy segments" vs. the paradoxes of segment length: the evidence of Tiberian Hebrew. *Linguistics* special issue: 119–158.

    1984. Tiberian Hebrew phonology. ms., Barnard College. (To appear, Winona Lake, Indiana: Eisenbraun's.)

McCarthy, J.J. 1979. Formal problems in Semitic phonology and morphology. Ph.D. dissertation, MIT.

    1981. A prosodic theory of nonconcatenative morphology. *Linguistic Inquiry* 12: 373–418.

    1985. Features and tiers: the structure of Semitic roots. Talk presented at MIT.

    1986. OCP effects: gemination and antigemination. *Linguistic Inquiry* 17: 207–263.

    1988. Feature geometry and dependency: a review. *Phonetica* 45: 84–108.

    1989. Guttural phonology. ms., University of Massachusetts, Amherst.

    1991a. Semitic gutturals and distinctive feature theory. In B. Comrie and M. Eid (eds.) *Perspectives on Arabic Linguistics III*. Amsterdam: Benjamins, 63–91. (Also appeared 1990 in E. Dunlap and J. Padgett (eds.) *UMOP 14*. Amherst, MA: Graduate Linguistic Student Association, 29–50.

    1991b. The phonology of Semitic pharyngeals. ms., University of Massachusetts, Amherst.

    Forthcoming. Guttural transparency. ms., University of Massachusetts, Amherst.

Merlingen, W. 1977. *Artikulation und Phonematik des H*. Vienna: Verlag der wissenschaftlichen Gesellschaften Österreichs.

Mester, R.A. 1986. Studies in tier structure. Ph.D. dissertation, University of Massachusetts, Amherst.

Mitchell, T.F. 1960. Prominence and syllabification in Arabic. *Bulletin of the School of Oriental and African Studies* 23: 369–89.

Mrayati, M. 1987. Statistical studies of Arabic language roots. In Raymond Descout (ed.) *Applied Arabic Linguistics and Signal and Information Processing*. Washington: Hempishere Publishing, 97–103.

Odden, D. 1988. Dissimilation as deletion in Chukchi. ms., Ohio State University, Columbus, OH.

Padgett, J. 1991. Stricture in feature geometry. Ph.D. dissertation, University of Massachusetts, Amherst.

Palmer, F.R. 1956. "Openness" in Tigre: a problem in prosodic statement. *Bulletin of the School of Oriental and African Studies* 18: 561–577.

    1962. *The Morphology of the Tigre Noun*. London and New York: Oxford University Press.

Penfield, W. and T. Rasmussen. 1950. *The Cerebral Cortex of Man*. New York: Macmillan.

Perkell, J. 1971. Physiology of speech production: a preliminary study of two suggested revisions of the features specifying vowels. *MIT Research Laboratory of Electronics Quarterly Progress Report* 102: 123–139.

1980. Phonetic features and the physiology of speech production. In B. Butterworth (ed.) *Language Production 1: Speech and Talk.* London and New York: Academic Press, 337–372.

Prince. A. 1975. The phonology and morphology of Tiberian Hebrew. Ph.D. dissertation, MIT.

Prochazka, T. 1988. *Saudi Arabian Dialects.* London: Kegan Paul International.

Prunet. J.-F. 1990. The origin and interpretation of French loans in Carrier. *International Journal of American Linguistics* 56: 484–502.

Raz, S. 1983. *Tigre Grammar and Texts.* Afroasiatic Dialects 4. Malibu, CA: Undena Publications.

Ringel, R.L. 1970. Oral region two-point discrimination in normal and myopathic subjects. In J.F. Bosma (ed.) *Second Symposium on Oral Sensation and Perception.* Springfield, Ill.: Charles C. Thomas. 309–321

Sagey. E. 1986. The representation of features and relations in nonlinear phonology. Ph.D. dissertation, MIT.

Sasse, H.-J. 1979. The consonant phonemes of Proto-East-Cushitic (PEC): a first approximation. *Afroasiatic Linguistics* 7: 1–67.

Schein, B. and D. Steriade. 1986. On geminates. *Linguistic Inquiry* 17: 691–744.

Selkirk, E.O. 1988. Dependency, place, and the notion "tier". ms., University of Massachusetts, Amherst.

1991. Vowel height features: evidence for privativity and dependency. Paper presented at Université du Québec à Montréal.

Shaw, P. 1987. Non-conservation of melodic structure in reduplication. In A. Bosch, B. Need, and E. Schiller (eds.) *Papers from the 24th Annual Regional Meeting of the Chicago Linguistic Society. Part Two: Parasession on Autosegmental and Metrical Phonology.* Chicago: Chicago Linguistic Society, 291–306.

Steriade, D. 1982. Greek prosodies and the nature of syllabification. Ph.D. dissertation, MIT.

1987. Locality conditions and feature geometry. In J. McDonough and B. Plunkett (eds.) *Proceedings of NELS 17.* Graduate Linguistic Student Association, University of Massachusetts, Amherst, 595–618.

Stevens, K.S. and A. House. 1963. Perturbation of vowel articulations by consonantal context: an acoustical study. *Journal of Speech and Hearing Research* 6: 111–128.

Trigo, L. 1991. On pharynx-larynx interactions. *Phonology* 8: 113–136.

Wehr, H. 1971. *A Dictionary of Modern Written Arabic,* J. M. Cowan (ed.) Ithaca, New York: Spoken Language Services.

Williamson, K. 1977. Multivalued features for consonants. *Languages* 53: 843–871.

Wood, S. 1979. A radiographic analysis of constriction locations for vowels. *Journal of Phonetics* 7: 25–43.

Yip, M. 1989. Feature geometry and co-occurrence restrictions. *Phonology* 6: 349–374.

John J. McCarthy

1991. Coronals, consonant clusters, and the coda condition. In C. Paradis and J.-F. Prunet (eds.) *The Special Status of Coronals: Internal and External Evidence.* New York: Academic Press.

Younes, M.A. 1982. Problems in the segmental phonology of Palestinian Arabic. Ph.D. dissertation, University of Texas, Austin.

13

Possible articulatory bases for the class of guttural consonants

LOUIS GOLDSTEIN

McCarthy's paper argues convincingly that "guttural" consonants in Semitic languages constitute a natural phonological class. In attempting to specify what it is that the gutterals have in common, articulatorily and/or acoustically, McCarthy is led to propose a different conception of features than is typically assumed at present, a conception based on orosensory patterns rather than on controlled articulators. In these comments, the assumptions about features implicit in McCarthy's proposal(s) will be examined and some alternative assumptions will be explored, leading to additional hypotheses about the physical basis for the natural class of guttural consonants.

13.1 The argument for orosensory features

McCarthy argues that the best candidate for a physical property shared by all the gutturals is the *region* of the vocal tract in which they are produced – anywhere between the larynx and the oropharynx – and he defines the feature [pharyngeal] to refer to articulations in this region. This definition in terms of region is incompatible, however, with articulator-based feature theories, which have defined place features in terms of the "active articulator": the lips for [labial], the tongue tip or blade for [coronal], and the tongue body for [dorsal]. In the case of gutturals, the evidence presented suggests that three different active articulators (or combinations of them) are involved; tongue body and root for /χ, ʁ/, tongue root and larynx for /ħ, ʕ/, and glottis for /h, ʔ/. McCarthy proposes that this conflict can be resolved by defining features as orosensory patterns (Perkell 1980), rather than as active articulators. In the case of the oral place features, he reasons that orosensory properties could do as good a job as active articulators at partitioning consonants into three place types.

[pharyngeal] consonants are hypothesized to produce a single orosensory pattern (despite the differences among them) because of the relatively poor sensory acuity in this region, compared to the lips and tongue. Thus, the [pharyngeal] place of articulation is "larger" (covers more of the length of the vocal tract) than the oral places, and is composed of a number of distinct active articulators.

13.2 Orosensory patterns VERSUS active articulators?

In principle, it is unneccessary to assume that *all* phonological natural classes will be based on the same type of physical property. Even in the standard feature-geometry view (that assumes an active articulator approach, e.g. as discussed in McCarthy 1988), there are some features that cannot use active articulator as a basis for distinguishing classes. Obviously, the "minor" place features such as [anterior] and [distributed] (that only apply to [coronal] articulations) are examples. In these cases, orosensory properties may be quite relevant. For example, Perkell *et al.* (1979) have shown that orosensory contact patterns can be used to distinguish [+anterior] versus [−anterior] sibilants in English. /s/ showed contact between the tongue tip and *lower* alveolar ridge in their study while /ʃ/ did not. In view of this, it would be useful to explore the possibility that [labial], [coronal] and [dorsal] classes could be defined in terms of active articultors, and an additional feature defined that could separate pharyngeal articulators from the others in terms of orosensory patterns. Before fleshing out this view and its possible advantages, one possible objection should be considered. The class of [pharyngeal] consonants is clearly a "major" place of articulation grouping, ostensibly parallel to [labial], [coronal], and [dorsal], and it could be reasonably expected to have a parallel physical basis. However, as McCarthy notes in the last section of his paper, the parallelism is not, in fact, complete. There is evidence (based on "guttural transparency" – McCarthy, forthcoming) that the three oral places share a property not shared by the [pharyngeal] place, and he represents this in the geometry shown in example (36) of his paper by grouping the three together under an Oral Place node. This effectively removes the foregoing objection.

My hypothesis is that a relatively simple property can be used to distinguish guttural from non-guttural consonants: contact along the upper surface of the vocal tract (from the soft palate to the upper lip) made by the tongue or the lower lip. Gutturals are hypothesized to lack such contact, and nongutturals always to have it. For some nonguttural consonants, there will be contact along the sides of the palate and teeth but none mid-sagittally (e.g. for central approximants), but all nonguttural consonants are hypothesized to have contact somewhere along that upper surface. The gutturals, however, seem to lack such contact (if we rule out the very tip of the uvula that might touch or trill in /ʀ/). Note that this view classifies the uvular stop /q/ and the uvular approximants /χ, ʀ/ in just the right way. The stop obviously has contact between the tongue and the soft palate, and it is not a member of the guttural class (as McCarthy notes). The approximants lack such contact and pattern with gutturals.

In this view, one can maintain a definition of the [labial], [coronal], and [dorsal] classes based on active articulator, and add an additional one, e.g. [radical], to account for the consonants that actively retract the tongue root (the uvular and pharyngeal approximants /χ, ʀ, ħ, ʕ/). The guttural/ nonguttural distinction is made by a separate, more global articulatory property: contact anywhere along the upper vocal tract surface. Exactly how such a property could be built into a feature geometry like McCarthy's (indeed, whether it would require anything different from the geometry in McCarthy's [36]) is beyond the scope of these remarks.

There are some advantages to keeping the basic place features defined in terms of active articular. First, this view dovetails nicely with the view that speech is composed of Gestures formed by the independently controllable articulator sets within the vocal tract (Browman and Goldstein 1989). The relation between the active articultors and the Gestures of articulatory phonology will be discussed below.[1] Second, it is not clear that it is possible to come up with a definition of [coronal] and [dorsal] in purely orosensory terms that will categorize articulations in just the right way. At the very least, the definitions are going to have to be somewhat complex (e.g. coronals involve contact of the sides or centre of the tongue tip or blade with the palate, alveolar ridge, or teeth). And crucially, such definitions do not distinguish active control from passive consequences (see Browman, this volume). For example, it is possible that in some environments the production of a [dorsal] stop may result in a (passive) raising of the blade of the tongue, so that the sides of the blade may touch the palate or teeth. If it is just the orosensory pattern that matters, how can this articulation be distinguished from a coronal? If classes are distinguished on the basis of the articulator set that is being actively controlled, however, then this is not a problem. Finally, in this view, there is a difference between classes based on active articulators (that can be simply related to the structures directly controlled in speech in an articulatory phonology model) and classes based on a property like "upper surface contact" that results from gestural events of a number of different types, but is not itself directly controlled. It would be interesting if it turned out that the kinds of phonological behaviors shown by these different classes were, in fact, different.

13.3 Active articulators and articulatory phonology

A second approach to specifying the class of guttural consonants requires a closer look at the notion of active articulator, and its relation to the model of articulator coordination developed within articulatory phonology (Browman and Goldstein 1989, 1992; Saltzman and Munhall 1989). In this approach, phonological units are modeled as dynamic articulatory actions called *Gestures*. Each Gesture involves the coordinated activity of a set of (potentially) independent articulators that are (temporarily) yoked into a single "coordinative structure" (Fowler *et al.* 1980). Each articulator set, or coordinative structure, can be thought of as functioning as a constricting system whose action produces a local constriction within the vocal tract. The articulator sets that have been hypothesized (Browman and Goldstein 1989) and the independent articulators that they harness are shown in table 13.1. (The TR set has not yet been implemented in the computational simulation and is, therefore, noted with an asterisk.) Note that it is the articulator *sets* (not the individual articulators) that correspond to the "active articulators" of feature theory (LIPS = [labial], TT = [coronal], TB = [dorsal]).

The Gestures underlying the consonants discussed by McCarthy (setting aside voicing distinctions) can be characterized as follows. For the laryngeal gutturals (h, ?), the GLO articultor set is involved, producing a {wide} glottal constriction for /h/, and a {closed} glottal constriction for /?/. For

Table 13.1. *Articulator sets and individual articulators (Browman and Goldstein 1989)*

Articulator Set	Articulators
LIPS	upper lip
	lower lip
	jaw
TT	tongue tip
(tongue tip/blade)	tongue body
	jaw
TB	tongue body
(tongue body)	jaw
*TR**	tongue root
(tongue root)	epiglottis
	others???
VEL	velum
GLO	glottis

the pharynheal gutturals (ħ, ʕ), lower pharyngeal constrictions are presumably produced by the TR articulator set. While this articulator set has not yet been explicitly modeled, the associated articulators would presumably include the tongue root and the epiglottis (and possibly the hyoid bone and the walls of the pharynx itself, through the sphincteral action of the pharyngeal constrictor muscles – Hardcastle 1976). For the uvular gutturals (χ, ʁ), constrictions both of TB and TR seem be required, and thus they would be described as constellations involving two Gestures. Interestingly, Delattre's (1971) description of these articulations in Lebanese Arabic notes that the lower pharyngeal constriction is formed first and that tongue-dorsum raising follows, supporting the supposition that there are really two Gestural events here. This description also parallels McCarthy's treatment of these consonants as "complex segments" (involving both [dorsal] and [pharyngeal] specifications).

This kind of Gestural specification for gutturals leads to roughly the same problem McCarthy confronts in featural terms: there are phonologically natural classes defined by the articulator set employed in the case of LIPS, TT, and TB gestures, but the gutturals constitute a mixed bag of articulator sets (TB + TR, TR, GLO). However, examining the individual articulators that make up the sets leads to a possibly interesting generalization. For both the GLO and TR, the jaw is not hypothesized as participating in the coordinative structure. The assumption seems uncontroversial in the case of GLO constrictions. In the case of TR constrictions, it is not clear that positioning the jaw contributes substantially to the production of a constriction in the lower pharyngeal region. (But there may be some small indirect effects. For example, mandible position and hyoid position interact through the geniohyoid muscle – see Hardcastle 1976: 70 – which attaches to both, and hyoid position may, in turn, affect pharynx width.) In general, however, the role of the jaw seems very different in the TR and GLO coordinative structures than it is in for LIPS, TT, and TB, where it serves to directly raise or lower the other articulators with which it cooperates (the tongue body, tongue tip, lower lip) toward the constriction goal. I hypothesize, then, that the class of guttural consonants could be defined as involving Gestures that are produced with coordinative structures in which the jaw does not participate (assuming VEL Gestures can be excluded on some other basis). Note that the uvular gutturals would qualify since one of their component Gestures involves a "jawless" constriction.

With data currently at hand, the hypothesis that the jaw does not participate in the coordinative structure for TR and GLO constrictions cannot be directly tested. Evidence for coordinative structures typically comes from data showing that the participating articulators display compensatory relations with one another, with their relative contributions to the constriction varying interdependently as a function of context (Kelso *et al.* 1986; Macchi 1988), token (Gracco and Abbs 1986), or mechanical perturbation (Folkins and Abbs 1975; Kelso *et al* 1984; Shaiman 1989). Such data do not exist for TR (or GLO) constrictions, as far as I know, and thus the issue cannot be decided definitively. A suggestive, but less conclusive, test could come from data on the jaw positions for both vowels and consonants in VCV utterances. If there is no change in jaw position from V to C to V for guttural consonants across a variety of symmetric vowel environments that show different jaw heights, then it would be reasonable to infer that the jaw is not contributing to the constriction for the guttural consonant. In fact, the data of Keating *et al.* (1990) show this type of pattern for /VhV/ sequences in English and Swedish. However, there seems to be no data of this kind for the Semitic gutturals.

Another suggestive test would be to examine the jaw positions for different guttural consonants in the same vowel environment. If the gutturals show different jaw positions from each other, then it would be reasonable to infer that the jaw was contributing differentially to the consonants. Data of this kind can be found in Boff-Dkhissi (1983), where jaw openings for guttural consonants in /VCV/ utterances are reported for a speaker of Moroccan Arabic. A relevant subset of the data is shown in table 13.2. In both the low and high vowel environments, there are small differences between the three classes in jaw opening: uvular consonants have the smallest opening and pharyngeal consonants the greatest. If we assume that there really is no jaw contribution (relative to the surrounding vowels) in the laryngeal case (as is suggested by the /VhV/'s of English and Swedish), then the uvular gutturals show a small amount of raising (smaller jaw opening compared to the laryngeal control), which is to be expected since they have a TD Gesture as well as a TR one. However, the pharyngeals show a small amount of jaw lowering, particularly for /ħ/ (larger jaw opening compared to the laryngeal control). If the lowering were a regular feature of the production of this kind of consonant, this could be interpreted as evidence that the jaw is involved in the production of the constriction. However, the data in Delattre (1971) for Lebanese Arabic show a quite different pattern, with the jaw *higher* for the pharyngeal gutturals than for the uvular gutturals. Such inter-speaker (or inter-language) variability might be expected if the jaw were not intrinsically involved in producing these constrictions, and was free to take on speaker-preferred postures. Overall, then, it seems premature to either discard or accept the hypothesis.

Finally, even if we assume that the hypothesis turns out to be correct, and that "jawlessness" is a characteristic shared by the coordinative structures for guttural consonants, we could ask why it is that this distinction is actually used by speakers to form a phonological class. One possible answer

Table 13.2. *Jaw opening in mm: Moroccan Arabic (data from Boff-Dkhissi 1983)*

		a___a	i___u
uvular	ʁ	3	2
	χ	3.25	2
pharyngeal	ʕ	5	4
	ħ	7	4
laryngeal	ʔ	4.5	3
	h	3.75	2.5

is that jaw movement is relatively accessible to speakers' awareness. Subjective awareness of jaw movements in speech was investigated by Lindblom and Lubker (1985), who found that it was much easier for subjects to consistently estimate the amount of jaw movement involved in a particular syllable than to estimate the amount of tongue movement.

In general, then, McCarthy's paper presents an interesting challenge to find the basis of the natural class of guttural consonants. In addition to the answer he provides, I have suggested two alternatives that I think are worth exploring, and that lead to differing conceptions of how languages form natural classes.

Note

This work was supported by NSF grant 8820099 and NIH grant DC-00121 to Haskins Laboratories. Thanks to Alice Faber for comments on an earlier draft.

1 The word "Gesture" is capitalized in this book for this technical usage in articulatory phonology, to distinguish it from more ordinary-language uses elsewhere in the book.

References

Boff-Dkhissi, M.-C. 1983. Contribution à l'étude expérimentale des consonnes d'arrière de l'arabe classique (locuteurs marocains). *Travaux de l'Institut de Phonétique de Strasbourg* 15: 1–363.

Browman, C. P. This volume. Lip aperture and consonant releases.

Browman, C. and L. Goldstein. 1989. Articulatory gestures as phonological units. *Phonology* 6: 201–251.

Browman, C. and L. Goldstein. 1992. Articulatory Phonology: an overview. *Phonetica* 49: 155–180.

Delattre, P. 1971. Pharyngeal features in the consonants of Arabic, German, Spanish, French and American English. *Phonetica* 23: 129–155.

Folkins, J. and J. Abbs. 1975. Lip and jaw motor control during speech: responses to resistive loading of the jaw. *Journal of Speech and Hearing Research* 18: 207–220.

Fowler, C.A., P. Rubin, R.E. Remez, and M. Turvey. 1980. Implications for speech production of a general theory of action. In B. Butterworth (ed.) *Language Production*. New York: Academic Press, 373–420.

Gracco, V. and J. Abbs. 1986. Variant and invariant characteristics of speech movements. *Experimental Brain Research* 65: 156–166.

Hardcastle, W. 1976. *Physiology of Speech Production*. New York: Academic Press.

Keating, P., B. Lindblom and J. Kreiman. Jaw position in English and Swedish VCVs. *UCLA Working Papers in Phonetics* 74: 77–95.

Kelso, J.A.S., E.L. Saltzman, and B. Tuller. 1986. The dynamical perspective on speech production: data and theory. *Journal of Phonetics* 14: 29–59.

Kelso, J.A.S., B. Tuller, E. Vatikiotis-Bateson, and C.A. Fowler. 1984. Functionally specific articulatory cooperation following jaw perturbations during speech: evidence for coordinative structures. *Journal of Experimental Psychology: Human Perception and Performance* 10: 812–832.

Lindblom, B. and J. Lubker. 1985. The speech homunculus. In V. Fromkin (ed.) *Phonetic Linguistics*. New York: Academic Press, 169–192.

Macchi, M. 1988. Labial articulation patterns associated with segmental features and syllable structure in English. *Phonetica* 45: 109–121.

McCarthy, J.J. 1988. Feature geometry and dependency: a review. *Phonetica* 45: 84–108.

Forthcoming. Guttural transparency. ms., University of Massachusetts, Amherst.

Perkell, J., S. Boyce, and K. Stevens. 1979. Articulatory and acoustic correlates of the [s–š] distinction. In J. Wolf and D.H. Klatt (eds.): *Speech Communication Papers (from the 97th meeting of the Acoustical Society of America)*. New York: Acoustical Society of America, 109–113.

Perkell, J. 1980. Phonetic features and the physiology of speech production. In B. Butterworth (ed.) *Language Production*. New York: Academic Press, 337–372.

Saltzman, E. and K. Munhall. 1989. A dynamical approach to gestural patterning in speech production. *Ecological Psychology* 1: 333–382.

Shaiman, S. 1989. Kinematic and electromyographic responses to perturbation of the jaw. *Journal of the Acoustical Society of America* 86: 78–88.

14

Phonetic evidence for hierarchies of features

KENNETH N. STEVENS

14.1 Introduction

When one attempts to specify the acoustic and articulatory correlates of distinctive features, one is often frustrated by the apparent many-to-one relations that exist between acoustic or articulatory properties and the abstract features which appear to be a part of a speaker/listener's knowledge of language. One step toward resolving this difficulty is to organize the features into hierarchies similar to those used in current approaches to phonology (Clements 1985; McCarthy 1988). On the basis of acoustic articulatory data, the features can be organized roughly into three classes (Halle and Stevens 1991): (1) articulator-free features that indicate whether a narrow constriction is made in the vocal tract and, if so, whether or not a complete closure is formed and whether pressure is built up behind the constriction; (2) articulator-bound features indicating the primary articulator that is active in forming the constriction (whether it be a narrow consonantal constriction or a less severe vocalic constriction), and specifying further details about the placement of the constriction; and (3) articulator-bound features indicating active adjustments of secondary articulators (i.e. articulators other than the primary ones), such as larynx, the soft palate, and the tongue body (for cases in which the tongue body is not the primary articulator). This hierarchical organization can serve as a basis for ordering the identification of features from the acoustic signal, with the more context-independent features being identified first and the more context-dependent features identified later.

A second proposal that may help to clarify the acoustic and articulatory correlates of the features is to give greater attention to the concept of landmarks in the sound that are produced by implementing articulator-free features. In the case of a consonant, a landmark is a point in the sound stream where an articulator creates a narrow constriction in the vocal tract. It is manifested in the sound either as an acoustic discontinuity (at the consonantal implosion and at the release) or as a minimum in amplitude (or in a related acoustic parameter). For a vowel, a landmark occurs at a point where the vocal tract is maximally open, generally corresponding to a maximum in amplitude and in the frequency of the first formant. The acoustic manifestations of the features for a particular segment occur in the vicinity of these landmarks. The landmarks provide the listener with regions in the signal where attention is to be focused in order to identify the features for the segments.

Placing emphasis on acoustic landmarks in the sound has implications for models of speech production as well as speech perception. If the acoustic manifestations of the features for particular segments are centered around these landmarks, then the speaker is constrained to coordinate the movements of his/her articulators so that these movements are appropriately represented in the sound near these landmarks.

In this paper we shall first review the articulatory and acoustic manifestations of the features in each of the classes, and we shall attempt to demonstrate the role of acoustic landmarks as events around which acoustic properties are centered. We shall then consider how this view of features and their correlates places constraints on the control and coordination of the articulatory structures during speech production.

14.2 Articulator-free features and landmarks

Among the articulator-free features (roughly the manner features or stricture features of Clements 1985 and Sagey 1986), we shall focus our attention initially on the features of consonantal segments. When a [+consonantal] segment is produced, a narrow constriction is formed at some point along the midline of the vocal tract above the glottis. The acoustic consequence of manipulating an articulator to form such a narrow constriction or to move away from a constricted position is to introduce a particular type of discontinuity in the acoustic signal. If the constriction is formed or is released adjacent to a vowel or some other sound produced with a vocal-tract configuration that is more open than that of the consonant, then the acoustic discontinuity is characterized by a rapid change in the spectrum shape, with rapid movements of some prominences in the spectrum.

When a segment is [+consonantal], there must always be a specification of the feature [continuant]. If the consonant is [−continuant], then a complete closure is made in the midline of the vocal tract at the point where the consonantal constriction is formed. The feature [+continuant] signifies that the closure at the constriction is not complete.

When a consonantal constriction or closure is formed at some point along the vocal tract, certain additional articulator-free features must be specified. These additional features indicate how the airstream is manipulated when the articulator forms the constriction. For example, it is necessary to specify whether or not the forming of the constriction causes pressure to build up behind the constriction. The buildup of pressure can be prevented if a bypass is provided for the airflow, either by opening the velopharyngeal port or by allowing the flow of air around the sides of the tongue blade. If pressure does build up as a consequence of the consonantal constriction, then the [+consonantal] segment is [−sonorant]. If there is no pressure buildup, then the discontinuity identifies a segment that is [+consonantal, +sonorant].

For a segment that is [+consonantal, +continuant], it may be possible to shape the articulator forming the constriction in such a way that the airstream that passes through the constriction is directed against an obstacle or surface. The consequence of this action is to generate a strong source of turbulence noise, stronger than the source that would be produced without such an obstacle. A consonant produced in this way is classified as [+strident].

Another articulator-free feature that is appended as a modifier to the feature [+consonantal] is [lateral] (which is specified for segments that are [+sonorant, −continuant] in English). For a consonant that is [+lateral], the airstream is directed around one or both sides of the tongue blade.

In summary, then, it is postulated that there are four articulator-free features that can operate when a [+consonantal] segment is formed, i.e. when a narrow constriction is made in the vocal tract. Not all combinations of these features are possible, however. For example, [+sonorant] is incompatible with [+strident], and [+strident] consonants are always [+continuant]. The five combinations that are possible are displayed in table 14.1. In this table, we place in parentheses the entries for which the feature is constrained to take on just one value. At the top of each column is an example of a consonant that has the given combination of the articulator-free features.

The acoustic manifestation of the production of the implosion or release for a consonant is an event that can take several forms depending on whether the consonant is sonorant or continuant, and depending on the state of the glottis. In general, however, the acoustic event must satisfy three requirements: (1) the spectrum should remain relatively constant or change only slowly within the constricted interval adjacent to the implosion or release; (2) a rapid change in the spectrum amplitude should occur over at

Table 14.1. *Listing of possible combinations of articulator-free features. An entry in parentheses indicates that the feature is constrained to take on a particular value. An example of a consonant with the given combination of features is given at the top of each column.*

Features	t	l	n	s	θ
Consonantal	+	+	+	+	+
Continuant	−	−	−	+	+
Sonorant	−	+	+	(−)	(−)
Lateral	(−)	+	−	(−)	(−)
Strident	(−)	(−)	(−)	+	−

least some part of the frequency range as the constriction is formed or as it is released; and (3) there should be a rapid change in the frequency of one or more peaks in the spectrum at these points. The first of these requirements indicates that, when the articulator is in the constricted configuration, the vocal-tract shape anterior or posterior to the constriction will tend not to change enough to cause a significant modification of the spectrum shape or the amplitude. The second and third requirements are a consequence of the fact that an articulator is moving toward or away from a constricted configuration, resulting in changes in some natural frequencies of the system and an abrupt shift in the acoustic source (e.g. from a glottal source to frication noise) and/or the acoustic path through the system (e.g. from mouth to nose output).

In the case of segments that are [−consonantal], any constriction that is formed above the glottis is not sufficiently narrow to create a rapid change in the spectrum shape when the constriction is formed or when it is released. For [−consonantal] segments, therefore, it is usually not necessary to specify additional articulator-free features. A discontinuity in the spectrum that is a consequence of adduction or abduction movements of the glottis or a constriction formed in the lower pharynx does not qualify as a consonantal event. Such a discontinuity is not characterized by a rapid movement of a spectral prominence, since there is not a rapid change in the vocal-tract shape that is the cause of the spectral prominences.[1]

Examples of some acoustic discontinuities that mark consonantal events are shown in figure 14.1. For example, at around 400 ms, a labial closure is produced. Smoothed spectra sampled 13 ms apart near the closure are shown in the left panel under the spectrogram. Immediately prior to the closure, there are rapid downward movements of the first three formants, as the spectra indicate. The amplitude drops abruptly at the instant of closure, and the spectrum remains weak and constant during the closure interval,

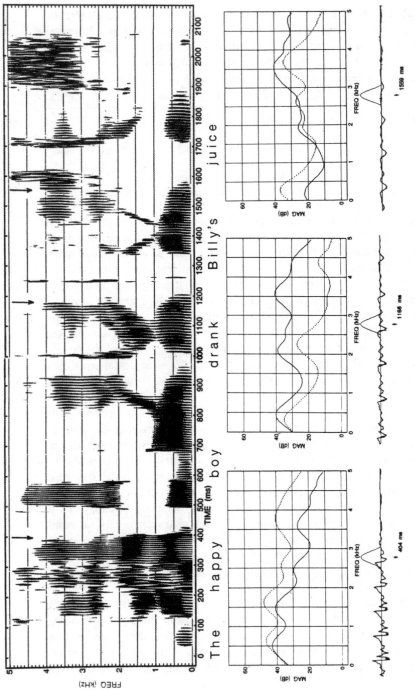

Figure 14.1. (Top) Spectrogram of the utterance 'The happy boy drank Billy's juice.' (Bottom) Smoothed spectra sampled at several points within the utterance. Each panel contains two spectra, sampled at points spaced 13–24 ms apart as described in the text. The first spectrum of the pair is the spectrum with the greatest amplitude at low frequencies. The three panels show the changing spectra near three points marked by arrows: the implosion of /p/ in *happy* (left), the implosion of /ŋ/ in *drank* (middle), and the implosion of /z/ in *Billy's* (left).

246

except for a brief interval of weak glottal vibration immediately following the implosion. Another example of an implosion and a release for a stop consonant is at about 580 and 680 ms.

At time 1180 ms, a closure is made by raising the tongue body to form a velar nasal, leading to an abrupt change in spectrum amplitude at mid and high frequencies. The middle panel under the spectrogram in figure 14.1 shows smoothed spectra sampled 19 ms apart near the time of closure for this consonant. There is a fall in the first-formant frequency (F_1) as the closure is made, and a single spectral peak appears at about 2200 Hz in place of the two peaks corresponding to F_2 and F_3. In this case, the consonant is sonorant, and this fact is represented in the sound by continuity in the amplitude of the first harmonic at low frequencies (not shown in the figure). A postvocalic fricative consonant is initiated at about 1540 ms, and two spectra sampled 24 ms apart near this point in time are displayed in the right panel in figure 14.1. Again there is a rapid change in the spectrum, but there is a relatively stationary spectrum shape in the few tens of milliseconds following the beginning of frication noise.

In the time interval centered around 260 ms, there is aspiration noise which excites all of the formants. This fact, together with the observation that there are no rapid changes in formant frequencies associated with a constriction formed by an articulator, is evidence that the only significant constriction in the airway is in the laryngeal region. Thus there is no [+ consonantal] segment in this region.

14.3 Articulator-bound features

As we have observed, the articulator-free features associated with consonantal segments indicate that a particular type of constriction has been formed in the vocal tract. The articulator-bound features that characterize a segment with a specified set of articulator-free features are of two types. One of these specifies which articulator is active in producing the constriction, i.e. which articulator is responsible for the acoustic discontinuity that occurs at the formation or release of the constriction. For [+ consonantal] segments, any one of three different articulators can be the active articulator: the lips, the tongue blade, and the tongue body. The first type of articulator-bound feature indicates how the primary articulator is to be shaped or located to produce the constriction. In terms of the geometrical arrangement of features proposed by Sagey (1986, based on the original proposal of Clements 1985), the primary articulator characterizes the node to which the pointer from the stricture features is directed. The second type of feature specifies how other articulators are to be manipulated in coordination with the primary articulator. These secondary articulators do not form the constriction that gives rise to the acoustic discontinuity; rather, they modulate the acoustic pattern in the vicinity of the discontinuity.

Some examples of this division of the articulator-bound features into these two classes are given for several different consonantal segments in table 14.2. The articulator-free features are listed at the top. Below this is the list of the three primary articulators, any one of which can be active in producing the consonantal constriction. A partial list of the articulator-bound features constitutes the remainder of the table. Some of these articulator-bound features are enclosed in boxes. These are features that specify how the primary articulators are to be manipulated. The remaining articulator-bound features are the secondary group. The features that specify velopharyngeal, pharyngeal, and laryngeal configurations and states are always associated with secondary articulators for [+consonantal]

Table 14.2. *Expansion of table 14.1 to include primary articulator-bound categories and articulator-bound features. The features enclosed in boxes are features that specify the placement of the primary articulator.*

		t	n	f	g	l
Articulator-free features	consonantal	+	+	+	+	+
	continuant	−	−	+	−	−
	sonorant	−	+	(−)	−	+
	strident					
	lateral	(−)	−	(−)	(−)	+
	strident	(−)	(−)	+	(−)	(−)
Primary articulator	lips			x		
	tongue blade	x	x			x
	tongue body				x	
Articulator-bound features	round			−*		
	anterior	+*	+*			+*
	distributed	−*	−*			−*
	high				+*	−
	low				−	−
	back				+*	+
	spread glottis	+		+	−	
	stiff vocal folds	+		+		
	slack vocal folds				+	
	adv. tongue root	−		−		
	const. tongue root					
	nasal		+			

*Values marked with an asterisk are enclosed in boxes in the original.

Table 14.3. *Representation of some nonconsonantal segments in terms of two types of categories: articulator-free features and articulator-bound features. The features enclosed in boxes are features that specify the placement of the primary articulator.*

		e	u	w	j	h
Articulator-free features	consonantal	−	−	−	−	−
	continuant					
	sonorant					
	lateral					
	strident					
Primary articulator	lips			x		
	tongue blade				x	
	tongue body	x	x			
	larynx					x
Features classifying	round		+	[+]		
articulator-bound	anterior				[−]	
categories	distributed				[+]	
	high	[−]	[+]	+	+	
	low	[−]	[−]	−	−	
	back	[−]	[+]	+	−	
	spread glottis					[+]

segments, whereas the lips, tongue blade and tongue body can be either primary or secondary articulators. For example, for the lateral consonant in table 14.2, the tongue body is a secondary articulator, and the features *high*, *low*, and *back* indicate the activity of this articulator.

In the case of nonconsonantal segments, a primary articulator is also designated, but, in contrast to consonantal segments, the primary articulator can be drawn from a wider inventory.[2] Table 14.3 lists some nonconsonantal segments, and gives for each segment the primary articulator, the features (in boxes) specifying the manipulation of this articulator, and the remaining articulator-bound features. For vowels the primary articulator is always the tongue body, whereas for the glides it can be the tongue blade (for /j/), the lips (for /w/), or the glottis (for /h/). A nasal glide, for which the soft palate is the primary articulator, appears also to be possible (Trigo 1988). As with consonantal segments, secondary articulators (and their associated features) can be specified for nonconsonantal segments.

There appear to be some features that specify the state of an articulator rather than its movement or position. These are features that characterize the stiffness or slackness of the vocal folds or of the laryngeal or pharyngeal surfaces immediately above the glottis. The acoustic correlates of these features are the changes in fundamental frequency of vocal-fold vibration and, for obstruents, the inhibition or facilitation of glottal vibration during the obstruent interval. When the laryngeal and pharyngeal structures are used in this way, they are never primary articulators.

14.4 Acoustic manifestation of articulator-bound features for consonantal segments: the role of acoustic landmarks

We have seen that the acoustic consequence of the articulator-free features for a consonantal segment is a particular type of discontinuity in the signal. The properties of the sound that signal which articulator is responsible for this discontinuity, and how this articulator is to be placed, are located in regions of the sound immediately adjacent to the discontinuity. These are the regions of the sound where the primary articulator is moving toward or away from the constricted configuration, or has achieved the constricted state. The literature contains a wealth of information indicating that the acoustic properties signaling the secondary articulator-bound features are also concentrated in the vicinity of the consonantal landmarks. Thus, for example, information about the laryngeal state or the state of the velopharyngeal opening for a consonant is located in regions near the acoustic landmarks that are correlates of the articulator-free features.

In a sense, the acoustic discontinuities produced by forming a constriction with the primary articulators constitute the glue that binds together the various features of a consonant to constitute a "segment." The acoustic manifestation of each of the features for the consonant segment normally appears in the vicinity of this discontinuity.

The spectrogram and the spectra in figure 14.1 illustrate the way in which acoustic evidence for articulator-bound features is located in the vicinity of the consonantal landmarks. The downward movement of F_2 and F_3 near the closure for [p] (left panel below the spectrogram) is evidence for a labial closure, whereas the rapid extinction of glottal vibration at this point (before F_1 has reached a low value), together with other low-frequency spectral changes just prior to closure, signals the fact that the glottis is spreading. In the middle panel of figure 14.1, the proximity of F_2 and F_3 and the spectral prominence in this frequency range indicate a closure in the mid-palatal region with a raised tongue body. And the raised F_2 in the third panel, together with the strong prominence (relative to that in the vowel) in the F_4

region (around 3500 Hz) is evidence for a constriction produced with the tongue blade in the alveolar region. The continued presence of low-frequency energy for a few tens of ms immediately following the closure signals that the glottis remains in a position that facilitates continued vocal-fold vibration during this obstruent interval.

The examples show that the acoustic manifestations of articulator-bound features for consonants often reside in the sound on both sides of an acoustic discontinuity. When a consonantal constriction is formed with the primary articulator, this constriction in effect divides the lumen of the vocal tract into two parts: a portion anterior to the constriction and a portion posterior to the constriction. The acoustic attributes that signal the identity and positioning of the primary articulator and of the other articulators will be different when the constriction is in place than when the articulator is moving toward or away from the constricted position. For example, for an obstruent consonant the acoustic signal can potentially provide information only about the portion of the vocal tract anterior to the constriction during the constricted interval when turbulence noise is being generated in the vicinity of the constriction.[3] After the release of the consonant, however, the source reverts to the glottis, and the radiated sound reflects the shape of the entire vocal tract as the cross-sectional area of the consonantal constriction increases. In the case of a nasal consonant, information about the vocal-tract configuration during the closure interval is sampled, in effect, by observation of the sound passing through the velopharyngeal opening and radiated from the nose, whereas the mouth output provides this information after the consonant is released. Similar kinds of statements can be made for a lateral consonant. It is evident from these and other observations that the acoustic properties signaling the identity of the primary articulator depend on the positioning of secondary articulators, such as the vocal folds and the soft palate. The acoustic correlates of some features seem to be more readily interpreted if other features have already been identified. There appears, then, to be a preferred order or hierarchy in the process of extracting the acoustic properties that lead to the features.

The examples in figure 14.1, as well as other data on the acoustic manifestations of features for consonants, illustrate three different points. One point is that the acoustic pattern on both sides of the acoustic discontinuity, and at the discontinuity itself, contribute to identification of articulator-bound features. The second point – which is perhaps of only indirect relevance to the present discussion – is that the diverse acoustic attributes signaling that an articulator-bound feature has been implemented are perhaps most easily interpreted if the relation between articulatory shapes and acoustic outputs for constricted configurations is taken into account. Thirdly, since identification of some features for a segment is facilitated if other features of the segment (such as continuancy or sonorancy) are known, an optimum strategy for a human or machine recognizer of speech is to identify features according to a particular order.

In the case of nonconsonantal segments, no abrupt discontinuity appears in the signal to serve as a focus for implementing the features of the segment. Nonconsonantal segments are characterized by points or regions in time at which certain articulatory structures reach an extreme position or state. At these points in time, some acoustic parameter, such as a formant frequency, achieves a maximum or minimum value, or may remain at a relatively fixed value over a time interval.[4] It is postulated that these points identify acoustic landmarks for nonconsonantal segments.

Acoustic interpretation of the various articulator-bound features for these nonconsonantal regions involves examining acoustic data in the vicinity of the acoustic landmark defined in this way, as well as changes in the spectrum preceding and following the landmark. The extent to which this view of an acoustic landmark can be applied to nonconsonantal segments is unclear, and requires further study. It is expected, for example, that tongue-body movements that are used to produce a labiovelar glide are adjusted to achieve an extreme high back configuration in synchrony with an extreme lip rounding. This synchrony would lead to a minimum in F_1 and F_2 and a maximum in the increased F_2 bandwidth that is characteristic of this glide and that signals the presence of a narrow tongue-body constriction. On the other hand, there may be other situations in which some asynchrony in the movements of a secondary articulator (such as the tongue root) in relation to the primary articulator may help to enhance the acoustic manifestation of the secondary articulator-bound features. For example, the distinction between vowels in English is carried in part by the way in which the spectrum changes with time. It appears that for some vowels the implementation of a feature specifying the configuration in the pharyngeal region is sequential with the implementation of features indicating the tongue-body position. Acoustic and perceptual studies of vowels in English have consistently shown that accuracy of machine identification of vowels is enhanced by examining formant trajectories over time rather than at a single point in time (Nearey and Assmann 1986; Leung 1989; Huang 1991).

As with the consonantal segments, the acoustic properties required to identify certain features appear to be independent of other features for a segment, whereas knowledge of context may be needed for identifying some features. Thus, for example, the acoustic properties used to identify the feature *nasal* or the feature *tense* are most readily identified if the feature *back* and perhaps *high* and *low* are known.

14.5 Constraints on the implementation of articulator-bound features

We have presented arguments for the view that there are consonantal landmarks in the speech signal and that the acoustic manifestations of articulator-bound features are represented in the signal in the vicinity of these landmarks. A consequence of this view is that, if the various articulator-bound feature are to be represented adequately in the sound, there must be constraints on the timing of the movements of the secondary articulators in relation to the primary articulators. Manipulation of a primary articulator creates an acoustic landmark. The movement of secondary articulators must be coordinated with the primary articulators so that acoustic evidence for the secondary features appears around the landmarks. This principle governing the coordination of different articulators during speech production has been proposed by Kingston (1990), who use the term "articulatory binding" to describe the process. Further discussion of the generality and possible limitations of the principle is given by Ohala (1990), Goldstein (1990), and Huffman (1990).

Some variability in the timing of the secondary articulators in relation to the primary ones is possible without doing damage to the ability of a listener to uncover the articulator-bound features that are associated with the secondary articulators. However, too large a deviation in the relative timing will result in an acoustic output that does not provide information about the intended features of the segment, or indicates feature values different from those intended (Goldstein 1989). In some cases, the influence of a secondary articulation might spread over such a wide time interval that it appears to be aligned with the landmark of an adjacent segment as well as (or instead of) its parent landmark. Adjustment of the timing and extent of the movement of secondary articulators can have an influence not only on the features for these articulators but also on the salience with which the articulator-free and the articulator-bound features for primary articulators are represented in the sound.

These influences on the sound of the relative timing of the movements of different articulatory structures have been examined for a variety of movement patterns by Browman and Goldstein (1986), although details of the acoustic consequences of these timing changes were not examined. In the present discussion we consider more closely the acoustic manifestations of these articulatory movements and we attempt to develop some principles, based on acoustics and perception, that might help to delineate constraints on the implementation of the features for an utterance. In this sense, therefore, we are drawing on the work of a number of investigators who have used phonetic data and models to show the kinds of constraints under which speakers operate when they produce an utterance in a given language (Manuel and Krakow 1984; Manuel 1990; Ohala 1990).

Several examples can be cited to illustrate how the movements of secondary articulators need to be properly timed in relation to the primary articulators. (See also Kingston 1990.) A familiar example is a voiceless aspirated stop consonant such as [pʰ]. Here the relevant articulator-bound features associated with a secondary articulator are [+spread glottis] and [+stiff vocal folds], using the laryngeal features that are accepted by some phonologists. The feature [+spread glottis] is implemented by adjusting the glottal abducting movement in such a way that the glottis is maximally open at the time of release of the primary articulator (Dixit 1975, 1989). In this way, the presence of aspiration noise and of a subsequent breathy-voiced onset is evident in the sound in the few tens of milliseconds following the release. Presumably the timing of the glottal adduction following the release is adjusted so that the movement of the supraglottal articulator that forms and releases the constriction is essentially complete by the time glottal vibration begins. The glottal spreading maneuver also contributes to inhibition of vocal-fold vibration immediately following the implosion. The feature [+stiff vocal folds] is implemented during the consonantal closure interval so that vocal-fold vibration does not occur within this interval when there is an increased intraoral pressure, or at the consonant release. Evidence for the feature [+stiff vocal folds] appears not only as inhibition of vocal-fold vibration within the closure interval but also as a raised fundamental frequency at the onset of vocal-fold vibration.

A somewhat more complex example is that of the voiced aspirated stop consonant as it occurs in Hindi and other languages. In this case again, the feature [+spread glottis] must be implemented in a way that shows aspiration noise and breathy onset of vocal-fold vibration following the consonantal release. The glottal spreading need not be as great as it is for a voiceless aspirated consonant since there is not a requirement that vocal-fold vibration be inhibited during the aspiration interval. However, the feature [+slack vocal folds] requires that vocal-fold vibration be evident in the sound prior to the consonant release. Because there is an interaction between the glottal spreading movement and the maintenance of vocal-fold vibration, it is necessary to preserve a reasonably adducted glottis throughout most of the consonantal closure interval, together with a slack state of the vocal folds. Glottal abduction is initiated only toward the end of the closure interval (Dixit 1975, 1989). Maintenance of glottal adduction and vocal-fold vibration is assisted by a vigorous active expansion of the vocal-tract walls, which helps to keep the supraglottal pressure low and the transglottal pressure high.

As another example of acoustic requirements influencing how a secondary articulator is controlled, we consider events at the release of a nasal consonant (cf. Huffman 1990; Ohala 1975). The velopharyngeal port is normally caused to close *following* the acoustic event created by the consonantal release. This temporal sequence guarantees that evidence of the feature [+ sonorant] remains represented in the sound. An early closing of the velopharyngeal port, prior to the consonantal release, will result in a buildup of intraoral pressure, and consequent noise generation at the release. Thus a relatively small change in the timing of the velopharyngeal closure (the velum being a secondary articulator) results in an abrupt switch in the properties of the sound, from characteristics indicating [+ sonorant] to [− sonorant].

Not only must the timing of the velopharyngeal opening in relation to the release of the primary articulator closure be appropriately adjusted, but it is probable that the amount of velopharyngeal opening that exists at the instant of the consonant release must be controlled depending on the following vowel (Abramson *et al*, 1981). When a nasal consonant is released into a high vowel, the velopharyngeal opening should be relatively small compared to the oral constriction for the vowel, to ensure the required rapid shift in output from the nose to the mouth. For a following low vowel, this requirement can be achieved with a larger velopharyngeal opening. Proper selection of the timing and degree of velopharyngeal opening, then, appears to enhance the strength of the acoustic discontinuity that occurs at the consonantal release.

Similar constraints on the timing and degree of movement of secondary articulators appear to play a role in the production of nonconsonantal segments. For example, the amount of lip rounding or spreading that is used to contrast rounded and unrounded vowels is different for different vowel heights and degrees of backness. Presumably the amount of lip rounding is selected to enhance the acoustic and perceptual contrast, and this amount may vary from one vowel to another. Similarly, the area of the velopharyngeal opening that is required to produce a nasal vowel is different depending on the vowel height. Data are needed to determine how the timing of the lip rounding or velum movements are adjusted in relation to movements of the tongue body, which is taken to be the primary articulator for vowels.

These and other examples illustrate how acoustic requirements constrain the coordination of secondary articulators with the primary articulators, particularly for consonants. There are many situations in which the acoustic consequences of manipulation of the timing of the secondary articulators are quantal. When the relative timing exceeds certain limits, there are abrupt changes in the characteristics of the sound in the vicinity of the consonantal landmark. Furthermore, the degree of movement of the secondary articulators appears often to be adjusted so as to enhance the acoustic representation of the various articulator-free and articulator-bound features (Stevens and Keyser 1989).

Notes

The influence of discussions with Morris Halle, Marie Huffman, Jay Keyser, and Sharon Manuel in developing the ideas in this paper, and the comments of John Ohala, who reviewed the paper, are gratefully acknowledged. The preparation of this paper was supported in part by grants from the National Institute of Health (grant DC-00075) and the National Science Foundation (grant IRI-8910561).

1 There are several situations for which a rapid change in spectrum amplitude in a particular frequency range can occur without a rapid movement of the lips, tongue blade, or tongue body toward or away from a constricted position. Examples are: the initial release of an affricate (for which the principal release of the primary articulator follows the initial release by a few tens of milliseconds); the shift from a voiceless condition to a condition with glottal vibration for /h/ or for a voiceless glide (for which spectral change is due primarily to a laryngeal adjustment rather than a movement of an articulator in the oral cavity); and the abrupt acoustic change that results at the time when velopharyngeal closure occurs during a prenasalized stop. In all of these cases, the acoustic signal does not indicate a closing or opening movement of an oral articulator and therefore does not provide direct evidence for the feature [+ consonantal]. For an affricate or a prenasalized stop, however, the spectral change signalling that an articulator has been released (evidence, therefore, for [+ consonantal]) usually appears a few tens of milliseconds later than the discontinuity noted here.

2 John Ohala (personal communication) has pointed out that the concept of a primary articulator being designated for every segment, whether consonantal or nonconsonantal, has a long history. See also Halle (1991).

3 An exception to this statement is that the presence or absence of glottal vibration during the constricted interval can be observed in the sound that is radiated from the neck.

4 For each nonconsonantal segment we might also postulate that there is a primary articulator (and a corresponding feature or features) that acts as a focus for the implementation of the other features that form the segment.

References

Abramson, A. S., P. W. Nye, J. B. Henderson and C. W. Marshall. 1981. Vowel height and the perception of consonantal nasality. *Journal of the Acoustical Society of America* 70: 329–339.

Browman, C. and L. Goldstein. 1986. Towards an articulatory phonology. *Phonology Yearbook* 3: 219–252.

Clements, G.N. 1985. The geometry of phonological features. *Phonology Yearbook* ~ 2: 223–250.

Dixit, R.P. 1975. Neuromuscular aspects of laryngeal control with special reference to Hindi. Ph.D. dissertation, University of Texas, Austin.

1989. Glottal gestures in Hindi plosives. *Journal of Phonetics* 17: 213–237.

Goldstein, L. 1989. On the domain of the quantal theory. *Journal of Phonetics* 17: 91–97.

1990. On articulatory binding: comments on Kingston's paper. In J. Kingston and M.E. Beckman (eds.) *Papers in Laboratory Phonology I: Between the Grammar and Physics of Speech*. Cambridge: University Press, 445–450.

Halle, Morris. 1991. Features. In W. Bright (ed.) *Oxford International Encyclopedia of Linguistics*. New York: Oxford University Press.

Halle, M. and K.N. Stevens. 1991. Knowledge of language and the sounds of speech. In J. Sundberg, L. Nord and R. Lund (eds.) *Music, Language, Speech, and Brain*. London: Macmillan, 1–19.

Huang, C. 1991. An acoustic and perceptual study of vowel formant trajectories in American English. *Research Laboratory of Electronics Technical Report 563*. Cambridge, MA: MIT Press.

Huffman, M.K. 1990. Implementation of Nasal: timing and articulatory landmarks. *UCLA Working Papers in Phonetics*, 75: 1–149.

Kingston, J. 1990. Articulatory binding. In J. Kingston and M.E. Beckman (eds.) *Papers in Laboratory Phonology I: Between the Grammar and Physics of Speech*. Cambridge: University Press, 406–434.

Leung, H.C. 1989. The use of artificial neural networks for phonetic recognition. Ph.D. dissertation, MIT.

Manuel, S.Y. 1990. The role of contrast in limiting vowel-to-vowel coarticulation in different languages. *Journal of the Acoustical Society of America* 88: 1286–1298.

Manuel, S.Y. and R.A. Krakow. 1984. Universal and language particular aspects of vowel-to-vowel coarticulation. *Haskins Laboratories Status Report on Speech Research*, SR–77/78: 69–78.

McCarthy, J.J. 1988. Feature geometry and dependency: a review. *Phonetica* 43: 84–108.

Nearey, T. and P. Assmann. 1986. Modeling the role of inherent spectral change in vowel identification. *Journal of the Acoustical Society of America* 80: 1297–1308.

Ohala, J.J. 1975. Phonetic explanations for nasal sound patterns. In C.A. Ferguson, L.M. Hyman, and J.J. Ohala (eds.) *Nasalfest: Papers from a symposium on nasals and nasalization*. Stanford University, Language Universals Project, 289–316.

1990. The generality of articulatory binding: comments on Kingston's paper. In J. Kingston and M.E. Beckman (eds.) *Papers in Laboratory Phonology I: Between the Grammar and Physics of Speech*. Cambridge: University Press, 435–444.

Sagey, E. 1986. The representation of features and relations in nonlinear phonology. Ph.D. dissertation, MIT.

Stevens, K.N. and S.J. Keyser. 1989. Primary features and their enhancement in consonants. *Language* 65: 81–106.

Trigo, L. 1988. The phonological derivation and behaviour of nasal glides. Ph.D. dissertation, MIT.

15

Do acoustic landmarks constrain the coordination of articulatory events?

LOUIS GOLDSTEIN

Over the last few years, research in phonology and phonetics has begun to investigate the coordination of articulatory events (or gestures) in speech – describing the coordinative patterns that characterize particular phonological structures and developing principles that underlie the patterns. In his paper, Stevens proposes some enrichments to the theory of distinctive features designed to allow the theory to come to grips with aspects of the coordination problem. It is the account of coordination that emerges from his proposal that I will evaluate critically in these remarks.

Specifically, Stevens proposes that articulator-bound features (those that specify the movement of a particular articulator in forming and releasing a constriction) are divided into two types: primary and secondary (with a given segment typically having at most one primary feature). Formation and release of a constriction using the primary articulator is seen as creating an acoustic "landmark." In the case of [consonantal] segments, this landmark is an acoustic discontinuity involving rapid spectral change. The coordinative principle is that secondary features must be coordinated with respect to the primary ones such that the acoustic evidence for the secondary features appears near the primary feature's acoustic landmark, on both sides of the discontinuity. The motivation for this is that "acoustic properties signaling the identity of the primary articulator depend on the positioning of secondary articulators" (section 14.4). Thus, Stevens seems to be suggesting that it is easier for the listener to sort out the interdependent acoustic influences of the entire ensemble of features when they are localized near these critical points.

I note, first of all, that Stevens's principle at the very least fails to account for the distinct modes of gestural coordination in speech that have been uncovered in recent work. For example, Krakow (1989, forthcoming) found a "bistable" relation between velic and lower-lip gestures in the production of American English nasal consonants. In syllable-initial position (e.g. "see *more*") the gestures were coordinated so as to be synchronous (maximum velic lowering coordinated with maximum lip raising), while in final position (e.g. "see*m* ore") they were asynchronous with the velic gesture leading (maximum velic lowering coordinated with the *onset* of lip raising). Browman and Goldstein (1992a) have proposed that these differences reflect general differences in coordination mode between initial and final position, pointing to the parallel between Krakow's results for nasals and Sproat and Fujimura's (1989, 1992) results for American English /l/. Sproat and Fujimura found that the two gestures for /l/ (tongue-tip raising and tongue-dorsum backing) are coordinated differently in different prosodic contexts, with the gestures again being roughly synchronous in word-initial position, but with the dorsum gesture leading substantially in word-final position. Both of these are examples that Stevens would treat as coordination of a secondary articulator-bound feature ([nasal], [back]) with a primary one ([labial], [coronal]). Yet nothing in Stevens's proposal predicts the systematic differences in coordination mode as a function of position.

Although Stevens's proposed constraint does not predict the different patterns of coordination as a function of position, one might try to argue that both patterns are consistent with it. That is, it might be possible to show (for the cases so far discussed) that in both coordinative patterns, there is an acoustic effect of the secondary feature on both sides of the landmark created by the primary feature. Since the secondary feature either leads or is synchronous, it will typically be in evidence around the time at which the primary constriction is formed and released. However, there are examples of these same phonological structures (nasals and /l/) that argue that even this view cannot be correct. These are examples in which the entire ensemble of gestures is coordinated in such a way that the primary feature regularly fails to produce the expected acoustic landmark at all. Even in these cases, however, the proposed coordinative generalizations outlined above still hold. Obviously, however, the patterns of coordination are not producing the expected acoustic effects at the (nonexistent) landmarks, and it is hard to imagine that such a principle is guiding their coordination in any way.

One such example showing a missing acoustic landmark can be seen in the data presented by Fujimura (1981), and discussed in Browman and Goldstein (1992b). He compared the production of final nasals in words like "pine" and "pined," whose acoustics show nasal murmurs, with words like "pint," where the murmur is absent, as is regularly the case in English for words ending in "nt" (Malecot 1960; see also Cohn 1990 for an analysis of such cases as involving "deletion" of the nasal consonant). As Fujimura notes, the movements of the tongue tip are quite similar in all these cases, with the lack of nasal murmur in "pint" being due to an additional laryngeal constriction typical of voiceless syllable codas in English. Despite the absence of the nasal murmur in "pint" (the spectral change into which would presumably constitute an acoustic landmark), the velum and tongue-tip movements exhibit the coordinative pattern predicted by Krakow's principle for final position: the maximum velic lowering is synchronized with the onset of tongue-tip raising. Figure 15.1 shows examples from the part of Tokyo x-ray microbeam corpus that was the basis of Fujimura's paper. Note that while the spectrograms show a clear nasal murmur for "pine," but not for "pint," the achievement of maximum velic lowering is coordinated with the onset of tip raising in both cases (as indicated in the figure by the vertical lines). Obviously, the basis for the common coordination pattern cannot lie in regulating the acoustic events.

A similar point can be made involving the production of /l/ in American English. Recasens and Farnetani (1992) compared electropalatographic data for /l/ in utterance-initial and utterance-final positions for speakers of Italian, Catalan, and American English. The patterns shown by their American English speaker are very similar to those of Sproat and Fujimura discussed above. Gestures of the tongue dorsum and tongue tip are roughly synchronous in initial position, while the tip-raising gesture lags substantially in final position, its movement onset roughly synchronized with the attainment of the maximum retraction of the dorsum. What is most interesting in the current context is that the tip raising for the speaker examined by Recasens and Farnetani takes place *after* phonation has already ceased. (This could not have been observed in the Sproat and Fujimura data, since they did not look at utterance-final position.) Thus, the gesture corresponding to the primary feature ([coronal]) again produces no acoustic landmark. However, the coordination pattern seems typical of (word- or syllable-final) /l/. Again, presence or absence of an acoustic property associated with a primary feature does not alter the coordination of the gestures.

To the extent that the observations made here continue to be borne out, it appears that there are regular patterns of coordination among articulatory events that are part and parcel of the phonological structure of a given language, but which are not constrained by the local requirements of some acoustic landmark. In general, the evolution of stable patterns of gestural coordination is likely to be subject to *many* pressures and boundary conditions (cf. Lindblom, MacNeilage, and Studdert-Kennedy 1983 for related ideas in the realm of inventories). Acoustic properties and how they can be used by listeners to specify the gestural structure should surely be included in the list, alongside anatomical, physiological, mechanical, and dynamical considerations. The system of coordination that evolves is

Feature Theory

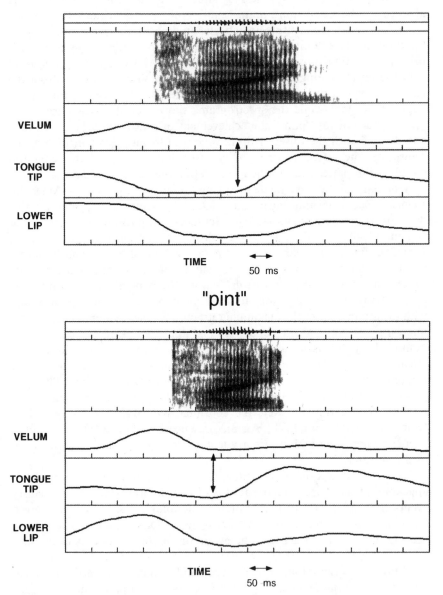

Figure 15.1. Top: Waveform (top panel) and spectrogram (second panel from top) synchronized with x-ray microbeam data (bottom three panels) for the utterance "pine". For microbeam data, the vertical position is displayed for pellets placed on the indicated articulators. For the panel labeled 'TONGUE TIP,' the pellet is actually positioned behind the tip, on the blade surface. Bottom as in top, for the utterance "pint."

presumably an overall, "global" solution that does not place rigid requirements on particular local events in the acoustic signal.

Note

This work was supported by NIH grant HD-01994 to Haskins Laboratories. Thanks to Rena Krakow and Edda Farnetani for helpful discussions.

References

Browman, C.P. and L. Goldstein. 1992a. Articulatory phonology: an overview. *Phonetica* 49: 155–180.

1992b. Replies to commentaries. *Phonetica* 49: 222–234.

Cohn, A. 1990. Phonetic and phonological rules of nasalization. *UCLA Working Papers in Phonetics* 76: 1–224.

Fujimura, O. 1981. Elementary gestures and temporal organization – What does an articulatory constraint mean? In T. Myers, J. Laver, and J. Anderson (eds.) *The Cognitive Representation of Speech*. Amsterdam: North-Holland, 101–110.

Krakow, R.A. 1989. The articulatory organization of syllables: a kinematic analysis of labial and velar gestures. Ph.D. dissertation, Yale University.

Forthcoming. *Articulatory Organization of Syllables: Patterns of Velum and Lip Movements*. Berlin: Mouton de Gruyter.

Lindblom, B., P. MacNeilage, and M. Studdert-Kennedy. 1983. Self-organizing processes and the explanation of phonological universals. In B. Butterworth, B. Comrie and O. Dahl (eds.) *Explanations of Linguistic Universals*. The Hague: Mouton, 181–203.

Malecot, A. 1960. Vowel nasality as a distinctive feature in English. *Language* 36: 222–229.

Recasens, D. and E. Farnetani. 1992. Spatiotemporal properties of different allophones of /l/: phonological implications. Presented at the International Conference on Phonology and Morphology, Krems und Stein, Austria, July 1992.

Sproat, R. and O. Fujimura. 1989. Articulatory evidence for the non-categoricalness of English /l/ allophones. Presented at the annual meeting of the Linguistic Society of America, Washington, DC, December 1989.

Sproat, R. and O. Fujimura. 1992. Allophonic variation in English /l/ and its implications for phonetic implementation. ms., AT&T Bell Labs. and Ohio State University, submitted for publication.

Part IV
Phonetic Output

16

Phonetic evidence for sound change in Quebec French

MALCAH YAEGER-DROR

16.1 Introduction

This paper will discuss the vowel phonology of Montreal French, based on the results of perceptual and acoustic analysis of a large corpus of Montreal French casual interviews (Sankoff and Sankoff 1973; Thibault and Vincent 1990; Cedergren *et al.* 1992). One underlying assumption behind this study is that language variation and change can efficiently be analyzed from the casual speech of a large number of speakers from different subgroups within a community. Another assumption is that rules for vowel shifting (or other linguistic changes) which are found to operate in one speech community help formulate theoretical and cognitive components of their grammar, and, by extension, they help to determine the typological possibilities available for all human languages. The Montreal French data to be discussed are especially interesting in that they provide evidence for sound changes that are systematically different from those which occur in English dialects (Labov 1991, 1983, and references cited there), or other languages (Labov *et al.* 1972).

Three issues relevant to changes in this vowel system will be discussed

the typology of vowel shifts (16.2),
the lexicon and phonological theory (16.3), and
cognitive abilities as they are revealed by evidence of phonological
change (16.4).

Each of these issues will be raised in turn; the perspective provided by the results of earlier studies will be outlined. Section 16.5 will describe the corpus, 16.6 will describe the analysis techniques, 16.7–8 provide discussion of the results, and conclusions will be presented in 16.9.

16.2 The typology of vowel variation and vowel shifts

Over the years, linguists have found that even in casual speech, when plotted on a two-dimensional grid representing phonetic "space," stressed vowels before high-sonority consonants (like voiced fricatives) are longer, and reach or even overshoot their vowel target (Labov *et al.* 1972; Edwards and Beckman 1988; Yaeger-Dror 1990; Beckman *et al.* 1991). Evidence was presented in Labov *et al.* (1972) that these long vowels are generally [+ peripheral]: that is, they systematically plot at the outer (peripheral) edges of the vowel space.

Stressed tokens of unstable long vowels will tend to rise and will plot across a broad segment of the periphery of a speaker's "vowel space." As a vowel reaches the upper edge of that space ([i], [y] or [u]), it is possible that its nucleus will then fall to a very low position within the vowel space ([a] or [ɑ]) with a glide. Most such changes which have been studied follow Pattern 1 for vowel shifting, found in the schematic drawing of figure 16.1 adapted from Labov *et al.* (1972).

In contrast, the shortest vowels – those before low-sonority consonants (like voiceless stops, cf. Lehiste 1970), and in less stressed positions – are the most reduced and centralized (Lindblom 1963; Delattre 1966, 1969; Beckman and Edwards, this volume; Veatch 1991); when these short vowels shift to a new position it will be toward this more neutral centralized position. Labov *et al.* (1972) refer to this as Pattern 1' for chain shifting, which can be seen in figure 16.1.

In French it is the mid-low lengthened vowels which until recently were unstable in France, and which are still unstable in New World dialects like

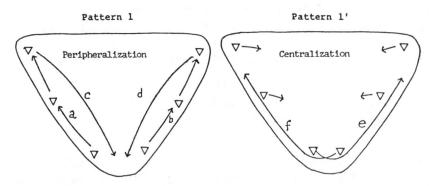

Figure 16.1. Patterns 1 and 1' for sound change of long and short vowels, respectively; adapted from Labov *et al.* (1972).

Montreal French.[1] Since they are long, therefore peripheral, they would be expected to rise. Thurot (1881–1883), in his historical review of French grammars, found that as far back as the mid-seventeenth century mid–low lengthened (ɛː), (ɔː), and (œː)[2] nuclei would rise to mid-high (as predicted by Pattern 1), while shortened mid-low vowels – primarily in the same syllable with an *r*-cluster – would centralize and fall slightly (as predicted in Pattern 1′). In the late nineteenth century, Geddes (1894) reported that the Quebec pronunciation of mid-low lengthened vowel nuclei appeared to be stable [e, ø, o], and that in a syllable with a cluster the mid-low short vowel nuclei still centralized and fell. These changes are consistent with those shown as Pattern 1 and 1′ in figure 16.1. We would expect any further changes in the current century to continue this pattern, for example continued raising of the mid-low vowels to high vowels. However, modern researchers have maintained that no vowel shifts are in progress in Montreal French (Gendron 1966; Santerre 1974). It is true that the shortened mid-low vowels (as in *perte* "loss") have not changed position in the Quebec dialects (Gendron 1966). Nonetheless, as we shall see, the lengthened mid-low vowels in *père* "father," and similar words – which had previously raised to mid-high – have more recently gone through a major shift of vowel *lowering*. This shift, which is counter to the expected Pattern 1, is quite similar for (ɛː, ɔː, œː). In all three cases, the expected Pattern 1 is not followed. Both perceptual and acoustic analysis reveal that the mid-low lengthened vowels of Montreal French are shifting downward while remaining peripheral: older men still realize these vowels as [eː[(i)], oː[(u)], øː[(y)]], respectively, while younger speakers are more likely to realize them as [aː[(i)], ɑː[(u)], ɑː[(y)]], respectively. Our focus here will be on this symmetric lowering of mid-low lengthened vowels in Montreal French, along with some of the lexical constraints on this vowel-shifting pattern.

16.3 The lexicon and phonological change

Labov (1981, 1988) demonstrated that certain types of linguistic change can be explained only if both the Neogrammarian Hypothesis and the Lexical Diffusion Hypothesis (Schuchardt 1885; Wang 1977) are considered to be active forces in the change. A neogrammatical change may be phonologically conditioned, while a lexical change is lexically conditioned. That is, while a neogrammatical change affects all lexical items within a class at once, lexical diffusion entails that different lexical items shift at different rates. Since the chain shift to be discussed here is complicated by lexical diffusion, this is an important point.

16.3.1 Etymological lexical classes

In some cases an etymological residue of older lexical classes remains. Evidence of a pseudomerger of older etymological classes in English is presented in J. Milroy (1980) and Harris (1985), who showed that the purported merger of the *meet/meat/mate* classes in Hiberno-English never took place, since the lexical classes remain distinct today. Pseudomergers in American English have also been studied (Labov *et al.* 1972; DiPaolo 1992; Labov *et al.* 1992). Unmerged etymological groups such as these will be referred to here as *etymological lexical classes*. Such classes are attested for mid-low lengthened vowels of Montreal French (Thurot 1881–1883; Dumas 1987) and can be seen in table 16.1. This table shows how words divide into different etymological classes depending on whether they demonstrate vowel lengthening. The first column gives the word classes, and the other columns give example words for each of three different vowels. The word classes are organized into groups according to the postvocalic consonant(s). The first group consists of cases where loss of a consonant resulted in compensatory vowel lengthening. The second group consists of cases where lengthening occurred consistently without consonant loss and is attributed to the consonant's sonority. The third group consists of cases where lengthening is less consistent, and the fourth group consists of cases where lengthening never occurred; here /N/ represents all nasal consonants and /K/ all stops and nongeminate voiceless fricatives. These groups were believed to be merged (cf., for example, Martinet 1969; Yaeger 1979; Paradis 1985), but they have proven to be still phonologically distinct (Yaeger-Dror and Kemp 1992).

Table 16.2 shows that, historically, compensatory lengthening (for the most part) preceded lengthening conditioned by the sonority of the following consonant. (Discussion of the historical evidence can be found in Yaeger-Dror 1990 and papers cited there.) Synchronically, length is determined by lexical class. For this study, words were coded both for following consonant (sonority) and for etymological class. Table 16.2 shows the difference between the order for sonority and that for etymological class. The hierarchy for etymological class is the same as that given in table 16.1.

16.3.2 Exceptional lexical patterns

In others cases, differences between lexical classes arise because a split occurs in a class when some words shift to a new vowel target, leaving other words behind, as occurred with the (æh/æ) split in American English (Labov *et al.* 1972; Labov 1981, 1991; Kiparsky 1988): words which either lead the

Table 16.1. *Etymological classes for French mid-low vowels*

V change Èxs:	(ɛ:)	(ø/œ:)	(O:/ɔ)
Compensatory lengthening:			
VSK > V̂:K^{cl}	bête	jeûne	côte
VN > Ṽ:^{cl}	ben	jeun	bon
Vss > V:s^{cl}	baisse	(loess)	bosse
Vrr > V:r^{cl}	guerre	beurre	—
Consistently lengthened by following consonant's sonority:			
Vz > V:z	pèse	vendeuse	rose
Vr > V:r	paire	peur	port
Less consistently lengthened:			
V3 > V:3	beige	—	loge
Vv ~ V:v	lèvre	fleuve	(ove)
Vr ~ V(:)r	mer	—	—
Unlengthened:			
VN	laine	jeune	bonne
VK	lettre	neutre	botte

cl = compensatory lengthening

Table 16.2. *Proposed hierarchy of sonority, as compared with an etymologically based hierarchy*

Consonant sonority	Etymological class
z, 3	^
	z
r/R	s, ʃ
v	r/R
s, ʃ	3
other voiceless fricatives/	v
& all stops	other voiceless fricatives/
	& all stops

shift, or remain behind when most other words have shifted, will be referred to here as *lexical exceptions.*

Figure 16.2 can be used as a wave model for lexical diffusion (Ogura *et al.* 1991): first a small group of innovative words "split off" and shift, followed by the bulk of "regular" lexical items, and lastly by the more conservative words. The wave theory projects that ultimately the lexical diffusion should be resolved as a change comes to completion. As a result, speakers at either extreme of the change would show less extreme vowel diffusion than those in the mid range, whose innovative words in a given lexical class would have reached the new target, while the conservative words would not be shifted yet. In their Middle English data Ogura *et al.* (1991) found that only a few words are clearly innovative, the majority of the lexicon shifts together, but several words are conservative. Vowel-color distinctions between classes are most salient as the vowel shift gets underway; as the "wave" of change nears completion, the conservative words shift, and the "lexical diffusion" is resolved among the younger speakers when the lexical groups remerge as the shift reaches completion.

Previous studies of this corpus have shown that there is evidence for such lexical diffusion in the 1971 corpus. The perceptual analysis found that such lexical diffusion exists for Montreal French (ε:) (Yaeger-Dror and Kemp

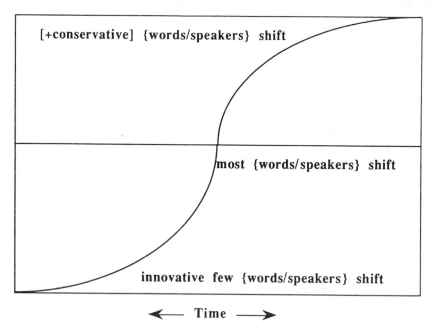

Figure 16.2. Wave model for sound change, adapted from the discussion in Guy 1988.

Table 16.3. *Exceptional lexical class words compared with similar words not in that class*

Regular class			]Lexical exceptions		
Word	Gloss	[Transc]	Word	Gloss	[Transc]
[−conservative]			[+conservative]		
paire	pair	pɛːr[3]	père	father	peːr
maire	mayor	mɛːr	mère	mother	meːr
mer	sea	mɛːr	hiver	winter	iveːr
infirmière	nurse	..mjɛːr	glacière	ice box	glasjeːr
frigidaire	fridge	friʒidɛːr			
terre	land	tɛːr	guerre	war	geːr
mords	bite	mɔːr	mort	dead	moːr
			d'abord	at first	daboːr
			encore	again	ãkoːr
leur	theirs	lœːr	leur	their (clitic)	ljør
			coeur	heart	kjør
[−conservative]			[+innovative]		
or	but	ɔːr	alors	therefore	alɒːr

1992), (œː), and (ɔː) (Yaeger-Dror 1989). (Further discussion of how the lexical groups were determined can be found in Kemp and Yaeger-Dror 1991, and in Yaeger-Dror 1992a.) Table 16.3 presents members of the exceptional lexical classes, which will be referred to as [+conservative], since they are generally realized with a more conservative (that is, raised) articulation. The acoustic data to be reported below confirm the earlier evidence for these lexical classes, and also the importance of these classes in the stepwise regression analysis of formant positions for all the speakers studied. The results permit us to discuss the relative robustness of the exceptional class variable over time.

16.4 Linguistic change and cognitive abilities

Labov (1983[1966]) demonstrated the possibility of analyzing sound change by comparing the speech of older and younger speakers from the same community, whose speech was gathered at the same time. In casual speech older individuals speak quite differently from their juniors, and this difference is assumed to reflect a shift from an older form of the dialect (spoken by the older individuals), toward the newer form of the dialect (spoken by younger speakers). In most phonological shifts studied to date, older women shift from an older variant, while men still retain it, and all younger speakers appear to follow the lead of the older women; gender and class distinctions are eliminated as the change reaches completion (Guy 1988). These studies of older and younger speakers interviewed at the same time appear to reveal actual phonological change as it progresses.

However, Chambers and Trudgill (1980: 164ff.) pointed out that while this "change in apparent time" could be determined by comparing interviews of older and younger speakers, it was not proven that this degree of change accurately reflected the actual change, which they referred to as "change in real time." They maintained that only a series of studies, done several years apart, preferably of the same speakers, could provide conclusive evidence of this "real" change.

Basing themselves on studies of speakers who have switched dialect areas (Payne 1980), both Labov (1982) and Trudgill (1986) presented supportive evidence for our ability to study linguistic change through studies in apparent time, while making a very strong claim about cognitive development: they both conclude that while *lexical* changes can continue after adolescence, a speaker's *dialect phonology* is "hard wired" or "fixed" into the brain by adolescence, or perhaps even by age eight. It is this latter hypothesis which will be of primary concern here. The present study is the first to permit actual acoustic analysis of a potentially changing dialect, and will therefore have a strong impact on our understanding of the theory of sound change, and on our understanding of cognitive development.

16.5 Corpus for the present analysis

The corpus used for this study was gathered in 1971 and was originally designed to permit study of casual speech to maximize our ability to determine change in "apparent time" (Sankoff and Sankoff 1973); subsequently, it was supplemented by additional older speakers from William Kemp's 1978 expansion of that corpus and by the inclusion of radio-archive speech (Kemp and Yaeger-Dror 1991). In 1984, Thibault and Vincent (1990) reinterviewed 60 of the original 120 speakers, in order to test the hypothesis that after adolescence a given speaker's vowel system will remain stable.

A subset of speakers was selected from this sample for the acoustic analysis. The subset permits a viable judgment sample including the following demographic cells (L. Milroy 1987): sex (2), socioeconomic group (2), and age (4).

Sex. Both men and women of contrasting social groups were included in the original sample for the perceptual analysis. However, given that even the oldest women had lowered the realization of mid-low lengthened vowels by 1971, it was assumed that only men's speech would warrant acoustic analysis, since men were more likely to continue to advance this shift after 1971.

Socioeconomic groups. Speakers were chosen from the social extremes, so "middle-class" (MC) speakers (doctors, lawyers, college deans) are contrasted with "working-class" (WC) speakers (with blue-collar jobs).

Age. Initially, speakers were divided by birth date, and the patterns which evolved were later built into the analysis. Speakers born before 1900 were separated from those born between 1900 and 1920, and from those born after World War II; those speakers who were born just prior to the post-World War II baby boom are more similar to the older generation than to their near age-mates, necessitating a separate group for speakers who were born just prior to the baby boom (born 1940–1946). For the acoustic analysis, men from all four groups were included.

Register. In order to determine the lexical classes which should be distinguished, and to determine the relevant speaker variables, time variables, and register variables, the perceptual analysis was made on a sample of 40 speakers in two registers: some had been casually interviewed in 1971–1978, and some had been broadcast on the radio prior to 1960. All acoustical analyses were run on speakers for whom two lengthy high-sound-quality interviews, 13 years apart (1971, 1984), were available. Of those, analysis based on data from the casual interviews for 13 speakers will be presented here.

16.6 Analysis techniques for this study

There are two methods for the analysis of vowel variation which have become generally accepted within the sociolinguistic community. Both of these methods have been used for this study.

16.6.1 Perceptual phonetic techniques

The first, initially pioneered by Labov (1983 [1966]), uses trained phoneticians' perceptual transcription of vowel color, dividing relevant phonetic distinctions for the phonological unit under analysis into a significant number of vowel heights (3–4). In this case, although initially [æ:], [a:], and [ɑ:] tokens were counted separately, under the assumption that more extreme lowering and backing would be correlated with social or phonological parameters, they were later recombined when neither

Table 16.4. *Template of variable realizations of mid-low lengthened vowels, used for perceptual analysis*

	Monophthong			Diphthong		
Raised	e:	ø:	o:	e:^{i}	ø^{y}	o:^{u}
	ɛ:	œ:	ɔ:	ɛ:^{i}	œ:^{y}	ɔ:^{u}
Lowered	æ:	a:	ɑ:	æ:^{i} /a:^{i}	ɑ:^{y}	ɒ:^{u}/ɑ:^{u}

phonological, generational, nor class-based criteria seemed to be consistently correlated with the degree of lowering and backing.

Table 16.4 shows the extent of dispersion for phonetic realizations of mid-low lengthened vowels. It is clear from the table that two parameters were isolated:

> vowel height and
> potential diphthongization.[4]

Unfortunately, space considerations preclude discussion of diphthong variation, so only vowel height distinctions will be discussed in detail here.

The primary advantage of the perceptual method is that all tokens of a variable can be categorized in less time than a few tokens of the variable can be analyzed acoustically; furthermore, one only needs to categorize tokens of the variable under analysis, while an acoustic analysis requires measurement of tokens of many different vowels, to determine the limits of the phonological space, in order to permit judgment of "raising" and "lowering" relative to the other vowels in the speaker's system. For that reason, acoustic analysis is generally preceded by a perceptual analysis, to determine relevant social and linguistic variables.

16.6.2 Acoustic phonetic techniques

The second technique pioneered by Labov (Labov *et al.* 1972) relies on acoustic analysis of the vowel tokens, measuring the first two (or more) formants of vowel nuclei for all vowel "classes" considered relevant, and placing the variable tokens within a given speaker's vowel "space" as determined by measurements of stressed tokens for all the vowels in an individual's vowel system. The advantage of the acoustic method is that often the differences among allophones of an unstable vowel are so small as to remain unperceived, but are consistently maintained; this patterned variation is of great theoretical interest, but is likely to be unheard or lost as "measurement error" in a perceptual study.

The present analysis has taken advantage of both methods: perceptual analysis was used to determine the relevant speaker groups, lexical classes, and stress factors which should be considered, and acoustic analysis was introduced to confirm the diagnosis, and to verify evidence of real-time change.

16.6.3. Stress levels

The data were coded for vowel color (as shown in table 16.4), as well as for sociolinguistic (speaker and register) variables discussed in section 16.5. In addition, all data were coded for etymological class (as in section 16.3.1), exceptional lexical class (as in section 16.3.2), and what will be referred to here as stress, since that is the term most common in the discussion of French prosody. (Whereas in English "stress" often connotes "accent" (cf. Beckman and Edwards's definition of "accent" in this volume), in French "stress" is primarily discussed as it relates to durational variation.)

Since as a rule only word-final syllables "carry" stress in French, only word-final syllable vowels were analyzed. As implied in section 16.2, vowels with more stress should be not only longer, but more peripheral. Therefore, when a change is taking place, the stressed unstable vowels, in overshooting their targets, will display the most extreme shifting toward the newer target.

It will be obvious to listeners who have ever tried to categorize intonational groups for a conversational speech style that classification is much more complex than the classification of intonation for a more controlled database (Ladd, this volume; Cedergren *et al.* 1992; Price *et al.* 1991). Phrasal stress levels assigned to conversational material do not invariably match the stress level that would be assigned on a theoretical basis, since influences relevant to discourse quite often outweigh more theoretical considerations. (See, for example, Yaeger-Dror 1985, and Liberman *et al.* 1991.) The classification used here reflects that complexity.

Initially five distinct stress groups were isolated for the analysis. These were later reduced to three:

1. In French, prepausal, "breath-group final" words are considered "stressed", and the final-syllable vowels are almost invariably the longest in the sentence. The final syllable of words at the end of exclamations or questions, generally with high or rising pitch and high amplitude, and following marked pause, were categorized separately from the final syllable of unmarked declarative statements, with low falling pitch and low amplitude, and following marked pause. These two articulatorily and acoustically very different groups were later combined and defined as

"breath-group final,"[5] because no significant differences between them could be found for duration or vowel color. It is already known that vowels in both these breath-group final positions are generally longer than vowels in other positions, and that even the vowels in syllables immediately preceding the final syllable are significantly longer than equivalent vowels in other positions (Boudreault 1968; Benguerel 1970; Klatt 1975; Kloker 1975; Yaeger 1979; Beckman and Edwards 1988; Fletcher 1991; Cedergren *et al.* 1992; Paradis and Deshaies 1990).

2. Similarly, emphatically or semantically stressed sentence-internal vowels, with high or rising contoured pitch and amplitude, and little or no following pause, were coded separately from vowels at the end of sentence-internal syntactic units, which are generally realized with low or falling contoured pitch[6] and possible short pause. However, these groups were combined for the statistical analysis when it was found that they could not be consistently distinguished; nor did there appear to be any appreciable difference between the vowel positions of those vowels which could be unambiguously determined to belong to one of these groups. These vowels were considered to be under "secondary" or "intermediate" stress.

3. The last stress level considered was "unstressed."

Both perceptual and acoustic analyses were coded for all stress levels, with subsequent recoding into these three groups. Section 16.7 provides an example of results of the perceptual analysis for one of the mid-low lengthened vowels – (ε:); 16.8 discusses the acoustic analysis.

16.7 Perceptual results for (ε:)

Yaeger-Dror and Kemp (1992) present a detailed analysis of the "apparent time" shift in (ε:), based primarily on the evidence from the 1971 corpus.[7] In the course of the study, each token for each word was coded separately. Percentages of raising, lowering, and diphthongization were determined for each individual speaker, and for the pooled speakers. Lexical class, age groups, and other factors were determined by perusal of the data after which analyses of variance were run on data for individual speakers, with age, socioeconomic group, gender, and register as variables (with all but unstressed tokens pooled) to confirm the analysis.

16.7.1 Raised vowels

While I stated earlier that there has been a shift from an older raised [e:] nucleus to a new lowered [æ:] nucleus, I have not yet presented evidence of this shift. Figure 16.3 shows the perceived percentages of [e:] nuclei for (ε:), for the pooled speakers from each of these demographic groups. It is clear that the older men are the only ones to retain the more conservative nucleus. All interviewed social groups reveal change in progress, except for working-class women who had apparently carried the change to completion by the 1970s. Stress does not appear to affect the incidence of [eː], which is consistent with the evidence that the change in progress is not toward [eː].

These data fit the "classic" wave pattern for sound change in progress, shown in figure 16.2. Older women have already shifted from the older variant, while men still retain it, and all younger speakers appear to follow the lead of the older women; gender and class distinctions are eliminated as the change reaches completion (Guy 1988). Differences between the genders and between the social classes are highly significant ($p < 0.0001$, $p < 0.007$), as are the age-related differences ($p < 0.0001$) (Yaeger-Dror and Kemp 1992). The pattern revealed in figure 16.3 is quite similar to the symmetrical pattern for the other mid-low lengthened rounded vowels (Yaeger-Dror 1989).

16.7.2 Shift toward [æ, aː]

Figure 16.4 documents the lowering of the (εː) nucleus toward [æ, a] or [ɑ]. None of the men recorded before 1960, nor middle-class men interviewed as late as 1978, used any appreciable percentage of lowered tokens, and only three of eight working-class men use even 10%. On the other hand, while *no* [æ] nuclei appear in radio broadcasts before 1960, and only one of six middle-class women interviewed later used any appreciable percentage, by the 1970s six of ten working-class women used [æ] nuclei more than 50% of the time, with the other four women not far behind. Figure 16.4 also reveals that lowering is most advanced in stressed syllables, where target overshoot can be most extreme during a vowel shift (Labov *et al.* 1972). This fact provides supporting evidence that the change is advancing.

Here again, the downward shift is almost complete for older working-class women, while the change is clearly progressing for all other social groups. Yaeger-Dror and Kemp (1992) found that here too the differences between men and women, between the socioeconomic groups, and between speakers of different ages, are all highly significant ($p < 0.0001$). The pattern is only slightly less advanced for mid-low lengthened rounded vowels (Yaeger-Dror 1989).

As mentioned in section 16.2, theoretically, the mid-low lengthened vowels could have continued to rise past [eː] along the peripheral track, and, in fact, some older rural speakers in the Kemp corpus (not included in the present sample) sporadically raise these vowels. However, /i, y, u/ are not stable in Montreal French, while the mid-high vowels, /e, o/ and (to a lesser extent) /ø/, are. In fact, while Dumas (1987) presents a few near-minimal

Phonetic Output

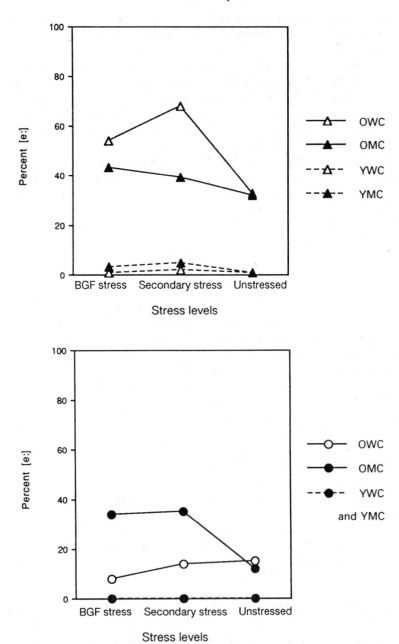

Figure 16.3. Pooled percentages of raised [eː] nuclei for Montreal-French-speaking (top) men (triangles) and (bottom) women (circles). Older speakers (solid lines) are distinguished from younger (broken lines). Middle-class speakers (filled symbols) are distinguished from working-class speakers (unfilled symbols). Note that stress does not appear to either favor or disfavor [eː].

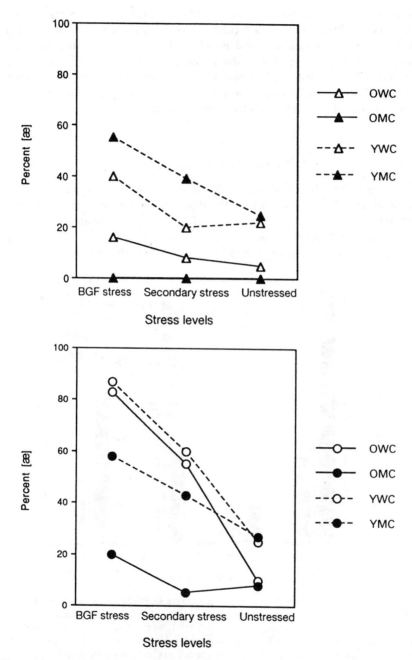

Figure 16.4. Pooled percentages of lowered [{æ:, a:, ɑ:}] nuclei for Montreal-French-speaking (top) men (triangles) and (bottom) women (circles). Middle-class speakers (filled symbols) are distinguished from working-class speakers (unfilled symbols). Note that stressed vowels are more likely to shift toward the newer pronunciation.

pairs for the long mid-high versus mid-low contrast – where one of the members is a loan from English (like *steak*) – there are no actual minimal pairs of mid-low lengthened and mid-high vowels. In contrast, there are many minimal pairs for the mid-low lengthened versus high lengthened vowel distinction, so there is a much greater functional load on the latter contrast. This might be one reason why raising, the "preferred" route for sound change (Labov *et al.* 1972), is not followed.

16.7.3 Exceptional lexical diffusion

Figure 16.5 shows the incidence of (perceived) [e] nuclei in stressed syllables for these lexical subsets of (ε:) for the interviewed speakers, demonstrating that the wave-like distribution projected for lexical diffusion in sections 16.3.2 and 16.4 does occur: the two lexical classes are most clearly distinguished not for the older speakers who had hardly started to shift the

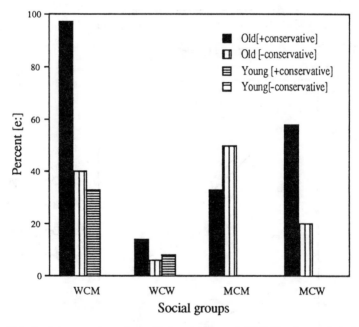

Figure 16.5. Pooled percentages of raised [e:] nuclei in stressed syllables for two lexical groups. The [+conservative] class is marked with a darker plot symbol, and is more conservative in pronunciation for all speakers except MC men (MCM). Note that among the younger speakers, first the [−conservative] words have no raised tokens (for younger WC speakers), and then the older pronunciation is lost for all the words in the (ε:) lexicon (among the younger MC speakers).

vowels, or for those who had completed the shift, but for younger working-class men, who have greatly reduced their apparent reliance on an [e] nucleus for (ɛ:) when the [+conservative] class is separated off from other (ɛ:) words. Yaeger-Dror (1989) found the same wave-like model to be useful in understanding the evidence for exceptional lexical classes with (ɔ:) as well.

As Ogura *et al.* (1991) had found, only a few words are clearly innovative, several words are conservative – on the tag end of the wave for the phonetic shift from a mid-high to low nucleus – and the bulk of the lexicon changes together. The words which shift last were classified as [+conservative] in table 16.3. As the "wave" of change nears completion, these conservative words shift, and the "lexical diffusion" is resolved among the younger speakers. Vowel-colour distinctions between classes are most salient as the vowel shift gets underway, but the lexical groups remerge as the shift reaches completion.

Both etymology and word frequency have been suggested as possibly related to lexical diffusion. Yaeger-Dror and Kemp (1992) present evidence that most lexical diffusion found in this corpus appears to be more closely related to lexico-semantic rather than phonological or etymological considerations, although Kemp and Yaeger-Dror (1991) cite a case whose causes are more difficult to determine.

It has been considered important to document perceptual evidence with further acoustic studies. While perceptual evidence can show that there are several independent variables which all influence a given dependent variable, it is only possible to determine the relative importance of different independent variables by performing regressions on the acoustic data. There is another important reason for including acoustic analysis in the present study. While a speaker's vowel formants may not move over time, as people age many paralinguistic features change radically. An acoustic analysis avoids the possibility that a change "heard" by the analyst reflects effects of aging rather than of chain shifting. Section 16.8 will provide evidence that would not have been available without an acoustic study.

16.8 Acoustic results

As explained in section 16.5, based on the conclusions of the perceptual analysis, men were chosen for whom long casual interviews were available from 1971 and 1984. Lengthened vowels classed as phonologically mid-low and low (as well as the first ten stressed /i#/, /e#/, /o#/ and /y#/) were measured, coded, and spliced onto a tape file which was then digitally analyzed, using the ILS program package (Markel *et al.* 1985), and LPC formants were proposed. Computer-analyzed vowels were measured immediately after the transition from the preceding consonant, and again immediately before the transition to the following consonant. (Yaeger, 1979, found that these transitions are longer in Montreal French than in the English dialects reported in earlier studies.) F_0 and F_1–F_4 frequencies, amplitudes and bandwidths, along with relevant duration and coding, were stored in a file.[8]

Stepwise regressions were run on the coded output of the acoustic analysis, showing the relative significance of different influences on the vowel shift. F_1 and F_2 data, and the first principle component of the F_1/F_2 data, for each speaker were each used as the dependent variable,[9] and ridge regression results were computed for each variable vowel, with the independent linguistic variables listed in table 16.5a.

Regressions were run for each speaker separately, as well as for the pooled speakers. Table 16.5b presents the results of the stepwise ridge regressions run on the acoustic data for each speaker, using the independent variables shown in table 16.5a. Results in table 16.5b confirm that:

1. *EtymL*: The etymological classes are a primary determinant of vowel color for all speakers, even for Speaker #73, an older medical specialist whose vowel system is the most "standard" of those studied. Etymological distinctions were consistently maintained for all speakers in both years. In contrast, when the following consonant was coded as relative sonority, the results were not significant (that is, Sonority did not enter the regression).

2. *ExcL*: The exceptional lexical classes are significant determinants of vowel position for all but the most middle-class speakers (#73, 25, 88) and the youngest working-class speaker (#52). While all speakers maintain the lexical split in the 1971 interview, for many speakers these are reduced or disappear in the 1984 interviews. As predicted in section 16.3.2, the lexical split remerges. The surprising fact is that this occurs within the speech of a single speaker as the change progresses. In contrast, the etymological classes are not being merged.

3. *D*: Diphthongization entered the equation for all speakers.

4. *Str/Dur*: Stress level enters the regression for only one speaker here. This is the case partly because of the strong interaction between Diphthongization (D) and Stress (Str) (Yaeger-Dror 1992b). When Diphthongization is forced out of the regression, Stress is quite a significant factor; in contrast, even without Diphthongization and Stress, Duration only entered the regression for one speaker.

Most important for this study,

5. *Yr*: The year of the interview entered into the regression analysis for all speakers except one most standard older speaker (#73). The speakers were all past adolescence in 1971, and all but two were already in the workforce. Thus, according to the theory (Labov 1982; Trudgill 1978), these speakers should all have been quite unlikely to change their phonology significantly

Table 16.5a. *Factor groups/variables relevant to the stepwise regressions on F_2 or F_1/F_2 factor*

Factor Group	Members of the group	Relevance to analysis	Inclusion
Speakers (Sp)	30, 90, 2, 6, 27, 52; 73, 25	Do all speakers change?	−
Year (Yr)	71, 84	Is there change in real time?	+
Vowels (V)	ε, ø–œ, o–ɔ, ɑ	Are all lengthened Vs shifting?	+
1a. Consonant sonority	Stops, nasals, fricatives	Does immediate environment influence a V?	−
1b. Etymological Lex. gps. (*EtymL*)	ˆ, Z; r/R; 3;v	Do all lexical classes shift together?	+
2a. Exceptional Lex. gps. (*ExcL*)	FA;X;ENC;AL	Are residual and exceptional classes similar?	+
2b. Syllable-internal cluster (Cl)	KL, KR	These can influence duration and color.	+
3. Diphthong (D)	D, M, Y	Diphthongs have more extreme positions	±
4a. Stress levels (Str)	Z,,,;?,Q,.	Stress influences diphthongization and color	±
4b. Duration (Dur)		Duration and stress levels are closely correlated; which is more important?	±

Table 16.5b. *Factors included in the stepwise regressions run for front-lengthened vowels ML. = "Marché Linguistique" rating, a single number between 0 and 1 characterizing a speaker's participation in the "linguistic market," explained most cogently by Laberge and Sankoff (1978).*

Speaker	Birth date	ML	Factors included in the analysis					
90°	1923	0.17	*EtymL*		*ExcL*	D	Yr	
73*	1920	0.84	V	EtymL				
30	1914	0.33	*EtymL*		Yr	D	V	*ExcL* Cl
27	1942	0.01	Yr	*EtymL*	*ExcL*	D	V	
25*	1944	0.84	V	*EtymL*		Yr		
6°	1946	0.14	*EtymL*	D	V	Yr	Stress Cl *ExcL*	
2°	1946	0.09	V	Yr	*ExcL*	D	*EtymL*	
52	1948	0.08	*EtymL*		Yr	V	D	

*Medical doctors. The younger speaker was a medical resident at the time of the first interview and a doctor at the second.
°Blue-collar at the time of both interviews

between 1971 and 1984. The results demonstrate that on the contrary native speakers continue to advance their dialect toward a newer phonology well into middle age. There is evidence that after retirement there may be a tendency to return to a more conservative phonology, rather than advance toward the newer vowel target. As already mentioned, there is an interaction between Year and Exceptional Lexical class, since for many speakers these classes are evident in the 1971 interview, but have merged with the unmarked lexicon by the 1984 interview.

16.9 Conclusions

Evidence has been presented that significant changes are occurring in the Montreal French realization of mid-low lengthened vowels:

1. Lowering of mid-low lengthened vowels is a "change from below" and conforms to the "wave-like" pattern of change described in Labov's classic studies. The older working-class women appear to have initiated the change, and all younger speakers have adopted the newer low vowel realization, following the classic model for sound change.

2. The lengthened vowels do not follow Pattern 1 (Labov *et al.* 1972), instead shifting from a raised position to a lowered position without having gone through high position. Labov (1991) has already pointed out that while

Romance languages often do follow the shifting pattern hypothesized in Labov *et al.* (1972), they do not always do so. Guy (personal communication) considers that the preference for lowering without passing through a [+high] position may be linked to those language families that permit falling glides (ie, ue ...) as well as rising glides (ei, ow).

3. Labov (1981) suggested that the shifting pattern of an unstable vowel will generally be (neogrammatically) phonologically conditioned, and that even where phonological conditioning is evident, there may well be lexical diffusion as well; he pointed out that this phenomenon was worthy of study, and hypothesized that "simple" changes (in which only one feature need change), and "changes from below" (unconscious changes), are less likely to trigger lexical diffusion than complex changes and changes from above. The present analysis of a simple unconscious change confirms that even with this least-likely case scenario, lexical splits do occur.

4. Two very distinct sorts of lexical diffusion were found in these data, although there was only time to discuss one here. There is, first of all, lexical diffusion which arises from some *etymological* distinction in the language, like the *meet/mate/meat* distinction discussed by J. Milroy (1980) for Hiberno-English. The regressions reported here confirm that this etymological distinction is found for all speakers analyzed here, and is not lost as the change advances.

Exceptional lexical diffusion also occurs. The regressions reported here confirm that this exceptional distinction is quite evident for most working-class speakers, but is merged for middle-class speakers and for younger working-class speakers.

5. The perceptual evidence in figures 16.3–5 revealed sound change in apparent time, and statistical tests of the acoustic evidence demonstrate significant change in real time. Sound change is advancing even for speakers well past middle age, especially among speakers who were relatively conservative in 1971 (like speaker 2), but also among speakers (like speakers 25 and 30) whose vowel phonologies were fairly advanced in 1971.

Our initial expectations has been that the vowel system would not change for the old speakers, but detailed analysis for speakers who had retired by 1984 shows that there is a tendency for old men to become more conservative after retirement, which has been confirmed by some studies of lexical choice (Thibault and Vincent 1990). This tendency definitely warrants further exploration.

Labov's work has provided us with many questions concerning the etiology of language change. Only detailed phonetic analysis of language variation and change in many different language groups will permit us to answer these questions and to formulate the rules which govern language change. It is hoped that this study has been able to provide some evidence which will help determine rules for linguistic evolution, and will convince other researchers to make use of phonetic techniques for the analysis of linguistic variation and change.

Notes

I would like to acknowledge the Fonds pour la Formation de Churcheurs et l'Aide à la Recherche (FCAR), which funded the collection of the data in the Montreal French corpus, and the National Science Foundation (#860-8714-3), which funded the acoustic analysis of the data. The work could not have been completed without the data and support provided by Pierrette Thibault's Ethnolinguistics group, and acoustical facilities provided by Laurent Santerre, of the Université de Montréal. Statistical advice was provided by David Sankoff, and statistical programming by Marc Bourdeau, P. K. Kannen, and Hillel Vardi. ILS programming was done by Robert Marchand. I am grateful to Terry Rew-Gottfried, Kerry Green, Bruno Repp, David Sankoff and Walt Wolfram for constructive suggestions at different points along the way, although the shortcomings which remain are mine. Earlier versions of the analysis have been delivered at the York Sociolinguistics Symposium in 1988, and at the Third Conference in Laboratory Phonology at UCLA in 1991. Address all correspondence to Dr. Malcah Yaeger-Dror, Linguistics Dept., University of Arizona, Tucson, Arizona, 85721. E-mail: Malcah@ccit.arizona.edu.

1 In Montreal French the long low vowel is also unstable, as are the high vowels. See Yaeger 1979; Dumas 1987.

2 Following Labov (1972), a variationist convention encloses unstable ("variable") phonological units in parentheses to differentiate them from stable units and from phonetic transcription. This phonological transcription should not be confused with the use of parentheses to signify an "optional" realization of a phonological unit; e.g. below, where the parenthetical glide "[e:$^{(i)}$]" signifies that the diphthong is optional.

3 [r] is the older vernacular pronunciation in Montreal. Unless otherwise specified, [r] will be used throughout this paper, since [r/R] variation in no way impinges on the variation under discussion here.

4 The evidence does not support Dumas's (1981) conclusions about Quebec diphthongization, on which the discussion in Hayes (1990) is based. A preliminary quantitative analysis of diphthongization can be found in Yaeger-Dror and Kemp (1992).

5 Note that to the degree that conversational-style materials can be interpreted using models developed for analysis of more careful styles of speech, the BGF contour should conform to Martin's (1987) C_0 for French, or Beckman and Pierrehumbert's (1986) "intonational phrase." The interested reader should also see Boudreault (1968), Benguerel (1970), and Fletcher (1991), for discussion of prosody in a more controlled register of European French.

6 Note that the intonational contour most commonly found for Martin's (1987) C_1 for French (comparable to Beckman and Pierrehumbert's (1986) "intermediate phrase") is not rising in Quebec French conversational-style material.

7 In the perceptual analysis, there was a high degree of intra-analyst and inter-analyst agreement for vowel color, diphthongization, and stress determination. The primary analysis was done by Yaeger, with periodic checks by Kemp. A formal check of 50 tokens for two different "difficult" speakers showed 95% agreement for vowel height, 97% agreement for diphthongization, and 89% agreement for the three stress levels.

8 If problems were evident from the tracked formants as presented, stress codings and LPC glitches (when necessary) were corrected before their entry into the permanent memory. Remeasurement of 120 vowels showed that virtually all coding, 96% of formant measurements, and 90% of duration measurements were reliably reproduced.

Paradis (1985) found that even measuring with the Real Time Analyzer, using only fully stressed tokens, approximately 20% of his measurements had to be discarded. Since this project attempted to analyze unstressed as well as stressed vowels, the abort rate was presumably higher. Vowel nuclei shorter than 55 ms were not retained in the figures or statistical analysis presented here, because they were found to be too centralized by vowel reduction. Note that the majority of (even) the unstressed vowels had nuclei longer than 55 ms, permitting their inclusion in the analysis. The F_0 and first two formant measurements were stored for the beginning and end of these vowels, along with the vowel duration, the coding, and the position on the transcript and on the ILS files where the data can be found.

9 These gave substantially the same results.

References

Beckman, M. and J. Edwards. 1988. The phonological domains of final lengthening. In B. Joseph and A. Zwicky (eds.) *A Festschrift for Ilse Lehiste. Ohio State Working Paper in Linguistics* 35: 167–176.

This volume. Articulatory evidence for differentiating stress categories.

Beckman, M., J. Edwards and J. Fletcher. 1991. Prosodic structure and tempo on a sonority model of articulatory dynamics. *Journal of the Acoustical Society of America* 89: 369–382.

Beckman, M. and J. Pierrehumbert. 1986. Intonational structure in Japanese and English. *Phonology Yearbook* 3: 255–309.

Benguerel, A.-P. 1970. Some physiological aspects of stress in French. *Natural Language Science Studies* 4. Ann Arbor: University of Michigan Phonetics Laboratory.

Boudreault, l'abbé M. 1968. *Rythme et mélodie de la phrase parlé en France et au Québec*. Quebec: Presses de l'Université Laval.

Cedergren, H., L. Levac, and H. Perreault. 1992. Durational effects of prosodic structure in spontaneous spoken French. *Journal of the Acoustical Society of America* 91: 2387(A).

Chambers, J. and P. Trudgill. 1980. *Dialectology*. Cambridge: University Press.

Delattre, P. 1966. Comparison of syllable length among languages. *International Review of Applied Linguistics* 4: 183–198.

Delattre, P. 1969. Acoustic and articulatory study of vowel reduction in four languages. *International Review of Applied Linguistics* 7: 295–325.

DiPaolo, M. 1992. Hypercorrection in response to the apparent merger of [a] and [ɔ] in Utah English. *Language and Communication* 12: 267–294.

Dumas, D. 1981. Structure de la diphtongaison québecoise. *Revue canadienne de linguistique* 26: 1–61.

Dumas, D. 1987. *Nos façons de parler*. Montreal: Université de Québec Press.

Edwards, J. and M. Beckman. 1988. Articulatory timing and the prosodic interpretation of syllable duration. *Phonetica* 45: 156–174.

Fletcher, J. 1991. Rhythm and final lengthening in French. *Journal of Phonetics* 19: 193–212.

Geddes, H. 1894. (Pub. 1908.) *Study of an Acadian-French Dialect Spoken off the North Shore of the Baie-des-Chaleurs*. Halle: Max Niemeyer.

Gendron, J.-D. 1966. *Tendances phonétiques du français parlé au Canada*. Paris: Klincksieck.

Guy, G. 1988. Language and social class. In F. Newmeyer (ed.). *Cambridge Survey of Linguistics* IV. Cambridge: University Press, 37–63.

Harris, J. 1985. *Phonological Variation and Change*. Cambridge: University Press.

Hayes, B. 1990. Diphthongization and coindexing. *Phonology* 7: 31–71.

Kemp, W. and M. Yaeger-Dror. 1991. Between /asjɔ̃/ and /ɔːsjɔ̃/: Changes in the realization of the process suffix in Quebec French. In P. Eckert (ed.) *New Ways of Analyzing Sound Change*. San Diego: Academic, 127–184.

Kiparsky, P. 1988. Sound change. In F. Newmeyer (ed.) *Cambridge Survey of Linguistics* I. Cambridge: University Press, 363–415.

Klatt, D. 1975. Vowel lengthening is syntactically determined in a connected discourse. *Journal of Phonetics* 3: 129–140.

Kloker, D. 1975. Vowel and sonorant lengthening as cues to phonetic phrase boundaries. *Journal of the Acoustical Society of America* 57: S33–34.

Laberge, S. and D. Sankoff. 1978. The Linguistic Market and the statistical explanation of variability. In D. Sankoff (ed.) *Linguistic Variation*. New York: Academic Press, 239–250.

Labov, W. 1981. Resolving the Neogrammarian controversy. *Language* 57: 267–308.

1982. Building on empirical foundations. In W. Lehmann and Y. Malkiel (eds.) *Building on Empirical Foundations*. Philadelphia: Benjamins, 17–92.

1983. *The Social Stratification of English in New York City*. Washington, DC: Center for Applied Linguistics. [1966]

1991. The three dialects of English. In P. Eckert (ed.) *New Ways of Analyzing Sound Change*. San Diego: Academic, 1–44.

Labov, W., M. Karen and C. Miller. 1992. Near mergers and the suspension of phonemic contrast. *Language Variation and Change* 3: 33–74.

Labov, W., M. Yaeger and R. Steiner. 1972. *A Quantitative Study of Sound Change in Progress*. Philadelphia: U.S. Regional Survey.

Ladd, D.R. This volume. Constraints on the gradient variability of pitch range.

Lehiste, I. 1970. *Suprasegmentals.* Cambridge, MA: MIT Press.

Liberman, M., C. Maclemore, and A. Woodbury. 1991. On the nature of prosodic phrasing. Presented at the conference on Grammatical Foundations of Prosody and Discourse, LSA Linguistic Institute, UC Santa Cruz.

Lindblom, B. 1963. Spectrographic study of vowel reduction. *Journal of the Acoustical Society of America* 35 (11): 1773–1781.

Markel, J. *et al.* 1985. The ILS Program Library. Speech Communication Research Laboratories ms.

Martin, P. 1987. Prosodic and rhythmic structures in French. *Linguistics* 25: 925–950.

Martinet, A. 1969. *Le français sans fard.* Paris: Presses Universitaires de France.

Milroy, J. 1980. Lexical alternation and the history of English. In E. Traugott, R. La Brum and S. Shepherd (eds.) *Current Issues in Linguistic Theory,* Vol. 14. Amsterdam: Benjamins, 355–361.

Milroy, L. 1987. *Observing and Analyzing Natural Language.* Oxford: Blackwell.

Ogura, M., W. Wang, and L. L. Cavalli-Sforza. 1991. The development of Middle English in England. In P. Eckert (ed.) *New Ways of Analyzing Sound Change.* San Diego: Academic, 63–106.

Paradis, C. 1985. An acoustic study of variation and change in the vowel system of Chicoutimi and Jonquière. Ph.D. dissertation, University of Pennsylvania.

Paradis, C. and A. Deshaies, 1990. Rules of stress assignment. *Language Variation and Change* 2: 135–54.

Payne, A. 1980. Factors controlling the acquisition of the Philadelphia dialect by out of state children. In William Labov (ed.) *Locating Language in Time and Space.* New York: Academic Press, 143–178.

Price, P.J., M. Ostendorf, S. Shattuck-Hufnagel and C. Fong. 1991. The use of prosody in syntactic disambiguation. *Journal of the Acoustical Society of America* 90(6): 2956–2970.

Sankoff, D. and G. Sankoff. 1973. Sample survey methods and computer assisted analysis in the study of grammatical variation. In R. Darnell (ed.) *Canadian Languages in their Social Context.* Edmonton: Linguistic Research, 7–64.

Santerre, L. 1974. Deux E et deux A phonologiques en français québecois. *Cahiers de linguistique* 4: 117–146.

Schuchardt, H. 1885: Über die Lautgesetze: Gegen die Junggrammatiker. (Translated in Theo Vennemann and T. Wilbur (eds.) 1972. *Schuchardt, the Neogrammarians and the Transformational Theory of Phonological Change.* Frankfurt: Athenäum, 39–72.

Thibault, P. and D. Vincent. 1990. *Un corpus de français parlé.* Quebec: National Library.

Thurot, C. 1881–1883. *De la prononciation française depuis le commencement du XVIe siècle d'après les témoignages des grammaires.* Paris: Imprimerie Nationale. (Geneva: Slatkine Reprints 1966.)

Trudgill, P. 1978. *Sociolinguistic Patterns in British English.* London: Arnold. 1986. *Dialects in Contact.* Oxford: Blackwell.

Veatch, T. 1991. English vowels: their surface phonology and phonetic implementation in vernacular dialects. Ph.D. dissertation, University of Pennsylvania.

Wang, W. S.-Y. (ed.) 1977. *The Lexicon in Phonological Change*. The Hague: Mouton.

Yaeger, M. 1979. Context-determined variation in Montreal French vowels. Ph.D. dissertation, University of Pennsylvania.

Yaeger-Dror, Malcah. 1985. Intonational prominence on negatives in English. *Language and Speech 28: 197–230*.

1989. Patterned symmetry in the Montreal French vernacular. In R. Fasold and D. Schriffin (eds.) *Language Change and Variation*. Philadelphia: Benjamins, 59–84.

1990. Formulating new rules for sound change. In J. Edmonson, C. Feagin and P. Mülhäusler (eds.) *Development and Diversity: Linguistic Variation across Time and Space*. Austin: Summer Institute in Linguistics, 35–70.

1992a. Word frequency as an influence on lexical diffusion: the case of Montreal French (ɛ:) and (ɔ:). University of Arizona manuscript, in revision.

1992b. Concerning the Hayes/Dumas analysis of Quebec French diphthongization. ms., University of Arizona.

Yaeger-Dror, M. and W. Kemp. 1992. Lexical classes in Montreal French: the case of (ɛ:). *Language and Speech 35: 251–293*.

17

Polysyllabic words in the YorkTalk synthesis system

JOHN COLEMAN

17.1 Introduction

The YorkTalk laboratory phonology speech generation system (Coleman 1992a, 1992b; Local 1992) implements two radical hypotheses about phonology and phonetics: (i) There are no *segments* in phonological or phonetic representations; (ii) There is no need for *rewriting rules* in the expression of phonological relations, regularities and generalizations, or in the phonetic interpretation of phonological representations. Instead, phonological representations are hierarchically structured graphical objects, and phonological relations, regularities and generalizations, and phonetic interpretation, are represented and solved by a declarative system of simultaneous constraints. Previous descriptions of the YorkTalk system have concentrated in particular on three areas: (i) The phonological structure and phonetic interpretation of single syllables in English (Coleman 1992a); (ii) The representation and interpretation of assimilation in English (Local 1992); (iii) Declarative analyses of apparently procedural phenomena, such as epenthesis, metathesis, and elision (Coleman 1990, 1992b).

In this paper, I shall describe the extension of the system from monosyllabic words (and assimilation between monosyllabic words) to polysyllabic words, with special attention to phonetic variability contingent on foot structure and the position of syllables within feet. Variability of this kind includes a diverse set of reduction phenomena, including vowel-quality reduction, vowel devoicing, vowel elision, flapping, and syllabic sonorants. All of these phenomena are modeled without rewrite rules in an explanatory, unified way within the YorkTalk system, and the quality of the resulting synthetic speech is both highly intelligible and natural.

The structure of this paper is as follows. In the second section, I shall briefly describe the theory of segmental phonology which underlies most current text-to-speech systems. I shall outline some practical problems and theoretical objections to this model of speech generation. In the third section, I shall outline the main features of an alternative phonological theory within the framework of Unification Grammar. In the fourth section, I shall briefly describe the YorkTalk model, a speech-generation system which implements this Unification-based theory of phonology. In the fifth section, I shall describe the phonological representation of monosyllables employed in the model, and their phonetic interpretation in terms of the parameters for the Klatt formant synthesizer. In the sixth section, I shall describe the principal details of the structure and interpretation of polysyllabic words. In the seventh section I shall describe the treatment of phonetic variability contingent on foot structure and the position of syllables within feet within the model, including vowel-quality reduction, vowel devoicing, vowel elision, flapping, and syllabic sonorants.

17.2 Transformational grammars and synthesis-by-rule

Most current text-to-speech systems (e.g. Allen, *et al.* 1987; Hertz 1982, 1990) are, at heart, un-constrained string-based transformational grammars based on the phonological theory developed by Halle (1959), Chomsky and Halle (1968), and subsequent work in that framework. Generally, text-to-speech programs are implemented as the composition of three noninvertible mappings: (i) grapheme-to-phoneme mapping (inverse spelling rules + exceptions dictionary); (ii) phoneme-to-allophone mapping (pronunciation rules); (iii) allophone-to-parameter mapping (interpolation rules).

For example:

(1)　　*p*it　↘　　　　↗　[p^h]　　→ AH = 65dB
　　　si*p*　→　/p/　→　[p$^‘$]　　→ AH = 57dB
　　　s*p*it　↗　　　↘　[p$^-$]　　→ AH = 0/dB

graphemes → phonemes → allophones → parameters

These mappings are usually defined using an ordered sequence of rules of the form A → B/C__D, usually called "context-sensitive," but which in phonology and speech-generation systems often in fact define unrestricted rewriting systems, since B may be the empty string. Since *any* computational procedure can be computed by an unrestricted rewriting system, the use of such systems constitutes the null hypothesis about human linguistic competence or synthesis design – that it is a computational procedure of some otherwise unconstrained kind: "if all we can say about a grammar of a natural language is that it is an unrestricted rewriting system, we have said nothing of any interest" (Chomsky, 1963: 360). Grammars made with rules of this type may sometimes be *contingently* quite restricted. For instance, if the rules apply in a fixed order without cyclicity, they may be compiled into a finite-state transducer (Johnson 1972). But in general such conditions do not obtain, and there is thus no guarantee that a program which implements such a grammar will halt.

The appeal of transformational grammars to phonologists and speech technologists is perhaps due to the fact that the basic operations of a transformational grammar – deletion, insertion, permutation, and copying – are apparently empirically instantiated by such well-established phonological phenemona as elision, epenthesis, metathesis, assimilation, and coarticulation. But the formal, empirical, and practical problems inherent in this approach are many. In addition to being excessively unconstrained: (i) there is no principled way of limiting the domain of rule application to specific linguistic domains, such as syllables; (ii) using *sequences* as the data structure for phonetic representations would be phonetically plausible only if all speech parameters changed with more or less equal regularity (although multiple parallel sequences, as in Hertz's 1990 Delta system, partially overcome this problem); (iii) as practical research in text-to-speech testifies, the task of developing and debugging a rule set is complicated by the derivational interactions between rules. Altering a rule earlier in the derivational sequence may have unforeseen and undesired consequences for the application of later rules.

17.3 Declarative lexical phonology of polysyllabic words

Between 1986 and 1991, in collaboration with phonologists and phoneticians at the University of York (where I was then employed), I have been developing a phonological theory and a speech-generation program which does not employ such string-to-string transformations (Local 1992; Coleman 1992a, 1992b, forthcoming). An underlying hypothesis of this research is that there is a trade-off between the richness of the rule component and the richness of the representations (Anderson 1985). According to this hypothesis, the reason why transformational phonology needs to use transformations is because its representations, strings, are not sufficiently richly structured. Consequently, it ought to be possible to considerably simplify or even completely eliminate the transformational rule component by using more structured representations. For instance, if we use graphs such as figure 17.1 to represent phonological objects, then instead of copying or movement, we can implement phonological harmony and agreement phenomena by structure sharing (cf. the distribution of the feature [chk] and the ambisyllabic C in figure 17.1).

Phonetic Output

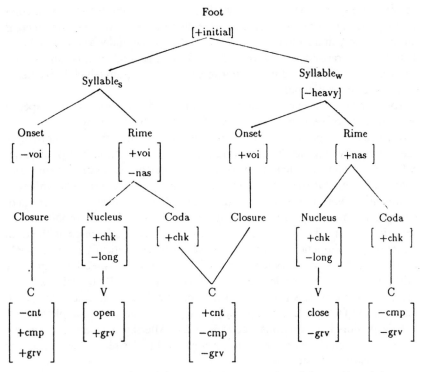

Figure 17.1. Part of a nonsegmental phonological representation of the word 'cousin.'

Phonological representations, such as figure 17.1, and phonetic representations, such as the parametric control matrices for speech synthesizers, are very different kinds of objects (cf. Ladefoged 1977). The mapping between these two kinds of objects cannot be applied more than once, because its codomain is not of the same *type* as its domain. This has two important consequences. The first is that the mapping is *arbitrary*: there is no free ride in relating phonetics to phonology. (This is true of parametric interpretation in most speech synthesizers, of course.) The second is that the phonetic-interpretation mapping is *highly constrained*: it is a homomorphism between parts of phonological representations and parts of parametric phonetic representations, so it must get it right in one step. There is no possibility of applying subsequent rules to fix up intermediate phonetic representations that are not surface-true. (Some examples of phonetic interpretation statements are presented in section 17.5 below.) The mapping underdetermines the phonetic descriptions, to the extent that nonsignificant variability is permissible.

Work in Metrical Phonology (Church 1985) and Dependency Phonology (Anderson and Jones 1974) has shown how stress assignment, a classical success of transformational phonological analysis, can be given a declarative analysis. Inkelas (1989) gives an essentially declarative account of the interactions between morphological and prosodic structure in Lexical Phonology, and Coleman (forthcoming) gives a declarative account of the phonological transformations presented in Halle and Mohanan's (1985) analysis of the Lexical Phonology of English.

It is important not to "jump out of the frying-pan into the fire," however, and introduce new formal devices such as *autosegmental transformations* which might undermine the computational benefits of using hierarchically structured phonological representations. For this reason, we employ a mildly context-sensitive type of grammar, which goes beyond context-freeness in only two respects:

1. A *terminal* phonological unit may be in two constitutents at once, so a weak degree of overlap between syllable onsets, nuclei, and codas is permitted. For example, in the analysis of between-word assimilation such as *ra*[ŋ] *quickly*, the place of articulation of the coda of the first syllable [ŋ] is inherited from the place of articulation of the first consonant in the onset of the following syllable [k], although the other features of the [ŋ] must still form a coda, since short vowels such as [æ] may not occur in open syllables. Cf. Local (1992).

2. Two sister categories in a phrase-structure rule may dominate the *same* substring, rather than consecutive substrings. For example, Greco-Latinate words in English have separate, noncongruent morphological and metrical structures. The morphological structure of the word "photographic," for instance, is *photograph-ic*, whereas its division into metrical feet is *photo-graphic*. A nearly-context-free analysis of the structure of such words is possible if context-free-type rules such as

$$\begin{array}{ccc} \text{Word} & \rightarrow & \text{Stress} & \cap & \text{Morphology} \\ \text{[+ Latinate]} & & \text{[+ Latinate]} & & \text{[+ Latinate]} \end{array} \text{ are permitted.}$$

This type of rule is employed in an analysis of morphological structure and phonological vowel harmony in Warlpiri by Sproat and Brunson (1987: 69).

There is an obvious sense in which a context-free phrase-structure grammar could be said to be nonderivational: any order of application of a particular set of rules to a given string assigns the same phrase marker to that string (excepting structural ambiguity). For example, the contemporary view of stress assignment and syllable-structure assignment is essentially a context-free analysis which can be implemented by simultaneous application of independent foot- and syllable-structure context-free rules (cf. figure 17.2).

Constraint				Example
a.	$\begin{array}{c}\text{Word}\\ \text{[+inflected]}\end{array} \rightarrow \begin{array}{c}\text{Word}_s\\ \text{[−inflected]}\end{array}$ Inflection$_w$			e.g. cat-s, underdetermine-s
b.	$\begin{array}{c}\text{Word}\\ \text{[−inflected]}\end{array} \rightarrow \begin{array}{c}\text{Word}\\ \text{[−inflected]}\end{array} \begin{array}{c}\text{Word}\\ \text{[−inflected]}\end{array}$			e.g. black-bird
c.	$\begin{array}{c}\text{Word}\\ \text{[−Latinate]}\end{array} \rightarrow \begin{array}{c}\text{Prefix}_w^*\\ \text{[−Latinate]}\end{array} \begin{array}{c}\text{Word}_s\\ \text{[−inflected]}\end{array} \begin{array}{c}\text{Suffix}_w^*\\ \text{[−Latinate]}\end{array}$			e.g. over-disorder-ly
d.	$\begin{array}{c}\text{Word}\\ \text{[+Latinate]}\end{array} \rightarrow \begin{array}{c}\text{Stress}\\ \text{[+Latinate]}\end{array} \cap \begin{array}{c}\text{Morphology}\\ \text{[+Latinate]}\end{array}$			e.g. photo-graphic ∩ photograph-ic
e.	$\begin{array}{c}\text{Stress}\\ \text{[+Latinate]}\end{array} \rightarrow \left(\begin{bmatrix}\text{Foot}_w\\ +\text{initial}\\ -\text{em}\end{bmatrix}\right) \begin{array}{c}\text{Foot}_w^*\\ \text{[−em]}\end{array}$ Foot$_s$			e.g. re-activ-ation
f.	$\begin{array}{c}\text{Foot}\\ \langle -\text{initial}\rangle\end{array} \rightarrow \left\langle\begin{array}{c}\text{Syllable}_s\\ \text{[+heavy]}\end{array}\right\rangle \left(\begin{array}{c}\text{Syllable}_w\\ \text{[−heavy]}\end{array}\right)$			e.g. ⟨∅⟩-re-, áct-∅, áct-ive (∅ denotes absence of a syllable, and ⟨ ⟩ denotes codependent units)
g.	$\text{Foot} \rightarrow \text{Syllable}_s \begin{array}{c}\text{Syllable}_w\\ \text{[−heavy]}\end{array} \begin{bmatrix}\text{Syllable}_w\\ +\text{em}\\ -\text{heavy}\end{bmatrix}$			e.g. áct-i-on
h.	$\begin{array}{c}\text{Morphology}\\ \text{[+Latinate]}\end{array} \rightarrow \begin{array}{c}\text{Prefix}^*\\ \text{[+Latinate]}\end{array} \begin{array}{c}\text{Stem}\\ \text{[+Latinate]}\end{array} \begin{array}{c}\text{Suffix}^*\\ \text{[+Latinate]}\end{array}$			e.g. in-ert-ia
i.	$\begin{array}{c}\text{Syllable}\\ \text{[}\alpha\text{heavy]}\end{array} \rightarrow (\text{Onset}) \begin{array}{c}\text{Rime}\\ \text{[}\alpha\text{heavy]}\end{array}$			e.g. (p)it
j.	$\begin{array}{c}\text{Onset}\\ \text{[}\alpha\text{voi]}\end{array} \rightarrow \left(\begin{array}{c}\text{Closure}\\ \text{[}\alpha\text{voi]}\end{array}\right) (\text{Glide})$			e.g. ((s)p)(r)
k.	$\begin{array}{c}\text{Closure}\\ \text{[−voi]}\end{array} \rightarrow (\text{[s]}), \text{C}$			(Either order) e.g. (s)p, p(s)
l.	(Constraint: in onsets, [s] < C)			e.g. sp
m.	$\begin{array}{c}\text{Rime}\\ \text{[}\alpha\text{heavy]}\end{array} \rightarrow \begin{array}{c}\text{Nucleus}\\ \text{[}\alpha\text{heavy]}\end{array} \left(\begin{array}{c}\text{Coda}\\ \text{[}\alpha\text{heavy]}\end{array}\right)$			e.g. eat, ant

etc.

Figure 17.2. Simple Unification-based phrase-structure grammar of English phonotactic structure.

It is not normal to think of a set of phrase-structure rules as a sequence of mappings from strings to strings which apply in sequence (though they can be thought of in this way, cf. Chomsky 1957: 27–28). The same selection of phrase-structure rules can be applied top-down, bottom-up, left-to-right, right-to-left, outside-in, inside-out, breadth-first, depth-first or even head-first to yield the same set of hierarchical phrase-structure relations.

Unification Grammar regards linguistic rules (such as phrase-structure rules) as partial *descriptions* of linguistic objects (such as trees or strings).[1] In this way, the *formal* distinction between rules and representations is entirely eliminated. Rules are just partial representations. According to this view, the yield of the grammar is a set of representations which are formed by combining lexical representations (encoding nonpredictable information) with rules (partial structural representations encoding predictable information) using the technique of constraint satisfaction. This combining operation involves two operations, concatenation and unification. Concatenation acts as syntagmatic "glue," and unification acts as paradigmatic "glue." A unification grammar, then, yields a set of linguistic structures (e.g. trees), the frontiers of which define a set of well-formed strings.

Under this direct interpretation of Unification Grammar, rules are not devices which maps strings to strings in an ordered sequence of steps. Since unification and concatenation are both associative operations, the constraint-satisfaction mechanism is intrinsically unordered. This has two consequences, one of linguistic importance, the other of computational importance. Firstly, a unification grammar defines a single level of representation, and different orders of rule application do not have different results. Analyses which require rule ordering of any kind are thus inexpressible. Secondly, the absence of rule ordering and the presence of a single level of representation makes the formalism somewhat simpler to debug than theories with rule ordering and derivations. These properties are the hallmarks of declarative formalisms. Since there are various possible declarative theories of phonology, I shall employ the terms "Declarative Lexical Phonology" and "Declarative Metrical Phonology" for the YorkTalk phonological theories.

There are at least two senses in which phonological representations such as figure 17.1 are nonsegmental. Firstly, the parts of such a representation corresponding to a segment in a segmental theory are root-to-frontier PATHS through the graph. Since every path shares some initial portion with some other path, they are not discrete, in the way segments are. For example, in a consonant cluster such as /nt/, the only distinction at the terminal level is [+nas][–nas]: the combination of all other features is a property of the whole cluster, not its two leaves. Secondly, the phonological representations employed here are largely unordered (see below). The frontier is thus not a sequence, but a bag (multiset), and cannot be interpreted except by including the paths which dominate it. Since discreteness of segments, and sequential (concatenative) organization, are the hallmarks of segmental representations, these representations are justifiably called nonsegmental.

Although Declarative Lexical Phonology is nonsegmental, features are used to represent phonological distinctions, drawing upon the (by now) extensive study of feature-value categories (cf. Gazdar *et al* 1985: 17–42; Shieber 1986; Gazdar *et al.* 1988). Every phonological feature has to be assigned an interpretation, and that interpretation is structure sensitive. The adoption of an interpretive rather than a transformational phonetics does not mean that phonetic interpretation of phonological representation is completely unsystematic, though. Just as in semantic interpretation, the Principle of Compositionality must be observed.

Feature-value categories in unification grammar can also be represented as a particular kind of graph: a directed, acyclic graph, or *dag*. Dags are like trees, except in three respects: (i) dags are unordered; (ii) some nodes may have more than one mother; (iii) and therefore, unlike trees, dags may have more than one root. These three properties hold of phonological representations, too.

Firstly, order is in general redundant in structured phonological representations (Cheng 1977). In languages with quite complex syllable structures, such as English, the ordering of consonants and vowels is predictable if syllables are given hierarchical representations as in figure 17.1. In such a representation, the order of nucleus with respect to coda is completely predictable: since codas always follow nuclei, this information should be expressed as a general ordering principle (Nucleus < Coda), rather than encoded in each phonological representation. Likewise, onsets always precede rimes, and so their relative order is completely predictable. Even in consonant clusters and diphthongs, the order of the parts follows general principles (but cf. figure 17.2(l)) and thus their order has no more place in a phonological representation than does the statement that nasality is accompanied by voicing in certain contexts in English.

The second property of dags, that some nodes (*reentrant* nodes) have more than one mother, is also applicable to phonological representation. For instance, the phenomenon of ambisyllabic consonants (consonantal forms which occur only at the junction between two syllables, such as the [ɾ] in North American pronunciation of words like "butter" [bʌɾə] or "Betty" [bɛrij]) may be analyzed as being constituents of two syllables at once. They are neither just the coda of the first syllable (assuming isolation pronunciations such as [bʌɾ] for "but" or [bɛɾ] for "bet" are not found), nor just the onset of the second syllable, since [ɾ] is never otherwise found syllable-initially. In addition, in their phonetic interpretation, they have a

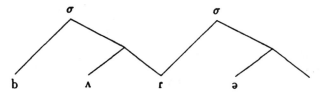

Figure 17.3. Ambisyllabicity represented by a reentrant graph ("butter").

transition *into* the tap like a coda, and a transition *out of* the tap like an onset. The simplest analysis,[2] then, is that they are simultaneously both coda of one syllable and onset of the next (cf. Turk, this volume). The representation of this phenomenon (figure 17.3) assigns more than one mother to such nodes. Sharing or spreading of features across adjacent nonsisters (as is found in cases of assimilation) admits of a similar representation (Local 1992).

Having more than one root in a phonological representation may also be desirable. Semitic languages, for instance, have a nonconcatenative inflectional morphology in which vowels and consonants form disjoint, but intercalated morphemes.

The nodes of representations such as figure 17.1 are labeled with complex phonological categories. This development enables phonological oppositions to be expressed between constituents of any category, not just over terminal symbols. So, for instance, it is possible to express contrasts between rounded versus unrounded syllables, nasal versus nonnasal rimes, voiced versus voiceless clusters, as well as the more conventional oppositions such as high versus low vowels or velar versus alveolar consonants. Each position in structure, in other words, each node in the phonological graph, is the locus for systems of oppositions between distinct utterances. Phonological oppositions may be expressed between constituents of any type.

For instance, in morphophonological representations, phrasal stress is located at the phrasal node; compound stress is represented at the Compound (level 3) stress node; the stress of morphemes of Greek or Germanic origin is represented at the Greco-Germanic Stress (level 2) node; Latinate main stress over the Main Stress domain (level 1); syllable weight is a property of rimes; nasality, frontness, rounding, and voice are onset/rime-level features; consonantal place of articulation is a terminal-domain feature; and vowel height is a nucleus-domain phonematic feature.

Dags may be represented and constructed using a small extension of the techniques used to represent trees. It is possible to represent a dag as a collection of trees which share some nodes. For example, the dag in figure 17.4 is equivalent to the join of two unordered trees at XY. This is done by *unifying* X and Y, adding the equation X = Y to the descriptions of the two

Phonetic Output

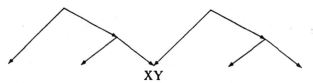

XY

Figure 17.4. A reentrant dag.

dags. This type of sharing is employed in the construction of larger phonological structures from smaller ones. Phrase-structure rules are used to build (unordered) trees, and unification equations are used to join them together into reentrant dags.

17.4 Overview of text-to-parameter conversion in *YorkTalk*

17.4.1 The York Model

The YorkTalk system has two main components: a *phonotactic parser*, which constructs headed phonological structures from strings of letters (the input to the system), and a *phonetic interpreter*, which determines parametric phonetic descriptions from the phonological structures. The parametric phonetic descriptions are suitable for high-quality generation of natural-sounding speech by the Klatt formant synthesis software (Klatt 1980; Allen *et al.* 1987). The YorkTalk system is implemented in Poplog Prolog and runs in several times real time on a MicroVAX 3400 or a VAXstation 2000. The system currently assumes a spelling normalization front-end, which is similar to a standard grapheme-phoneme algorithm, except that the linguistic plausibility of the normalized spelling is of no consequence, since the phonological representations used by the system are generated from the normalized spelling by a phonological parser. This parser could be tailored to the analysis of any context-free set of strings, so in future it is hoped that the parser might generate phonological structures directly from ortho-graphic input.

The model of speech employed in the YorkTalk system is an acoustic model. The outputs of the model are the various independently variable parameters of the Klatt formant synthesizer (Klatt 1980). In some respects, the YorkTalk phonetic model is a refinement of previous (partial) acoustic models of speech production. In particular, the YorkTalk model is indebted to the following studies: (i) Öhman's (1966) theory of Consonant–Vowel transitions. (ii) Fant's (1969) model of the structure of Consonant–Vowel transitions. (iii) Kewley-Port's (1982) study of Consonant–Vowel transitions. (iv) Klatt's "modified locus theory" of Consonant–Vowel transitions

John Coleman

(Allen *et al.* 1987: 109–115). (v) Fowler's (1980, 1983) theory of Consonant–Vowel timing. (vi) Browman and Goldstein's (1985, 1986, 1989, 1990, 1992) theory of articulatory motion.

The system is presently limited to the generation of single words. In our phonological theory, however, even single words and syllables are richly structured objects (cf. figure 17.1). However, they are not qualitatively different from larger units such as phrases or sentences, so we concentrated on perfecting the quality and naturalness of smaller units such as words and parts of words before moving on to work on larger units.

Although YorkTalk is a declarative system, it is possible to give a procedural description of its run-time operation. First of all, an input string in normalized orthography is *parsed*, using a Unification Grammar of English words. Part of a simplified version of such a grammar is shown in figure 17.2. YorkTalk includes a comprehensive and detailed grammar of English syllables, and a grammar of word structure and stress. These grammars are used to assign phonological structures such as figure 17.1 to input strings of phoneme symbols, determining stress, syllabification, rhythm, and many other phonological phenomena. Following the construction of such phonological representations, the input string of phoneme-like symbols is *discarded*. The parser returns a graph, representing the intended phonological structure.

As well as determining the phonological structure, the parser distinguishes one constituent in each subtree as the *head* of that subtree. In the string /pijt/ ("peat"), /ijt/ ("eat") is the head; and in /ijt/ ("eat"), /ij/ ("ea") is the head. The theoretical relevance of headed structures is discussed in Coleman (1992), but headedness also has practical importance in declarative speech generation from structured phonological representations, because it is used to determine which constituent should be interpreted first in the model of coarticulation described below (see section 17.5).

YorkTalk began merely as an experimental demonstration of the *possibility* of speech generation from nonsegmental phonological representations, but it is now designed to demonstrate the applicability of these methods in a text-to-speech system. It is intended to replace the phoneme-to-allophone rule component of a segmental synthesis-by-rule system, as well as the allophone-to-parameter component and the prosodic component. YorkTalk thus does rather the same sort of task as a synthesis-by-rule system, but without using context-sensitive rewrite rules or transformations. Instead, it employs more sophisticated ways of representing phonological information, together with the declarative constraint-satisfaction mechanism for constructing phonological representations on the basis of a grammar, and providing a phonetic interpretation for those representations.

As well as being computationally "clean", highly constrained, and efficient, this method of generation is nonsegmental at both the phonological and phonetic levels. Phonetic segmentation, which cuts across all phonetic parameters at the same point in time, is a poor phonetic model for two reasons. Firstly, it forces one to make arbitrary decisions about where to place segmental boundaries. For example, in a vowel-to-nasal consonant transition, a segmental boundary would be placed at the time of oral closure for the consonant. Since the nasality begins quite some time earlier, the nasal parameter is unnaturally divided into two portions at the time of oral closure, necessitating a rule of anticipatory nasality, or a set of partially nasalized vowel segments. Segmenting each parameter independently of the others obviates such a proliferation of rules or phonetic units. Secondly, the dynamics of articulators (and consequently of acoustic parameters) are mostly independent of one another, and are subject to different inertial and other physical constraints. Segmental-synthesis models fail to reflect this fact, and consequently discontinuities and rapid cross-parametric changes are often manifested around segment boundaries, resulting in clicks, pops, and other dysfluencies typical of synthetic speech. By segmenting parameters independently, the speech produced by YorkTalk is fluent, articulate and very human-like. When the model is wrong in some respect, it often sounds like a speaker of a different language or dialect, or someone with dysfluent speech (except, of course, if there is an actual bug in the software, in which case more undesirable dysfluencies sometimes arise!). With a nonsegmental, parametric phonetic model, it becomes very easy to provide a phonetic interpretation for nonsegmental phonological statements such as "the domain of nasalization is the Rime," or "there is only one distinctive occurrence of the feature [±voice] for the Onset." Consequently, we regard the combination of nonsegmental phonology and phonetics to be a twin merit.

17.5 Parametric phonetic interpretation of monosyllables

Phonetic interpretation of the structures generated by the parser involves two interacting tasks: (i) the assignment of temporal "landmarks" to each node in the graph, relative to which the parametric time functions will be calculated (temporal interpretation); and (ii) the determination of such time functions within specific temporal limits, which typically differ from parameter to parameter within the interpretation of a single phonological constituent (parametric interpretation). The following temporal constraints are obvious: (i) syllable start time = onset start time (ii) syllable end time = rime end time (iii) rime end time = coda end time. A number of other

John Coleman

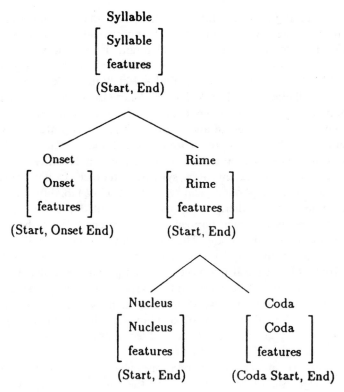

Figure 17.5. Syllable tree after constraint satisfaction.

important temporal constraints concerning constituent overlap are discussed in section 17.5.1.

After temporal interpretation, each syllable's structure can be represented as in figure 17.5. Note that as a result of temporal interpretation, the onset costarts with the nucleus, and the coda coends with the nucleus, which implements the coproduction model of coarticulation discussed above. (The parametric aspects of coarticulation are discussed below.)

After temporal interpretation, the structure is assigned a parametric interpretation. The parametric phonetic interpretation is simply a *relation* between phonological categories at temporally interpreted "places in structure" (i.e. nodes in the syllable tree) and sets of *parameter sections*. A parameter section is a sequence of ordered pairs, each of which represents the value of that parameter at a particular (salient) time. For instance, the parameter section $[(t_1, v_1), (t_2, v_2), (t_3, v_3)]$ denotes value v_1 at time t_1, value v_2 at time t_2 and value v_3 at time t_3 for some parameter. The times may be constants, denoting absolute times in ms, or they may be functions of the start and end times of the constituent being evaluated, denoting relative times. For instance (Onset End, Value) might denote the value of some parameter at the notional transition point that marks the boundary between onset and nucleus. Likewise, (Coda End − 100, Value), (Rime End − 100, Value) and (Syllable End − 100, Value) all denote the same parameter value at a point in time 100 ms from the end of the syllable, given that the temporal constraints presented above hold. Although they are *extensionally* equivalent, these three pairs are *intensionally* distinct, a circumstance which sometimes demands close attention. For example, if labiality is observed throughout the entire extent of a syllable utterance, it is necessary to determine whether the phonological representation of labiality is located at the syllable node, or whether, for instance, it is located at a lower node, the phonetic exponents of which happen to be coextensive with the phonetic exponents of the syllable node. The first analysis takes labiality to be a syllable-level phonological distinction, and its whole-syllable extent follows for free from the temporal interpretation of the syllable node; the second analysis requires the "excessive" duration of labiality to be explicitly specified in the phonetic interpretation component by temporal constraints. Thus the *phonological* domain of a phonetic phenomenon cannot be determined simply by measurement and comparison of its extent with *phonetic* phenomena of similar extent.

The parametric interpretation relation, which is called *exponency*, is simply a (large) set of ordered pairs of the form (Category, Parameter Definition) which can also be represented Category $\xrightarrow{e}$ Parameter Definition. The parameter definitions may be descriptions of parameter sections (e.g. 5), or definitions of particular parameter values (e.g. 2) or salient times (e.g. 6). These definitions are not rewrite rules; the arrows simply denote a (possibly many-to-many) mapping between two dissimilar domains of description; linguistic feature structures, representing distinctions and similarities between phonological objects, and the phonetic parameters of the speech model.

Some example exponency statements used in the interpretation of the word "take" are the following:

$$(2) \quad \begin{bmatrix} \text{N:} & \begin{bmatrix} \text{long: +} \\ \text{V1: [height: mid]} \\ \text{V2: [height: close]} \end{bmatrix} \end{bmatrix} \xrightarrow{e} \text{Fl}_{start} = 540 \text{ Hz}$$

$$(3) \quad \begin{bmatrix} \text{N:} & \begin{bmatrix} \text{long: +} \\ \text{V1: [height: NOT(close)]} \\ \text{V2: [height: close]} \end{bmatrix} \end{bmatrix} \xrightarrow{e} \text{Fl}_{end} = 380 \text{ Hz}$$

Note that the feature structure relevant to the determination of Fl_{start} is different from that relevant to Fl_{end}. (2) applies to all mid-closing diphthongs, such as /ej/ and /ow/, and (3) applies to all closing diphthongs, including open-closing diphthongs such as /aw/ and /aj/. Both statements are oblivious to whether the diphthongs are front or back. This underspecification ability is a further notable characteristic of Unification-based nonsegmental phonological representation.

The interpretation of the second-formant bandwidth B2 in (4) is insensitive to whether the nucleus is a monophthong or diphthong, treating mid-front vowels such as /ɛ/ and diphthongs which begin mid-front, such as /ej/, alike. In nonsegmental phonetic terminology, it can be said that B2 is monophthongal even in a phonologically diphthongal nucleus.

$$(4) \quad \left[N: \left[V1: \begin{bmatrix} \text{grv:} & - \\ \text{height: mid} \\ \text{rnd:} & - \end{bmatrix} \right] \right] \xrightarrow{e} B2 = 130 \text{ Hz}$$

Example (5) constructs a description of the amplitude of voicing, AV, for the nucleus between time points 200 ms following the start of the nucleus to 200 ms before the end of the nucleus. Thus the nucleus is regarded as an interval of voicing (the audible part of the vowel) flanked by 200 ms silences within which onset and coda exponents may lie. These periods without voicing are regarded as part of the nucleus exponency, however, because the vocalic place of articulation is maintained throughout the onset and coda in the form of consonantal secondary articulation (cf. the discussion of coarticulation above). The interpolation $\xrightarrow{1}$ is also shown.

$$(5) \quad N \xrightarrow{e}$$
$$AV [(N_{start} + 200, 60), (N_{end} - 200, 60)] \xrightarrow{i}$$
$$AV = 60 \text{ dB} \left| \begin{matrix} t = N_{end} - 200 \\ t = N_{start} + 200 \end{matrix} \right.$$

The interpretation of the coda depends on the interpretation of the nucleus, because it coarticulates with it. As shown above, the coda is temporally coproduced with the nucleus by equating the end of the coda with the end of the nucleus. The beginning of the coda is therefore the difference between the end of the coda and the duration of the coda. The duration of the coda in its turn depends on its phonological representation. For example, in the YorkTalk system, voiceless codas are regarded as being longer than voiced codas (6). The consequence of this is that voiceless codas start earlier in the rime than voiced codas. The difference between the end of the onset and the beginning of the coda (that is, the audible portion of the nucleus) is thus less for voiceless codas than for voiced codas. The distinction in coda duration, then, gives rise to the effect that vowels are shorter before voiceless codas than before voiced codas, a well-known exponent of the coda voiced/voiceless opposition in English. This effect is not achieved by manipulating the duration of the nucleus at all, though. It follows as a consequence of the locally defined coda duration and its interaction with other independently motivated temporal exponents of syllable structure.

(6) $[\,\text{Co:}\,[\,\text{C:}\,[\text{voi:} -]\,]\,]\overset{e}{\rightarrow}\text{Co}_{\text{dur}} = 250$ ms

Dennis Klatt in Allen *et al.* (1987: 113–115) presents a theory of onset formant-frequency transitions which takes account of the formant-frequency motions of the nucleus. Klatt's method is as follows, using the second-formant frequency motion of the syllable "go" by way of example. Firstly, the motion for the *isolation form* of the nucleus F_2 is determined. The onset part of the second-formant motion is then evaluated over the overlapping interval from the time at which the velar closure is released to the time at which the underlying formant motion for the nucleus appears independent of the onset. The value of the second-formant frequency at release time is a function of three variables: a backward-extrapolated locus L for the F_2 value during the closure, the value V of the second formant at the consonant–vowel boundary, and a measure of coarticulation C between the (extrapolated) consonant locus and the (observed) vowel value. This function is

(7) $F2_{\text{burst}} = L + C\,(V - L)$

Consequently, in YorkTalk, parametric phonetic interpretation of the syllable tree is performed top-down and head-first (i.e. heads are interpreted before nonheads). The motivation for this flow-of-control regime is so that the parameters of the nucleus (syllable head) are evaluated before onset and coda (nonheads), both of which are dependent on the nucleus. Formant transitions are modeled using Klatt's locus theory. The values of the terms in the locus-theory equation are usually somewhat different for onsets and codas, even for units that are regarded as the same unit in segmental accounts, e.g. onset /t/ and coda /t/.

After every applicable parametric interpretation statement has been evaluated, it is possible to determine a unique value for each parameter at every moment during the utterance. Parameter values are calculated at 5 ms intervals. The result of this process is a two-dimensional array of parameter values and times. Such an array is an appropriate input to the Klatt formant-synthesis program.

17.5.1 Temporal interpretation and overlap

Common to YorkTalk and Browman and Goldstein's model of the phonetics–phonology interface is the formal inclusion of (at least) two temporal relations, precedence and overlap.[3]

In structured phonological representations, the phonetic exponents of smaller constituents overlap the phonetic exponents of larger constituents. Thus the *default* temporal interpretation of syllable structure is figure 17.6, in which the onset exponents and the rime exponents overlap (indeed are part of) the syllable exponents, and the nucleus exponents and the coda exponents overlap the rime exponents and the syllable exponents.

The temporal constraints which express this state of affairs are:

(8)	syllable start time = onset start time
(9)	syllable end time = rime end time
(10)	onset end time = rime start time
(11)	rime start time = nucleus start time
(12)	rime end time = coda end time
(13)	nucleus end time = coda start time

If phonetic representations were made up exclusively of well-ordered sequences of elementary phonetic objects, then such a set of temporal constraints would suffice to divide up and group together phonetic subsequences into phonological constituents. This, it seems, is the strategy offered by Generative Phonology in its original form and in more modern versions, such as Autosegmental, Metrical and Dependency Phonology.

But speech is not so neat, and the exponents of one constituent may overlap those of another. This is a well established observation. For instance, Öhman (1966) noted that in V_1CV_2 sequences, the transition from V_1 to V_2 does not necessarily occur at the V_1C boundary nor the CV_2 boundary but, depending on various factors, may fall either somewhat before or somewhat after the C. This suggests the existence of an underlying vowel-to-vowel movement, upon which the C is overlaid. Such a model of articulation has been proposed by Liberman *et al.* (1967), Perkell (1969), Mermelstein (1973), Gay (1977) and Bell-Berti and Harris

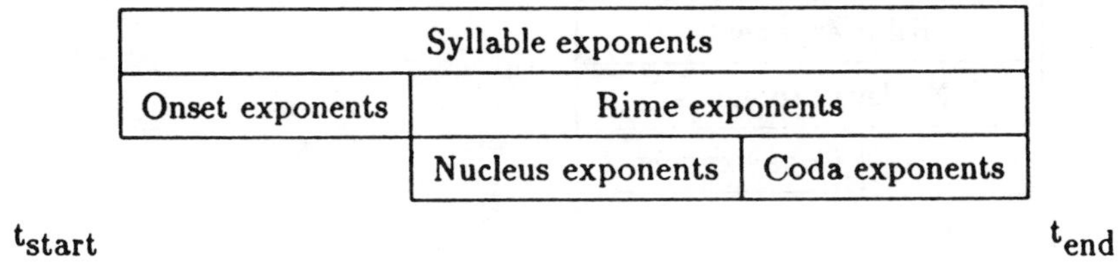

Syllable exponents		
Onset exponents	Rime exponents	
	Nucleus exponents	Coda exponents

t_{start} $\qquad\qquad\qquad\qquad\qquad\qquad\qquad\qquad\qquad\qquad\qquad\qquad\qquad$ t_{end}

Figure 17.6. Default temporal interpretation of syllable structure.

(1979), and proposed as a basis for nonlinear phonological organization by Firth (1937), Fowler (1980, 1983), and Griffen (1985). It has not been generally adopted in Generative Phonology, however, and even Autosegmental Phonology continues to present phonological representations constructed from well-ordered sequences of consonants and vowels, with no account of their temporal synchronization or qualitative coarticulation. Mattingly (1981) describes a generation model which, like YorkTalk, uses a pattern of overlaying, directed by syllable structure, to generate smooth parametric representations. Concatenation is not employed at all.

In YorkTalk, the overlay account of VCV articulatory timing has been applied to the interpretation of onsets and codas. In the case of codas, temporal constraint (13), which means that the coda follows the nucleus, must be replaced by (14), which ensures that the coda and the nucleus end at the same time.

(14)   nucleus end time = coda end time

Taken together with the contingent fact that the exponents of codas are (generally) shorter than the exponents of nuclei, we can portray the temporal interpretation of nucleus and coda as figure 17.7.

This is done by augmenting the rime structure with temporal constraint (14). It follows from constraints (11), (12) and (14) that the exponents of rimes are coextensive with the exponents of nuclei (figure 17.8).

Onsets come in for similar treatment in the overlaying model. Rather than *prefixing* the exponents of the onset to the exponents of the rime, we state

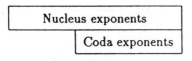

Figure 17.7. Temporal interpretation of nucleus and coda.

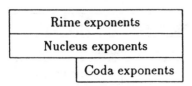

Figure 17.8. Temporal interpretation of rime structure.

that the exponents of onsets are overlaid on the exponents of rimes starting at the beginning. This is done by replacing constraint (10) by (15).

(15)   onset start time = rime start time

Since rimes and nuclei are coextensive, the consequence of this is that the exponents of onsets are also overlaid on the exponents of nuclei.

From constraints (8), (9) and (15) it follows that the exponents of syllables are coextensive with the exponents of rimes, and that the temporal interpretation of figure 17.2(i) is figure 17.9.

Combining figures 17.8 and 17.9 gives the temporal interpretation of syllable structure in which syllable, rime, and nucleus are coextensive in time (figure 17.10). (This does not mean that the phonological distinctions and the nontemporal phonetic distinctions between syllable, rime, and nucleus have been lost, of course. The *categories* syllable, rime, and nucleus have not become conflated.)

Compare figures 17.9 and 17.10. Note that in figure 17.10 the onset exponents are overlaid on the nucleus by virtue of the facts that the onset is overlaid on the rime, by constraints (8), (9), and (15), and that the rime is coextensive with the nucleus, by constraints (11), (12), and (14). This is despite the fact that onset and nucleus are not sisters in the phonological structure, and yet it is exactly the desired result, according to the phonetic model. Exactly the right phonetic interpretation for onset timing arises from the interaction of all six temporal constraints, simultaneously according with the established view of English syllable structure and the overlay model of timing.

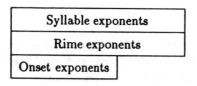

Figure 17.9. Temporal interpretation of syllable, rime, and onset exponents.

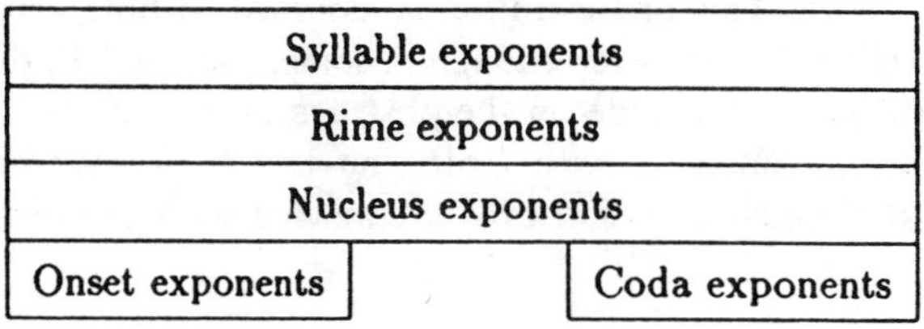

Syllable exponents	
Rime exponents	
Nucleus exponents	
Onset exponents	Coda exponents

Figure 17.10. Non-concatenative temporal interpretation of syllable constituents.

17.5.2 Clusters

In 1987, while modeling consonant clusters in the YorkTalk system, Adrian Simpson proposed that obstruent + glide clusters also have an overlaid, rather than concatenative, temporal structure. Simpson's proposal modeled the timing of obstruent + glide clusters similarly to onset + rime structures, as in figure 17.11. Mattingly's (1981) proposed generation model also has this analysis of clusters.

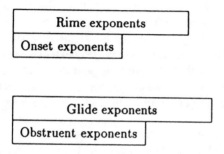

Figure 17.11. Simpson's analogy.

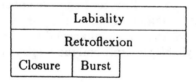

Figure 17.12. Labiality and retroflexion of /r/ are present throughout /pr/.

This analysis is borne out by a detailed examination of the phonetic exponency of obstruent + glide clusters such as /pr/ and /pl/. These two differ in that in /pr/ the strong labiality which is a characteristic exponent of /r/ is present throughout the cluster, and the "spooning" of /r/ is audible throughout the burst of /p/, suggesting the temporal orchestration illustrated in figure 17.12. This orchestration is assumed to hold generally for all obstruent + glide clusters, even though in some, such as /pl/, there is little or no audible effect of the glide on the obstruent.

In the cluster /spr/, compared with /spl/, the two /s/s have audibly different qualities, a distinction which can be modeled with the temporal organization:

/r/ exponents	
/s/ exponents	/p/ exponents

In an onset cluster such as /pr/, which is the head, /p/ or /r/?[4] Neither is obligatory; each may occur independently of the other. But the theory of head-first phonetic interpretation employed in YorkTalk demands that one be taken to be the head, and the other to be dependent. Experimentation with the model has confirmed that in this theory, the glide must be taken to be the head.

17.6 Structure and interpretation of polysyllabic words in the metrical component of Declarative Lexical Phonology

In Metrical Phonology, constituent structures are almost always binary branching. One sister of each pair is labeled "s(trong)" and the other "w(eak)", corresponding to head and nonhead respectively. In Dependency Phonology and Metrical Phonology, the difference in the location of the main and secondary stresses in a morphologically related pair of words such as "photograph" and "photographer" is ultimately attributed to the fact that the number of syllables is different, so the constituent structures of the metrical feet are different, and thus the (metrical) head is a different syllable in the two cases.

As an illustration of Declarative Metrical Phonology, I will briefly discuss some aspects of the representation of stress placement in English words. In English, there is a close relationship between morphological structure and lexical metrical structure (i.e. lexical stress). A compound word has two constituents, one stronger than the other (e.g. *black*bird). The lexical constituent structure and the lexical metrical structure are congruent (binary branching); see figure 17.2b. Similarly, words of Germanic origin can be divided morphologically into prefixes and stems. It is the stem which bears the stress, relative to the prefix. Again, the lexical constituent structure and the lexical metrical structure are congruent (figure 17.2c).

In words of Latinate extraction or form, however, morphological structure and metrical structure are not congruent. For instance, the morphological structure of the word "photographical" is *photo + graph + ic + al*, whereas the metrical structure places a foot division between *photo* and *graphical*. As a rule, Latinate stress falls on the rightmost heavy syllable of the last three syllables of the word (Lass 1988: 114). A metrical representation, therefore, could divide Latinate words into a beginning part of zero or more feet which are of no relevance to main-stress placement, and a final foot from the rightmost heavy syllable of the last three syllables of the word up to the end (figure 17.2e). If this is done, a declarative, structural characterization of Latinate stress placement can be formulated: *Latinate stress falls on the first syllable of the last foot*. The validity of the division of Latinate words into a beginning part of indeterminate length, and a final foot Main Stress Domain of finite length, is demonstrated by the fact that the final foot, as a whole, is more strongly stressed than the beginning part. When the parts of this analysis are drawn together, Declarative Metrical Phonology can be employed to assign relative prominence to every syllable in the string.

The representation-based approach to stress assignment proposed in Declarative Metrical Phonology is attractive because it does not require the cyclic application of relatively complex stress-manipulating transformations as in SPE phonology or cyclic assignment of metrical structure as in, for example, Kiparsky (1979) or Hayes (1980), and yet it is conceptually simple. Being declarative rather than procedural, it is susceptible to computational implementation in a relatively straightforward fashion.

17.6.1 Syllable linkage

The minimal requirement of the polysyllable grammar is that the set of strings that it defines, at least, must be right, irrespective of the structures it assigns to those strings. It must include all the actual polysyllabic words of English, but must not include any impossible strings. The account of English lexical structure given above is not sufficient to meet even this minimal requirement, however. This is because each terminal symbol of the lexical grammar is a syllable, which means the set of strings defined by the lexical grammar is a subset of the concatenation closure of the set of syllables. But some ill-formed sequences of syllables are not precluded by this grammar, namely those containing "over-long" sequences of concatenated coda and onset at the junction of two syllables. For example, the syllables "osp" and "sprey" are both well-formed, but the polysyllabic string "ospsprey" is ill-formed. Clearly, then, defining the set of polysyllables is more complicated than simply plugging syllables into metrical or lexical structures. The grammar of polysyllables must also be sensitive to transsyllabic coda-onset constraints.

Since the set of intervocalic clusters is a proper subset of the concatenation of the codas and onsets, it should not be necessary to have an independent category of intervocalic clusters. The set of intervocalic clusters should be defined, compositionally, as a function of the set of codas and the set of onsets. The set of intervocalic clusters should be the product of concatenating syllables while observing certain coda–onset constraints.

A preliminary attempt to define the set of intervocalic clusters is the following: (i) in compound words, any coda–onset combination is a legal cluster; (ii) the left quotient of the cluster must be a well-formed coda; (iii) the right quotient of the cluster must be a well-formed onset; (iv) the left and right quotients must be either concatenated or overlapping (in other words, every part of the cluster is in either the coda or the onset or possibly both); (v) the cluster must not be too long.

We do not yet have a motivated definition of which clusters are too long. We hypothesize that the clusters which are too long are those which involve the repetition of an element in both coda and onset, such as geminate consonants and sequences like "spsp" and "ktt." This hypothesis is based on the supposition that there is an algebraic account of the statistical constraints on the set of intervocalic clusters presented by Pierrehumbert (this volume). We can simultaneously enforce the constraint that the left and right quotients of the cluster are a coda and onset respectively, and that repetition is prohibited, by enforcing the predominance of ambisyllabic constituents. For example, the account we propose for the prohibition of "ospsprey" is that if "sp" is in a coda and in an onset, then the structure defined by the grammar is not the sequence "spsp," but the single constituent "sp" shared by both the coda and the onset.

I shall show in the next section that ambisyllabic constituents are not just a convenient phonological construct for accounting for the pattern of intervocalic clusters. They are also exactly right for the phonetic interpretation of intervocalic consonants using the existing account of the phonetic interpretation of onsets and codas.

17.7 Phonetic variability contingent on foot structure

We shall describe phonetic interpretation of polysyllables in two parts. Firstly, we shall consider how syllables are linked together in phonological and phonetic representations, paying attention to intersyllable "glue." Secondly, we shall consider the phonetic interpretation of the metrical structures assigned to joined-up syllables.

17.7.1 Phonetic interpretation of ambisyllabic constituents

Let us now consider the phonetic interpretation of intervocalic consonants such as that in "butter." For the phonetic interpretation of the intervocalic consonant to sound natural, it must coarticulate properly with its flanking vowels. Under the nonsegmental theory of phonetic interpretation described in section 17.5 coarticulation is not the mechanical effect arising from the temporal smearing of neighboring segments, but is part of the phonetic interpretation of the phonological domains Onset and Coda. For intervocalic consonants to coarticulate with their flanking vowels, therefore, we need to ensure that they are interpreted just like codas with respect to the preceeding vowel, and just like onsets with respect to their following vowel. As well as making them sound right, this hypothesis would also allow us to use the existing definition of the exponency function to generate intervocalic consonants using some of the statements for codas and some of the statements for onsets. However, we cannot simply represent intervocalic consonants as a concatenative sequence of phonologically similar coda and onset, as the phonetic interpretation of codas includes a syllable-final release. We do not want the coda to be released and then followed by an onset. We want the phonetic interpretation of the intervocalic consonant to start off like a coda, and then turn into an onset.

This is done as follows. Observe that coda stops have an internal sequential structure – a closing phase $Closing_{Coda}$, a closure phase $Closure_{Coda}$, and a release phase $Release_{Coda}$ – as do onset stops, which have just a closure phase $Closure_{Onset}$ and a release phase $Release_{Onset}$. In voiceless stops, the closure phase is acoustically silence. Our hypothesis (contra Turk, this volume) is that up to closure, intervocalic consonants are like codas, and after closure, they are like onsets. The internal temporal structure of an intervocalic consonant, then is $Closing_{Coda}$ $Closure_{Coda}$ $Closure_{Onset}$ $Release_{Onset}$.

By way of an informal experiment, we generated a sequence of two syllables, /part/ and /tij/, and then spliced out everything from the end of the coda closure to the beginning of the onset closure. In other words, we removed the coda release, and the period of silence between the two syllables. The result was a very natural-sounding intervocalic *geminate* consonant – the duration of the period of closure being too long. We then calculated the initial difference between the start of the onset release and the coda release, and on a second attempt spliced out that portion. The intervocalic consonant constructed in this was was completely natural-sounding in its duration and coarticulation with its neighbouring vowels.

This method was then formally implemented into the system in the following way. In the phonetic interpretation program, the interpretation given to the rule in figure 17.2f was at first the concatenative interpretation:

$$\text{Syllable}_{(\text{Start, } t_1)} \wedge \text{Syllable}_{(t_1, \text{ End})} \Rightarrow \text{Foot}_{(\text{Start, End})}$$

where t_1 is the end of the first syllable and the beginning of the second syllable. This interpretation produces two separate monosyllables separated by a period of silence, because onsets and codas in monosyllables are respectively preceded and followed by a short period of silence. If a certain period of time T is subtracted from the start time of the second syllable, that syllable is generated T time-units earlier. If T exceeds the duration of the period of silence which separates the isolation-form monosyllables, then the second syllable will be generated at a time which *overlaps* the end of the first syllable. By setting T to the difference between the release of the coda and the release of the onset, then the closure period of the intervocalic consonant has just the right duration:

$$\text{Syllable}_{(\text{Start, } t_1)} \wedge \text{Syllable}_{(t_1 -T, \text{ End})} \Rightarrow \text{Foot}_{(\text{Start, End})}$$

By increasing T yet further, so that the steady-state closure period tended to zero, a continuous sinusoidal transition into and out of the intervocalic closure could be modeled. This transition sounded like the ballistic motion heard in flaps in North American English.[5]

This overlaying account of syllable juncture in intervocalic voiceless closure works well for voiced stops too. In these stops, overlay is preferable to simple deletion of the coda release and between-syllable silence, as the AVS (amplitude of sinusoidal voicing) parameter for voiced stops in coda position is not overwritten by the onset closure, a detail which is in fact needed for naturalness, but which would be lost if a simple concatenative model was employed. Likewise, intervocalic consonant clusters containing stops can also be generated in this way. For example, the cluster /nt/ can be modeled as an onset /t/ overlaid on a coda /nt/. In such a case, therefore, we regard the /t/ alone as ambisyllabic.

To sum up, the ambisyllabic account of the pattern of intervocalic consonant clusters can be given a compositional phonetic interpretation. The phonetic interpretation of ambisyllabic consonants is the interpretation of their first mother, the coda node, combined with the interpretation of their second mother, the onset node, combined with the interpretation of ambisyllable disyllables, which is temporal overlap.

17.7.2 Phonetic interpretation of metrical structure

Although the intervocalic constituents produced by the above method sound extremely fluent and naturally "glued together," the F_0 pattern was not at all natural-sounding, since it was simply two monosyllabic falls. Normally, the pitch of a disyllable with a falling intonation contour can be expected to be either a single fall, or a rise-fall, corresponding to the metrical patterns stressed–unstressed and unstressed–stressed respectively.

The falling pitch contour of an isolated monosyllable consists of a linear falling F_0, which starts at 120 Hz and finishes at about 55 Hz. These values give a good mid-range fall, ending in creaky voice. In disyllables, this fall is duplicated. Let us refer to the start and end points of the first fall as $Fall1_{start}$ and $Fall1_{end}$, and of the second fall as $Fall2_{start}$ and $Fall2_{end}$. If the same start and end F_0 values (i.e. 120 Hz and 55 Hz) are used for a single fall from $Fall1_{start}$ to $Fall2_{end}$, a very fine falling contour on a stressed–unstressed metrical pattern is produced. For the consonantal perturbations to F_0 by the coda and onset to be produced, the disyllabic fall must be generated before the interpretations of its constituent syllables are evaluated. This will also work for trisyllables of which the first syllable is stressed and the remaining two unstressed. In other words, the falling F_0 pattern as already applied to monosyllables can be applied more generally to all metrical feet.

We have also done some experimental prototypes of the second disyllabic stress pattern, unstressed–stressed. The first such experiment was in fact an attempt to model nuclear elision in unstressed syllables, as in words such as "support", which may often sound as if the vowel has been removed, e.g. "s'pport." According to the declarative account of this phenomenon to be described in more detail in the following section, the vowel is not deleted in these cases. It is simply that the coda of the first syllable, /p/, starts so soon after the onset that the vowel is eclipsed by the coda. We attempted to model this in a similar way to the overlapping account of ambisyllabic constituents, as follows. A clause was added to the statements of coda duration to say that codas in unstressed syllables were as long in duration as codas in stressed syllables ("normal" codas) plus almost the complete duration of the audible period of the vowel. The effect of this is that when the coda of an unstressed syllable is generated, it is so long that it almost completely overlaps the audible part of the vowel. If the degree of overlap between the syllables is increased by the same amount, the timing of the intervocalic consonant and the second syllable is entirely normal. This produces a very convincing falling contour on an unstressed–stressed pattern, since the first syllable appears to be much shorter in duration, its nucleus is eclipsed by its coda, and its isolation-form falling F_0 is also eclipsed.

If there is a sonorant in the coda, as in disyllables such as "intend," the period of low F_0 during the sonorant (the residue of the isolation-form falling F_0 contour) is an additional part of the falling contour as seen on the unstressed–stressed pattern.

17.7.3 Vowel reduction and elision

Further evidence for the nonderivational account of syllable organisation is provided by cases of apparent vowel deletion in unstressed prefixes in words such as "prepose," "propose," and "suppose." In Declarative Lexical

Phonology, no material is removed or lost in these examples, so no deletion rules or processes are required. (None are possible, of course.)[6] In my analysis of this phenomenon, the phonological representation of these items is invariant, but may receive various possible temporal interpretations, depending on phonological factors (e.g. metrical structure) and/or phonetic factors (e.g. speech rate). The unreduced forms of these prefixes have the temporal organization shown in figure 17.13.

In the reduced forms, the nucleus duration can be reduced up to the point at which the end of the nucleus coincides with the end of the onset (figure 17.14).

This analysis is supported by the fact that the exponents of onset are those appropriate to the presence of the exponents of the nucleus in each case, and that the qualities of the release/glide differ in the expected way in the

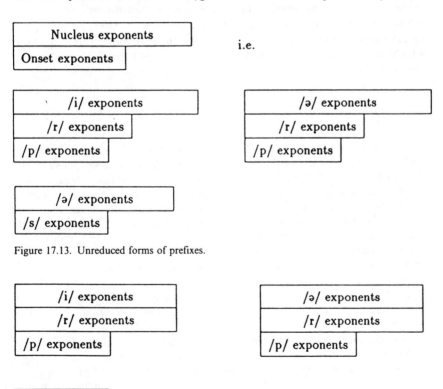

Figure 17.13. Unreduced forms of prefixes.

Figure 17.14. Reduced forms of prefixes.

reduced forms of "prepose" and "propose."[7] These observations present serious problems to procedural segmental phonology (deletion involves the removal of a segment; coarticulation demands its presence). The overlay analysis suffers from no such problems.[8]

17.8 Conclusion

In this paper, I have sketched the principal characteristics of a Unification-based phonological theory, Declarative Lexical Phonology, and the York model of phonetic interpretation. I showed how the maintenance of a rigid distinction between phonological structure (which is unordered) and phonetic interpretation (which includes timing) enables many phonological phenomena to be modeled without the use of transformations or even strings of segments. The price of this benefit is that phonological representations must have more structure than simple strings, a detail which is, however, borne out by many phonological and phonetic considerations.

Notes

I would like to record my thanks to John Local, Adrian Simpson, and Richard Ogden, who have all personally contributed extensively to the development of the YorkTalk system. Rob Fletcher of the University of York Computing Service wrote an interactive graphics editor for synthesizer parameter files, described in Fletcher *et al.* (1990), which has been an invaluable and much-used tool. Since 1987, this research has been supported by British Telecom plc. I would also like to thank Keith Johnson for his helpful comments on an earlier draft of this paper, and for his sensitive written commentary. Steven Bird and Bob Ladd have also raised probing questions on various occasions that it has been useful to address.

1 Contrast this with Chomsky's (1957: 27) presentation of trees, which was simply a declarative notation for the sequential application of a set of phrase-structure rules.

2 Not everyone would agree with this. An alternative analysis proposed in Kiparsky (1979) and Nespor and Vogel (1986) is that such elements are in one place in structure at one step in the derivation, and in another at a later step in the derivation. Such movement or resyllabification rules, however, are not expressible in this framework, which is more constrained, and contains no structure-changing operations. Some linguists regard improper bracketing with horror, but providing the number of mothers a node can have is finitely bounded, it is nowhere near as damaging to the goal of producing a constrained grammar formalism as the use of structure-changing rules.

3 The YorkTalk system in fact contains two types of temporal overlap: coproduction of *different* phonetic parameters, and overlap of the parameters of one constituent on top of the *same* parameters of another constituent, a distinction which parallels in some respects the distinction which Browman and Goldstein (1990: 360–362) make between within-tier *blending* and between-tier *hiding.*

4 I overlook for the moment that some properties of this cluster, such as voicelessness, are properties of the whole constituent.

5 The absence of aspiration in intervocalic /t/ in these dialects is not explained by this mechanism, however. It is necessary to restrict the distribution of aspiration to foot-initial position, unlike British and other dialects, in which aspiration may also be foot-internal.

6 Browman and Goldstein (1990) present a very similar account to this in the analysis of consonant elision in casual speech renditions of phrases such as "perfec(t) memory."

7 A similar phenomenon is voiceless vowel elision in Japanese, cf. Coleman (1991).

8 As well as complete onset-nucleus overlap, complete nucleus-coda overlap is also found, e.g. in the pronunciation of (i)mportant, (o)f, (a)n, etc.

References

Allen, J., S. Hunnicutt and D. Klatt. 1987. *From Text to Speech: The MITalk System.* Cambridge: University Press.

Anderson, J. and C. Jones. 1974. Three theses concerning phonological representations. *Journal of Linguistics* 10: 1–26.

Anderson, S. R. 1985. *Phonology in the Twentieth Century.* Chicago: University of Chicago Press.

Bell-Berti, F. and S. Harris. 1979. Anticipatory coarticulation: some implications from a study of lip rounding. *Journal of the Acoustical Society of America* 65: 1268–1270.

Browman, C.P. and L. Goldstein. 1985. Dynamic modeling of phonetic structure. In V. A. Fromkin (ed.) *Phonetic Linguistics: Essays in Honor of Peter Ladefoged.* Orlando, Florida: Academic Press, 35–53.

1986. Towards an articulatory phonology. *Phonology Yearbook* 3: 219–252.

1989. Articulatory gestures as phonological units. *Phonology* 6.2: 201–251.

1990. Tiers in Articulatory Phonology, with some implications for casual speech. In J. Kingston and M. E. Beckman (eds.) *Papers in Laboratory Phonology I: Between the Grammar and the Physics of Speech.* Cambridge: University Press, 341–376.

1992. "Targetless" schwa: an articulatory analysis. In G.J. Docherty and D.R. Ladd (eds.) *Papers in Laboratory Phonology II: Gesture, Segment, Prosody.* Cambridge: University Press, 26–55.

Cheng, R.L. 1977. *Economy and Locational Information in Phonology.* Indiana University Linguistics Club.

Chomsky, N. 1957. *Syntactic Structures*. The Hague: Mouton.

1963. Formal properties of grammars. In R.D. Luce, R.R. Bush and E. Galanter (eds.) *Handbook of Mathematical Psychology* Vol. II. New York: John Wiley, 323–418.

Chomsky, N.A. and M. Halle. 1968. *The Sound Pattern of English*. New York: Harper and Row.

Church, K. 1985. Stress assignment in letter to sound rules for speech synthesis. *Proceedings of the Conference*, 23rd Annual Meeting of the Association for Computational Linguistics, Chicago: 246–253.

Coleman, J. S. 1990. Unification Phonology: Another look at "synthesis-by-rule". In *Proceedings of the Thirteenth International Conference on Computational Linguistics. COLING 90* 3: 79–84. International Committee on Computational Linguistics.

1991. Non-pitch exponents of accent and structure in Japanese. *York Papers in Linguistics* 15: 41–92.

1992a. The phonetic interpretation of headed phonological structures containing overlapping constituents. *Phonology* 9.1: 1–44.

1992b. "Synthesis-by-rule" without segments or rewrite rules. In G. Bailly and C. Benoît (eds.) *Talking Machines: Theories, Models, and Applications*. Amsterdam: Elsevier, 43–60.

Forthcoming. Declarative Lexical Phonology. To appear in J. Durand and F. Katamba (eds.) *Frontiers of Phonology: Primitives, Architectures and Derivations*. London: Longman.

Fant, G. 1969. Stops in CV-syllables. In G. Fant 1973. *Speech Sounds and Features*. Current Studies in Linguistics Series 4: pp. 110–139. Cambridge, MA: MIT Press.

Firth, J.R. 1937. The structure of the Chinese monosyllable in a Hunanese dialect. *Bulletin of the School of Oriental Studies* 8: 1055–1074.

Fletcher, R.P., J.K. Local and J.S. Coleman. 1990. Speech Synthesis – How to do it, and using graphics to get it right. In *Proceedings of the DECUS (UK, Ireland and Middle-East) Conference*, Keele University, March 1990, 101–111.

Fowler, C.A. 1980. Coarticulation and theories of extrinsic timing. *Journal of Phonetics* 8: 113–133.

1983. Converging sources of evidence on spoken and perceived rhythms of speech: cyclic production of vowels in monosyllabic stress feet. *Journal of Experimental Psychology: General* 112(3): 386–412.

Gay, T. 1977. Articulatory movements in VCV sequences. *Journal of the Acoustical Society of America* 62: 183–193.

Gazdar, G., E. Klein, G. Pullum, and I. Sag. 1985. *Generalized Phrase Structure Grammar*. Oxford: Blackwell.

Gazdar, G., G. Pullum, R. Carpenter, E. Klein, T.E. Hukari and R.D. Levine. 1988. Category structures. *Computational Linguistics* 14(1): 1–19.

Griffen, T.D. 1985. *Aspects of Dynamic Phonology*. Amsterdam Studies in the Theory and History of Linguistic Science, series 4: Current Issues in Linguistic Theory, Vol. 37. Amsterdam: Benjamins.

Halle, M. 1959. *The Sound Pattern of Russian*. The Hague: Mouton.

Halle, M. and K.P. Mohanan. 1985. Segmental phonology of modern English. *Linguistic Inquiry* 16.1: 57–116.

Hayes, B. 1980. *A metrical theory of stress rules*. Ph.D. dissertation, MIT.

Hertz, S.R. 1982. From text to speech with SRS. *Journal of the Acoustical Society of America* 72(4): 1155–1170.

    1990. The Delta programming language: an integrated approach to non-linear phonology, phonetics and speech synthesis. In J. Kingston and M. Beckman (eds.) *Papers in Laboratory Phonology I: Between the Grammar and Physics of Speech*. Cambridge: University Press.

Inkelas, S. 1989. Prosodic constituency in the lexicon. Ph.D. dissertation, Stanford University.

Johnson, C.D. 1972. *Formal Aspects of Phonological Description*. The Hague: Mouton.

Kewley-Port, D. 1982. Measurement of formant transitions in naturally produced stop consonant-vowel syllables. *Journal of the Acoustical Society of America* 72(2): 379–389.

Kiparsky, P. 1979. Metrical structure assignment is cyclic. *Linguistic Inquiry* 10: 421–442.

Klatt, D.H. 1980. Software for a cascade/parallel formant synthesizer. *Journal of the Acoustical Society of America* 67(3): 971–995.

Ladefoged, P. 1977. The abyss between phonetics and phonology. *Proceedings of the 13th meeting of the Chicago Linguistic Society:* 225–235.

Lass, R. 1988: *The Shape of English*. London: Dent.

Liberman, A.M., F.S. Cooper, D.P. Shankweiler, and M. Studdert-Kennedy. 1967. Perception of the speech code. *Psychological Review* 74: 431–461.

Local, J.K. 1992. Modelling assimilation in non-segmental rule-free synthesis. In G. J. Docherty and D.R. Ladd (eds.) *Papers in Laboratory Phonology II: Gesture, Segment, Prosody*. Cambridge: University Press, 190–223.

Mattingly, I.G. 1981. Phonetic representations and speech synthesis by rule. In T. Myers, J. Laver and J. Anderson (eds.) *The Cognitive Representation of Speech*. Amsterdam: North-Holland.

Mermelstein, P. 1973. Articulatory model for the study of speech production. *Journal of the Acoustical Society of America* 53: 1070–1082.

Nespor, M. and I.B. Vogel. 1986. *Prosodic Phonology*. Dordrecht: Foris.

Öhman, S.E.G. 1966. Coarticulation in VCV utterances: spectrographic measurements. *Journal of the Acoustical Society of America* 39: 151–168.

Perkell, J.S. 1969. *Physiology of Speech Production: Results and Implications of a Quantitative Cineradiographic Study*. Cambridge, MA: MIT Press.

Pierrehumbert, J. This volume. Syllable structure and word structure: a study of triconsonantal clusters in English.

Shieber, S.M. 1986. *An Introduction to Unification-Based Approaches to Grammar*. Stanford University: Center for the Study of Language and Information.

Sproat, R. and B. Brunson. 1987. Constituent-based morphological parsing: A new approach to the problem of word-recognition. *Proceedings of the 25th Annual Meeting of the Association for Computational Linguistics:* 65–72.

18

Phonetic arbitrariness and the input problem: comments on Coleman's paper

KEITH JOHNSON

YorkTalk is an impressive accomplishment because it is an explicit implementation of a formal phonological system and its phonetic interpretation; explicit enough to produce speech. John Coleman could very well answer criticism by saying, "that's an interesting idea, does it work?" Undaunted by my own lack of an explicit implementation of anything, I will raise some points of concern, and react to some of the issues brought into focus by the explicitness of YorkTalk.

The YorkTalk synthesis system contains two mappings and three levels of representation. A phonotactic parser constructs hierarchical phonological structures from transcription (using "phoneme-like symbols"). These phonological structures are then used to determine parametric values for a software formant synthesizer. Some general issues arise in connection with (1) the mapping from phonological structure to synthesis parameters as it relates to the arbitrariness of phonetics, and (2) the mapping from transcription to phonological structure as it relates to the input problem in phonological theory.

18.1 The arbitrariness of phonetics

In discussing the mapping between phonological structure and synthesis parameter tracks, Coleman points out that because phonological representations and parametric phonetic representations are "very different kinds of objects," the mapping between them is by necessity arbitrary. The implementation of a phonetics/phonology interface in YorkTalk emphasizes both the one-to-many and the many-to-one nature of the mapping between phonological features and parametric phonetic values.

Concerning the one-to-many nature of the mapping, consider the phonological feature [$\pm$ voice]. There is a parameter in the Klatt synthesizer called AV (amplitude of voicing), so we might hypothesize that to phonetically implement [−voice] one simply sets the AV to zero. However, such a nonarbitrary mapping from the feature value to the synthesis parameter will not produce natural-sounding speech because there are many other acoustic correlates of the property we call "voiceless." For instance, Lisker (1986) identified 16 acoustic cues associated with the distinction between voiced and voiceless medial stops in English, including vocal-cord vibration during stop closure, relative durations of the preceding vowel and the stop closure, and F_1 transition duration following the stop release.

An example of the many-to-one nature of the mapping has to do with the feature [grave]. In YorkTalk, the acoustic definition of [grave] is not uniform across segment classes; it differs for consonants versus vowels. This is specified by saying that it depends on the position of the feature in a hierarchical structure (whether the feature is dominated by [+cons] or by [−cons]). The phonetic correlates of [±grave] are determined by reference to the position of the feature in a hierarchical structure and are therefore not expected to remain invariant over all contexts. Thus, by making phonetic implementation sensitive to hierarchical information, YorkTalk can incorporate acoustic definitions of features which differ arbitrarily across segment classes. This approach solves the problem of phonetic arbitrariness by throwing out the concept of phonetic "natural class." If phonetic implementation (and presumably the listener's knowledge of similarity relations between sounds) is to be stated in terms of hierarchical structures of features rather than stating some phonetic property which all [nasal] sounds share, how is it that [nasal] sounds in a language may group together in phonological processes?

The many-to-one type of arbitrariness illustrated by the implementation of [±grave] in YorkTalk comes about primarily because Coleman is concerned only with a mapping from phonological features to acoustic/ phonetic parameters. In terms of articulation, the feature may have a single phonetic interpretation. Where the acoustic description of [grave] may be dependent on the other features of a segment, an articulatory description of [coronal] is very straightforward and can (to a first approximation) be independent of the other features in the segment.

The choice of a domain of description (acoustic versus articulatory) is relevant for the proposed distinction between one-mouth and two-mouth theories of phonological feature sets. Some phonological phenomena seem to require a single set of features for the description of vowels and consonants because consonants and vowels may interact with each other in assimilatory processes, while other phonological processes seem to require a separate set of features for consonants and vowels because consonants may be transparent in processes of vowel harmony (Clements 1990). From the considerations of phonetic implementation discussed above we could hypothesize that these different requirements of phonological processes may reflect different domains of similarity: auditory similarity affecting vowel harmony (a two-mouth type of process because vowels and consonants are quite different auditorily) and articulatory similarity affecting consonant-vowel assimilation (a one-mouth type of process because vowels and consonants utilize the same articulators).

It is important to note, furthermore, that although in many cases the set of acoustic cues associated with a particular distinctive feature seems to arise from a single articulatory gesture, there is evidence that even in the articulatory domain phonetics is arbitrary. For instance, in English (but not in Polish, Keating 1985), stop voicing is cued by the length of the preceding tautosyllabic vowel. Thus, there is a set of articulatory dimensions involved in making the [± voice] distinction in English, related to (although smaller than) the set of acoustic dimensions involved.

So, on the one hand we use words like "voiced" to describe a constellation of observable properties in the speech signal and use instruments to determine whether a particular interval of speech has those properties or not. And on the other hand, we use the same terms to describe patterns among the lexical items in a particular language. So, for example, the distinction between /t/ and /d/ in English is realized differently in utterance-initial and medial positions. In initial position the distinction is cued primarily by the presence or absence of aspiration noise at the release of the stop closure, while in medial position the distinction is largely neutralized. In what sense can we say that the initial /t/ and the medial /t/ are instances of the same sound? The answer is that American English speakers have learned that utterances like [bʌɾɚ] and [bʌtʰɚ] are instances of the same word ("butter"). The identity between the allophones of /t/ occurs at the lexical level and so the possible pronunciations of words define phonological sets. Note also that the phonetic similarity between initial and medial /t/ is increased in hyperarticulated speech and reduced in less careful speech. The phonological similarities and differences expressed by distinctive features are present in the speech stream (and thus available for the listener) in hyperarticulated productions but not always in normal speech. This observation led Jakobson and Halle (1956: 6) to state, "The slurred fashion of pronunciation is but an abbreviated derivative from the explicit clear-speech form which carries the highest amount of information . . . When analyzing the pattern of phonemes and distinctive features composing them, one must resort to the fullest, optimal code at the command of the given speakers." Thus, the phonetic arbitrariness put into focus by YorkTalk leads us to consider the possibility that the phonetics/ phonology interface might be best stated with emphasis given to the role of clear-speech forms.

18.2 The input problem

The phonotactic parser in YorkTalk takes as input a string of "phoneme-like symbols" and through the application of a unification grammar constructs a hierarchical phonological structure. Coleman plays down the importance of the input string, stating that its "linguistic plausibility is of no consequence" and pointing out that "the input string is discarded" after the structures are built.

The input string is interesting for two reasons. First, it may be considered to be the result of a prior phonological analysis. The symbols are "phoneme-like." So, we should keep in mind the limits of the phonological analysis being performed by the system. Decisions about distinctiveness (and to a certain extent alternation) are a part of the input and not the result of the parsing algorithm. So, the nature of the input limits the analytical work performed by the system.

Second, the fact that YorkTalk uses phonemic transcription as an input string is interesting because in this regard the system is a reflection of the noncomputational process of constructing phonological representations. In constructing phonological representations in a computational system, the role played by the input in the eventual properties of the phonological representations constructed by the system cannot be disregarded. Perhaps we should also recognize the crucial nature of the input to noncomputational phonology.

The discussion of phonetic arbitrariness above lays a groundwork for further discussion of the input problem in noncomputational phonology. First, upon consideration of phonetic arbitrariness we realize that distinctive features are cover terms for phonetic complexes. Second, cross linguistic phonetic research (Ladefoged 1980; Lindau 1984; Keating 1985) has led to the conclusion that there is no universal phonetic interpretation of these cover terms. So, for instance, the phonetic complex which characterizes voiced stops in one language may be different from the complex found for voiced stops in another. Therefore, the phonological preprocessing of the input to non-computational phonology must be theoretically justified.

Obviously, any adequate account of phonological structure and patterning must be learnable. If the child learning a language builds a phonological system around distinctive features, we are under obligation to account for the preprocessing (represented by YorkTalk's "phoneme-like symbols") which produces the distinctive feature representation in the first place. The "preprocessing" that I'm talking about is normally performed by the field linguist in the course of transcribing a language.

Chomsky and Halle (1968) provided a theoretical solution to the input problem by asserting that there is a universal phonetic component which provides a mapping from the speech signal to distinctive features. But cross-linguistic phonetic research in the intervening years has indicated that this proposal is untenable. The arbitrariness of phonetics, and the cross-linguistic variability in the phonetic implementation of phonological distinctions, suggests that the child learning language must learn some phonetics (thus, phonetic knowledge is part of the speaker/hearer's linguistic knowledge). Moreover, these facts suggest that in real life the input to the phonology is phonetic.

One type of phonetic input which might serve as an adequate input for the development of a phonology is clear speech. Hyperarticulated forms exhibiting important contrasts which are generally left unrealized in normal speech may serve as a source of phonological knowledge for the child: the complexity and indeterminacy of ordinary speech is left unanalyzed until more completely elaborated lexical representations can be internalized. This solution to the input problem sees, then, a somewhat sanitized and simplified input as fundamental to the process of constructing phonological representations, and in this regard is not much different from YorkTalk. However, it is assumed here that the phoneme-like symbols are actually a part of the experience of the language learner. Finally, although clear-speech forms may solve one aspect of the input problem (reducing the amount of "phonetic implementation" that the child has to undo in recovering the distinctive properties of sounds) there remains a problem in positing a universal set of distinctive features. In a general sense the human speech-production capability is limited by the physical equipment; however, the range of possible constellations of phonetic properties, and variations on those constellations from which the languages of the world construct phonological distinctions, may well be unlimited. We should therefore expect to have a better understanding of the phonological patterning of sounds synchronically and diachronically as we learn more about patterns of phonetic arbitrariness and the nature of the phonetic input to the phonology.

References

Chomsky, N. and M. Halle. 1968. *The Sound Pattern of English.* New York: Harper & Row.

Clements, G.N. 1990. Place of articulation in consonants and vowels: a unified theory. In B. Laks and A. Rialland (eds.) *L'architecture et la géométrie des représentations phonologiques.* Paris: Editions du Centre National de la Recherche Scientifique.

Jakobson, R. and M. Halle. 1956. *Fundamentals of Language.* The Hague: Mouton.

Keating, P. 1985. Universal phonetics and the organization of grammars. In V. Fromkin (ed.) *Phonetic linguistics: Essays in Honor of Peter Ladefoged.* Orlando: Academic Press, 115–132.

Ladefoged, P. 1980. What are linguistic sounds made of? *Language* 56: 485–502.

Lindau, M. 1984. Phonetic differences in glottalic consonants. *Journal of Phonetics* 12: 147–155.

Lisker, L. 1986. "Voicing" in English: A catalog of acoustic features signalling /b/ versus /p/ in trochees. *Haskins Laboratories: Status Report on Speech Research* SR-86/87: 45–53.

19
Lip aperture and consonant releases

CATHERINE P. BROWMAN

19.1 Introduction

The focus of this paper is, simply put, how the mouth is opened during vowels in CV (sub)syllables. Such a question is intimately related to the nature both of consonant releases and of lip control (as in rounding). The function of controlling the lips for vowels might be to ensure that the mouth is open during the vowel, so that there will be radiated sound. If this is the case, then actively controlled consonant-release movements, which would serve the same purpose, might not be necessary; the mouth might open sufficiently, given the lip control, if the consonant is simply turned off without actively moving away from its position of closure.

Much previous work has viewed the relation between consonants and vowels as a linear phenomenon. In a CV syllable or subsyllable, the consonant is considered to occur first, followed by the transition from consonant into the vowel, and finally the vowel. In the acoustic instantiation of such a perspective, the transition from consonant to vowel often consists of two parts, at least for plosives: a burst (plus any aspiration) followed by formant transitions (e.g. Cooper *et al.* 1952; Fant 1973). The importance of the acoustic properties of the release for characterizing stop consonants has been emphasized by authors such as Stevens and Blumstein (1981).

However, it is in fact not possible to separate consonantal and vocalic information temporally. As emphasized by Liberman *et al.* (1967), both the burst and the formant transitions are affected by both the vowel and the consonant, due to the overlapping articulations involved. Articulatorily, consonants and vowels are not linearly organized. Articulations for the vowel and consonant can cooccur (e.g. Gay 1977); that is, articulation is inherently multilinear. In the simplest cases, for example that seen in [ba], the consonant and vowel articulations use different articulators (the lips for

[b] and the tongue for [a]), and the tongue movements for [a] cooccur with, or overlap, the lip movements for [b]. In such a case, both the tongue movements into the vowel and the lip movements out of the consonant might affect the resulting linear acoustic signal. The linear acoustic transition from consonant to vowel can be affected both by the release movement out of the consonant and by the tongue-body movement into the vowel. This paper will attempt to separate the vocalic and consonantal influences in at least some instances.

The framework of articulatory phonology (e.g. Browman and Goldstein 1986, 1989, 1990a; also Goldstein, this volume), which provides a natural way of characterizing such overlapping, linguistically significant articulations, will be used in this paper. Articulatory phonology is an approach to phonology in which characterizations of the movements of speech articulators, both through space and over time, are considered to be the primitive units constituting the utterances of a language, for the purposes of phonological patterning as well as for phonetic description. Articulatory movements are characterized in terms of underlying articulatory *Gestures* that can be specified dynamically in terms of a *task-dynamic* model (e.g. Saltzman and Kelso 1987; Saltzman 1986; Saltzman and Munhall 1989). One aspect of a Gestural approach that is directly relevant to the questions being considered here is that oral Gestures are coordinative structures (see e.g. Turvey 1977); that is, characterizations of constrictions formed with sets of articulators, not with single articulators. Thus, the lip-closing constriction associated with the beginning of the utterance [ba] is achieved by the coordinated action of the upper lip, lower lip, and jaw, termed a Lip Aperture (LA) Gesture. Dimensions of the constriction that use these coordinated sets of articulators are referred to as *tract variables*, for example, the tract variables of constriction location and constriction degree.

It is very important to note that there need not be a one-to-one relationship between Gestures or tract variables and the movements of the articulators. For example, the distance between the upper- and lower-lip articulators can vary, either because it is actively and directly controlled, as in a Lip Aperture (LA) Gesture, or as a passive consequence of the movement of an articulator, such as the jaw, that has been activated as part of another Gesture. In the first case, active control, the lip aperture would be considered specified, whereas in the second case the lip aperture is unspecified. The question of specification is phonologically important regardless of the phonological framework being invoked. While the question of active articulatory control, or specification, is of course a central question in the framework of an articulatory phonology, it is also relevant to other phonologies. No phonology would wish to claim as phonologically important a movement that was simply a passive side-effect of some other movement. This issue is particularly relevant for any theory of representation that gives special status to some, but not all, consonant releases. For example, Steriade (1993), theorizes that stops and affricates have two phonologically relevant aperture specifications, one each for closure and release, while fricatives have a single phonological specification for aperture value. This proposal could be interpreted as hypothesizing an active release gesture for the plosives but a passive one for fricatives.

Returning now to the specification or nonspecification of lip opening to see how lip opening can change when it is unspecified, consider that the lower lip rides upon the jaw, and therefore as the jaw moves, the opening between the lips will automatically change. The movement of a single articulator such as the jaw may be affected in turn by the simultaneous activation of several Gestures, for example, overlapping consonant and vowel Gestures (since the movement of the tongue body for a vowel is achieved by the coordinated action of the jaw and the tongue body). Thus a change in lip opening might occur either because the lip aperture is directly specified and controlled, or because the jaw is moving due to the activation of another Gesture. Any investigation into how the mouth is opened during the vowel must consider "passive" or "unspecified" hypotheses in addition to "active" or "specified" hypotheses such as a controlled vocalic lip Gesture (as for rounding). In fact, one kind of hypothesis of unspecified lip opening during front unrounded vowels was proposed by Fromkin (1964), who showed that, during the acoustic vowel, lip opening for front unrounded vowels appeared to result from the lowering of the jaw for the vowel. (The lips were assumed to be controlled for back rounded vowels.)

Because the Gestural model has been implemented as a computational model at Haskins Laboratories (Browman *et al.* 1986), it was possible to test the hypothesis that lip position should only be specified for rounded vowels, and not for unrounded vowels. While this approach worked fine for low vowels (as in [bɑb]), it did not work for high vowels (as in [bib]), in which the lips did not open sufficiently after the first bilabial consonant to permit vocalic resonance. This result can be understood as follows. In the computational model, the jaw did not lower much during the movement towards the vowel [i], and therefore the lower lip did not move a distance from the upper lip sufficient to open the vocal tract for sound radiation. Inspection of x-ray data confirmed that at least for some subjects, the jaw did not lower during the vowel [i]. One motivation for this paper was to attempt to refine our understanding of those situations in which the lips are actively controlled, and those in which lip opening appears to be a passive consequence of jaw movement.

The presupposition above was that mouth opening during the vowel was basically lip opening associated with the vowel, either from direct specification (as in rounding) or as a passive consequence of jaw lowering. It is, of course, also possible that the mouth opening during the acoustic vowel interval could arise from the release of the consonant. Here too it is necessary to distinguish the "active" and "passive" hypotheses, although the passive hypothesis in this case focuses on the posited tendency of articulators to return automatically to a neutral position when not actively controlled. This tendency is simulated in the computational task-dynamic model by having each articulator return to a neutral position when it is not participating in any active Gesture. In the case of the lips, the neutral position is defined with respect to the jaw. Thus, the work reported in this paper investigates whether mouth opening always needs to be specified, or whether it is sometimes passive; and whether mouth opening during vowels is a result of vocalic Gestures, consonantal releases, or both.

19.2 Stimuli

Articulatory data for two-syllable American English nonsense utterances were collected from a single speaker using the x-ray microbeam facility in Madison, Wisconsin. The utterances all had the same syllable structure – CVCVC – with stronger stress on the first syllable. Each utterance used only one vowel from the set [i, e, ε, æ, a, o, u] and one consonant from the set [p, t, k, s]; some sample utterances are ['pipip], ['titit], ['tɑtɑt], ['sɑsɑs], etc. The utterances were collected in blocks with no carrier phrase, in each of which the vowel was the same. For example, in one block the speaker read "PEEpeep TEEteet KEEkeek SEEseece TEEteet SEEseece." A total of about 80 analogous blocks produced three usable tokens of each vowel–consonant combination, with movement data from pellets placed on the upper and lower lips, the jaw (lower incisors), the tongue tip, the tongue dorsum, and two intermediate tongue points.

For each of the three tokens from each of the 28 CVCVC utterances, lip opening was computed by subtracting the vertical position of the pellet on the lower lip from the vertical position of the pellet on the upper lip. Two maxima and one minimum were found in the lip-opening movement trace, the maxima corresponding to maximum openings during the acoustic vowels, and the minimum to the minimum opening during the intervocalic consonant closure. As shown in figure 19.1, the curves for lip opening (LO) and for vertical position of the jaw (JY) were compared at the LO maxima and minimum. Visual inspection of the curves confirmed that the LO maxima and minima usually fell close to maxima and minima in the JY curves. (In the major exception, utterances containing [o], JY tended to reach its maximum height during the intervocalic consonant closure roughly 25 ms later than the LO minimum, and the jaw minima during the vowels

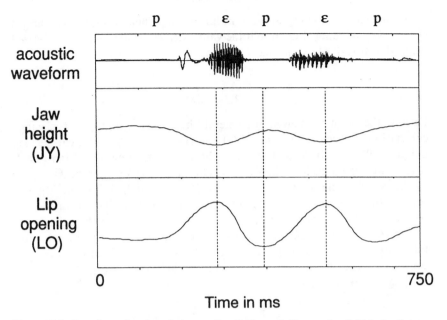

Figure 19.1. Transformed and marked x-ray data for [pɛpɛp]. Lip opening (LO) is the distance between pellets on upper and lower lips. The range is 35 mm in both movement channels.

were slightly later than the corresponding LO maxima. Nevertheless, the same selection procedure was followed for [o] as for the other vowels: the amplitudes thus selected seemed fairly close, by eye, to the relevant extremes.)

19.3 Passive versus controlled lip opening

The first analyses attempted to determine whether or not lip opening was actively controlled in particular circumstances, or whether, in some situations, lip opening might be a passive consequence of the movement of the jaw. In the stimuli being tested, jaw movement associated with the vowel was assumed to be the result of the vocalic coordinative structure, in which both the jaw and tongue-body articulators participated in the vowel constriction. This assumption was tested in the computational model, in which for isolated vowels jaw height was always found to have the same rank order as the tongue height, being lower as the tongue height lowered, although only the constriction location and degree for the tongue body were controlled. Thus, given that jaw variation can be predicted in this, or some other, independent manner, a significant negative correlation between jaw height and lip opening (the higher the jaw, the smaller the lip opening) would indicate a passive variation in lip opening. Therefore, the jaw height (JY) and lip opening (LO) amplitude values described above were correlated using the BMDP 6D statistical package.

19.3.1 Vowels

During the acoustic vowel, in general there was a significant negative correlation between lip opening (LO) and jaw height (JY). This can be seen in figure 19.2, which shows LO and JY at the LO maxima for all 168 vowels (two vowels from each of the three repetitions of the 28 utterances) labeled by the vowel in the utterance (p < .001, R = −0.769). While the negative correlation between lip opening and jaw height shows that lip opening is strongly affected by jaw height, there are also differences in the behavior of the vowels which indicate that some vowels directly control lip behavior. Interestingly, this vowel difference can be seen most clearly during the consonant, and in particular in differential behavior during bilabial and nonbilabial consonants.

19.3.2 Consonants

Considering all the consonants together, there was not a significant correlation between LO and JY at the LO minimum (i.e. during the consonant). However, as can be seen in figure 19.3, this lack of correlation is due to the much smaller lip opening (LO) for the labial consonant [p], which

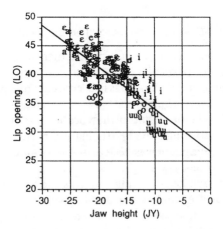

Figure 19.2. Scatter plot of jaw height (JY) versus lip opening (LO), both in mm, for the vowels in both syllables of the utterances.

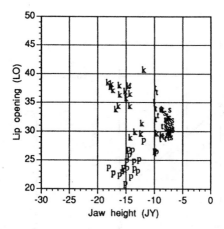

Figure 19.3. Scatter plot of jaw height (JY) versus lip opening (LO), both in mm, for the intervocalic consonant.

has about the same jaw height (JY) as [k] but by far the smallest lip opening of any consonant. Indeed, the nonlabial consonants [k], [t], and [s], considered together, do show a significant negative correlation between LO and JY (p < 0.001, R = −0.687). (Note that the alveolars, both [t] and [s], have the highest jaw position, and in fact have a fairly tight JY distribution, as expected from Keating *et al.* 1990; Kiritani *et al.* 1983; Perkell 1969). These results for the consonants show that there is a difference between the labial and the nonlabial consonants: lip opening is correlated with jaw height only for the nonlabial consonants. This in turn suggests that, while lip aperture is probably controlled for the labial consonant, lip opening appears to be a passive consequence of jaw height for the nonlabial consonants – not a surprising result (although one which, as we shall see, needs to be moderated a bit).

Figure 19.4 demonstrates differential behavior for nonlabial and labial consonants by displaying the correlation between JY and LO during the LO minimum separately for the four consonants [k], [t], [s], and [p]. The labels in the figure indicate the vowel in the utterance. Thus, in figure 19.4a, the three values labeled "u" reflect the point during the intervocalic [k] in the three tokens of [kukuk]. For the nonlabial consonants [k] and [t] (figure 19.4a and b), LO and JY are significantly negatively correlated (p < 0.005, R = −0.588 and p < 0.001, R = −0.705, respectively). JY and LO are so tightly bunched for [s], seen in figure 19.4c, that they are not significantly correlated. However, for the labial consonant [p] (figure 19.4d) the correlation between LO and JY is categorically different from that of the nonlabials, being positive (p < 0.004, R = 0.607). Thus, it is clear that the

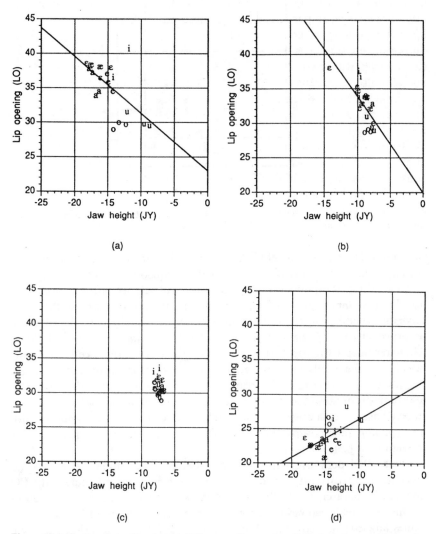

Figure 19.4. Scatter plot of jaw height (JY) versus lip opening (LO), both in mm. Each point corresponds to the measurements for a single intervocalic consonant, labeled by the vowel in the utterance. (a) utterances with [k]. (b) utterances with [t]. (c) utterances with [s]. (d) utterances with [p]. 'a' = [ɑ] in these plots.

behavior of lip opening during the labial consonant is categorically different from what it is during the nonlabial consonants, as the vowels in the utterance change. In particular, as can be seen in figures 19.4a and b, when lip opening is unspecified for the consonant ([k] and [t]), then the lip opening during the consonant is smallest for utterances containing rounded vowels (the vowel [i] will be considered separately below, and is excluded from these and all following discussions of round/unround comparisons). However, as seen in figure 19.4d, when Lip Aperture is controlled for the consonant ([p]), lip opening during the consonant is *largest* for utterances containing rounded vowels.

The unexpected difference in lip opening during the consonant described above – smaller for rounded vowels than for unrounded vowels when the consonant is nonlabial, but larger when the consonant is labial – is predicted by the Gestural model, adding only the assumption that the rounded vowels (but not unrounded vowels) are controlled for lip movement, with the control affecting lip opening. The two crucial aspects of the model are (1) the overlapping of vocalic and consonantal Gestures, and (2) the fact that overlapping Gestures that use the same tract variable are blended. A brief discussion of each of these aspects follows.

(1) Vowel–consonant overlap is currently incorporated in the linguistic-gestural component of the Gestural computational model (Browman and Goldstein 1990b). Such overlap between vowels and consonants has been reported by a variety of researchers (e.g. Gay 1977; Borden and Gay 1979; Browman and Goldstein 1990b). Moreover, the fact that there are jaw-height differences during the intervocalic consonant that are attributable to the vowels in the present data indicates that these data are also consistent with vowel–consonant overlap (although the identity of the vowels in the two syllables means these data cannot provide unambiguous evidence). (2) The task-dynamic component of the Gestural computational model blends overlapping (simultaneously active) Gestures that use the same tract variable (Saltzman and Munhall 1989), and thereby predicts that the resultant tract-variable motion should be intermediate between the two targets in such a case.

The key fact captured by the Gestural model is that, in an utterance containing bilabial consonants and rounded vowels, during the bilabial consonant the lips will be affected by both the consonant and the vowel, given vowel–consonant overlap. In figure 19.5a, using Lip Aperture (LA) activation boxes as an indication of controlled lip Gestures, an estimated LA Gestural score for "Poe" is presented, showing the overlap of controlled lip Gestures for the consonant and the vowel. This contrasts with "pa" (figure 19.5b), with lip control only for the consonant; "toe" (figure 19.5c), with lip control only for the vowel; and "ta" (figure 19.5d), which does not have lip control at all. The observed lip opening in utterances with nonlabial consonants such as [t] should only be a consequence of the lip opening associated with the vowel. This means that lip opening should be smaller during the [t] in "toe" than during the [t] in "ta," given that vowel-related lip opening is less for rounded vowels (see figure 19.2); this is confirmed by the data in figure 19.4b. However, for labial consonants, the lip opening will result solely from the consonant when the vowel has no lip control (as in "pa"), and will be some kind of blend of the consonant and vowel target values when the lips are controlled for the vowel (as in "Poe"). That is, the very small constriction for the bilabial stop will become larger when it is blended with the overlapping lip Gesture associated with the rounded vowel (which has a wider lip constriction). Thus, the Gestural model accounts for the fact that the relative size of lip opening between unrounded and rounded vowels switches between labial and nonlabial consonants, as shown in figure 19.4. Moreover, the Gestural model also accounts for the fact that the numerical values of lip opening for the rounded vowels are smaller during labial than during nonlabial consonants, as seen in figures 19.4d and 19.4a for [p] and [k]. While the differences in lip opening for rounded vowels during labial and nonlabial consonants are probably not large enough to be very important in the overall characterization of linguistically significant articulations, nevertheless, since only a model with vowel-consonant overlap and blending can account for such behavior in a general way,[1] the differences serve as support for the Gestural approach.

To confirm that the model could simulate the results, Gestural scores were created for utterances with the corresponding voiced stop using the computational model, with the additional assumption that lip aperture was controlled for rounded vowels. For the sake of simplicity, and given the results of Bell-Berti and Harris (1982), the timing of the lip-aperture Gesture for rounded vowels was assumed to be identical to the timing of the tongue-body gesture (because the vowels were identical in both syllables, the data could show no more, regarding timing, than that the posited vocalic lip-aperture Gesture was active by the time of closure for the intervocalic consonantal Gesture). As seen in the sample gestural score of figure 19.6, during the intervocalic consonant in an utterance such as [bobob] a vocalic LA Gesture and also a consonantal LA Gesture are simultaneously active. In such a case, the targets of the two Gestures are blended. Since the LA target for a rounded vowel is wider than that for a bilabial closure, the resultant lip opening during the intervocalic bilabial is larger (wider) in the context of a rounded vowel (when the small consonantal LA is blended with the larger vocalic LA) than in the context of an unrounded vowel (when the only control of the LA is the small consonantal LA). This is exactly what was observed in the x-ray microbeam data described above (figure 19.4d).

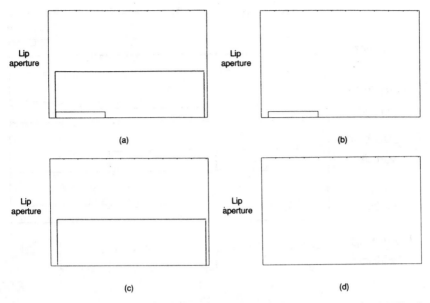

Figure 19.5. Partial schematic Gestural scores for different labial aperture scenarios. (a) "Poe," (b) "pa," (c) "toe," (d) "ta." Boxes indicate the estimated extent of Gestural control.

19.3.3 Spread vowel(s)

In addition to the evidence that is consistent with rounded vowels having controlled lip Gestures, there is evidence that [i] also has a controlled lip Gesture, although presumably lip spreading rather than lip rounding. Note that during both labial and nonlabial consonants (figure 19.4) [i] has a lip opening as large or larger than the other unrounded vowels, even when the jaw is high (which would result in a smaller lip opening if lip opening were uncontrolled for [i]). However, this controlled lip gesture for [i] differs in its behavior from that of the rounded vowels. Recall that, unlike the case for [i], lip opening during the consonant for the rounded vowels changes its relation to the unrounded vowels as the consonant changes from labial to nonlabial: lip opening is smaller for rounded than for unrounded vowels during the nonlabial consonants, and the reverse during the labial consonant. The lip-opening behavior of both [i] and the rounded vowels appears consistent with the lip control NOT being that of lip aperture per se, but rather something else such as a constraint against contact between the sides of the lips (for [i] and possibly unrounded vowels in general) or requiring a certain minimum contact between the sides of the lips (for rounded vowels), as suggested in

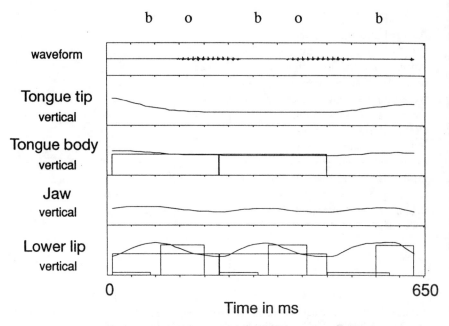

Figure 19.6. Gestural score for [bobob]. Boxes indicate the extent of active Gestural control, and the curves indicate transformed movements in space of ASY (vocal tract model) articulators. In the lower lip channel, the boxes refer to lip aperture activation, and in the tongue body channel, the curve refers to the position of the ASY tongue ball center in space, and the boxes to the activation for the tongue body tract variables. The range is the same in each channel, to facilitate comparison, with the exception of the jaw channel, in which the range is half that of the other channels. Each bilabial consonant also has a release Gesture, presaging later results.

Goldstein (1991). Lip opening presumably would reflect such a side-contact constraint only imprecisely. While the side-contact hypothesis cannot be directly tested with the current data, in which there is no interpretable information about the frontal view of the lips, it is interesting to notice that the numerical values for lip opening during the consonant in figures 19.4a–d for [i] are quite variable, whereas the values for the rounded vowels are quite stable, differing only between the nonlabial and labial consonants. Such behavior would be consistent with the differing nature of the constraints – for [i], there can be any degree of openness as long as side contact is avoided, whereas for the rounded vowels, there is a minimum amount of side contact required.

19.4 Consonant releases

As a result of the above analyses, it appears that the lips (LA in the current version of the computational model) are controlled for rounded and spread vowels, but for no other vowels. The question then remains as to the necessity of active consonant releases. Harking back to the basic question, would the mouth be adequately opened during all the vowels, unrounded as well as spread and rounded, without the use of an active consonant release? (Recall that there is always a "passive" consonant release present, in that the individual articulators return to an articulator-neutral position when not under active control, as simulated by the computational task-dynamic model.) The hypothesis that no active consonant releases were necessary was tested using the computational mode, and found to be wanting in some utterances with unrounded vowels, in which the mouth simply did not open enough for vowels as low as [ɛ]. Figure 19.7 shows a Gestural score for

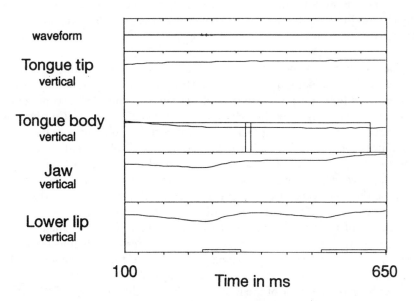

waveform

Tongue tip
vertical

Tongue body
vertical

Jaw
vertical

Lower lip
vertical

100   **Time in ms**   650

Figure 19.7. Gestural score for [bɛbɛb], without active releases. Boxes indicate the extent of active Gestural control, and the curves indicate transformed movements in space of ASY (vocal-tract model) articulators. In the lower lip channel, the boxes refer to lip aperture activation, and in the tongue body channel, the curve refers to the position of the ASY tongue-ball center in space, and the boxes to the activation for the tongue body tract variables. The range is the same in each channel, to facilitate comparison, with the exception of the Jaw channel, in which the range is half that of the other channels. No segment label is given because no acoustic signal is produced.

[bɛbɛb], generated using the above assumptions. The mouth did not open enough to permit an acoustic signal to be generated for the vowels in the utterance.

In tracking down the problem, the simulated motions of the various model tract articulators were compared to the x-ray data. The lower lip was apparently correct in that it both raised and lowered for the bilabial closure. The tongue-body motion was very accurately simulated. Indeed, both the simulated tongue-body position in [bɛbɛb] (figure 19.7) and the position of the tongue body in the x-ray data in [pɛpɛp] (figure 19.8a) were stable. The problem appeared to be with the jaw. That is, in the simulation, the jaw continued to raise throughout the utterance, unlike in the x-ray data (figure 19.8a), indicating that something else needed to be controlled. However, the motion of the jaw could not be a result of the positioning of the tongue body required for the vowel, given that the tongue body basically did not move once the target had been achieved. Rather, the jaw motion had to arise from some other kind of control. Three possibilities suggest themselves: that the jaw is moving because the tongue tip is moving; that there is some kind of direct vowel-related control of the jaw; or that the jaw is moving as part of an active consonant release. These three hypotheses will be considered in turn.

The movement of the tongue tip during a bilabial consonant, as seen in figure 19.8a, is actually quite puzzling. Moreover, the apparent correlation between the tongue-tip movement and the jaw movement is also puzzling, given that the tongue body, which lies between the tongue tip and jaw anatomically, is not moving. This apparent correlation is quite real: for all utterances containing nonhigh vowels, the vertical displacements of the jaw and tongue tip during [p] were highly correlated (see table 19.1; utterances with high vowels [i] and [u] probably did not show tip–jaw correlations because they had very little movement of either the tongue tip or the jaw). This tongue-tip movement was probably a passive consequence of the movement of the jaw, which raised for the bilabial. The movement of the tongue tip was likely due to the fact that it was "resting" behind the lower teeth for the front vowels, presumably a side-effect of the action of the anterior genioglossus (Hardcastle 1976; see also Baer *et al.* 1988), and was further back on the floor of the mouth for the nonhigh back vowels. That is, the movement of the tongue tip during the bilabial was probably a consequence of the tongue tip riding along on the jaw.

Of the other two hypotheses, direct vowel-related control of the jaw would mean undesirable redundancy, since, as discussed earlier, in many kinds of environments the jaw is automatically lowered as a consequence of the tongue-body movement for the vowel. Moreover, since for alveolars (in which the tongue tip is raised, i.e. not resting on the floor of the mouth) the

Table 19.1 *Results of step-wise multiple regression for displacements during intervocalic [p]. Dependent variable: TTY (vertical position of the tongue tip); possible independent variables: TB2Y (vertical position of the second tongue-body pellet), JY (vertical position of the jaw).*

Vowel in word	Step1		Step 2	
	var.	R	+ var.	R
i	TB2Y	0.89	—	—
e	JY	0.85	—	—
ɛ	JY	0.93	TB2Y	1.0
æ	JY	0.97	—	—
ɑ	JY	0.81	—	—
o	JY	0.09	—	—
u	TB2Y	0.84	—	—

tongue tip as well as the jaw lowered out of the consonant, some kind of active consonant release was deemed necessary. While it is possible that a lowering "kick" should be used, i.e. a "Gesture" with no target, that is not possible to test with the current version of the task-dynamic model. Therefore, a consonant release with constriction-degree and constriction-location targets was added to the computational Gestural model, basically in order to test whether the tongue body could remain in a constant position even in the presence of an active release. Releases for bilabial and alveolar voiced stops, in bisyllabic words with each of the seven vowels in this study, have been tested and appear to provide adequate simulations of the x-ray movement data as well as correct perceptual results; simulations with velars have not yet been successful with a context-independent release. The constriction-degree target for the bilabial and alveolar releases (11 mm) was always independent of the vowel; the constriction-location target was also independent of the vowel, and was vertical in the inferior–superior plane.

Figure 19.9 shows the results of adding a labial-release component to the simulation of [bɛbɛb]. Note that, unlike the simulation shown in figure 19.7, the mouth is now open enough to produce radiated sound during the vowel. Moreover, the jaw now raises and lowers, albeit slightly, as in the x-ray data shown in figure 19.8a, and unlike the earlier simulation without the active release in figure 19.7. The tongue body does not move. The combination of both a labial consonantal release and a rounded vowel was seen in figure 19.6, which showed the Gestural score for [bobob]. Note the additional lip

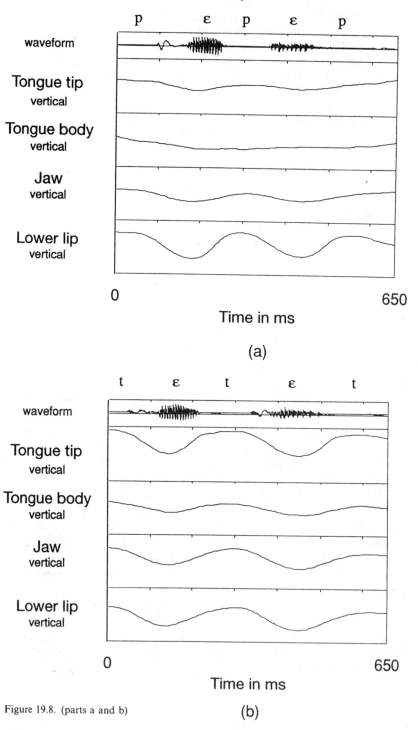

Figure 19.8. (parts a and b)

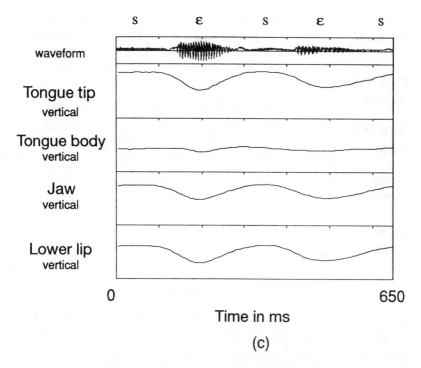

Figure 19.8. (part c) Vertical x-ray pellet positions over time for three utterances with vowel [ɛ]. The range is 35 mm in each channel. The tongue body channel represents the movement of the TB2 pellet, the tongue pellet second from the rear, approximately 50 mm back from the tip. Utterances with consonants (a) [p], (b) [t], (c) [s].

Gestures associated with the rounded vowels in [bobob]. In general, in utterances with bilabials the lip opening is effectively decomposed into two context-free components, one associated with the vowel and one associated with the consonant.

19.4.1 [s]

It is interesting to note that in the x-ray data [s] also shows lowering of the jaw out of the consonant with little concomitant tongue-body motion when the word contains the vowel [ɛ] (figure 19.8c). In other contexts, [s] shows evidence of additional tongue-body shaping, with a lowered tongue-body pellet during the consonant and a raising of the tongue body at release (see, for example, figure 19.10c as compared with figures 19.10a and 19.10b).

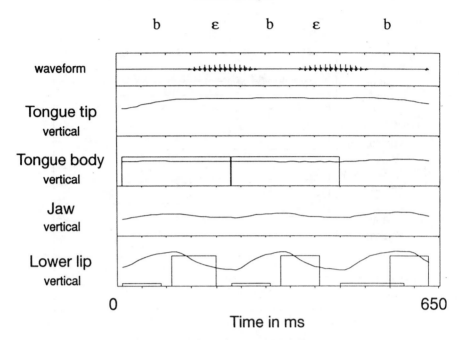

Figure 19.9. Gestural score for [bɛbɛb], including active releases. Boxes indicate the extent of active Gestural control, and the curves indicate transformed movements in space of ASY (vocal-tract model) articulators. In the lower lip channel, the boxes refer to lip aperture activation, and in the tongue body channel, the curve refers to the position of the ASY tongue-ball center in space, and the boxes to the activation for the tongue body tract variables. The range is the same in each channel, to facilitate comparison, with the exception of the Jaw channel, in which the range is half that of the other channels. In this simulation, as in the above simulations, the movements began from the neutral configuration, often leading to initial differences between the simulations and x-ray data, which started from the configuration of the preceding utterance.

Here, too, the jaw lowers. Thus, for [s] as well as the stops, the lowering of the jaw cannot result from the tongue-body movement in the cases where the tongue body does not change position (or, worse, raises). Therefore, the same logic that suggests an active release for the stops suggests there is also an active release for [s]. Active releases for [s] were not tested using the computational model, since it does not currently generate an adequate acoustic signal for fricatives. However, a simulation of [sɛsɛs] without an active release and with a tongue-body target for [s] showed the same continually rising jaw as in the simulations of stops without active releases, even when the vowel and consonant Gestures were sequential rather than overlapping. This result supports the suggestion that for [s] as well as for stops something about the release needs to be controlled.

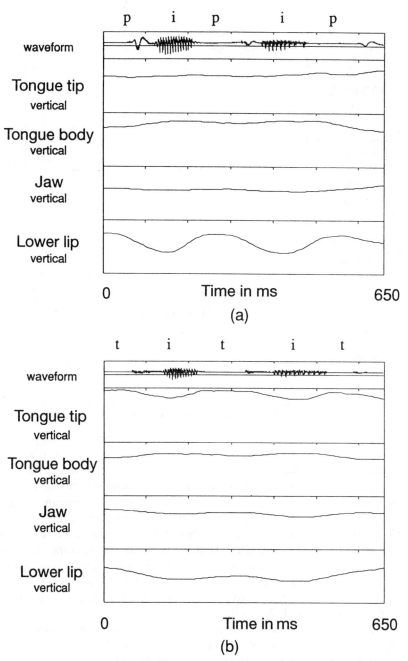

Figure 19.10. (parts a and b) Vertical x-ray pellet positions over time for three utterances with vowel [i]. The range is 35 mm in each channel. The tongue body channel represents the movement of the TB2 pellet, the tongue pellet second from the rear, approximately 50 mm back from the tip. Utterances with consonants (a) [p], (b) [t], (c) [s].

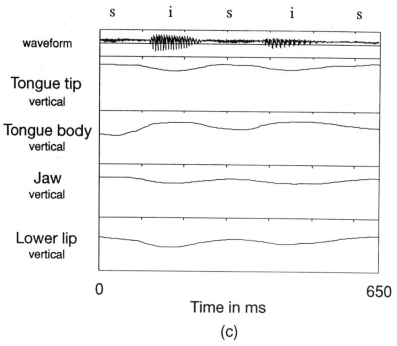

Figure 19.10. (part c)

19.5 Summary and discussion

Analyses of x-ray data of American English utterances provided support for
a decomposition of lip movement into a consonantal component and a
vocalic component. Rounded vowels and spread vowels showed evidence of
controlled lip Gestures, whereas unrounded (and [−spread]) vowels did not.
Moreover, the computational Gestural model, in which consonant and
vowel Gestures overlap and are blended (when the same tract variables are
used), correctly predicted the differences in lip opening observed during
labial and nonlabial consonants as the vowels in the utterance differed
between rounded and unrounded. In addition, active consonant release
movements for stop consonants, and probably for [s], were shown to be
necessary, and labial and alveolar stop releases were plausibly simulated
with the computational Gestural model.

The similarity between the stops and [s], in terms of both appearing to
have an actively controlled release, provides no support for Steriade's (1993)
suggestion that the phonological difference between (audibly released)

[−continuant] plosives and affricates, on the one hand, and [+continuant] fricatives, on the other hand, should be coded in terms of differential release behavior. Recall that Steriade proposes that stops and affricates have two phonologically relevant aperture specifications, one each for closure and release, while fricatives have a single phonological specification for aperture value. The current data, which suggest that [s] is similar to the stops in having an active release, imply that the differences between the [−continuant] and [+continuant] sounds are probably better related to some other aspect of their production than the presence or absence of a specified release.

Notes

Thanks to an anonymous reviewer and the editor of this volume for helpful comments on a preliminary version of this paper. This work was supported by National Science Foundation grant BNS 8820099 and National Institutes of Health grants HD-01994 and DC-00121 to Haskins Laboratories.

1 In the case of the labial consonants, it might be possible to analyze the increased value of lip opening in utterances with rounded vowels as resulting from lip curl associated with possible protrusion for the rounding. However, such an analysis does not account for the striking numerical similarity of lip openings across utterances containing rounded vowels for different nonlabial consonants. That is, if lip opening were simply increased by lip curl for all rounded vowels, then lip opening should be different across the utterances with different consonantal jaw heights, which it is not.

References

Baer, T., P.J. Alfonso and K. Honda. 1988. Electromyography of the tongue muscles during vowels in /axpVp/ environments. *Annual Bulletin of the Research Institute of Logopedics and Phoniatrics* 22: 7–19.

Bell-Berti, F. and K.S. Harris. 1982. Temporal patterns of coarticulation: lip rounding. *Journal of the Acoustical Society of America* 71: 449–454.

Borden, G.J. and T. Gay. 1979. Temporal aspects of articulatory movements for /s/-stop clusters, *Phonetica* 36: 21–31.

Browman, C.P. and L. Goldstein. 1986. Towards an articulatory phonology, *Phonology Yearbook* 3: 219–252.

1989. Articulatory gestures as phonological units, *Phonology* 6: 201–251.

1990a. Gestural specification using dynamically-defined articulatory structures, *Journal of Phonetics* 18: 299–320.

1990b. Tiers in articulatory phonology, with some implications for casual speech. In J. Kingston and M. E. Beckman (eds.) *Papers in Laboratory Phonology I:*

Between the Grammar and Physics of Speech. Cambridge: University Press, 341–376.

Browman, C.P., L. Goldstein, E. Saltzman and C. Smith. 1986. GEST: A computational model for speech production using dynamically defined articulatory gestures. *Journal of the Acoustical Society of America* 80: S97.

Cooper, F.S., P.C. Delattre, A.M. Liberman, J.M. Borst and L.J. Gerstman. 1952. Some experiments on the perception of synthetic speech sounds. *Journal of the Acoustical Society of America* 24: 597–606.

Fant, G. 1973. Stops in CV-syllables. In G. Fant (ed.) *Speech Sounds and Features.* Cambridge, MA and London: MIT Press, 110–139.

Fromkin, V. 1964. Lip positions in American English vowels. *Language and Speech* 7: 215–225.

Gay, T. 1977. Articulatory movements in VCV sequences. *Journal of the Acoustical Society of America* 62: 183–193.

Goldstein, L. 1991. Lip rounding as side contact. *Proceedings of the XIIth International Congress of Phonetic Sciences* 1: 97–101.

Goldstein, L. This volume. Possible articulatory bases for the class of guttural consonants.

Hardcastle, W.J. 1976. *Physiology of Speech Production.* London, New York, San Francisco: Academic Press.

Keating, P.A., B. Lindblom, J. Lubker and J. Kreiman. 1990. Jaw Position in English and Swedish VCVs. *UCLA Working Papers in Phonetics* 74: 77–95.

Kiritani, S., S. Tanka, T. Tanka, K. Hashimoto, S. Masaki and K. Shirai. 1983. Contextual variation of the jaw movement for the intervocalic consonant in VCV utterances. *Annual Bulletin* 17: 45–53.

Liberman, A.M., F.S. Cooper, D.P. Shankweiler and M. Studdert-Kennedy. 1967. Perception of the speech code. *Psychological Review* 74: 431–461.

Perkell, J. S. 1969. *Physiology of Speech Production: Results and Implications of a Quantitative Cineradiographic Study.* Cambridge, MA: MIT Press.

Saltzman, E. 1986. Task dynamic coordination of the speech articulators: a preliminary model. In H. Heuer and C. Fromm (eds.) *Generation and Modulation of Action Patterns.* New York and Berlin: Springer Verlag. (Volume 15 of Experimental Brain Research Series), 129–144.

Saltzman, E. and J.A.S. Kelso. 1987. Skilled actions: a task dynamic approach. *Psychological Review* 94: 84–106.

Saltzman, E.L. and K.G. Munhall. 1989. A dynamical approach to gestural patterning in speech production. *Ecological Psychology* 1: 333–382.

Steriade, D. 1993. Closure, release and nasal contours. To appear in M. Huffman and R. Krakow (eds.) *Nasals, nasalization, and the velum.* Phonetics and Phonology 5. San Diego: Academic Press.

Stevens, K.N. and S.E. Blumstein. 1981. The search for invariant acoustic correlates of phonetic features. In P.D. Eimas and J.L. Miller (eds.) *Perspectives on the Study of Speech.* Hillsdale, NJ: Lawrence Erlbaum Associates, 1–38.

Catherine P. Browman

Turvey, M.T. 1977. Preliminaries to a theory of action with reference to vision. In R. Shaw and J. Bransford (eds.) *Perceiving, Acting, and Knowing: Toward an Ecological Psychology.* Hillsdale, NJ: Lawrence Erlbaum Associates, 211–265.

20

Change and stability in the contrasts conveyed by consonant releases

JOHN KINGSTON

20.1 Introduction

This commentary on Browman's paper explores the phonetics and phonology of two interactions between a consonant's release and the nature of the following sound. In the first interaction, a following vowel's place of articulation alters the consonant's, while in the second, the following sound's openness determines whether the consonant contrasts for laryngeal and other articulations. Both interactions come about because the following context influences the spectrum and/or audibility of the consonant's release. Browman's data show that the blending of vocalic and consonantal Gestures affecting lip aperture should produce different effects on the acoustics of the consonant's release in [p] than in [t, s, k], which may explain differences between labials and nonlabials in their susceptibility to assimilation to the place of adjacent vowels. These differences are explored in section 2 of this commentary, through examination of pervasive consonant-to-vowel place assimilations in Bantu languages. Browman argues that active release Gestures are necessary to achieve a sufficiently open vocal tract to produce a vowel after a stop closure. Section 3 of this commentary summarizes a variety of data suggesting that many consonantal contrasts depend on, or are best conveyed by, the release of an oral closure into an open vocal-tract configuration, and thus that an active release might be essential for conveying these contrasts.

20.2 Changes in place

Consonants' place of articulation is frequently altered by assimilation to the place of adjacent, particularly following, vowels. A set of sound changes pervasive in the Bantu languages shows that places of articulation differ in their susceptibility to assimilation to a following vowel's place. Proto-Bantu is reconstructed (Guthrie 1967) with seven vowels; two are "super-high" or "super-close" *$i̧$ and *$u̧$ (IPA [i̧] and [u̧]) and the remainder the common five-vowel system *i, *e, *u, *o, and *a. Before the super-high vowels, stops frequently change place of articulation, becoming [coronal] before *$i̧$ and [labial] before *$u̧$, and even more frequently change manner of articulation, becoming fricatives; in (1), /s, z/ and /f, v/ are both the most common reflexes before the super-high vowels and represent [coronal] and [labial] reflexes as a class:[1]

(1)   a. Typical changes in place and manner of Proto-Bantu stops before super-high vowels:

   (i) Coronalization before a front vowel.

   *p, *t, *k > s; *b, *d, *g > z / __ i̧

   (ii) Labialization before a rounded vowel.

   *p, *t, *k > f; *b, *d, *g > v / __ u̧

   b. The proportion of sample of stops that both spirantize and assimilate to the [coronal] or [labial] place of a following *super-high vowel (top row) versus the proportion which spirantizes without also assimilating in place (bottom row):

Place	*p, *b		*t, *d		*k, *g	
Vowel	*i̧	*u̧	*i̧	*u̧	*i̧	*u̧
Place and manner:	0.244	0.054	0.042	0.464	0.571	0.548
Manner alone:	0.369	0.536	0.780	0.274	0.000	0.018

However, dorsals are much more likely[2] to undergo either of these changes in place than coronals or labials, and the coronals much more likely than the labials.[3] Furthermore, if [labial] stops become [coronal] before *$i̧$ or [coronal] stops become [labial] before *$u̧$ in a language, the [dorsal] stops will nearly always undergo the same changes, too. Since changes in place of [dorsal] stops are much more common, this means that a change in a labial's or coronal's place implies a change in the corresponding dorsal's, but not vice versa. Finally, there is a weaker, but statistically significant tendency for the [labial] stops to coronalize and the [coronal] stops to labialize together rather than for just one of the changes to occur alone.

In Browman's results, lip aperture is unsurprisingly smaller during [p] than [t, s, k]. In addition, lip aperture during the consonant is smaller for flanking rounded than unrounded vowels when the consonant is one of [t, s, k], but larger for rounded than unrounded vowels when it is [p]. Finally, lip aperture tends to be relatively larger during all the consonants when the flanking vowel is [i] than when it's some other unrounded vowel. Jaw height during the consonant varies directly with vowel height for the noncoronals [p, k], but is quite invariantly high for the coronals [t] and (even more so) [s].

In the Gestural scores (Browman and Goldstein 1990, 1992) of these utterances, the lip and jaw Gestures for each vowel and consonant are supposed to be the same in all contexts, and the differences observed are supposed to be the result of blending the flanking vowel Gestures with those of the consonants they overlap with in the task dynamics. If an articulatory dimension such as lip aperture varies with the vowel during the consonant, then the consonant is assumed not to have a Gesture controlling that articulatory dimension; invariance, on the other hand, implies the consonant does have such a Gesture. Rounded vowels are produced with a lip Gesture that specifies a relatively narrow lip aperture, though one larger than in [p]; this Gesture is presumably more extreme for higher than lower rounded vowels (cf. Linker 1982). Higher front vowels may also entail a lip Gesture, one which produces a certain relatively large opening as a probable side-effect of lip spreading. [k] apparently has neither a lip nor jaw Gesture, so an overlapping vowel's lip and jaw Gestures determine both lip aperture and jaw height during the [k]. From Browman's data, we can correctly predict that [dorsal] stops would readily assimilate to either a following [labial] or [coronal] vowel's place. At the opposite extreme, [s] must specify both a very high jaw and an intermediate lip aperture, which override the vowel's lip and jaw Gestures. With respect to the jaw, [t] is similar to [s], but it must lack a lip Gesture, since lip aperture varies with the vowel's rounding. The small lip opening during [t] between rounded vowels also correctly predicts that a [coronal] consonant should assimilate to a following [labial] vowel's place. Unlike the coronals, [p] must entail a lip Gesture but perhaps no jaw Gesture. The small lip aperture in [p] between all vowels predicts, again correctly, that a [labial] consonant would not often assimilate to a following [coronal] vowel. The consonant's labial Gesture overrides that of the vowel. The lip opening in [p], larger between labial than between nonlabial vowels, should not influence its place of articulation, but the larger lip opening produced by spreading the lips in a high, front vowel may have been enough to cause a [labial] stop to coronalize occasionally in front of *i̯ (see also Ohala 1978 for discussion of the acoustic effects of the lingual articulation specified by this [coronal] vowel). From Browman's data we can thus predict the asymmetries observed between the proto places of articulation in susceptibility to the [coronal] or [labial] articulations of the super-high vowels.

20.3 Release audibility and neutralization

The other question addressed by Browman's modeling of her data is whether in the transition from consonant to vowel the vocal tract will open enough on its own, through relaxation to a neutral configuration, to produce a vowel, or if instead an active release Gesture is required to achieve a sufficiently open configuration. She finds that a separate release Gesture is required. Other evidence suggests that the acoustics of a stop consonant's release into a following open vocal-tract configuration are important for conveying the laryngeal and other properties of the consonant. That is, these properties will be conveyed if the stop consonant's release and the modifications of its acoustics by various simultaneous articulations are audible. Furthermore, articulatory evidence suggests that some articulations that produce these properties are coordinated with the release of the stop consonant in this context, which makes sense if the release itself is a specified articulatory event, rather than simply a passive product of relaxation of the vocal tract to a more open configuration once a closing articulation is complete.

Stop consonants are more likely to contrast for laryngeal articulations before sounds which specify more open vocal-tract configurations, ideally [+sonorant] sounds, than before those which convey less open ones (Kingston 1985, 1990; Keating 1990; Lombardi 1991); the release Gesture could in fact be interpreted as the implementation of the [+sonorant] specification. The reason why laryngeal contrasts are conveyed best in this context is that the acoustic characteristics of the glottal source will be distributed across a broad range of frequencies if the stop is released into an open(ing) vocal tract configuration. More specifically, releasing a stop into an open vocal tract configuration makes audible differences in (1) the relative intensity of F_1 versus the higher formants that correlate with the presence and onset time of vocal-fold vibration, i.e. whether a stop is aspirated or not; and (2) if the folds are vibrating, in the tilt of the glottal source spectrum (how rapidly energy falls off with increasing frequency), properties that correlate with a tense, constricted versus lax, spread glottis. Since evaluating either property involves comparing energy levels across the spectrum, they will both be more readily detected if the vocal tract is relatively open and the higher frequencies are not attenuated.

Releases also contribute to conveying place contrasts in stops, whether oral or nasal, in a way they probably do not in continuants, because the acoustic events at the release of a noncontinuant differ markedly from those at a continuant release. The noncontinuants have a burst of noise at this moment if oral, or an abrupt increase in energy across the spectrum and a frequency shift in the F_2 region if nasal; in both cases a sharp acoustic discontinuity.[4] In continuants, on the other hand, there is no burst at the release and the onset of energy across the spectrum is more gradual. In the noncontinuants, these events at the release of the oral closure contribute substantially to conveying their place of articulation, since the complete closure of the mouth during the consonant's articulation so severely attenuates the spectrum above F_1 that the essential cues to place in the region of F_2 and F_3 are inaudible until the release. In continuants, on the other hand, the spectrum during the consonant itself may convey the consonant's place, either (as in continuant sonorants) because the vocal tract is more open and the essential higher frequencies are less attenuated, or (as in fricatives) because there is a local oral sound source.

Noncontinuants' reliance on release acoustics to convey their place of articulation predicts that they would be more susceptible to assimilating to following consonants' place of articulation and to neutralizing place contrasts syllable-finally than continuants, because the noncontinuants are likely to lack an audible release in these contexts. Observed patterns of place assimilation in noncontinuants differ from these predictions in obeying a further constraint: that the sound which is assimilated be itself a noncontinuant. The most common case is a nasal assimilating to a following stop's place, but not to the place of a following fricative or non-nasal sonorant (see Padgett 1991, for extensive discussion).[5] Fricatives do assimilate less often to the place of a following consonant than non-continuants (Kohler 1990; Padgett 1991), apparently because the place of a preconsonantal fricative is reliably conveyed by the spectrum of the noise produced during the constriction, while a release-less stop or nasal's place is not conveyed so reliably in that context (Hura *et al.* 1992).

These differences in susceptibility to assimilation between noncontinuants and continuants support Steriade's (1991) argument that the nature of their releases differs, and suggest that Browman has rejected this argument prematurely.

Finally, place-of-articulation contrasts are frequently neutralized in both oral and nasal noncontinuants when they occur syllable-finally independent of any assimilation to a following consonant's place. A very elaborate example of such attrition of place contrasts can be found in the developments of syllable-final stops and nasals between Middle Chinese and the modern dialects (Chen 1973). A comparison of dialects that have undergone different degrees of attrition shows that *-p* and *-t* merged first with *-k* and then collapsed to glottal stop, while *-m* and *-n* merged first with *ŋ* and were then all replaced by nasalization of the preceding vowel. Place attrition clearly began with the stops, since it has gone further in many dialects than in the nasals, and it probably began with them because they were unreleased syllable-finally. While pattern congruity might have made place attrition likely in the nasals as well, the fact that they weren't followed immediately by a more open vocal-tract configuration also made their place less discernible.

These remarks are intended merely to show that an active release Gesture is likely to serve many other purposes than ensuring that the vocal tract is open enough for a vowel to be produced. What they suggest is that the opening of the vocal tract specified by such an active Gesture is what allows properties of laryngeal, oral, and soft palate articulations to be conveyed (see also Ohala 1990), and if, before a consonant or at the end of a syllable, no such Gesture occurs or it is inaudible, contrasts for these articulations are likely to neutralize.

Notes

1 This change in manner was a consequence of intra-oral air pressure building up so much behind the very close articulation of these vowels that air flow through the constriction stayed noisy for some time after the release of the stop (see Jaeger 1978 for other examples), turning it initially into an affricate. The modern reflex of the stops before the super-high vowels is thus an affricate in many Bantu languages. However, in most of the languages, the consonant lost its [−continuant] specification and became a fricative. The sustained noisiness of the release and transition to the following vowel was apparently more salient.

2 Frequencies of each type of change were determined from a comprehensive sample of the languages compiled in Guthrie (1967). Guthrie divides the Bantu languages among 15 zones and then within each zone among a number of "sub-zones." The sample was constructed by taking one language from each sub-zone, yielding 84 languages. Similar asymmetries can be observed in Nurse's (1979) more detailed sample of languages from the northeastern part of the Bantu-speaking area.

3 A change in manner alone for [labial] and [coronal] stops is all that's expected before a homorganic vowel, but it is unexpected that the change in manner before super-high vowels should be so much more common for [coronal] than [labial] stops. That [dorsal] stops are so susceptible to a change in place as well as manner is what makes the frequency of manner changes alone so low for this place.

4 This discontinuity will occur only if the soft palate is not too low when the oral closure is released (Manuel 1991). If the soft palate is high enough, oral resonances, especially in the region of F_2, will suddenly become quite pronounced, but if it's too low, the oral resonances will not increase in intensity so noticeably. Data both in Huffman (1989) and in Krakow (1989) show that speakers control the timing and size of soft-palate movements relative to oral ones in nasals and nasal–oral stop clusters to produce this discontinuity at the release.

5 Nasals do assimilate to a following fricative or continuant sonorant's place, but only when that segment has apparently been hardened to a stop by the nasal.

What appears to be hardening may actually be nothing more than prolongation of the nasal's [−continuant] articulation beyond the moment when the soft palate was raised. A brief oral stop would result. This suggestion is in line with proposals of Steriade (1993), who argues that an apparently assimilated nasal-fricative sequence such as [nz] can be analyzed as an affricate, differing from [dz] in that the closure interval is nasal rather than oral, but resembling [dz] in being released into the narrow oral constriction of a fricative. This analysis provides a different perspective on the other process common to nasal–fricative sequences, deletion of the nasal. If these nasal–fricative sequences are really prenasalized affricates, then deletion of the nasal could simply be a side effect of the loss of the [−continuant] interval (the closure) which turns an affricate into a fricative. The loss of the closure, leaving the fricative behind, is in fact a quite common change in affricates whose closure is oral in the Bantu languages, which provide much of the data on the behavior of nasal-consonant clusters, see note 1. A problem remains, however, with the cases where the fricative hardens as a result of prolonging the oral closure of the nasal. The resulting oral stop should have the place of the nasal rather than of the following consonant, because making a stop closure entails that it be made somewhere, i.e. a place of articulation (cf. Padgett 1991). If producing the closure specified by [−continuant] during the nasal entails a place specification, then there's no reason to expect the place of that closure to change as it's prolonged. Why does the nasal nonetheless assimilate to the place of the following consonant after hardening? The reason must be that the following consonant's place information is more salient than the nasal's. Greater salience is likely because the following consonant's articulation should acoustically dominate the transition into a following vowel, and its oral articulation may begin before the nasal's is released, so it will also influence the acoustics of the release of the oral closure. The greater salience of the following consonant's articulation thus causes a substitution of its place for the nasal's, despite the fact that achieving hardening by prolonging the nasal's oral closure also extended the nasal's place of articulation into the following consonant.

Reference

Browman, C. and L. Goldstein. 1990. Tiers in articulatory phonology, with some implications for casual speech. In J. Kingston and M. Beckman (eds.) *Papers in Laboratory Phonology I: Between the Grammar and Physics of Speech.* Cambridge: University Press, 341–376.

1992. Articulatory phonology: an overview. *Phonetica* 49: 155–180.

Chen, M. 1973. Cross-dialectal comparison: a case study and some theoretical considerations. *Journal of Chinese Linguistics* 1: 39–63.

Guthrie, M. 1967. *Comparative Bantu: An Introduction to the Comparative Linguistics and Prehistory of the Bantu Languages.* 4 vol. Hants, UK: Gregg Press.

Huffman, M. 1989. Implementation of nasal: timing and articulatory landmarks. Ph.D. dissertation, University of California, Los Angeles. (*UCLA Working Papers in Phonetics* 75.)

Hura, S., B. Lindblom and R. Diehl. 1992. On the role of perception in shaping phonological assimilation rules. *Language and Speech* 35: 59–72.

Jaeger, J. 1978. Speech aerodynamics and phonological universals. *Proceedings of the Fourth Annual Meeting of the Berkeley Linguistics Society*, 311–329.

Keating, P. 1990. Phonetic representations in generative grammar. *Journal of Phonetics* 18: 321–334.

Kingston, J. 1985. The phonetics and phonology of the timing of oral and glottal events. Ph.D. dissertation, University of California, Berkeley.

1990. Articulatory binding. In J. Kingston and M. Beckman (eds.) *Papers in Laboratory Phonology I: Between the Grammar and Physics of Speech.* Cambridge: University Press, 406–443.

Kohler, K. 1990. Segmental reduction in connected speech: phonological facts and phonetic explanations. In W. Hardcastle and A. Marchal (eds.) *Speech Production and Speech Modeling.* Dordrecht: Kluwer Publishers, 69–92.

Krakow, R. 1989. The articulatory organization of syllables: a kinematic analysis of labial and velar gestures. Ph.D. dissertation, Yale University.

Linker, W. 1982. Articulatory and acoustic correlates of labial activity in vowels: a cross-linguistic study. Ph.D. dissertation, University of California, Los Angeles. (*UCLA Working Papers in Phonetics* 56.)

Lombardi, L. 1991. Laryngeal features and laryngeal neutralization. Ph.D. dissertation, University of Massachusetts, Amherst.

Manuel, S. 1991. Some phonetic bases for the relative malleability of syllable-final vs. syllable-initial consonants. *Proceedings of the XIIth International Congress of Phonetic Sciences*, Aix-en-Provence. Vol. 5: 118–121.

Nurse, D. 1979. *Classification of the Chaga Dialects: Language and History on Kilimanjaro, the Taita Hills, and the Pare Mountains.* Hamburg: Helmut Buske Verlag.

Ohala, J. 1978. Southern Bantu versus the world: the case of palatalization of labials. *Proceedings of the Fourth Annual Meeting of the Berkeley Linguistics Society:* 370–386.

The phonetics and phonology of aspects of assimilation. In J. Kingston and M. Beckman (eds.) *Papers in Laboratory Phonology I: Between the Grammar and Physics of Speech.* Cambridge: University Press, 258–275.

Padgett, J. 1991. Stricture in feature geometry. Ph.D. dissertation, University of Massachusetts, Amherst.

Steriade, D. 1993. Closure, release and nasal contours. In M. Huffman and R. Krakow (eds.) *Nasals, nasalization, and the velum.* Phonetics and Phonology 5. San Diego: Academic Press.

Index of subjects

Index of names (major citations only)

Adriaens 96
Al-Ani 193, 194
Al-Mozainy 214–215

Beckman 8, 18
Beckman and Kingston 3
Beckman and Pierrehumbert 35, 46–48, 58
Beckman *et al.* 15, 39
Blanc 214
Boff Dkhissi 194, 239
Bolinger 37, 57–58, 64
Borden and Harris 2
Broe 2
Browman and Goldstein 260, 332
Bruce 47, 57
Butcher and Ahmad 194–195
Bybee 173

Catford 195, 196, 223–224
Chen 358
Chomsky 294–295
Chomsky and Halle 196–197, 329
Clark and Yallop 2
Clements 196
Clements and Keyser 108, 136
Cooper and Eady 15, 39
Cooper and Sorenson 60–61

Delattre 152, 194, 239
Dell 149

El-Halees 194, 225

Fromkin 333
Fry 13
Fujimura 260–261

Geddes 269
Ghazeli 193, 194–195, 226
Goldsmith 2
Grossman 200
Gussenhoven 15, 36
Gussenhoven and Rietveld 49–55, 61, 64
Guthrie 359
Guy 272

Hammond 8
Hardcastle 238
Hayes 3, 15
Hayward and Harward 192, 195, 213
Herzallah 208, 219
Hess 201–202, 224
Horne 15, 39–40
Huss 15

Irshied and Kenstowicz 215
Ito 183

Jacobs 53ff
Jakobson 196
Jakobson and Halle 327
Jakobson *et al.* 196
Johnstone 212

Kahn 107, 125
Keating *et al.* 239

Index of names